the Unofficial Guide™ to

Distance Learning

Shannon Turlington

IDG Books Worldwide, Inc.
An International Data Group Company
Foster City, CA • Chicago, IL • Indianapolis, IN
• New York, NY

First Edition

IDG Books Worldwide, Inc.
An International Data Group Company
919 E. Hillsdale Boulevard
Suite 400
Foster City, CA 94404

For general information on IDG Books Worldwide's books in the U.S., please call our
Consumer Customer Service department at 800-762-2974. For reseller information,
including discounts and premium sales, please call our Reseller Customer Service department at 800-434-3422.

Library of Congress Number information available on request

ISBN: 0-02-863756-9

Manufactured in the United States of America

10 9 8 7 6 5 4 3 2 1

Acknowledgments

The work of many people went into this book. I would like to particularly thank my agent, Martha Kaufman-Amitay, my editor, Dave Henthorn, and all the people at Arco who helped make this book a reality.

Contents

The Unofficial Guide™
Declaration of Independence

So, you're thinking about going back to school, perhaps just to take a few courses or maybe even to earn a degree. And you've decided that distance learning is the way to do it. Distance learning enables you to take higher education courses without leaving your job, moving away from home, or disrupting your family life. It's the ideal option for many working adults who want to return to school.

But the process of choosing a distance-learning program, applying, and taking courses can be confusing. So many choices are open to you, not only in terms of which courses you can take and which schools you can attend, but also which technologies you can use. From old-fashioned correspondence courses to the latest Internet-based programs, you have literally thousands of choices.

To survive the process—and to get into the right distance-learning program for you—you need help.

You Need a Helpful Guide

This book is designed to help you make sense of it all. Inside, you won't find any misinformation or myths, only facts. Since this book is "unofficial," you can trust it to give you only the insider scoop—how to choose the best distance-learning program to fit your needs and lifestyle, how to avoid the numerous scams, and how to stick with the program despite the distractions of everyday life.

And this book is complete. It covers the entire process of finding a distance-learning program. You will start by choosing the right type of program and move all the way through to when you start your first class. You won't have to buy additional books for learning about applying for financial aid or how to avoid fraudulent programs. This is the only guide you need.

Finally, this book will be a practical aid for you. It's bursting with uncensored strategies, tips, and facts that you can put to use right away. It includes an extensive guide to distance-learning programs offered by accredited, well-known schools, ranging from high school diploma programs to individual college courses to full-fledged Ph.D. programs. The important facts are right at your fingertips, including the degrees you can earn, the cost, the length of the program, and how to be admitted. Finally, several helpful appendices help you locate the program you need based on its location, the field you want to study, or the degree you want to earn.

So, get ready to have the entire process of getting into college demystified. By the time you're done with this book, you'll feel fully prepared to go back to school and join the growing ranks of distance learners.

How This Book Is Organized

This book is divided into two parts:

- *Part I: All About Distance-Learning* gets you started in the right direction—learn how to evaluate distance-learning programs, how to apply, and how to pay.

- *Part II: Directory of Distance-Learning Programs* is an extensive directory of major, accredited community colleges, four-year colleges, universities, and technical and vocational schools offering individual courses and degree programs via distance learning. Each listing tells you what courses and degrees are available through the program, how much it costs, how long it takes to complete the program, the technologies used, any entrance requirements and restrictions, and other important facts.

Special Features

To help you get the most out of this book, quickly and easily, the text is enhanced with the following special sidebars:

- "Time Saver"—tips and shortcuts to save you time.
- "Money Saver"—tips and hints to save you money.
- "Watch Out!"—cautions and warnings about pitfalls to avoid.
- "Bright Idea"—strategies that offer an easier or smarter way to do something.
- "Unofficially…"—an insider's fact or anecdote.
- "Quote"—statements from real people that can give you valuable insights.

You also need to have quick information at your fingertips. Thus, I have included the following helpful sections at the back of the book:

- Appendices of the distance-learning programs, organized by geographical location, field of study, and degrees offered by each program.

- Contact information of the nationally recognized accrediting agencies that evaluate and approve distance-learning programs in the United States.
- A glossary of distance-learning terms.
- A selection of Internet resources where you can find even more information about distance learning.

My Pledge to You

You can trust me to give you only the straight scoop. I have no bias. I'm not affiliated with any particular distance-learning program nor do I have an agenda to sell you. I'm here to tell you the truth about how to choose a distance-learning program, get in, and succeed while avoiding pitfalls and scams.

I don't have any reason to hide information from you. My only concern is to offer you the most efficient, accurate, and useful guidance for finding the best distance-learning program for you—and then getting admitted to that program. As a result, you can focus your time and energy on evaluating programs, completing applications, and fulfilling your goals and dreams, worry-free.

That's why this book proudly bears the banner of the *Unofficial Guide*. Authorized and controlled by no one, I serve only one master—you, the reader.

Letters, Comments, and Questions from Readers

I've learned a great deal over the years from students like yourself. I've heard from many people just like you who have generously shared their stories with me—helpful tips, mistakes they made along the way, and approaches they'd recommend to other students who want to enter the world of distance learning. Many of the tips and suggestions scattered throughout the book have benefited from their input.

If you have questions, comments, suggestions, or ideas for future editions of this book, I'd like to hear from you. Write to me at this address:

Shannon Turlington
The Unofficial Guide™ to Distance Learning
IDG Books Consumer Reference Group
10475 Crosspoint Boulevard
Indianapolis, IN 46256

Thanks for making the *Unofficial Guide™* your guide to entering the exciting world of distance learning. I hope that you'll enjoy using it to help make your dreams come true.

How to Use the Listings

This section of the guide profiles accredited distance-learning programs. Only large, established programs offering a wide range of courses, certificates, diplomas, and degrees to students in North America (and often beyond) are profiled. The profiles are designed to help you quickly and easily locate the most important information about the distance-learning programs. Use these profiles to find programs that meet your needs and academic goals.

The distance-learning program profiles are organized alphabetically by the name of the school sponsoring the program. To find programs located in a particular state or country, check Appendix A, "Index of Distance-Learning Programs by Location." To find degree-, diploma-, and certificate-granting programs in specific academic fields, turn to Appendix B, "Index of Distance-Learning Programs by Subject." And to quickly locate programs that offer a particular kind of course, check Appendix C, "Index of Distance-Learning Individual Course Programs by Subject."

Distance learning is the fastest-growing area of higher education. Please keep in mind that new programs are opening their "virtual" doors everyday, there is no way that any directory could list every program out there. Future editions of this book will profile even more programs as information about them becomes available.

Sample Profile

Take a look at the following sample profile to see exactly what information each profile provides and how it's formatted.

While every effort has been made to ensure that this information is as accurate and as up-to-date as possible, schools do often change tuition,

Name of the school sponsoring the program.

Charter Oak State College

Admissions Office

Contact address and phone number.

55 Paul Manafort Dr.

New Britain, CT 06053

860-832-3800

Program Web site and e-mail address.

Web: www.cosc.edu/

E-mail: info@mail.cosc.edu

Programs: AA/AS/BA/BS— General Studies; individual courses

Certificates/degrees that can be earned through the program; following the general degree designations are all majors or specialties in that degree offered by the program. If distance learners can take individual courses from the school, that's also indicated.

General subjects of individual courses that can be taken through the program.

Individual course subjects: anthropology, art, biology, business, communications, critical thinking, economics, English, film studies, geography, history, mathematics, philosophy, social sciences, sociology

Average cost of distance-learning courses/degrees.

Average tuition: $68–$135 per credit (depending on type of course and residency)

Length of program: degree programs—1–2 years

Average time it takes to complete distance-learning courses/ degrees.

Distance-learning technologies used in the program.

Technologies: correspondence, Internet, video

Accreditation: NEASC

Nationally recognized accrediting agencies that have accredited the school/department offering the program.

Basic requirements needed to apply to the program.

Entrance requirements: 9 college-level credits from any acceptable source (regardless of level of formal education)

Restrictions: Applicants must be at least 16 years old.

Geographic, age, or residency restrictions.

Special student services offered by the program.

Special services: academic advising; tuition payment plan

program specifics, and other factors. The specified tuition is an *average* amount and may vary depending on the course you want to take or the program you want to enter. Likewise, the individual course subjects represent the general kinds of courses you can take through distance learning; specific course offerings may differ from one academic term to the next. Once you find a program that you like, order the program's catalog by contacting the address or phone number given in the profile, and talk to an admissions officer to get the latest facts and figures.

Degree Abbreviations

In the profiles, the most common undergraduate and graduate degrees are referenced with the following abbreviations:

- Associate of Applied Science: AAS
- Associate of Arts: AA
- Associate of Business Administration: ABA
- Associate of General Studies: AGS
- Associate of Science: AS
- Bachelor of Arts: BA
- Bachelor of Business Administration: BBA
- Bachelor of Fine Arts: BFA
- Bachelor of General Studies: BGS
- Bachelor of Science: BS
- Master of Arts: MA
- Master of Business Administration: MBA
- Master of Divinity: MDiv
- Master of Education: MEd
- Master of Fine Arts: MFA
- Master of Library Science: MLS
- Master of Public Administration: MPA
- Master of Science: MS
- Master of Theology: ThM
- Education Specialist: EdS
- Doctor of Audiology: AuD
- Doctor of Business Administration: DBA
- Doctor of Education: EdD
- Doctor of Ministry: DMin
- Doctor of Pharmacy: PharmD
- Doctor of Philosophy: PhD

Accrediting Agency Abbreviations

In the profiles, nationally recognized regional accrediting agencies are referenced with the following abbreviations:

- Middle States Association of Colleges and Schools: MSACS
- New England Association of Schools and Colleges: NEASC
- North Central Association of Colleges and Schools: NCACS
- Northwest Association of Schools and Colleges: NASC
- Southern Association of Colleges and Schools: SACS
- Western Association of Schools and Colleges: WASC

Nationally recognized professional accrediting agencies that have accredited schools offering distance-learning programs are referenced with the following abbreviations:

- Accrediting Association of Bible Colleges: AABC
- Accrediting Board for Engineering and Technology: ABET
- Accrediting Commission of Career Schools and Colleges of Technology: ACCSCT
- Accrediting Commission on Education for Health Services Administration: ACEHSA
- Accrediting Council for Continuing Education and Training: ACCET
- Accrediting Council for Independent Colleges and Schools: ACICS
- American Association of Family and Consumer Sciences: AAFCS
- American Bar Association: ABA
- American Council on Pharmaceutical Education: ACPE
- American Dental Association: ADA
- American Dietetic Association Commission on Accreditation/Approval for Dietetics Education: ADiA
- American Library Association: ALA
- American Psychological Association: APA
- American Speech-Language-Hearing Association: ASHA
- Association of Theological Schools in the United States and Canada: ATS
- Commission on Opticianry Accreditation: COA
- Computing Sciences Accreditation Board: CSAB
- Council for Accreditation of Counseling and Related Educational Programs: CACREP
- Council on Education for Public Health: CEPH
- Council on Occupational Education: COE

- Council on Rehabilitation Education: CORE
- Distance Education and Training Council: DETC
- National Accrediting Agency for Clinical Laboratory Sciences: NAACLS
- National Association of Schools of Public Affairs and Administration: NASPA
- National Council for Accreditation of Teacher Education: NCATE
- National League for Nursing: NLN
- Transnational Association of Christian Colleges: TRACS

All About Distance
Learning

PART I

GET THE SCOOP ON...
What distance learning is ▪ Different types of distance-
learning programs available ▪ Degrees and certificates
you can earn through distance learning ▪ Types of schools that
offer distance-learning programs

The Lowdown on Distance Learning

In today's job market, it is more important than ever to have a college or graduate school degree. On top of that, many of us constantly reeducate ourselves to keep up with changes in our fields. But at the same time, our lives are busier than ever before. Many of us juggle family, friends, and hobbies in addition to our jobs. We can't simply take time out of our lives to go back to school.

That's where distance learning comes in. With distance learning, you can take classes, get a professional certificate, and even earn a college or graduate school degree without leaving your house. In the next few chapters, you'll find out just how easy it is to get started with a distance-learning program. You'll discover exactly what distance learning is, how it works, the kinds of degrees and certificates you can get, and where you can get them.

If you want to fit education into your busy life but you don't see how you can, distance learning may offer the perfect solution. Keep reading to discover how distance learning can benefit you.

What Is Distance Learning?

Distance learning is a form of education in which the instructor is geographically separated from the student. This broad term covers a wide range of educational programs, everything from correspondence courses to live lectures taking place over satellite television to classes that use the latest Internet technologies. But all distance-learning programs have three characteristics in common:

- The instructor and the student are separated from each other.
- In most cases, all of the students in the class are dispersed over a wide area—scattered across a state, a country, or even the entire world.

Chapter 1

- Communication between the students and the instructor often takes place using one or more communications technologies, such as the phone, fax, television, or computer.

A Brief History of Distance Learning

Many people mistakenly assume that distance learning is a relatively new phenomenon that originated with the advent of personal computers and the Internet. Actually, distance-learning programs have existed in one form or another for over a hundred years.

The first distance-learning programs began in the mid-1800s with the advent of correspondence courses, or courses taught entirely through the mail. Correspondence courses became prevalent throughout the late 1800s and early 1900s, when students could learn everything from stenography to farming techniques through mailed instructions.

The development of communications technologies like cable television, videotape, satellite broadcasting, teleconferencing, and the Internet, coupled with the falling costs of these technologies, have brought about a distance-learning boom over the last 30 years. During this time, more and more prestigious colleges and universities around the world have implemented distance-learning programs, and more and more students have turned to distance learning as a practical way to get an education while holding down a job and raising a family. The Distance Education and Training Council (DETC), which accredits distance-learning programs, estimates that there are three million distance learners in the United States today.

Unofficially...
Today, the largest distance-learning student body in the world is part of the University of South Africa, with more than 200,000 students enrolled worldwide.

The Typical Distance Learner

First, there is no such thing as a "typical" distance learner. Students of all ages, backgrounds, and walks of life turn to distance education for one reason or another.

Most distance learners are older than traditional-age college students and have had some college-level education. The majority of them work full-time, so they require flexible scheduling. A large percentage of distance learners are women, and many are single parents.

All of the following are examples of distance-learning students:

- The single parent who wants to complete an interrupted college degree
- The working adult who wants to earn a master's degree without quitting his or her job
- The professional who wants to further his or her education in order to obtain a better job or a promotion
- The employee who needs last minute job training but can't leave the workplace to get it
- The homemaker who wants to prepare to enter the workforce while raising a family

- The busy adult who lives too far from a college or university to attend nighttime classes

- The disabled student who is unable to attend on-campus classes

- The student who wants to further his or her education while caring for an elderly relative

- The homeschooler who needs to supplement parental teaching with outside classes

- The retiree who likes to learn for the fun of it

These are just a few examples of the many kinds of people who can benefit from distance learning. But whatever their reason for wanting to continue their education, these students choose distance learning because they need to learn at a time and place that is convenient for them. For many of these students, distance learning is the only practical way to earn an undergraduate- or graduate-level degree.

What Distance Learning Is Not

Many people believe that distance learning is an easier or faster way to earn a degree. This is because so many fraudulent distance-learning schools have sprung up in recent years that promise degrees in little or no time for little or no work. The preponderance of these "diploma mills" has led to the false perception that distance-learning degrees are somehow less legitimate than degrees earned the traditional way. (You'll learn more about diploma mills and how to avoid them in Chapter 3, "Choosing a Distance-Learning Program.")

Nothing can be farther from the truth. While diploma mills abound, many legitimate and prestigious colleges and universities offer distance-learning programs. A degree from Harvard or the University of California—Berkeley carries the same cachet no matter whether the student attended classes on campus or took them from a distance.

Distance-learning degree programs offered by reputable schools require just as much time and effort as their on-campus counterparts. In fact, the distance-learning degree program may be even more difficult than the traditional program. That's because completing a degree at a distance requires a high level of self-discipline, motivation, responsibility, and commitment. No one is looking over your shoulder or forcing you to do the work—you have to be your own slave driver.

Types of Distance-Learning Programs

Distance-learning programs are generally defined by the kind of technology used to conduct the course. These programs fall into four broad categories:

- Correspondence courses
- Audio-based courses

- Video-based courses
- Computer-based courses

Correspondence Courses

Correspondence courses rely solely on printed materials to conduct the class. The student receives course materials such as textbooks, study guides, and workbooks through the mail. The student completes the assignments at his or her own pace and returns them to the instructor, also via the mail. While correspondence courses enable students to work at their own pace, they can also be a slow way to get an education.

Courses by mail are the historic way to deliver distance education. Within the United States and Europe, though, the newer communications technologies have largely supplanted the traditional correspondence course.

This type of distance-education program still holds many advantages, though. Correspondence courses are low-tech and can be taken anywhere at any time, which means that the largest number of students can participate. Students don't have to purchase costly equipment and learn how to use it before they can start the program.

Correspondence courses are naturally very flexible. Students can move quickly through the easiest lessons and devote more time to the difficult ones. They can study when they want, whether that is late at night or during the lunch hour. They can also work anywhere—in the office, at the public library, or on the kitchen table at home. Finally, correspondence courses are inexpensive to implement, which means the student doesn't have to pay as much for an education.

But the by-mail type of distance-learning program has some drawbacks. For example, printed textbooks can't include valuable audio, video, or interactive learning aids. Students must read well in order to benefit from the course. Correspondence courses allow for little real-time interaction with instructors, and it can take a long time for students to receive feedback on assignments through the mail. (Some courses circumvent this problem by providing feedback via faxes, which means the student must also have access to a fax machine.) While print materials continue to serve as a major component of most distance-learning courses, the addition of other technologies has helped to alleviate the problems with the traditional correspondence course.

Audio-Based Courses

Like all of the distance-learning programs that rely on communications technologies, audio-based distance-learning programs can be either passive or interactive. Passive, or asynchronous, audio-based programs include classes that are taught on cassette tape or over the radio. Interactive, or synchronous, audio technologies include the telephone, voice conferencing, and shortwave radio. Radio courses were most popular in the 1930s and

1940s, when the radio was a major form of entertainment. Today, it is much more common for distance-learning classes to be broadcast on television rather than on the radio.

Audio-based distance-learning programs hold many advantages. It is relatively inexpensive to produce classes on cassette, especially when compared to filming classes for videotape or television, and this savings is usually passed on to the student. Audio-based programs take advantage of common technologies, such as the telephone and cassette player, which most students are already familiar. Audio-based course materials are more portable than videos or computers; you can listen to class lectures while driving to and from work, for instance (if you have a tape player in your car, that is).

Often, audio-course materials are used in conjunction with other types of technologies in distance-learning programs. For example, while the classes themselves may be on video, actual live interaction with the instructor and other classmates may be conducted through voice conferencing over the telephone, which is cheaper and easier to use than videoconferencing.

Video-Based Courses

Video-based distance-learning programs encompass all courses that are taught on videotape, on film, and on television through public, cable, and satellite broadcasting. It also includes live group and one-on-one interaction via videoconferencing.

Video is a very familiar medium to most people, and many students feel more comfortable watching a class lecture than they do reading a textbook or listening to a lecture on tape. Video is a more effective teaching tool, as well, because it can better illustrate difficult concepts. For example, students can literally look through the lens of a microscope or travel to the moon. Taking a video course requires less motivation than a correspondence course; it seems less like work. Finally, many students own the basic equipment needed to take a video-based course: a television and a VCR.

On the other hand, video-based courses are more expensive to produce, and you, the student, will end up paying a higher tuition to take them. Sometimes, student-teacher interaction is limited in these courses, and many video-based courses are entirely passive. But when used in conjunction with other technologies, video is one of the most effective teaching tools for distance-learning programs.

Computer-Based Courses

A computer-based course can simply be a class that is delivered via software, rather than by audiocassette or videotape. But more often, a computer-based course is one that is conducted over a computer network, such as the Internet.

Computer-based courses take advantage of a wide range of new technologies to publish course materials, complete assignments, and interact

Watch Out!
Since class members interact over the Internet primarily through text, a computer-based distance-learning program usually requires highly developed writing skills to express yourself properly through e-mail and in chat rooms. If you feel your writing talents aren't up to par, consider taking an introductory writing course before signing up for a computer-based program.

Bright Idea
If you plan to enter a computer-based distance-learning program, consider taking an introductory computing course first, so you'll feel comfortable with computers and the Internet before you start the program. Your school may offer such a course, or check out the noncredit course offerings at Tutorials.Com (tutorials.com/) and ZD University (www.zdu.com/catalog/catalog.asp).

with classmates and teachers. Often, course materials are published on a Web site, which students can access at any time over the Internet. These course materials can include text, video, audio, and even interactive simulations.

Classmates and instructors typically interact by exchanging messages via electronic mail. The instantaneous nature of e-mail enables students to turn in assignments and receive instructor feedback very quickly, often the same day. Class members may also post messages to a discussion group or electronic bulletin board system; any member of the class can log on to the Internet, read messages from the instructor and fellow classmates, and post responses whenever he or she wants to.

Computer-based courses also provide the means for real-time interaction between class members and the instructor. For example, class discussions may be held in a chat room or a virtual world, called a "MOO." A MOO (which stands for MUD—or Multi-User Dimension—Object-Oriented) is a text-based, multi-user simulation where all members of the class to meet and "talk" without actually having to go to class on a physical campus. Class members can also interact using shared software programs called groupware. For example, students can watch as the instructor draws or writes notes on a shred writing space, called an electronic whiteboard.

It's obvious that computer-based courses hold a lot of advantages for the distance learner, which explains why this is the fastest-growing area of distance education today. Students can work at their own pace, but still receive quick feedback from the instructor. There is plenty of opportunity for real-time interaction among all members of the class. Finally, many different technologies—such as print, audio, and video—can be linked on the computer to create effective lessons.

But if you don't already have the necessary equipment, a computer-based distance-learning program can require a significant up-front investment. Not only will you have to purchase a computer, but you will also need to pay for an Internet connection, a modem that connects your computer to the Internet, and any software that you might need for the course. Computer technology changes rapidly, which means that you might have to purchase additional hardware and software if you enroll in a long-term degree program.

Not only can computer-based distance learning be expensive, but it can also be intimidating for potential distance-learning students who have never used a computer before. You may actually have to take a course or two on how to use the computer and the Internet before you can even think about starting a computer-based distance-learning program.

Actually, it is very rare for a distance-learning program to rely on only one type of technology, and most utilize a combination of all four. For example, the main course materials may be printed textbooks and workbooks that students receive through the mail, while course lectures are provided on prerecorded videotapes. Real-time interaction with the instructor may occur over the phone, while students turn in assignments and receive feedback via e-mail. As technologies change and improve, it is inevitable that the number and kinds of distance-learning programs available to you will increase and that these programs will become better and better.

Degrees and Certificates You Can Earn

Don't make the mistake of thinking that distance learners are limited to only a few specialized degree programs. Actually, almost every degree program that you can pursue through traditional education is also available as a distance-learning program. Distance education spans a wide range of courses, from life-improvement courses like wine tasting to accredited graduate-level programs.

Students can earn any one of the following degrees and certificates through a distance-learning program:

- High school diploma

- Professional certificate, which prepares the student for a specific job or for professional certification or licensure

- Associate's (or two-year) degree, which typically requires 60 semester hours of undergraduate study

- Bachelor's (or four-year) degree, which typically requires 120 semester hours of undergraduate study

- Master's degree, which typically requires a bachelor's degree and 30 semester hours of study at the graduate level

- Doctorate (Ph.D.), which typically requires a bachelor's degree and 90 semester hours of study at the graduate level

There are exceptions, of course. For example, the American Bar Association (ABA) has not accredited any distance law program, and ABA accreditation is required if you want to take the bar exam in most states. Also, no Ph.D. program is completely nonresident; most have a short-term residency requirement ranging from a few days to a few weeks.

Taking Courses for Certification or Licensure

If you're an adult who would like to enter the workforce, get a promotion or a raise, or change careers, distance learning may be just the way to do it. Distance-learning certification programs can train you for a new career, even if you've already earned a college degree in an entirely different field. A certification program usually consists of around 10 courses, all focused on a single profession. These programs are often designed with the help of professional associations and licensing boards and thus encompass real-world, practical knowledge.

Many certification programs prepare students for professional certification or licensure. At the end of the program, the student sits for an exam and earns a state-recognized certificate from a certifying agency or licensing board. If this is your goal, you should make certain that the certification

Watch Out!
Degree requirements vary from school to school. The definition of a semester can also vary depending on the school and the country where it's located. (See the glossary in Appendix E at the back of the book for more information.) Always check with your chosen school to find out the degree requirements.

program you want to take meets the certifying agency's or licensing board's requirements. That way, you won't waste your time and money completing a program that won't help you meet your ultimate professional goals.

Before enrolling in a distance-learning certification program, ask the certifying agency or licensing board the following questions:

- What are the certification or licensing requirements?
- Does the program or course you intend to take have acceptable accreditation?
- How many credits toward certification or licensure can you earn through distance learning?

Taking Courses for Credit

In addition to entering a certification or degree program, you can simply take distance-learning courses for college credit. Successful completion of a credit course counts toward a degree at any college or university that will accept the credit. You may already attend a traditional college but decide to take a distance-learning course that your school doesn't offer and count it toward the requirements for your bachelor's degree. Or you may simply need a few course credits to finish an interrupted degree.

If you want to take distance-learning courses for college credit that you will then apply toward a degree at another school, it's a good idea to check with your school before enrolling to make certain that the credits will transfer. Many colleges and universities limit the number and kinds of credits they accept from outside programs. Degree requirements and policies vary from school to school and even among academic departments in the same school.

Ask your academic adviser the following questions before signing up for a distance-learning credit course:

- Will the school accept the course credit and apply it to graduation?
- Will your academic department accept credits earned by distance learning?
- How many credits by distance learning can be applied toward graduation?
- How must the distance-learning program be accredited?

Noncredit Distance-Learning Courses

Distance learning is also a good option for working adults whose professions require continuing education, even after they've earned their degree, certificate, or license. Many states mandate continuing education for professions like teaching, nursing, and accounting. Professionals in the health-care, engineering, business, and computer-science industries may also opt to take distance-learning courses to keep up with new developments in their fields.

Watch Out!
Transferring college credits can be a tricky business. Some schools limit the number of credits that you can earn via distance learning or require that students take certain courses on campus. Almost all schools won't accept credits that weren't earned from a properly accredited program. (Turn to Chapter 3 for more information about accreditation). Find out what the restrictions are at your school ahead of time, so you won't waste your time and money taking a course that won't earn you credit.

If you take a distance-learning course for career enhancement or just to satisfy a personal interest, you don't necessarily have to earn college credit for the course. These noncredit courses earn Continuing Education Units (CEUs), a nationally recognized system that provides a standard measure for accumulating, transferring, and recognizing participation in continuing education programs. It is still important to take the courses from a properly accredited program, however, so that employers and professional agencies will recognize them. (Chapter 3 teaches you all about accreditation.)

Who Offers Distance-Learning Programs?

A better question is: Who doesn't offer distance-learning programs? Colleges, universities, graduate schools, community colleges, technical schools, and vocational schools have all implemented distance-learning programs. These aren't just schools that you've never heard of, but household names like Harvard, Duke, Georgia Tech, Stanford, and the University of California (to name a few); and more schools open distance-learning programs every year.

The challenges presented by distance education have forced colleges and universities to be creative, which ultimately benefits you, the student. For example, some schools have formed partnerships with cable companies, public-broadcasting services, and satellite broadcasters to deliver high-quality distance education. Colleges and universities have also partnered with large corporations to deliver distance education to employees. Many schools have formed consortiums within a state, across a region, or even internationally, enabling students to take courses from all the participating institutions within one degree program and guaranteeing transfer of credits.

Finally, a few colleges and universities are virtual, which means that they don't have a physical campus. These schools are entirely devoted to providing degrees to their students through distance learning. While very few of these schools exist at the present time, the number is sure to grow as distance learning becomes more commonplace. In fact, several states are exploring distance learning as a low-cost way of opening new public universities to serve the growing number of college students.

But distance learning is not limited to the college and graduate level. Increasingly, high schools and elementary schools are developing distance-learning programs aimed at K–12 students. Using distance-learning technologies, these schools can offer classes to homeschooled students, students in rural areas whose hometown schools may not provide a wide choice of courses, and students whose schools are poorly funded or lack qualified teachers.

Corporations, hospitals, government agencies, and the military have also jumped on the distance-learning bandwagon. Distance education offers the ideal way to provide training to employees who are scattered

Bright Idea
If you're still in high school, taking a college-level dis-tance-learning course is a great way to earn advanced-placement credit. Having one or two college-level courses on your transcript will also make you a more attractive can-didate when it comes time to apply to colleges.

across a large geographical area. Distance learning also enables employers to bring the classroom to the work site to provide on-the-job training.

In Part II of this book, you'll find a comprehensive directory of hun-dreds of accredited distance-learning programs offered by high schools, community colleges, four-year colleges, and universities, as well as by the military, the government, professional organizations, and virtual universi-ties. Flip through that section to get a good idea of just how many options you have in distance education.

Just the Facts

- Distance learning encompasses all education where the student is physically separated from the instructor; for many busy adults, it's the only way to learn.

- Distance-learning programs usually make use of one or more commu-nications technologies, including print, audio, video, the computer, and the Internet.

- You can earn almost any degree or professional certificate through a distance-learning program; many distance learners also take credit courses to transfer to another school, to finish up an interrupted degree, or to prepare themselves for a promotion or a career change.

- Hundreds of prestigious community colleges, four-year colleges, and universities now offer distance-learning programs, as well as virtual universities, businesses, high schools, and the government.

Is Distance Learning Right for You?

While distance learning can fulfill diverse needs for a wide range of students, it's not for everyone. Some students don't have the study skills or the self-motivation necessary to succeed as a distance learner. Others have educational goals that cannot be met by a distance-learning program.

In this chapter, you will discover whether distance learning is the right solution for you. Don't get turned off if you don't think you have what it takes to succeed at a distance-learning program, or if you think that distance-learning programs can't possibly meet your needs. Distance learning offers more benefits and flexibility than you might have imagined. So, while distance learning is not the best option for everyone, it can offer the ideal way to get an education for many kinds of people with differing educational goals. Read on to find out how distance learning can benefit you.

Benefits of Distance Learning

The benefits of distance learning are diverse. That's why distance-learning programs meet the needs of so many different people of all ages, genders, professions, and educational backgrounds.

The following is a list of the benefits that distance-learning programs can provide. As you read over the list, ask yourself if any of these benefits provide a solution to an obstacle that is standing in your way when you think about going back to school. Do any of them make continuing your education a real possibility right now, rather than a vague goal for sometime in the future? If you answer yes, then distance learning is probably right for you.

Here are the major benefits of distance learning:

- *Distance learning is flexible.* You can learn when and where you want to, so you can more easily schedule your education around a busy work and home life. You can take just as many courses as you can handle at a time, and often you can start courses at the best time for you, instead of at the beginning of the school semester. And if your schedule changes frequently, distance learning can accommodate the changes.

- *Distance learning comes to you.* This makes distance learning ideal for students who can't get to the college campus—students who live in remote areas, who are single parents and can't afford childcare, or who don't have the time to commute to campus.

- *Distance learning goes at your pace.* Distance learning is ideal for students who can't keep up with the pace of a traditional classroom or who learn best on their own. You can work through the lessons at a pace that you set, spending more time on difficult concepts and less time on easier ones. If you must learn something quickly—to meet a need at work, for instance—distance learning makes it possible. A crisis at work or at home won't put you behind.

- *Distance learning saves money.* In most cases, distance-learning programs cost less than attending classes on campus. On top of that, you save money on childcare, gas, parking, and other commuting costs, and you won't have to take time off from work to attend classes.

- *Distance learning fits individual needs.* Often, you can tailor a distance-learning program to match your exact interests or professional goals. You aren't locked into a prescribed course of study.

- *Distance learning provides freedom of choice.* You aren't limited to schools that are close to home, but can select from a wide range of prestigious colleges and universities located around the world. Hundreds of distance-learning programs are now available and more are opening every year, giving distance learners more choices than ever before.

- *Distance learning teaches you more than just the course material.* Depending on the type of program you take, distance learning can help you develop your computer, Internet, reading, writing, and verbal communications skills, which benefit you no matter what kind of career you pursue.

- *Distance learning broadens your perspective.* Often, your classmates are scattered far and wide. In distance-learning programs with a high degree of class interaction, you'll meet others who live on the other side of the country or even on the other side of the globe.

Bright Idea
Distance learning is particularly well-suited to people who travel extensively—you can take your lectures on the road with you and fax in your assignments or send them in via e-mail.

Distance Learning Versus Traditional Education

Distance learning was developed as an alternative to traditional education, in which students attend courses on the college or university campus on a full- or part-time basis. Distance learning came about to meet the needs of those who desired a higher education but could not get to campus for one reason or another. But how does distance learning stack up against that traditional college experience?

Many people think of distance learning as traditional education's poorer cousin. They believe that getting a degree through distance learning is somehow less legitimate than earning one the traditional way, as if not setting foot in a classroom decreases the worth of the degree. They see distance learning as a last resort, something to turn to when it is impossible to get a degree by going the traditional route.

But this perception is simply wrong. Recent research comparing distance learning to traditional on-campus education has shown that distance learning is equally as effective as its traditional counterpart. Of course, there are a few caveats. The distance-learning program must encompass the following qualities in order to measure up to a traditional college education:

- The methods and technologies used in the distance-learning program must be appropriate to the subject matter taught in the program.

- The instructor of the distance-learning program must provide timely feedback on assignments.

- The distance-learning program must allow for interaction among all of the students taking the course.

With today's distance-learning technologies, particularly the computer and the Internet, it's easy to develop distance-learning programs with all of these qualities. In fact, you should look for these qualities in the programs you're considering before deciding which one to sign up for. (You'll find out how to evaluate distance-learning programs in Chapter 3, "Choosing a Distance-Learning Program.")

Therefore, if you take a well-designed distance-learning program, the degree you earn is every bit as worthwhile and valuable as if you followed the traditional route. But there are still some important differences between distance learning and traditional education that prevent some students from fully benefiting from distance learning:

- Dropout rates are higher for distance-learning programs than for campus-based programs. It requires a high degree of self-motivation and discipline to complete a distance-learning program. It's all too easy to allow pressures from work or family to get in the way of completing the program.

- Distance learning can be lonely. Some students require the stimulus of being around other students to get the most of out a class, so they can

Bright Idea
One side benefit of taking a computer-based distance-learning program is that you develop computer and Internet skills, which will help you stay competitive in today's high-tech job market.

discuss ideas and form study groups. Some distance-learning programs have compensated for this deficit by incorporating class interactivity over the Internet, but for many, this can't substitute for face-to-face interaction.

- Distance learning takes longer. Even if you attend on-campus classes part-time, you are more likely to finish your degree faster than you would through a distance-learning program. Because distance-learning programs are self-motivated, other demands in your life can easily take precedence over completing the program, making it easier for you to put off finishing your degree.

- On-campus students get better services. They have access to the school's library, academic advisers, job-placement services, tutoring, and study-abroad programs. Many distance-learning programs now offer valuable services to woo students, such as online libraries and technical support, but they still can't compare to the services that the on-campus student enjoys.

- On-campus students get the full "college experience"—the parties, the games, the dorm life, and the cultural activities that a college campus attracts (not to mention the food). For many distance learners, this isn't an important consideration, but for students who are going to college for the first time, the experience may be too valuable to pass up.

- A traditional college degree is a better choice to meet some future goals. For instance, a traditional degree may look more attractive when applying to graduate schools and professional schools, like law school or medical school. (You'll learn more about this later in this chapter.)

Unofficially...
While it's true that distance learning limits opportunities for face-to-face interaction, it doesn't have to be an impersonal, lonely process. Especially in Internet-based programs that offer many opportunities for interaction, you can get to know classmates very well and establish long-lasting friendships. In some distance-learning programs, you have more opportunities to interact with your instructor than in the traditional classroom setting.

As a nontraditional way of getting an education, distance learning seems best suited to the nontraditional student—the older, working adult who has already settled down and become part of a community. This kind of student often already possesses the necessary qualities to succeed in a distance-learning program.

Younger students who are new to college—recent high school graduates, for instance—don't make good candidates for distance learning. These students often haven't developed the necessary study skills and maturity level that a distance-learning program demands. These students benefit a great deal from the things that a college setting has to offer, such as student services, interaction with other students, and on-campus social activities. These are also the students who most crave the "college experience," which provides the ideal transition from high school to the adult world.

Before considering enrolling in a distance-learning program, you should evaluate your educational goals, your personality type, and your study skills. Most importantly, you should determine exactly what you want to get out of continuing your education. You may discover that a distance-learning program won't meet your goals, that you require all the benefits of being on campus, or that you just learn better in a traditional classroom setting. It's important to be honest with yourself; if distance learning truly isn't for you, your chances of finishing any distance-learning program that you start are low.

Necessary Skills for Success

As I mentioned in the previous section, taking a distance-learning program can actually be more difficult than pursuing a degree via traditional education. That's because distance learning requires several skills in addition to basic study, reading, and writing skills. To determine if you will be a successful distance learner, you need to evaluate how you work.

Evaluating Your Personal Skills

With distance learning, you are really on your own. You don't have to go to class everyday; no one is taking roll. No one is making sure that you are finishing your homework and turning it in on time. No one is forcing you to do the reading or the practice exercises. The only one who can ensure that you will succeed is you.

Because distance learning forces you to work on your own to such a high degree, it's vital that you have the necessary personal skills to succeed at the program. To determine if this is so, ask yourself the following questions (and be truthful about the answers):

- Are you strongly motivated to complete your education?
- Do you have the time to fit a regular study period into your schedule?
- Are your work and home schedules predictable enough to enable you to schedule time to study?
- Are you a good organizer?
- Do you plan ahead instead of tackling jobs at the last minute?
- Do you tend to complete a task once you start it?
- Do you regularly try to complete a task today rather than put it off until tomorrow?
- Can you complete a task without a preset deadline?
- Can you sustain your interest in learning without a great deal of interaction with others?
- Does your family strongly support your educational goals?
- Do you have a place to study without distractions?
- Do you have access to the necessary equipment, such as a computer, satellite television, or fax machine?
- Do you have access to a good library or to the Internet for research purposes?

If you answer yes to all of these questions, then you are an excellent candidate for distance learning. But distance learning doesn't just require

Unofficially...
Entrepreneurs, managers, and people who work at home are particularly well suited to distance learning—they are experienced working on their own and forcing themselves to meet deadlines without any outside encouragement.

highly developed personal skills. You also need basic academic skills in order to succeed.

Evaluating Your Academic Skills

In a distance-learning program, you rely heavily on your academic skills. The instructor isn't present to hold your hand or guide you the minute you drift off course. You need to be able to read well, comprehend what you read, write clearly, and think critically. Students who have some experience completing college-level work are the best prepared to enter a distance-learning program.

Evaluate your academic proficiencies by answering the following questions (again, you have to be honest with yourself):

- Do you read regularly?
- Can you easily comprehend and evaluate what you read?
- Can you skim text and quickly pick out the main ideas?
- Can you research a topic and then write about it?
- Do you have experience writing in the workplace (writing reports, proposals, or memos, for instance)?
- Can you take a test without getting stressed out?

Do you fit most or all of these qualifications? If so, then you are the ideal candidate for distance learning.

Fortunately, the very type of person who is drawn to distance learning is the type of person who is most likely to succeed at it. Distance learning tends to attract older students who have careers and families. These students have developed a high degree of self-discipline and maturity. They have voluntarily decided to continue their education, and they have clear educational goals that motivate them to finish what they started. They are used to working on their own and forcing themselves to meet deadlines without anyone looking over their shoulders. Through their jobs, they have honed their writing, reading, and communications skills. And they have usually completed at least some college work in the past, so they are used to working at the college level.

Does this description sound like you? Then you are the type of student that distance learning was made for. But don't worry if you don't precisely match this description. Even if you don't possess all of the personal and academic skills recommended for distance learning, chances are good that you can still find a distance-learning program at which you can succeed.

Selecting a Distance-Learning Program to Match Your Skills

While distance learning is not for everyone, it can work for most people. The key to success is to find a program that plays to your strengths and supports your weaknesses.

For example, you may work best when you interact to a high degree with the instructor and other students. You may require the structure and motivation that frequent interaction can bring. You may have trouble getting

Money Saver
Many distance-learning programs enable you to take a trial course before signing up for a long-term program, so you can figure out if distance learning is right for you before committing a lot of time or money. You might choose to take a trial lifestyle improvement, computer, or writing skills course.

things done without strict deadlines to keep you on task. If that's the case, look for a distance-learning program that offers a strict schedule for turning in assignments, frequent opportunities for instructor feedback, and real-time interaction with the rest of the class. An Internet-based program will work best for you.

On the other hand, you may develop a high level of self-discipline and motivation to keep up with your work and finish what you start. What you require is scheduling flexibility (to accommodate a busy home life or an unpredictable work schedule, for instance). If that describes you, then you should look for a distance-learning program that has no fixed start or end time and that allows students to work at their own pace, such as a correspondence course or a course on videotape.

Most people fall somewhere between these two extremes. For them, a hybrid course that combines a self-paced work course with some interaction, such as one class meeting a week, would work best.

Another quality that varies from student to student is learning style. Some people are strong readers and learn best from a textbook; for them, a correspondence course is a good choice. Others better absorb information when it is presented visually; they should choose a video-based course. Students who are experienced with the computer and comfortable with using the Internet benefit most from a computer-based course.

The trick is to evaluate how you work and what your needs are first, before considering distance-learning programs. Then, you can seek out a program that will be the best fit for you.

Employer's Perceptions of Distance-Learning Degrees

Many potential distance-learning students worry that future employers will consider a degree earned through distance learning to be inferior to a degree earned the traditional way. For students who want to use distance learning as the means of obtaining a job promotion or raise, or use a new degree or certificate to make a career change, this can be a very important concern.

The truth is that most employers don't care *how* you earn your degree—what's more important is *where* you earned it. In one study, 100 percent of human resources and personnel officers at major companies said that they would consider a job candidate with a distance-learning degree, as long as the degree came from an accredited program. (You'll learn more about accreditation in Chapter 3). Some people responsible for company hiring actually preferred the candidates with distance-learning degrees, because that demonstrated that the applicants were highly motivated, organized, and self-disciplined, and were capable of working independently.

Many long-established, highly prestigious colleges and universities are now establishing distance-learning programs. This means that more students than ever before are able to earn a degree from a big-name school, such as Harvard, Duke, or Stanford. What employer wouldn't find that impressive?

Unofficially...
You can't tell by looking at a diploma whether it was earned through distance learning or traditionally. So, unless you make a point of telling potential employers that you got your degree through distance learning, they probably won't ever know.

Going to Graduate School with a Distance-Learning Degree

Another major concern for many potential distance-learning students is whether graduate schools accept students who earn an undergraduate degree from a distance-learning program. Unfortunately, this situation isn't as clear-cut as with distance-learning students who go on to enter the job market.

At the graduate level, admissions decisions are not made by the school, but by the individual academic department where you want to study. Admissions policies can vary greatly even within the same university, and you just can't predict whether a distance-learning degree will make a real difference to the admissions committee.

For the most part, graduate schools accept distance-learning degrees if they are earned from a regionally accredited program. But a fair number won't accept degrees from schools that are accredited by the Distance Education and Training Council, the only nationally recognized agency that solely accredits distance-learning programs. Therefore, if you intend to get a master's or doctorate someday, you must be extremely careful about which distance-learning program you choose to earn your bachelor's degree from, as accreditation can make all the difference. It's also a good idea to find out what percentage of graduates of the distance-learning program is accepted to graduate school. Research a program as if you are applying to a traditional college.

Remember that many master's and doctorate programs are available through distance education. Increasingly, institutions of higher education perceive distance learning as a legitimate, effective means of getting an education. Because of this, you can expect a distance-learning degree to become much more widely accepted by graduate schools in the future.

Just the Facts

- Distance learning offers many benefits, including scheduling flexibility, an individually tailored course of study, and financial savings.

- While a well-designed distance-learning program is just as effective as a traditional education, some students will naturally learn better in the college or university setting.

- Distance learning requires many personal and academic skills for success; if you identify your strengths and weaknesses ahead of time, you're more likely to choose a program that works best for you.

- Most employers don't distinguish between a degree earned through distance learning and one earned the traditional way, and some even prefer the job applicant who is also a distance learner.

- While policies differ among academic departments and universities, distance-learning degrees from regionally accredited programs are becoming readily accepted by graduate and professional schools.

GET THE SCOOP ON...
Determining your goals for taking a distance-learning
program ▪ Evaluating distance-learning programs for
quality and how well they fit your specific needs ▪ The importance
of accreditation of distance-learning programs ▪ Avoiding scams,
worthless programs, and diploma mills ▪ Checklist for selecting a
distance-learning program

Choosing a Distance-Learning Program

Chapter 3

With the recent advent of computer and Internet technologies, the field of distance learning has exploded. The resulting smorgasbord of new programs gives distance learners lots of choices, but it can also make it difficult to choose the best program. Most distance-learning programs haven't been in operation long enough to really establish themselves as "the best." In addition, there are so many variables in distance-learning programs, such as the course structure and the technologies used in the program, that it's difficult to compare one program to another. Testing the quality of a distance-learning program and settling on one that meets your needs present real challenges.

In this chapter, you'll learn how to evaluate distance-learning programs and select one that will meet your educational goals and individual requirements. The first step is to determine what your goals are for continuing your education through distance learning. With those goals in mind, you can zero in on the programs that will best meet them while avoiding the duds.

Determining Your Goals

The first question you should ask yourself is: What exactly do you want to accomplish by continuing your education? Knowing your goals before you go looking for a distance-learning program will ensure that you make fewer mistakes when choosing a program.

The following are some examples of goals that distance learning can meet:

- Change careers
- Get a raise, promotion, or better job
- Finish an interrupted degree

- Earn a higher degree
- Take credit courses for transfer to a program you're already enrolled in
- Supplement a homeschooling education
- Learn a specific task or skill
- Improve your sense of self-worth and personal accomplishment

Once you've determined your end goal, that should naturally lead to questions about the distance-learning program that you want to take. For example, perhaps your goal is to earn a professional certificate. You should look for distance-learning certification programs that are recognized in your field and that meet all the requirements by the appropriate certifying agency or licensing board.

Or perhaps you want to get a better job or a promotion in your existing job. You must make certain that the distance-learning program you want to take will help you accomplish this goal. Find out your employer's requirements for promotion and choose a distance-learning program that meets those requirements.

Determining your educational goals before you start searching for a program has another benefit—it motivates you to complete the distance-learning program you eventually enroll in. If you know that at the end of the program you will possess the means to secure a better job or a higher salary, then you will be more likely to keep working until you accomplish that goal.

Evaluating Distance-Learning Programs

The directory of distance-learning programs in Part Two of this book should include several programs that you think will help you meet your educational goals. The next step is to evaluate the quality of the programs on your short list and determine which one best fits your needs and learning style.

Choosing a high-quality distance-learning program is all-important. For one thing, a well-designed and well-implemented distance-learning program is much more likely to sustain your interest, so that you'll stick with the program to the end. Also, a high-quality program results in a degree or certificate that is more valuable in the eyes of future employers, graduate schools, and professional agencies.

But how do you go about evaluating the quality of a distance-learning program? First, you should contact someone at the school, generally someone in the admissions department, and request a brochure and catalog for each program that interests you. These materials are good starting points for comparing the programs on your list. (The checklist at the end of this chapter will help you make those comparisons.)

Your contact in the admissions department should be able (and willing) to answer all of your questions about the program. Don't hesitate to call the school, no matter what your question is or how basic it may seem.

Time Saver
Many professionally oriented distance-learning program administrators will communicate directly with employers to explain the program and establish credentials. Not only can this help you ensure that taking the program will lead to a promotion, but it also may convince your employer to reimburse you for the cost of the program.

If information is missing from the catalog or if any of the details are confusing to you, call and ask about it. A sign of a good program is being able to easily contact someone who knowledgeably and cheerfully answers all of your questions.

If you have trouble getting your questions answered, then consider another program. There are so many distance-learning programs operating now that you should have plenty of choices. Therefore, you have the luxury of selecting the program that you feel most comfortable taking. Remember that you're investing a lot of money in your education, so you want to make sure that you're getting the most value for your investment from the start.

The following are the most important qualities to look for in a potential distance-learning program:

- Technologies used in the program
- Course structure and schedule
- Interaction with instructors
- Experience and expertise of the faculty
- Class size and interaction
- Longevity
- Student satisfaction
- Cost
- Student services and other extras
- Accreditation

When you turn to the program listings in Part II of this book, you'll find all of this important information listed, so you can determine at a glance whether a particular program is likely to meet your needs. But don't stop there. Always contact the program directly, request a catalog, and ask numerous questions to ensure that the program is right for you *before* investing your time and money in it.

Kind of Program

Your first consideration should be the kinds of technologies that are used to conduct the distance-learning program. Is the program essentially a correspondence course, or is it completely Internet-based? Does it use video or audio technologies? Does it combine a number of different technologies?

The answers to these questions should help you decide whether a particular program is a good fit for you. You've already given some thought to how you learn best. If you've determined that you're primarily a visual learner, then you know to avoid correspondence courses. If getting on the computer intimidates you, then an Internet-based course is probably not a good choice.

There are other considerations, as well. For example, what special equipment is required to complete the program? The cost of purchasing a new computer or satellite dish may be prohibitive. The course may require frequent use of a fax machine; would you be willing to buy one or run down to your local copy shop every time you need to send or receive a fax? Give careful thought to the equipment that the program requires and whether you're willing to invest the money to buy it and the time to learn how to use it.

Think about where you plan to complete your lessons, as well. If most of your free time is during the commute to and from work, an audio-based course taught on cassettes that you can play in your car is a good choice. If you plan to study during your lunch hour, you need a program type that's easily portable, such as a print- or audio-based course. But if you plan to work at home at night and on the weekends, a video- or computer-based course may be a better choice for you.

Course Schedule and Structure

Class schedules are an important consideration. If you choose a program with a schedule that conflicts too much with your work or home life, chances are good that you'll neglect your coursework. Some programs schedule a regular, live lecture on television, the radio, or the Internet that occurs once or twice a week. Some programs require regular, real-time class meetings through teleconferencing or over the computer. If the program you're considering has these features, will you be able to fit the scheduled class meetings into your schedule? If your schedule is too busy or too unpredictable to accommodate regular class meetings, then consider a distance-learning program that is completely asynchronous, such as a correspondence course.

Bright Idea
Ask to review the course syllabus or other course materials in order to judge the quality of the course content. Many programs even allow you to preview a lesson or sit in on a class session before signing up.

Course content is another important characteristic that you should look at. Will the program adequately meet your needs for the field that you're pursuing? Are the courses offered for a degree or certification program acceptable to employers, graduate schools, and certifying agencies? Do you have a lot of choice when it comes to course selection? Can you take electives? How is coursework evaluated—will you receive a grade or are courses pass/fail? (Note that some schools don't accept the transfer credits of pass/fail courses.) How are exams administered? Comparing course offerings to similar degree or certificate programs, particularly those offered by traditional schools, is a good way to judge the quality of course content.

Finally, find out how the courses and the program are structured. Find out how long the program usually takes to complete and if you are required to finish within a certain timeframe. A free-form structure with no strict starting and ending dates and no hard-and-fast deadlines better suits students who have busy, unpredictable schedules or who need to work at their own pace. On the other hand, a strict structure with preset deadlines, regularly scheduled class meetings, and specific starting and ending dates is the better choice for the student who needs more structure in order to stay motivated and disciplined. If you anticipate crises at work or major life changes, look for programs that you can leave and reenter with little trouble.

Instructor Interaction

As I mentioned in Chapter 2, "Is Distance Learning Right for You?" instructor interaction is a vital component of a high-quality distance-learning program. Frequent instructor interaction provides two benefits. First, you receive feedback on your assignments within a short amount of time, so you can better judge how you're progressing in the course. Second, you have a good resource to turn to if you have questions or get bogged down at some point.

In a good distance-learning program, the instructor should be readily available to you. While evaluating programs, ask how you will turn in assignments and how quickly you'll receive feedback on those assignments. Find out if you can easily contact the instructors by phone, fax, or e-mail with questions and concerns, and if instructors conduct regular office hours when you can be sure to reach them.

But keep in mind that programs that offer excellent opportunities for instructor-student interaction are only worthwhile if you take advantage of those opportunities. Don't be afraid to contact the instructor with any questions or concerns that you may have during the course of the program—you'll better ensure your success in the long run.

Faculty Experience and Expertise

Distance learning is very different from traditional education, and requires a different teaching style. Beware of programs where the instructors are faculty members who have been coerced into teaching a distance-learning course in addition to their traditional courses. Look instead for programs where the instructors are experienced with distance learning and have been teaching that way for a number of years.

You should also try to avoid programs where the instructors don't possess adequate expertise in the fields they are teaching. This is particularly important at the graduate level. You should easily be able to ascertain an instructor's credentials, credibility in the field, real-world experience (for professional programs), and educational background while researching the program.

Another important consideration, particularly if you plan to enter a long-term degree program, is faculty size. Will a large number of qualified instructors be available to you? How many members of the faculty teach full-time and how many teach part-time? High-quality programs have obvious ties to reputable professional organizations, colleges, and universities.

Class Size and Interaction

One important factor in any educational program, and one that many distance-learning programs neglect, is interaction among all the students in the class. As I mentioned in Chapter 2, classroom interaction is a vital component of an effective distance-learning program. Look for programs that offer opportunities to hold discussions with classmates. Computer technologies provide the best means of classroom interaction, with choices like

Money Saver
Many distance-learning programs provide toll-free telephone numbers where you can contact instructors.

Watch Out!
Find out where faculty members received their degrees. If too many of the faculty (more than 25 percent) earned their degrees from the same institution where they now teach, that's a sign that the program is of poor quality or perhaps an outright scam.

e-mail discussion groups, bulletin board systems, real-time chat rooms, and interactive virtual worlds.

Another important consideration is class size. This might not seem like a big deal in distance learning; after all, you don't actually have to get together in a classroom. But big classes can make a significant difference in the quality of a program.

Since there is no physical classroom in distance education, the temptation is to pack classes with as many paying students as possible. But too many students mean too much competition for the instructor's personal attention. Contact between the student and the instructor is vital to your success in the program, and anything that reduces the amount of student-instructor interaction is a drawback. Ideally, look for programs that assign no more than 25 to 30 students to each instructor.

At the same time, you should avoid programs that are too small. A small number of students may indicate that the program has too few faculty or resources to meet your needs.

Program Longevity

Distance education is very different from traditional education and cannot be structured the same way. You need to look for distance-learning programs that take advantage of available technologies to most effectively present the subject matter being taught.

You can't rely on name-brand schools to provide the best programs. Distance learning as it exists today is a relatively new area of education, and many colleges and universities are scrambling to get in on the distance-education boom. Their programs may be so new that they haven't yet ironed out the kinks, which means you won't receive the quality that you might expect from a well-known institution or what the on-campus students receive.

On the other hand, a small college that you've never heard of may have developed an innovative distance-learning program and tested it over a number of years. A program that's been in place longer is more likely to be of higher quality with more experienced instructors than one that was just started a year ago.

But don't expect to find distance-learning programs that have been operating for 50 or 100 years. Remember that distance education has only gained prominence in the last 30 years or so. Therefore, a "long-established" distance-learning program might be one that has been operating for 10 years, rather than 100.

Student Satisfaction

Another indication of an educational program's quality is student satisfaction with the program. When researching a program, find out what proportion of students who enroll actually complete the program. If there is a high dropout rate, try to discover why students drop out.

Bright Idea
Professional societies in your field and nationally recognized accrediting agencies can generally provide reliable information about the history and performance of a particular distance-learning program.

Determine what graduates do after finishing the program. How long does it typically take them to find employment? What percentage goes on to earn a higher degree? All of these numbers paint a good picture of how well students benefit from the program.

Program Cost

Of course, program cost is going to be a major consideration. You will surely be looking for a program that fits your budget. (Chapter 5, "Paying for It," provides information about getting help with the tuition.)

There are other considerations than just the base cost of the course or the program, though. For instance: Will you have to pay for course materials and extra services separately, or are they included in the base tuition? If you decide to leave the program, will you be able to receive reimbursement for all or part of your tuition? Will you have to pay the entire tuition up-front, or can you make spread payments out over time? Look for a program with flexible payment options and a reasonable refund policy.

Student Services and Other Extras

Distance-learning programs often skimp on student services, which can be a major drawback. Look for programs that offer student services you consider important, such as the following:

- Academic advising (an extremely important service for anyone entering a degree program)
- Tutoring
- Technical support
- Career counseling
- Digital library resources

Some services become even more important to students who lack local resources. For instance, your local library may not be adequate for your research needs. If that's the case, search for programs that allow distance-learning students access to a large, computer-based library, so that you can be assured of being able to complete your assignments.

All-Important Accreditation

Accreditation is probably the most important, and the most confusing, criterion when it comes to picking a distance-education program. Why is accreditation so important? In a nutshell, it determines whether the degree or certificate you earn through distance learning will be a valuable one that is universally respected by colleges, employers, and professional agencies, or whether it will be a worthless piece of paper.

Accreditation is a peculiarly American phenomenon. In every other country, a centralized government agency evaluates the quality of the schools within the country. But in the United States, we don't have such an agency. To take its place, private, nonprofit accrediting agencies have been established. These agencies evaluate the quality of schools within a particular region or professional field and accredit the schools that meet the standards established by the accrediting agency. Accreditation validates a school or academic department and ensures that students will receive a quality education from that institution.

The problem is that in the United States, there is not just one centralized agency that accredits all schools. On the contrary, there are hundreds of accrediting agencies in existence right now, and it is absurdly easy to establish a new agency. So, who accredits the accrediting agencies?

Two national organizations recognize accrediting agencies: the U.S. Department of Education and the Council for Higher Education Accreditation (CHEA). Accrediting agencies that are recognized by one or both of these organizations are said to be nationally recognized agencies.

Nationally recognized accrediting agencies are the only legitimate accrediting bodies in the United States. They follow the Generally Accepted Accredited Principles (GAAP). In the U.S., there is near-unanimous agreement on GAAP by institutions of higher education, businesses, and government agencies, so accreditation by a nationally recognized accrediting agency is the closest thing this country has to national accreditation.

The U.S. Department of Education and CHEA publish a list of the accrediting agencies that each organization recognizes. You can get a copy of the list and obtain more information about accreditation by contacting these organizations directly. (You'll also find a comprehensive list of nationally recognized accrediting agencies and contact information in Appendix D of this book.)

Here's how to contact the U.S. Department of Education:

> U.S. Department of Education
> Office of Postsecondary Education
> Regional Office Building 3
> 7th and D Streets SW
> Washington, DC 20202
> www.ed.gov/offices/OPE/index.html

And here's how you can get in touch with CHEA:

> Council for Higher Education Accreditation
> One Dupont Circle NW, Suite 510
> Washington, DC, 20036-1135
> 202-955-6126
> www.chea.org/

To make matters even more confusing, there are two kinds of accrediting agencies in the United States: regional accrediting agencies and professional accrediting agencies. Each kind serves a very different function in accrediting institutions of higher education.

Unofficially...
In foreign countries like the United Kingdom, Canada, and Australia, the country's centralized higher education evaluation process is generally accepted as accreditation under GAAP. Therefore, established foreign colleges and universities are generally accepted as accredited by American schools. Still, if you want to take a program from a foreign school, it's best to double-check that you can transfer credits or receive certification earned from that program in the U.S.

Regional Accrediting Agencies

Both the U.S. Department of Education and CHEA recognize six regional accrediting agencies. These agencies are responsible for accrediting schools within a particular region of the country.

The following are the six regional accrediting agencies:

- **Middle States Association of Colleges and Schools:** accredits schools in Delaware, the District of Columbia, Maryland, New Jersey, New York, Pennsylvania, Puerto Rico, the Republic of Panama, and the Virgin Islands

- **New England Association of Schools and Colleges:** accredits schools in Connecticut, Maine, Massachusetts, New Hampshire, Rhode Island, and Vermont

- **North Central Association of Colleges and Schools:** accredits schools in Arizona, Arkansas, Colorado, Illinois, Indiana, Iowa, Kansas, Michigan, Minnesota, Missouri, Nebraska, New Mexico, North Dakota, Ohio, Oklahoma, South Dakota, West Virginia, Wisconsin, Wyoming, and the Navajo Nation

- **Northwest Association of Schools and Colleges:** accredits schools in Alaska, Idaho, Montana, Nevada, Oregon, Utah, and Washington

- **Southern Association of Colleges and Schools:** accredits schools in Alabama, Florida, Georgia, Kentucky, Louisiana, Mississippi, North Carolina, South Carolina, Tennessee, Texas, Virginia, and most of Latin America

- **Western Association of Schools and Colleges:** accredits schools in California, Hawaii, American Samoa, the Federated States of Micronesia, Guam, Marshall Islands, Northern Marianas, and the Republic of Palau

Regional accreditation sets the standards regarding a school's faculty, the quality of the school's learning resources and facilities, and the school's financial strength. These standards are universally recognized by other accredited schools, as well as by employers.

Thus, regional accreditation provides a framework for transferring credits from one school to another and for earning advanced degrees. If you transfer course credits to another college or university, the courses must be from a regionally accredited school. If you want to earn a master's or doctorate degree, you must have received your bachelor's degree from a regionally accredited school.

When a regional accrediting agency accredits a school, it accredits the entire school and every academic program operating under the umbrella of that school, including distance-learning programs. Therefore, if you take a distance-learning program from a regionally accredited school, you can rest assured that the program has received regional accreditation as well.

Professional Accrediting Agencies

Professional accrediting agencies differ from regional accrediting agencies in that they only accredit a particular professional school or academic department within a college or university. Professional accreditation does not extend to the entire school, like regional accreditation does; if a college or university receives regional accreditation, then every program within that school is also regionally accredited, regardless of whether it receives professional accreditation.

Professional accreditation requires a particular academic department or professional school to stand on its own, outside the umbrella of its parent college or university. This type of accreditation evaluates the quality of the academic department's curriculum, faculty, and resources, and sets standards for admission requirements, faculty selection, and curriculum development. These standards can vary greatly, depending on the field.

Time Saver
Check with colleagues in your industry or professional associations to determine how important professional accreditation is in your chosen field.

The importance of professional accreditation varies greatly from industry to industry. In some fields, like business, professional accreditation is not very important. In others, like engineering, professional accreditation is vital and may stand in the way of getting a job in the industry. And some professions, like law, nursing, and psychology, require students to attend professionally accredited schools in order to receive a license to practice in that field.

Approximately 80 professional accreditation agencies are recognized by either the U.S. Department of Education or CHEA, or both. Turn to Appendix D at the back of the book for a list of these agencies and contact information.

Accreditation and Distance Learning

Accreditation by a nationally recognized accrediting agency is the No. 1 verification of quality of a distance-learning program. It is also the only way to guarantee that the distance-learning program meets current academic standards and isn't simply a scam or a diploma mill. Because so many fraudulent distance-learning programs are out there, accreditation should be the first thing you look for when choosing a program.

Seeking accreditation is entirely voluntary. Many perfectly legitimate schools have opted to forego accreditation because the process of becoming accredited is so expensive or because the schools are too experimental to meet the standards of the rather conservative accrediting agencies. Other schools may be too new to have received accreditation, which requires a lengthy review process.

But these schools are relatively few, especially when compared to the large number of outright scams that are posing as legitimate schools. It's much better to play it safe and pick an accredited school than to take a risk on an unaccredited one—even if you think that the unaccredited school is completely legitimate.

Getting a degree from an unaccredited school is likely to cause you problems down the line. Regional accreditation is required to transfer course credits, seek a higher degree, or gain employment at many companies. Even if you don't have any of these goals right now, you may change your mind (or your job) later. You don't want to end up having to get your degree all over again just because the first time you didn't earn it from an accredited school.

Even choosing a program that has received professional accreditation but not regional accreditation may pose some problems. Some colleges and universities only recognize regional accreditation; professional accreditation doesn't matter to them. For example, some regionally accredited schools won't accept credits from a school accredited by the Distance Education and Training Council, which accredits distance-learning programs, or by the Accrediting Association of Bible Colleges, which accredits Bible colleges, even though both agencies are nationally recognized by CHEA and the U.S. Department of Education. Therefore, your degree from a professionally accredited program still won't count when transferring course credits or applying to graduate school, unless a regionally accredited college or university offered the program.

To sum all of this up, you can't go wrong if you choose a distance-learning program offered by a regionally accredited school.

All of the distance-learning programs listed in Part II of this book are accredited by a nationally recognized accrediting agency. The agencies that have accredited the program are listed in the program description. To be safe, you should double-check any program's accreditation; accreditation can be withdrawn, or a program may have been put on probation since this book was written. Contact the accrediting agency directly and ask if the school or program has received accreditation. You'll find contact information for all of the nationally recognized accrediting agencies in Appendix D at the back of the book.

Avoiding Scams

Thousands of distance-learning programs are in operation today, and the majority of them are not accredited by any nationally recognized accrediting agency. These programs fall into three general categories:

- Legitimate programs that have elected not to pursue accreditation or that are too new to be accredited

- Programs that go just over the line by trying to trick potential students into thinking they are legitimately accredited

- Outright scams (also called diploma mills)

These three types of programs all have one thing in common. Because no nationally recognized accrediting agency accredits these programs, any

Unofficially...
Accreditation may not be all that crucial for students taking a single course to accomplish a specific goal—to learn a new skill needed for a job, for instance. Many business and computing courses are unaccredited but still considered valuable by employers. But accreditation becomes much more important if you intend to transfer course credits to a degree or certification program.

degree, certificate, or course they offer is not recognized by any legitimately accredited school—or by employers, certifying agencies, and licensing boards. Therefore, it's best to avoid all three programs.

The simplest way to avoid these is to only consider distance-learning programs offered by schools that have received accreditation from a nationally recognized accrediting agency. But this may be more difficult than it sounds, particularly when you're dealing with the fraudulent programs that employ all sorts of clever ruses in order to trick you into thinking they are legitimate. In this section, we examine some of the most common tricks used by these fraudulent distance-learning programs.

Accreditation Pitfalls

As you've already learned, accreditation alone doesn't guarantee a school's legitimacy. The school must be accredited by an agency approved by either the U.S. Department of Education or the Council on Higher Education Accreditation.

I stress the importance of this because it's all too easy to start an accrediting agency. Anyone can do it. And that's just what some fraudulent distance-learning programs do—start their own accrediting agency and then claim to be accredited by it. Often, the name of the accrediting agency is very similar to the name of a legitimate agency. The school may even try to lend credence to the phony accrediting agency by having the agency "accredit" well-known colleges and universities. But the accreditation is still worthless.

Furthermore, any school can claim to be accredited by any agency, whether it actually is or not. That's why it's crucial to double-check all claims of accreditation. There's nothing to stop a fraudulent distance-learning program from claiming accreditation by one of the nationally recognized accrediting agencies. But unless the agency itself verifies the claim, you can't trust it. That's why I've included contact information for all nationally recognized accrediting agencies in Appendix D of this book—so you can check a program's accreditation claims for yourself with a simple phone call or visit to a Web site.

Some schools may not be regionally accredited but may claim state approval instead. This is not a trick; these schools usually *have* been approved by their states. But state approval is not worth nearly as much as accreditation. Standards for state approval are often much less stringent than the standards set by the regional accrediting agencies. The states rely on the regional accrediting agencies to set and uphold academic standards, so they don't have to. Therefore, a program that has won state approval but hasn't received regional accreditation probably isn't worth very much, and certainly won't be recognized by other colleges and universities.

Another common ruse of fraudulent programs is to claim that the school is pursuing accreditation or that it intends to pursue accreditation. Or the school may claim to be chartered, licensed, registered, recognized, authorized, or approved. But these claims mean nothing. Just because a school pursues accreditation doesn't mean that it will actually be accredited. Until the school receives accreditation, any degrees earned there will not be worth much when you decide to pursue further education or employment.

Something for Nothing

Most people know that you can rarely get something for nothing, and usually what you do get isn't worth very much. But we're all tempted, especially when the alternative is to pay thousands of dollars. Diploma mills take advantage of this temptation to scam students out of their money in exchange for worthless, phony degrees. What's more, they're outright scams and completely illegal.

All a diploma mill asks for from its students is money. It doesn't require students to complete coursework, undergo testing, or otherwise earn the degree. And they employ all sorts of techniques to get students to fork over their hard-earned cash:

- They make phony accreditation claims.
- They advertise heavily, particularly on the Internet or in the back of magazines.
- They employ high-pressure telemarketing techniques.
- They make lofty promises, such as promising a bachelor's degree after taking just five courses or promising professional licensure without having to take a board examination.

What do you end up with? A degree that isn't worth the paper it's printed on. Diploma mills don't fool graduate schools, certifying agencies, licensing boards, and employers; none will accept an applicant who holds a degree from a mill. In fact, trying to pass off a fraudulent degree as legitimate is a good way to get yourself drummed out of your chosen profession, even if you don't know the degree is fraudulent.

So, the next time you see a distance-learning program advertising that you can earn a college degree in just six weeks or for just $500, beware. Getting a real degree requires years of hard work, whether you earn it through distance education or the traditional way. The work you put into earning a degree or certificate is what gives it its value. And if you want a high-quality education, you usually have to pay for it. Don't fall for the "something-for-nothing" trap.

Looks Can Be Deceiving

One common way that fraudulent or unaccredited distance-learning programs try to trick students into signing up is by making themselves look better than they really are.

For instance, the school may slap together a snazzy-looking Web site or a slick catalog. The Web site may include photographs of an impressive

Unofficially...
If you are considering taking a course from an unaccredited program—a single course to learn a new job skill, for instance—it's safer to take one from a school that doesn't claim accreditation at all, rather than from one that claims accreditation from an unrecognized or phony accrediting agency.

building—but you have no way of knowing whether this is the school's actual campus, a building where the school rents an office or two, or perhaps just a building in the school's city that has nothing to do with the school. The catalog may list a large number of faculty members, but without further investigation, you can't determine their qualifications. Some scams even list names of people who have nothing to do with the school or that are completely made up.

Don't be taken in by flash without any substance. You have to look deeper than the school's own literature when investigating a distance-learning program. Getting an unbiased, outside opinion on the program's worth is the best way to verify its quality—which is what accreditation is all about.

Spotting a Scam

Watch Out!
You should immediately suspect any distance-learning program that denies that it is a diploma mill; no legitimate program would feel the need to make such a statement.

When you're investigating distance-learning programs, be aware of signs that the program is a scam. The following are the most common signs to look for:

- *No printed catalog.* Legitimate schools always have a printed catalog that you can order, not just a Web site. Your first step when investigating a distance-learning program should be to obtain a copy of the catalog.

- *No physical address.* Legitimate schools have a physical campus or offices of some kind. Be wary of schools that list only a post office box as their address.

- *Frequent moves.* Schools that frequently move or that have relocated from one state to another are suspect. Relocating a legitimate college or university is a major move and rarely happens. A school that moves too often may be too small to meet your needs or may be trying to outrun the law.

- *No one to answer your questions.* When you call a legitimate school, the person on the other end of the line should be able to easily answer any questions you may have about the program. Be suspicious if you call repeatedly and are always told that the person you need to talk to isn't available and must call you back.

- *Super-easy admissions policies.* Even open-admission colleges require a high school diploma or GED, and no graduate or professional school will admit you without a bachelor's degree. Also, watch out for programs that readily give you credit for past experiences without careful examination or placement testing, or programs that don't request your academic transcripts from the schools you previously attended.

By purchasing this *Unofficial Guide*™, you save yourself the trouble of having to weed out diploma mills or worthless distance-learning programs. All of the programs listed in this book are accredited by one or more of the nationally recognized accrediting agencies. The accrediting agencies are listed in the program's description, so you can double-check the accreditation for yourself. Remember, just because a program isn't listed in this book doesn't automatically mean that it's a scam or even that it's not a good program; but to be safe, stick with the accredited programs.

Program Selection Checklist

It's time for you to start choosing which distance-learning programs you want to consider for enrollment. Part II of this book lists hundreds of programs from accredited schools, along with important information about each program. Your goals for continuing your education should be fixed in your mind before turning to Part II. Once this has been accomplished, seek out programs that you think best fulfill your goals. For each program that you find, contact the school directly to request a catalog.

The checklist on the following page will help you when you start evaluating your final list of distance-learning programs. Make one copy of the checklist for each program that you're seriously considering. When you receive the program's catalog, fill out the worksheet. This will ensure that you have all the important information in one place. After you read the catalog, call the school directly and request answers to any remaining questions.

When you're done completing the worksheet for each program, you can lay the worksheets side by side to directly compare different programs. This should help you easily choose the best program for you based on characteristics like cost, length of program, special services, and entrance requirements.

Just the Facts

- Before you start looking at distance-learning programs, establish clear goals for continuing your education; this will help you choose the right program, and it will motivate you to finish that program.

- It's important to evaluate all aspects of a distance-learning program before signing up, both for overall quality and for whether the program meets your individual needs. Don't be afraid to ask questions.

- Accreditation is the most important, and most confusing, requirement for a good distance-learning program; look for programs that have received accreditation from a nationally recognized accrediting agency, preferably one of the regional accrediting agencies.

- The distance-learning boom is spawning a large number of scams, diploma mills, and other shady programs; evaluate distance-learning programs carefully and double-check accreditation claims to ensure that you're not getting taken.

Bright Idea
If possible, try to visit the campuses of the schools offering the distance-learning programs where you want to enroll. This can help you form an impression of the school's quality, and talking face-to-face with admissions officers and distance-learning instructors can help you determine whether the program is right for you.

DISTANCE-LEARNING PROGRAM SELECTION CHECKLIST

School: _____

Kind of program: ☐ Professional certificate ☐ Associate's degree ☐ Bachelor's degree ☐ Master's degree ☐ Doctorate ☐ Credit courses only (no degree)

Major or field of study: _____

Accreditation: ☐ Regional accreditation (note accrediting agency: _____ _____) ☐ Professional accreditation (note accrediting agency: ____ _____)

Cost of program: _____

Cost of course materials: _____

Additional fees: _____

Financial aid/scholarships offered: ☐ Yes ☐ No

Payment plan: ☐ Yes ☐ No

Refunds offered for early withdrawal: ☐ Yes ☐ No

Trial course offered: ☐ Yes ☐ No

Technologies used (check all that apply): ☐ Correspondence course ☐ Audio tape ☐ Radio ☐ Voice conferencing ☐ Videotape ☐ Television broadcast ☐ Cable TV ☐ Satellite TV ☐ Interactive TV ☐ Software ☐ Internet ☐ Other: _____

Required equipment: _____
_____

Regularly scheduled class meetings: ☐ Yes ☐ No
Time/Day of meetings: _____

Means of instructor interaction: _____

Means of class interaction: _____

Program start date: _____

Length of program: _____

Number of students enrolled in program: _____

Dropout rate: _____

Faculty/student ratio: _____

Number of instructors:_____

Instructor credentials (degrees, professional experience, experience teaching at a distance): _____
_____

Year program was established: _____

Entrance requirements: _____
_____

Special services: _____
_____

Getting into a Program

O nce you've evaluated a variety of distance-learning programs and decided on one (or a few) that you think would be ideal for you, the next step is to get admitted to the program. As you've already learned, distance-learning programs vary greatly in terms of course content, structure, and the communications technologies used to facilitate the program. They also vary in their admissions policies and competitiveness. Some programs admit all comers who hold a high school diploma or a GED. Others are highly competitive and require a rigorous application process.

Once again, you should be thinking about your goals for continuing your education, as well as your personal qualifications, when deciding which kind of program to apply to. If you simply want to finish up an interrupted bachelor's degree or earn a professional certificate, you may choose to avoid the stress of applying to a highly competitive degree program. But if a degree from a prestigious, well-known school will greatly benefit you in your chosen field, or if you're planning to pursue graduate education, you should probably search out the best program in your area and go for it, regardless of how strict the admissions policies are.

In this chapter, you'll learn what to expect during the application process. You'll find out about the admission requirements for different distance-learning programs. And you'll discover how to succeed—regardless of which program you choose.

How to Apply

Application procedures for distance-learning programs vary greatly, depending on the school offering the program, the type of degree or certificate earned through the program, and the polices of the academic department offering the program.

If you simply want to take distance-learning courses for college credit, but you don't want to earn a degree or certificate, you will only have to fill out a short registration form or nondegree application form in most cases.

37

You should receive a copy of the registration form with the course catalog. At many schools, you can also register for courses by phone or fill out the registration form at the school's Web site. Before registering for the course, make certain that you have fulfilled all of the course's prerequisites and that you have all the required equipment. In most cases, you will have to pay the entire course fee when you register.

If you would like to enter a distance-learning degree program, you have to apply for admission to the college or university sponsoring the program. You must submit an application for admission, which you can obtain by contacting the admissions department at the school directly. Many schools now allow you to submit application forms online at the school's Web site as well.

In addition to the application form, you may have to submit any or all of the following:

- High school, community college, and/or college transcripts
- Standardized test scores
- A portfolio of your past experiences and accomplishments
- Letters of recommendation from teachers or employers
- An original essay
- Copies of diplomas or certificates that you have previously earned
- Your resume
- Application fee (ranging from $10 to $100)

No matter what kind of program you decide to enroll in, you should contact the admissions department directly before submitting an application. Take the time to find out what the application procedures are, what the admission standards are, what you need to submit in order to apply, and application deadlines. That way, you ensure that your application package is complete, increasing your chances for a quick acceptance. You also won't waste your time (and application fee) applying to a program where you don't meet the entrance requirements.

Meeting the Entrance Requirements

Some schools, particularly community colleges and four-year colleges geared solely toward working adults, maintain open admission policies. That means that all you need to be admitted to the program is a high school diploma or a GED.

Others, especially prestigious colleges, universities, and professional schools, maintain more stringent admission standards. At these schools, applicants compete for admission to a limited number of spots in the program.

These competitive schools strongly consider your past academic, professional, and personal achievements when considering your application. You are evaluated based on your grades, test scores, past achievements, letters of recommendation, and an essay. If you apply for admission to a competitive program, you must take pains to make yourself as attractive as possible in your application package.

If you do want to enroll in a competitive degree program, it's a good idea to apply to three or four programs to hedge your bets in case your top choice doesn't accept you. Ideally, you should select one program that is a "reach" (where you aren't sure if you meet all the entrance requirements) and one that's a "safety" (where you're sure you'll be accepted). The remaining choices should be mid-range programs, where you feel comfortable about your chances of being accepted. But most importantly, make certain that you only apply to programs that meet your requirements and that you will be happy participating in.

Academics and Work Experience

If you intend to enter an undergraduate degree program (bachelor's or associate's degree), you will need to submit your high school transcript along with your application. You can obtain a copy of your high school transcript by calling your high school and requesting one. You may also be asked to provide proof of graduation from high school by submitting a copy of your diploma or GED.

As a nontraditional older student, though, your high school grades are not as important as what you have accomplished since high school. In addition to your high school transcript, you should submit transcripts from any community colleges or four-year colleges that you have attended. In fact, several distance-learning undergraduate degree programs require students to have completed some college-level work—usually the equivalent of one to two years—before entering their program.

The admissions department will more heavily weigh your work at the college or community college level than your work in high school. You don't have to be an A student, but a C average or better will make you a more attractive candidate for admission. If you've taken college-level courses outside the college setting or you previously took credit courses without entering a degree program or completed college courses while in high school—the admissions department will count that work in with the bulk of your higher-education experience.

If you apply for admission to a master's or doctoral program, your past academic achievements become much more important. You need to submit an academic transcript from the college where you earned your bachelor's degree (and from the university where you earned your master's, if you are pursuing a Ph.D.). Most graduate schools require applicants to have obtained a certain grade point average (GPA) in college, usually 2.0 or higher. In addition, the graduate school will probably require at least one letter of recommendation from a college professor who worked closely with you and who can describe your academic achievements and skills.

As a working adult, your work experience will be extremely important to the admissions department. For some programs (such as master's programs in engineering or nursing), several years of experience working in the field

Bright Idea
Help your supervisor or coworker write a dynamite letter of recommendation. Provide a summary of your work and education history, along with details about the program where you're applying and admissions criteria. Also provide a stamped, addressed envelope. Give the person plenty of time to write the letter (two to three months), and check in about a month before the application deadline.

is a requirement. Other programs that are geared entirely to adult students may require that you are employed at least part-time before you apply for admission to the program. But for any competitive program, your work experience reveals to the admissions department your achievements outside the academic environment.

To demonstrate your work experience, you may be asked to submit a resume detailing your employment history, the positions you have held, and the job duties you performed. The school may require that you put together a personal portfolio showcasing your accomplishments, such as reports you have prepared or presentations you have given. Copies of professional certificates you have earned will also help demonstrate your achievements in your field. Finally, you will very likely have to submit one or more letters of recommendation from your supervisor or coworkers.

Even if you have no experience in the workplace, you may still have life experience that will make you a more attractive candidate for admission. For instance, you have extensive experience as a volunteer. Definitely mention such experience in your application, especially if the volunteer position is related in some way to the field you want to study. You can submit letters of recommendation from your supervisor or people you work with at the volunteer program.

If you pursue a talent or skill in your free time, that is also worth noting in your application. You may have joined an amateur theater company, taken dance lessons, or learned a foreign language on your own. Any hobby or skill that demonstrates your willingness to learn and a broad range of worthwhile interests will help your candidacy for admission.

Be honest about your past academic, work, and volunteer experiences. Remember that any of your past life or academic experiences may earn you college credit and thus help you move one step closer to your ultimate goal of obtaining your degree (more on this later in the chapter).

Standardized Tests

Nontraditional students who apply to an undergraduate degree program aren't usually required to take the standardized tests that graduating high school students must take (either the SAT or the ACT Assessment). If you take either test in high school, though, you have to submit your test scores. Standardized test scores are kept on file indefinitely, and you can request a score report at any time by contacting the test administrators (you have to pay a fee for each score report you request).

To request your score report for the ACT, contact:

ACT Records
P.O. Box 451
Iowa City, IA 52243-0451
319-337-1313
www.act.org/aap/

Time Saver
If you didn't take either the SAT or the ACT in high school and the distance-learning program you're applying to requires a standardized test score, you may be able to take the test or an equivalent one through the college itself. Contact the admissions department to find out if this is possible.

To request your score report for the SAT, contact:

College Board SAT Program
P.O. Box 6200
Princeton, NJ 08541-6200
609-771-7600
www.collegeboard.org/

If you apply for a graduate-level degree program, you have to take the Graduate Record Examination (GRE). The GRE is like a superversion of the SAT; some graduate schools also require a GRE subject test in the area that you intend to study. For more information about registering for and taking the GRE, contact:

GRE-ETS
P.O. Box 6000
Princeton, NJ 08541-6000
609-771-7670
www.gre.org/

If you plan to earn a Master of Business Administration (MBA) degree, you must take the Graduate Management Aptitude Test (GMAT) before applying to the MBA program. For more information about this standardized test, contact:

GMAT
Educational Testing Services
P.O. Box 6103
Princeton, NJ 08541-6103
1-800-GMAT-NOW
www.gmat.org/gmat_frames.html

Finally, if you apply to a distance-learning program from outside the United States and English is not your native language, you will probably have to take the Test of English as a Foreign Language (TOEFL). This demonstrates that you have achieved a level of proficiency in English required to do well in the program. Most colleges and universities require a minimum score between 450 and 550. A computerized version of the TOEFL is given in most countries. The fee for taking the test is $100.

To get started, order the appropriate Information Bulletin for the country or area in which you plan to take the test from your local distribution office. This free publication tells you how to schedule an appointment to take the TOEFL, where testing centers are located, identification requirements, and everything else you need to know. To find the address of your local distribution office, contact:

TOEFL/TSE Services
P.O. Box 6151
Princeton, NJ 08541 USA
609-771-7100
www.toefl.org/

Time Saver
You may not have to take the TOEFL if most of your formal schooling has been in English-speaking schools or if you completed your secondary education in an English-speaking country. Ask the admissions officer at the school where you're applying if the TOEFL requirement can be waived.

The Essay

You may be required to submit an original essay with your application. The essay fulfills three important functions:

- It tells the admissions department why you want to continue your education through distance learning or why you have chosen this particular program.

- It demonstrates your writing ability—how well you organize and express your thoughts, your grasp of the fundamentals of spelling and grammar, and your creativity and originality.

- It helps the admissions department get to know you as a person—what your personality is like, what your values are, and what your goals are.

The following are some examples of the kinds of essay questions you may be asked:

- Why have you decided to pursue a degree at this time in your life?

- Why have you decided to apply to this program?

- What characteristics do you have that will contribute to your success in distance learning?

- How will your personal and professional experiences contribute to your education?

- What do you expect to achieve from your studies?

On the other hand, the essay topic may be completely open-ended. For example, you may have to provide a personal statement, or you may be asked simply to tell the admissions officer about yourself.

If an essay is required with the application, you should treat it very seriously. It will most likely be a crucial part of the decision-making process for the admissions committee. Be prepared to spend some time writing and rewriting your essay.

Here are some tips to help you write a powerful, impressive essay:

- Use your essay to help explain your goals in continuing your education.

- Focus on one specific topic, instead of a very broad, general topic. Sticking to specifics results in a more powerful essay.

- Don't write what you think the admissions officer wants to read. This will result in an insincere, vague essay.

- Keep the introduction brief. Use it to hook the reader.

- Use vivid, precise language. Choose words that show rather than tell. Use fewer but more specific words to cut down on wordiness. Avoid passive verb constructions.

- After writing the first draft, let your essay sit for a day or two. Then, you can reread it with fresh eyes.

- Read your essay out loud. This will help you catch awkward sentences, passive voice, and stilted language.

- When rewriting your essay, focus on cutting repetition, awkward phrasing, and anything that doesn't directly relate to your main theme.

- Proofread for spelling or grammatical errors—they will count against you. Don't rely on your computer's spellchecker. Get someone to proofread after you've done it, as well.

- Have someone else read your essay. A friend, coworker, or spouse can give you valuable feedback on content.

Additional Requirements

Some distance-learning programs have special entrance requirements; for instance, some programs may be limited to a particular age level or to residents of a specific state, or some programs may specify prior work or academic experience. Determine what all the requirements of the distance-learning program are before applying for admission, so you can be sure that you meet the requirements.

In addition, some programs, particularly graduate-level programs, have residency requirements. This means that you will have to spend some time on campus, ranging from a weekend to six weeks, usually in the summer. Generally, residency requirements are short, and most students can fulfill them while taking short-term leave from work or while on vacation.

Typical Entrance Requirements for Different Degree Programs

The following overview of the typical entrance requirements for different degree levels should give you a good idea whether you are prepared, academically and professionally, to enter the degree program. Keep in mind that the requirements vary greatly depending on the school and the academic department where you are applying for enrollment. Generally speaking, the more competitive and prestigious the school, the stricter the entrance requirements will be.

The following are the typical requirements for admission to a bachelor's degree program:

- High school diploma or GED
- Official transcripts from high schools, community colleges, and colleges previously attended
- Work experience of two to five years
- Short personal essay (300–500 words)
- One or more letters of recommendation from instructors or people who have worked closely with you

The following are the typical requirements for admission to a master's degree program:

- Bachelor's degree from a regionally accredited college
- Official transcripts from colleges previously attended
- Grade point average of 2.0 or greater on a 4.0 scale

Bright Idea
Need help writing your essay? Consult a proven style guide like Strunk and White's *Elements of Style*, or buy an essay-writing guide like *The Best College Admission Essays* by Mark Stewart and Cynthia Muchnick (IDG Books Worldwide, 1997).

- GRE or GMAT (business school) score
- Personal written statement
- Two to three letters of recommendation from professors and people who have worked closely with you

The following are the typical requirements for admission to a doctoral degree program:

- Master's degree in the field of study from a regionally accredited university
- Official transcripts from colleges and universities previously attended
- Grade point average of at least 3.0 on a 4.0 scale
- Five years or more of work experience
- Personal written statement
- Two to three letters of recommendation from professors and people who have worked closely with you

Watch Out!
In most cases, you can't earn credit for life experience in a graduate-level degree program. That's because graduate degrees are based completely on academic learning, while undergraduate degrees can take into account learning acquired outside the classroom.

Getting Credit for Life Experience

If you plan to enter a distance-learning degree program and you have been out of school for a number of years, you may find that you can earn a significant number of college credits for your past experiences. The theory is that you should receive credit if you have the same level of knowledge as a student taking an undergraduate college course would have, regardless of how you acquired that knowledge.

All of the following activities can earn you college credit when you go back to school:

- Previous college-level coursework
- Work experience
- Corporate educational programs
- Professional certificates or licenses you have earned
- Military training
- Volunteer experience
- Self education

You can't simply convert every item on your resume into a college credit, though. You have to equate your past experiences and learning with college-level coursework. There are three ways you can do this:

- Earn credits by taking exams
- Earn credits based on established standards
- Put together a portfolio documenting your accomplishments

Policies of how credit for life experience is awarded vary from school to school. Some programs limit the number of credits you can earn this way, and some won't award credit for life experience at all. So, it's important to ask whether you can receive college credits for life experience, how you obtain those credits, and how many of those credits you can apply toward your degree before you apply for admission to a distance-learning degree program. Colleges geared exclusively toward adult learners are the most flexible when it comes to granting credit for life experience, with the average student receiving 15 to 18 credits through this process.

Credit by Exam

Credit by exam is the most popular and widely established way of earning college credit for past experience. Ninety-three percent of colleges award credit for prior learning based on exams that demonstrate acquired knowledge and skills at the college level. If you have taken college-level coursework in the past and you can't transfer the credits directly, taking an exam is a good way to demonstrate that you have completed those courses and get credit for them. Credit by exam is also a good option for you if you have done a lot of studying on your own or if you have acquired a high level of knowledge in a specialized subject.

Depending on the school's policies, you may be able to earn credits by exam in any of the following ways:

- Take the final exam for a course given by the school (this is a common way of testing out of prerequisite courses)

- Take the school's own placement exam

- Take an exam in the College-Level Examination Program (CLEP)

CLEP is by far the most common way for nontraditional students to earn college credit by exam. CLEP is the most widely accepted credit-by-examination program in the country. More than 2,800 colleges and universities currently participate in the program. Taking a CLEP exam, and scoring well, enables you to place out of prerequisite or entry-level college courses.

There are 34 CLEP exams in two broad categories: general and subject. You can take as many CLEP exams as you'd like. Most colleges specify a maximum number of credits that you can earn through testing, though.

The general exams cover material taught in required courses during the first two years of college. A satisfactory score on each general exam usually earns three to six semester hours of credit. The general exams cover the following broad subject areas:

- English composition

- Humanities (fine arts and literature)

- Math

- Natural sciences (biology, chemistry, and physical science)

- Social sciences and history (economics, anthropology, geography, political science, and world history)

Time Saver
Earning credit for life experiences is a good way to bypass the prerequisites for entering a certification or degree program or for taking a particular course.

The CLEP subject exams cover material taught in equivalent college-level courses. Typically, colleges grant the same course credit to students who earn a successful score on the CLEP exam as they do to students who successfully complete the course. You can take CLEP exams in the following specific subjects:

- American Government
- American Literature
- Analyzing and Interpreting Literature
- Calculus with Elementary Functions
- College Algebra
- College Algebra-Trigonometry
- College-Level French Language
- College-Level German Language
- College-Level Spanish Language
- English Literature
- Freshman College Composition
- General Biology
- General Chemistry
- History of the United States I: Early Colonizations to 1877
- History of the United States II: 1865 to the Present
- Human Growth and Development
- Information Systems and Computer Applications
- Introduction to Educational Psychology
- Introductory Business Law
- Introductory Psychology
- Introductory Sociology
- Principles of Accounting
- Principles of Macroeconomics
- Principles of Management
- Principles of Marketing
- Principles of Microeconomics
- Trigonometry
- Western Civilization I: Ancient Near East to 1648
- Western Civilization II: 1648 to the Present

Nearly 1,400 colleges and universities across the country administer CLEP exams. There are two types of CLEP test centers. Open test centers admit anyone who registers; they administer CLEP exams each month of the year. Limited test centers restrict testing to students who have been admitted to or are enrolled in the college where the test center is located. Contact the test center where you plan to take the CLEP to confirm which kind it is.

You must directly contact the college administering the test to determine the appropriate registration procedure and to order a registration form. You then send the completed registration form to the test center at that college, along with a check for the registration fee of $44 plus the test center administration fee, usually $10. Contact the CLEP program directly to get a list of test centers and obtain more detailed registration information:

CLEP
P.O. Box 6601
Princeton, NJ 08541-6601
609-771-7865
www.collegeboard.org/clep/students/html/student.html

Credit for Work and Military Training

In the past, you might have completed educational programs sponsored by your company, a professional association, a trade union, or a government agency. You might also have completed coursework or received specialized training while in the military. You can receive college credit for all of these programs.

The American Council of Education (ACE) has evaluated these educational programs according to college-level criteria and recommended how much college credit should be awarded for different programs. Many colleges and universities use these standards as guidelines for awarding credit based on educational programs that nontraditional students have completed in settings other than the college classroom. If you have taken educational or training programs in the workplace or in the military, ask your school whether it follows the ACE recommendations.

If the organization that administered the educational program you took in the workplace participates in ACE's College Credit Recommendation Service, you can obtain a transcript of all your college credit courses and examinations that you can then submit to your school for college credit. To participate, you must join the Registry of Credit Recommendations for a one-time fee of $25; call ACE at 202-939-9434 or send e-mail to credit@ace.nche.edu to request more information about joining the Registry.

If you are currently serving in the military, you can request college credit for military coursework by visiting your local Education Center and requesting a certified DD Form 295, "Application for the Evaluation of Learning Experiences During Military Service." If you have previously served in the Armed Forces, you should request a copy of your DD Form 214, "Armed Forces of the United States Report of Transfer or Discharge," by contacting the following address:

Time Saver
Interested in whether your college gives credit for CLEP exams or where the nearest test center is? Consult the searchable database at www.collegeboard. org/clep/students/ html/student.html and click on Colleges Granting Credit/Test Centers.

National Personnel Records Center
Military Personnel Records
9700 Page Ave.
St. Louis, MO 63132-5100

Submit this form to the admissions department or academic adviser for the program you plan to attend. Remember to request credit for all courses you completed while in the service, including basic training, correspondence courses, college-level examinations, and tests administered by the Defense Activity for Nontraditional Education Support (DANTES).

If you joined the Army after 1981, you can obtain a transcript that details all of your military training and education from the Army/ACE Registry Transcript Service. You can then submit the transcript to the school where you're applying just like any other academic transcript. To obtain a transcript, write:

AARTS Operation Center
415 McPherson Ave.
Ft. Leavenworth, KS 66027-1373

Prior Learning Assessment

Some types of experience, particularly work experience, are not so easily measured by examination. Over 1,000 colleges and universities allow nontraditional students to submit a portfolio of information about their work and accomplishments in a process called Prior Learning Assessment. Faculty members at the school review the portfolio and determine the equivalent amount of college credit.

Your personal portfolio is a formal written report that clearly and succinctly identifies your prior learning and explains how this learning relates to the degree program that you intend to pursue. It also includes supporting documentation, so that the college faculty reviewing your portfolio can accurately award credit for your prior experience. Supporting documentation can include writing samples like reports or articles, awards you have won, certificates or licenses you have earned, tapes of presentations you have given, copies of speeches you have written, and the like. You will be assigned an academic adviser at your school who will help you assemble your portfolio and identify those activities that are likely to result in college credits.

Succeeding in Your Distance-Learning Program

Once you get into a distance-learning program, you want to make sure that you stick to it and complete the program. After all, you've already invested a lot of time and money in this program, even before you've begun.

As you already know, completing a degree program can be especially challenging for distance-learning students, much more so than for traditional students living and studying on the college campus. Dozens of other things will constantly compete for your attention—your family, your job, your friends, housework, social events. Establishing good study habits from the start can be the key to success.

Follow these tips to excel in your distance-learning program:

- Set aside a regular study time, and stick to it. Schedule it in your calendar, and make it a major priority. Make it clear to your family that this period is your study time, and you can't be disturbed.

- Set up an appropriate study environment. It should be a room away from the main part of the house and free from distractions. If you can't find an appropriate place in your home, consider making the public library your study place.

- Pay attention to instructions, and make sure you understand exactly what is being asked of you for each assignment. If you have any questions, don't hesitate to contact your instructor.

- Get involved with your fellow classmates, especially if you have joined an Internet-based program. Regular participation in class discussions, no matter how they are conducted, will help you stay motivated.

Bright Idea
To keep yourself on track, commit to achieving one distance-learning goal per day, such as reading a certain number of pages in an assignment or completing a specific number of exercises.

Just the Facts

- Application procedures vary depending on the type of distance-learning program you're applying to and the school where you're applying; make certain that you understand the requirements and submit the appropriate application forms.

- Depending on the kind of degree program that you want to enter, you may have to meet specific entrance requirements to be accepted for admission to the program. You will most likely have to submit academic transcripts, a professional portfolio or resume, letters of recommendation, and an original essay or personal statement.

- Nontraditional students can often earn college credits for professional experience, previous college coursework, military training, volunteer experience, and self-education, which means that you can get your degree more quickly and for less money.

- Once you begin a distance-learning program, you should establish a study schedule and workspace right from the start to help you stick to the program through to the end.

GET THE SCOOP ON...
How much you can expect to pay for a distance-learning program
• Financial aid • How to apply for financial aid from the federal
government • Obtaining a private educational loan • Employer
reimbursement for tuition • How to get tax credits for going back
to school • Other forms of financial aid

Chapter 5

Paying for It

The major stumbling block for most adults returning to school is the cost. Even working adults may find it a struggle to meet the costs of a distance-learning program while paying the bills. Too many adult students don't even search for help with paying for their education, mistakenly believing that aid money is completely earmarked for traditional college students.

The reality is that there is a lot of financial aid out there for nontraditional students. Some of it comes from the federal government, but a lot of it comes from unexpected sources, like private loans, tax breaks, and even your employer. The key to financing your education is to be persistent about searching out all sources of aid and taking advantage of the aid programs that you do qualify for.

This chapter will help you make sense of financial aid. You'll learn how to apply for federal aid and where else you might find money to help pay for your education. By the time you're done, the cost of tuition should no longer stand in your way of continuing your education.

The Cost of Distance Learning

The costs of distance-learning programs vary greatly from school to school. But you should expect to pay less to complete a distance-learning degree program than you would if you earned the degree the traditional way. For one thing, tuition for distance-learning programs is often lower. Also, you won't have to pay all the associated costs of commuting to campus, such as gas, parking, and childcare.

What You Have to Pay

Distance-learning programs carry a bundle of costs that are typically billed separately. That's why you shouldn't merely look at the amount of tuition when figuring out how much your distance-learning program will cost you.

You also need to take into account related expenses to arrive at the total cost of your distance learning.

You can expect to be charged for all of the following:

- **Tuition:** The typical cost of a full-credit, college-level course in a distance-learning program ranges from $300 to $1,000. (The average tuition for each program listed in Part II of this book is provided in the program's description.)

- **Course materials:** These can include textbooks, workbooks, procedure manuals, software, videotapes, audiotapes, slides, photographs, and other audiovisual materials.

- **Special equipment:** This includes any new equipment that you will have to buy in order to participate in the course, such as a satellite dish, computer, modem, or Internet account.

- **Postage and handling:** Postage is charged for all course materials that must be mailed to you. Handling fees defray the costs of processing course registration and shipping course materials.

- **Special fees:** You may incur additional fees for transferring credits, extending a course, or enrolling in a program at an out-of-state public college or university.

Watch Out!
Course tuitions listed in this guide are subject to change. Check the most recent course catalog for the distance-learning program to find the latest rates.

You may not be able to reduce the cost of tuition, fees, or postage and handling, but you can probably cut costs when purchasing your course materials. Here are some suggestions:

- Purchase textbooks from local bookstores instead of directly from the school.

- Buy used materials, particularly textbooks, instead of brand-new ones.

- Some schools allow you to rent the more costly course materials.

- Most schools will buy back your course materials at the end of the course for a partial refund.

How to Pay

Generally, distance-learning programs charge by the course. That's because most distance-learning students only take one or two courses, rather than completing an entire degree program. At the time you register for a distance-learning course, you will have to pay the entire cost of tuition, course materials, equipment, and postage and handling fees for that course. Since most programs charge on a course-by-course basis, you can spread out the costs of completing the degree program over the entire length of the program.

Find out about the program's withdrawal and refund policies before you enroll. Unexpected emergencies can happen, forcing you to leave a program early or temporarily stop taking courses. In that case, you should be entitled to at least a partial refund of the tuition that you have already paid for the course you're taking. The admissions department should be able to answer all of your questions about payment and refund policies.

Paying the full cost of a distance-learning course all at once can be a great burden to those of us who don't have a bundle in our savings accounts. Some schools recognize this and have attempted to make paying for education easier by instituting payment plans. For example, some schools accept credit cards. Others allow you to pay with monthly installments.

Joining a payment plan has some added benefits. For one thing, the payment plan can keep you motivated. Every time you write a check, you'll get a reminder that you are taking the course to achieve a specific goal, a goal that is important to you, so you won't be as likely to drop out of the course halfway through. If you do have to withdraw for some reason, you won't have to go to the hassle of trying to get a partial refund of the course costs. You just simply stop making the payments. Be sure to inquire whether your school has any payment plans that can benefit you.

Understanding Your Financial Aid Options

Even with the most innovative payment plans, many students have trouble paying all of the costs of a distance-learning program out of their own pockets. But in many cases, they don't have to. Financial aid money is available even for nontraditional students to help defray the costs of education.

Financial aid comes from all of the following sources:

- Federal government
- State government
- The school's own funds
- Private organizations, such as professional associations and civic groups
- Employers
- Private lenders

Financial aid is typically awarded in one of the following forms:

- *Grants* are awarded based on financial need and don't have to be repaid.
- *Scholarships* are awarded based on merit or some quality other than financial need and don't have to be repaid.
- *Work-study* enables the student to work in exchange for aid money; this form of aid is not typically feasible for distance learners.
- *Employee educational benefits* are paid by employers; the schooling must usually be directly related to the employee's job.
- *Loans* must be repaid eventually; education loans typically carry lower interest rates and better repayment terms than other kinds of loans.

Money Saver
Another way to save on tuition costs is to obtain college credit for your life experiences or previous learning, which would allow you to place out of a course that you would otherwise have to pay for. The cost of documenting past experiences for college credit is very low, as low as $25 per credit.

Watch Out!
Some diploma mills offer blanket scholarships or tuition discounts in an effort to get you to enroll. While you should be on the lookout for scholarships and other aid opportunities, be suspicious when a deal seems too good to be true.

Don't expect a completely free ride in the form of grants and scholarships. The sad truth is that most federal, state, and institutional financial aid and most private scholarships go to first-time college students enrolled in traditional, on-campus degree programs. There just isn't a lot of money available for nontraditional students, although that should change as distance learning becomes a more established and widespread way of earning a degree.

But that doesn't mean that there's no financial aid available for you at all. You just have to know where to go looking for it.

Money Saver
It pays to shop around. Some schools have more financial aid to offer to distance learners than other schools.

Each school has its own policies on who receives financial aid and how that aid is awarded. The school that sponsors your distance-learning program should have a financial aid office that you can contact. Get in touch with a financial aid officer to find out what aid options are open to distance learners and the exact procedures for applying for financial aid.

Aid from the Federal Government

The first place any college or graduate school student should turn to for financial aid is the federal government. You may very well be eligible for federal need-based grants or low-interest student loans. Also, applying for federal aid is often the way to apply for aid from your state and from your school.

There is no age limit for receiving federal financial aid, but there are some restrictions:

- You must have a high school diploma or GED. If you don't, you must pass a test approved by the U.S. Department of Education or meet other standards established by your state that are approved by the department.

- You must be a U.S. citizen.

- You must have a valid Social Security number.

- You must be enrolled or be accepted for enrollment as a student working toward a degree or certificate. If you are simply taking a few distance-learning courses, even credit courses, you can't apply for federal financial aid.

- You must remain enrolled in the degree program at least half-time.

Half-time enrollment is a very specific term. This requirement alone may exclude many working adult students from eligibility for federal financial aid. Here's what it means:

- At schools measuring progress by credit hours and academic terms (semesters, trimesters, or quarters), half-time enrollment is equivalent to taking at least six semester hours or quarter hours per term.

- At schools measuring progress by credit hours but not using academic terms, half-time enrollment is equivalent to taking at least 12 semester hours or 18 quarter hours per year.

- At schools measuring progress by clock hours, half-time enrollment is equivalent to taking at least 12 hours per week.

The amount of federal financial aid that you qualify for is based on your financial need. In general, the difference between what the program costs (including course materials, required equipment, and additional fees) and what your financial circumstances indicate you can afford to pay determines the amount of your financial need, or the amount of federal financial aid you can receive. If you meet the eligibility requirements, you should apply for federal financial aid, regardless of whether you think you'll qualify.

After you apply for financial aid, you'll receive a form that indicates your Estimated Financial Contribution (EFC). This number is the total amount that the federal government estimates that you can contribute toward your educational costs each year. Your EFC is determined by analyzing your over-all financial circumstances. The major factor in determining your EFC is your income and your spouse's income, *not* the balances of your savings accounts or the worth of trust funds and other assets. If your EFC is less than the total cost of one year's worth of courses in your distance-learning pro-gram, then the difference is the amount of financial aid that you can receive.

Distance learners who qualify for financial aid can typically participate in one or both of the following federal aid programs: the Pell Grant pro-gram and the Stafford loan program.

Pell Grants

Students with extremely high need may qualify for the Pell Grant program. Pell Grants typically only go to the students with the lowest incomes and are thus very difficult to get. Everyone who qualifies for a Pell Grant receives one, regardless of whether they are a traditional student or are taking a distance-learning program.

The Pell Grant award changes from year to year, depending on how much funding Congress allocates to the program. For the 1998-99 school year, the maximum award was $3,000. The amount of the grant you may receive is not standardized. Different schools, with their varying tuition, dis-burse different amounts. In 1997-98, individual grants ranged from $400 to $2,700, with the average grant totaling around $1,700.

Stafford Loans

There are two main kinds of low-interest, federally guaranteed loans for stu-dents: the Federal Direct Student Loan (Direct Loan) Program and the Federal Family Education Loan (FFEL) Program. Collectively, they're called Stafford loans.

Direct Loans come directly from the federal government and are admin-istered by federally run Direct Loan Servicing Centers. FFEL loans involve private lenders like banks, credit unions, and savings and loans; your state's loan guaranty agency or a private agency chosen by the state administers

Money Saver
Distance-learning programs often reduce tuition by 50 percent or more for senior citizens.

these loans. Aside from that difference, the two loan programs are pretty much the same; which program you get your money from depends on which program your school participates in. As the Pell Grant program, an unlimited number of students can receive Stafford loans.

If financial need remains after subtracting your EFC, your Pell Grant eligibility, and your financial aid from other sources, you can borrow a subsidized Stafford loan to cover all or part of the remaining need. These are the best of the Stafford loans to get. With a subsidized loan, the government pays the interest while you're earning your degree and for six months after you graduate. So, the overall amount that you have to repay is lower.

If you don't have need remaining but you are eligible to receive federal financial aid, you can still borrow a Stafford loan to cover all or part of your EFC. But this is an unsubsidized loan; you must pay *all* of the interest. If you qualify for an unsubsidized loan, your interest charges begin accruing from the time you first get the loan until you pay it in full. You may opt to postpone repayment until you graduate, but interest will accrue during the entire time that you're taking distance-learning courses.

You can mix and match subsidized and unsubsidized loan money, so long as both loans come from the same program (either FFEL or Direct Loan). Depending on your financial need, Stafford loans can add up to a total of $46,000, with no more than $23,000 of that amount in subsidized loans.

The interest rate on Stafford loans varies from year to year, but it has consistently remained below market value. The maximum interest rate is 8.25 percent, and the rate is often lower while you are actually taking courses.

Stafford loans cost some money up-front. An "origination fee" of 4 percent plus an insurance fee of up to 1 percent, both of which are deducted directly from your loan disbursements in installments, are administered. The state guaranty agency may also take its cut—up to 3 percent—proportionately from each disbursement as an insurance premium. You may also be charged late fees and collection costs if you don't keep up with your payments.

You have to start paying back Stafford loans six months after you earn your degree, leave the program, or drop below half-time student status. (You can start repaying unsubsidized loans earlier than that, if you want to reduce the total amount of interest that you'll pay.) You usually have five years to repay the debt, though some lenders allow as many as 10 years, and perhaps as many as 12 to 30 years under the Direct Loan program. The amount of your payments (a minimum of $50 per month) and the length of the repayment period usually depend on how much you borrowed and whom you borrowed it from.

Applying for Federal Financial Aid

To apply for federal financial aid (and for aid from your school, in most cases), you must fill out the Free Application for Federal Student Aid (FAFSA). As implied by its name, submitting the FAFSA is free. Plan to submit the FAFSA as soon as possible after Jan. 1 in the year you intend to start the program (you can't submit the form before January). Otherwise, you may not be approved for aid until *after* the course has already started.

You have several options for obtaining a copy of the FAFSA and submitting it to a federal aid processing center:

- You can apply electronically through the U.S. Department of Education's Web site at www.fafsa.ed.gov/. According to the Department of Education, this is the fastest way to apply.

- You can use the FAFSA Express software; it runs on computers that use the Windows operating system and have a modem. You can find computers with the FAFSA Express program at many high schools, public libraries, and Educational Opportunity Centers. You can order the software on a disk by calling 1-800-801-0576, or download a copy yourself by going to www.ed.gov/offices/OPE/Students/apply/fexpress.html.

- You can forego technology altogether and get the version of the form that comes on old-fashioned paper. Ask at your school's financial aid office, or contact:

    Federal Student Aid Information Center
    P.O. Box 84
    Washington, D.C. 20044-0084
    1-800-4-FEDAID

Once you've applied, the processing agency takes between four and six weeks to turn your application around. You may be asked to confirm information or to correct the FAFSA and resubmit it. The reprocessing will add another two or three weeks to your wait.

In addition to the FAFSA, you may also have to fill out a financial aid application specific to the college or university sponsoring the distance-learning program that you plan to take. The financial aid office at the school can provide all of the necessary forms.

Looking into Loans

Private education loans are available to all distance learners. Although a loan isn't free money, education loans often carry lower interest rates and more flexible repayment terms than other kinds of consumer loans. Thus, they make an attractive alternative for the adult student. Eligibility is generally based on your creditworthiness, rather than on your financial need.

The terms of these supplemental-loan programs can differ greatly from lender to lender, so it's definitely worth your while to shop around for the best deal. Until recently, your lender was invariably a bank, but that's no longer the case. Now, educational organizations, associations, and even schools offer private student loans. Many lenders have education loan programs geared specifically toward working adult students.

Watch Out!
Don't send in the FAFSA by fax or overnight express mail; using anything but the regular postal service or the in-place electronic filing procedures only slows processing of your application.

The following nationwide lenders all offer private education loans for working adults who want to continue their education:

- *Key Bank:* Offers the Key Career Loan for students who work full-time while going to school and students participating in continuing education programs. Contact 1-800-KEY-LEND or www.keybank.com/educate/.

Money Saver
Even though you'll be taking classes at a distance, you can save money by searching for distance-learning programs close to home. Community colleges and public universities usually offer reduced tuition to distance learners who live in the same state.

- *The Education Resources Institute (TERI):* Offers a continuing education loan with an annual minimum borrowing amount of $500 and an annual maximum of $15,000. Borrowers only need to be enrolled in one course to qualify. Contact: 1-800-255-8374 or www.educaid.com/eduloan/extended.htm.

- *Wells Fargo:* Offers the Wells Fargo Alternative Education Loan for nontraditional students, whether they attend school full-time, part-time, or just take one class. You can borrow between $1,500 and $25,000 annually. Contact: 1-877-255-2431 or www.norwest.com/students/doc/graduate/success.htm.

Your bank may also provide an education loan. Graduate students should be able to find loan programs geared specifically to their needs. Be sure to shop around to find the loan and the lender that's the best match for your circumstances.

Tuition Reimbursement from Your Employer

Bright Idea
Unions often negotiate educational benefits into their contracts. If you're a member of a union, contact your union's business manager to find out if you're eligible for educational benefits.

If the course, degree, or certificate that you want to complete is essential for your job, then in many cases your employer will reimburse you for all or part of the tuition. This is the great unclaimed area of financial aid that you're always hearing about, with billions of dollars available to millions of employees. Although many companies offer tuition reimbursement programs, only about 5 percent of employees take advantage of them.

In reimbursement plans, you have to put up the tuition money at first; you get the money back only when you have successfully completed the course (in some programs, that means with a grade of B or better). In other programs, the company pays up-front, but you still have to repay the company if you drop out or fail to pass. Also, you may have to commit to stay with the company for a certain number of years after you get the degree or certificate. An understanding boss can help you to frame your educational needs in such a way that they fit in nicely with the company objectives.

Another stickler in this area is the IRS, which ruled that the courses you take have to be job-related to qualify as a benefit. If you take any course that isn't directly related to your work but your employer still pays for it, you have to declare the cost of the course as taxable income. But under the Tax-Reform Act of 1986, you can deduct up to $5,250 worth of employer-paid tuition, even if the courses you take don't directly relate to your job.

To find out if your employer has an educational-benefits program, check with the personnel or human resources department at your company.

Tax Credits for Education

The 1997 Taxpayer Relief Act introduced many tax benefits to help students pay for higher education. The Lifetime Learning Credit applies directly to nontraditional students. The Lifetime Learning Credit gives you a tax credit of 20 percent on the first $5,000 of total tuition you pay in a year (subtracting tax-free financial aid first), so you earn a maximum credit of $1,000. By the year 2002, you'll be able to claim a 20 percent tax credit on the first $10,000 of tuition. There's no limit to the number of school years you can claim for the Lifetime Learning credit.

The HOPE Scholarship tax credit, another provision of the Taxpayer Relief Act, may apply to you if you have never taken college-level coursework before. It can be claimed only for the first two years of higher education. A 100 percent tax credit applies to the first $1,000 of required tuition and fees (after deducting grants, scholarships, and other tax-free financial aid), and a 50 percent tax credit applies to the second $1,000—essentially paying for up to $1,500 of tuition per year. To qualify for the HOPE Scholarship tax credit, you must be enrolled on at least a half-time basis in a degree or certificate program.

The following are some other important restrictions on claiming a HOPE Scholarship or Lifetime Learning tax credit that you should know about:

- You can't claim the credits for any educational expense for which you have already claimed a tax deduction.
- Married couples must file jointly to claim the credit.
- The credit can be applied only to required tuition and fees, not to the cost of course materials.

Finally, the HOPE Scholarship and Lifetime Learning programs are designed to meet the needs of middle-class and low-income families. This tax credit is phased out for joint filers reporting between $80,000 and $100,000 of adjusted gross income and for single filers reporting between $40,000 and $50,000 of adjusted gross income. Once your income rises over $100,000 (for a married couple) or over $50,000 (for a single filer), you're no longer eligible for the tax credit.

If you want more information about these tax breaks, consult your tax adviser or go straight to the source—the IRS. IRS Publication 970, *Tax Benefits for Higher Education*, describes the HOPE Scholarship and Lifetime Learning Credit benefits, as well as other tax benefits for students paying for higher education. You can order the publication at no charge by calling the IRS at 1-800-TAX-FORM or by visiting the IRS Web site at www.irs. ustreas.gov/.

Watch Out!
You can't claim both the Lifetime Learning tax credit and the HOPE Scholarship tax credit for yourself in the same year.

Unofficially...
Keep in mind that these tax laws are brand-new, and it could take several years to clarify the restrictions and eligibility requirements. A knowledgeable, up-to-date tax adviser is your best asset for figuring out these complicated laws and for keeping abreast of changes in the next few years.

Other Sources of Aid

Here are some other possible sources of financial aid that you may have overlooked:

- Public school employees may be eligible to receive reimbursement for courses taken for college credit. Contact the coordinator of staff development in your district.

- Veterans are eligible for many educational benefits. Check with a local Veterans Administration (VA) office for more information. Some states also provide benefits to veterans; your state's veterans or military affairs office can tell you more.

- Members of the Armed Forces, including the National Guard and Armed Forces Reserve, can receive in-service benefits from the U.S. Department of Veterans Affairs, as well as tuition assistance from their services. The educational service officer of your base, post, or ship can provide more information.

- Almost all states provide educational benefits to students with disabilities. Your state's Department of Vocational Rehabilitation can give you more information.

Money Saver
If you plan to take a distance-learning course while overseas—for instance, if you're in the military—enroll in the program before you leave and carry your course materials with you to avoid postage and tariff costs.

Just the Facts

- The total cost of a distance-learning course includes not only the tuition for the course but also the cost of course materials, required equipment, and special fees.

- Financial aid for college and graduate students is available from many sources, including state and federal government, the school itself, private agencies, and employers.

- Although many distance learners aren't eligible for federal financial aid, those who are should apply; they may receive grants or low-interest loans.

- Private education loans often have lower interest rates and better terms than other types of consumer loans; many lenders offer education loans geared specifically toward adult students.

- Many employers provide education benefits, but too many employees don't take advantage of them; if your distance-learning program is job-related, your employer may reimburse you for all or part of the tuition.

- The Taxpayer Relief Act instituted several tax cuts to help defray the costs of higher education; distance learners should take advantage of them.

- Veterans, members of the Armed Forces, public school employees, and disabled students may also be eligible for additional money to help defray the costs of continuing their education.

Directory of Distance-Learning Programs

PART II

A

Adams State College

Division of Extended Studies

208 Edgemont, RH 143

Alamosa, CO 81102

1-800-548-6679

Web: www.adams.edu/exstudies/

E-mail: ascextend@adams.edu

Programs: individual courses

Individual course subjects: business, economics, education, English, environmental studies, journalism, leisure studies, mathematics, physical education, physical science, psychology, sociology

Average tuition: $240 per course

Length of program: 6 weeks–1 year per course

Technologies: audiocassette, correspondence, Internet, video

Accreditation: NCACS

Entrance requirements: none

Restrictions: none

Special services: use of the on-campus library

Aims Community College

Distance Learning, Aims Community College Corporate Education Center

P.O. Box 69

Greeley, CO 80632

1-888-644-3451 or 1-800-344-5209

Web: www.aims.edu/distance/

Programs: Certificate—Information Technology; AAS—Biomedical Electronic Technology; AA—Mortgage Banking; Certificate/AA—Telecommunications; Certificate/AGS—Broadband Communications

Average tuition: $125 per credit

Length of program: 10 weeks per course

Technologies: CD-ROM, correspondence, fax, Internet, video

Accreditation: NCACS

Entrance requirements: high school diploma or GED

Restrictions: none

Special services: academic advising

Amber University

1700 Eastgate Dr.

Garland, TX 75041

972-279-6511

Web: www.amberu.edu

E-mail: webmail@ambernet.amberu.edu

Programs: BS—Applied Studies in Management Technology; BA/MA—Professional Development; BS/MS—Human Relations and Business; MBA—General Business, Management, Strategic Leadership

Length of program: up to 6 years

Technologies: Internet

Accreditation: SACS

Entrance requirements: BA/BS—2 years of prior college coursework with a 2.0 GPA; MA/MBA/MS—bachelor's degree with a 3.0 GPA on the last 30 semester hours and a GRE score of 800 or a GMAT score of 400

Restrictions: Students must be at least 21 years old.

Special services: academic advising; financial advising; international student advising; online library; personalized degree plan

Time Saver
Amber University maintains its own computer network, accessible through the Internet or by modem, that enables distance-learning students to access their academic records, review their degree plans, chat with students or faculty, and visit libraries at any time.

American Academy of Nutrition

1204-D Kenesaw

Knoxville, TN 37919-7736

1-800-290-4226

Web: www.nutritioneducation.com

E-mail: aantn@aol.com

Programs: AS—Applied Nutrition; individual courses

Individual Course Subjects: comprehensive nutrition

Average tuition: individual courses—$1,790; AS—$5,980

Length of program: individual courses—15 months; AS—4 years

Technologies: correspondence, video

Accreditation: DETC

Entrance requirements: high school diploma or GED

Restrictions: none

Special services: academic advising; tuition payment plan

The American College

270 S. Bryn Mawr Ave.

Bryn Mawr, PA 19010-2196

1-888-AMERCOL

Web: www.amercoll.edu

E-mail: StudentServices@Amercoll.Edu

Programs: Certificate—Certified Financial Planner, Chartered Financial

Consultant, Chartered Leadership Fellow, Chartered Life Underwriter, Registered Employee Benefits Consultant, Registered Health Underwriter; MS—Financial Services

Average tuition: certificates—$300 per course; MS—$490 per course
Length of program: certificates—$2^1/_2$ years; MS—7 years
Technologies: audiocassette, CD-ROM, Internet, video
Accreditation: MSACS
Entrance requirements: certificates—3 years of full-time business experience (an undergraduate or graduate degree is equivalent to 1 year of work experience); MS—bachelor's degree
Restrictions: The MS program requires 2 residency sessions.
Special services: student counseling

American College of Prehospital Medicine

365 Canal St.
Suite 2300
New Orleans, LA 70130-1135
1-800-735-2276
Web: www.acpm.edu
E-mail: admit@acpm.edu
Programs: AS/BS—Emergency Medical Services
Average tuition: $250 per semester hour
Length of program: AS—15 months–2 years; BS—$2^1/_2$–3 years
Technologies: CD-ROM, Internet
Accreditation: DETC
Entrance requirements: all programs—high school diploma or GED, and emergency medical services certification at the Emergency Medical Technician—Basic level, registered nurse license with an involvement in emergency medical services, or military personnel having advanced emergency medical training; BS—paramedic certificate or the equivalent
Restrictions: none
Special services: academic advising; library materials (accessible through the mail); tuition financing plan

Money Saver
The American College of Prehospital Medicine annually awards a $4,000 scholarship to a bachelor's degree applicant outside the U.S. or Canada.

American Graduate University

733 N. Dodsworth Ave.
Covina, CA 91724-2499
626-966-4576
Web: www.agu.edu/selfstdy.htm
E-mail: Info@agu.edu
Programs: Certificate—Acquisition and Contracting, Finance and Pricing, Management, Project/Program Management; Master of Acquisition Management; Master of Project Management
Average tuition: $590 per course
Technologies: correspondence, Internet, teleconferencing, video
Accreditation: DETC

Entrance requirements: certificates—1 year of work experience in the certificate area; master's—bachelor's degree and 3 years of related work experience

Restrictions: The Master of Project Management requires some on-campus courses.

Special services: none

American Health Science University

1010 S. Joliet #107
Aurora, CO 80012
1-800-530-8079
Web: www.ahsu.com
E-mail: healthynin@earthlink.net
Programs: Certificate—Nutritional Science
Average tuition: $550 per course
Length of program: 2 years
Technologies: correspondence
Accreditation: DETC
Entrance requirements: bachelor's degree (students with a significant combination of work experience and college-level coursework may be admitted without a bachelor's degree)
Restrictions: none
Special services: internship placement program; Society of Certified Nutritionists membership; mentor program; student support; toll-free help hotline

American Institute for Paralegal Studies

17W705 Butterfield Rd.
Suite A
Oakbrook Terrace, IL 60181
1-800-553-2420
Web: www.aips.com/paralegal_training_via_distance_learning.html
E-mail: john@aips.com
Programs: Certificate—Paralegal Studies
Average tuition: $3,990
Technologies: Internet
Accreditation: ACCET
Entrance requirements: 42 semester hours of undergraduate education or 2 years of law-related work experience
Restrictions: none
Special services: course facilitators

American Institute of Applied Science

P.O. Box 639
Youngsville, NC 27596
1-800-354-5134
Web: www.aiasinc.com

E-mail: aias@mindspring.com

Programs: Diploma—Forensic Science

Average tuition: $20–$680 (depending on the specific course)

Length of program: 6 lesson examinations per month

Technologies: correspondence

Accreditation: DETC

Entrance requirements: high school diploma or GED

Restrictions: none

Special services: educational support; tuition payment plan

American Institute of Commerce

1801 E. Kimberly Rd.

Davenport, IA 52807

1-800-747-1035

Web: www.aicedu.com/aiconline/

E-mail: sbaker@aicedu.com

Programs: individual courses

Individual course subjects: Microsoft certification

Average tuition: $9,000–$12,000

Length of program: 36–38 weeks

Technologies: CD-ROM, Internet

Accreditation: NCACS, ACICS

Entrance requirements: high school diploma or GED, score of 65 on the Programming Battery Exam or score of 18 on the Computer Competency Exam, and work experience

Restrictions: none

Special services: academic advising; technical support; tuition payment plan

American Military University

9104-P Manassas Dr.

Manassas Park, VA 20111

877-468-6268

Web: www.amunet.edu

E-mail: admissions@amunet.edu

Programs: BA—Intelligence Studies, Military History, Military Management; MA—Military Studies

Average tuition: $750 per course

Length of program: 16 months–4 years (depending on the number of courses taken each semester and transfer credits)

Technologies: correspondence, fax, Internet

Accreditation: DETC

Entrance requirements: BA—high school diploma or GED and 2.0 high school GPA; MA—bachelor's degree and 2.7 GPA in final 60 undergraduate semester hours

Bright Idea
The American Institute of Commerce provides an online tour of their "CyberClass" so that potential students can find out what classes are like before they enroll.

Money Saver
American Military University provides technology grants to help students cover the costs of purchasing a computer and getting an Internet account. Students may also apply for merit scholarships, which can cover up to 25 percent of the tuition costs.

Restrictions: none
Special services: tuition payment plan

Anderson University

School of Theology
1100 E. 5th St.
Anderson, IN 46012
1-800-428-6414, ext. 4534
Web: www.anderson.edu/academics/sot/catalog/pdlp.html
Programs: Certificate—Theological Studies
Average tuition: $321 per credit hour
Length of program: 1 year per course
Technologies: audiocassette, correspondence, Internet, video
Accreditation: NCACS, ATS
Entrance requirements: bachelor's degree
Restrictions: none
Special services: none

Andrew Jackson University

10 Old Montgomery Hwy.
Birmingham, AL 35209
205-871-9288
Web: www.aju.edu
E-mail: info@aju.edu
Programs: BA—Communications; BS—Business; BS/MS—Criminal Justice; MBA; MPA
Average tuition: BA/BS—$3,350–$13,400 (depending on the number of transferred credits); MBA/MPA/MS—$4,950
Length of program: BA/BS—9 months–12 years; MBA/MPA/MS—1–5 years
Technologies: correspondence, video
Accreditation: DETC
Entrance requirements: BA/BS—high school diploma or GED; MBA/MPA/MS—bachelor's degree
Restrictions: none
Special services: interest-free tuition payment plan

Andrews University/Home Study International

Andrews University/HSI Office
Nethery Hall
Andrews University
Berrien Springs, MI 49104-0070
1-800-253-2874
Web: www.andrews.edu/AUHSI/
Programs: BA—Religion; AA/BA/BS—General Studies
Average tuition: $165 per credit hour

Technologies: correspondence
Accreditation: NCACS (Andrews University); DETC (Home Study International)
Entrance requirements: high school diploma or GED, completion of 13 units of college-preparatory work in high school, and surpass minimum high school GPA, GED test scores, or ACT/SAT test scores
Restrictions: none
Special services: library access via fax and the Internet; tuition payment plan

Watch Out!
Students of these programs must have access to a well-stocked medical library.

Anglia Polytechnic University
Radiography
School of Health Sciences
East Road
Cambridge
UK CB1 1PT
Web: www.cam.anglia.ac.uk/radiography/home.htm
Programs: BS—Health Sciences; MS—Medical Imaging, Radiography
Average tuition: Contact the program administrator.
Length of program: BS—2 years; MS—3–5 years
Technologies: correspondence
Accreditation: United Kingdom government
Entrance requirements: BS—diploma qualification in radiography; MS—degree or higher professional qualification, 2 years of clinical experience, and current employment in radiographic practice
Restrictions: The MS in Medical Imaging requires a residential weekend at the start of the program (residential weekends are run in countries outside the UK where there is significant demand).
Special services: academic support; personal tutoring

Aquinas Institute of Theology
3642 Lindell Blvd.
St. Louis, MO 63108
1-800-977-3869
Web: www.op.org/aquinas/
E-mail: aquinas@slu.edu
Programs: DMin—Preaching
Average tuition: $14,000
Length of program: 4 years
Technologies: Internet
Accreditation: NCACS
Entrance requirements: MDiv or the equivalent and 3 years of full-time ministry experience
Restrictions: requires 3 seminars on campus
Special services: none

Arizona State University

Distance-Learning Technology
Box 870501
Tempe, AZ 85287-0501
480-965-6738
Web: asuonline.asu.edu
E-mail: distance@asu.edu
Programs: individual courses
Individual course subjects: art, business, communication disorders, communications, criminal justice, education, engineering, English, French, German, history, humanities, Italian, mathematics, nursing, physical sciences, political science, psychology, social services, Spanish, women's studies
Average tuition: $92–$115 per credit hour
Length of program: up to 1 year per course
Technologies: CD-ROM, correspondence, interactive TV, Internet, teleconferencing, television, video
Accreditation: NCACS
Entrance requirements: high school diploma or GED and admission as a nondegree undergraduate or graduate student
Restrictions: none
Special services: access to the online library catalog; technical support

Art Instruction Schools

3309 Broadway St. NE
Minneapolis, MN 55413
612-339-6656
Programs: individual course
Individual course subjects: Fundamentals of Art
Length of program: self-paced
Technologies: correspondence
Accreditation: DETC
Entrance requirements: none
Restrictions: none
Special services: none

Athabasca University

Public Affairs
1 University Dr.
Athabasca
Alberta T9S 3A3
Canada
1-800-788-9041
Web: www.athabascau.ca
E-mail: auinfo2@athabascau.ca

Programs: Certificate—Accounting, Administration, Career Development, Computers and Management Information Systems, Counseling Women, English Language Studies, French Language Proficiency, Health Development Administration, Home Health Nursing, Labor Relations, Rehabilitation Practice; Diploma—Arts, Inclusive Education; Bachelor of Administration—Health Administration, Industrial Relations, Management, Organization; Certificate/Bachelor of Administration—Public Administration; BA—Anthropology, Canadian Studies, English, French, General Studies, History, Humanities, Information Systems, Psychology, Sociology, Women's Studies; Bachelor of Commerce; Certificate/BA—Labor Studies; BGS—Arts and Science, Applied Science; Bachelor of Nursing; Bachelor of Professional Arts—Communication Studies, Criminal Justice; BS—Human Science; Certificate/BS—Computing and Information Systems; Advanced Graduate Diploma—Advanced Nursing Practice, Distance Education, Management; MBA; Master of Distance Education; Master of Health Studies; individual courses

Individual course subjects: accounting, anthropology, art history, astronomy, biology, business, career development, chemistry, communications, computer science, criminal justice, economics, education, English, English as a second language, environmental studies, finance, French, geography, geology, German, health, history, humanities, labor studies, law, management, management information systems, marketing, mathematics, music, native studies, nursing, nutrition, organization, philosophy, physics, political science, psychology, public administration, religion, small-business management, social sciences, sociology, Spanish, women's studies, world studies

Average tuition: $404–$1,100 (Canadian) per course (depending on residency and the number of credits)

Length of program: 6–12 months per course; bachelor's—2–4 years; advanced graduate diploma—18 months–5 years; master's—$2^1/2$–3 years

Technologies: groupware, Internet, video

Accreditation: Canadian government

Entrance requirements: individual courses/certificates/diplomas/bachelor's—none; advanced graduate diploma—bachelor's degree and 2 years of professional experience; master's—bachelor's degree; MBA—bachelor's degree or accepted professional designation and 3–5 years of related professional experience

Restrictions: Students must be at least 18 years old. Students who attend another university must obtain a letter of permission from their home institution before taking individual courses. Biology, chemistry, and physics courses require on-campus lab sessions.

Special services: academic advising; career planning; library services; student counseling; technical support; tutoring

Atlantic Cape Community College

5100 Black Horse Pike

Mays Landing, NJ 08330-2699

609-343-4900

Web: www.atlantic.edu

Programs: AA—History, Liberal Arts; AS—Business Administration, General Studies; individual courses

Individual course subjects: accounting, anthropology, art, biology, business, computer information systems, criminal justice, economics, English, English as a second language, health, history, hospitality, humanities, mathematics, music, nursing, office technology, physical education, political science, psychology, sociology

Average tuition: $75 per credit

Technologies: Internet, television, video

Accreditation: MSACS

Entrance requirements: high school diploma or equivalent

Restrictions: Some courses require on-campus meetings.

Special services: academic advising; library services

Atlantic University

Building 330

Suite 100

397 Little Neck Rd.

Virginia Beach, VA 23452

1-800-428-1512

Web: www.atlanticuniv.edu

E-mail: info@atlanticuniv.edu

Programs: MA—Transpersonal Studies

Average tuition: $510 per course

Technologies: correspondence

Accreditation: DETC

Entrance requirements: bachelor's degree with a 2.5 GPA

Restrictions: none

Special services: none

Auburn University

Distance Learning

204 Mell Hall

Auburn University, AL 36849-5611

334-844-5103

Web: www.auburn.edu/outreach/dl/

E-mail: audl@uce.auburn.edu

Programs: MBA; Master of Engineering; MS—Nutrition and Food Science; individual courses

Individual course subjects: biology, communications, criminal justice, economics, engineering, entomology, film studies, geography, health, horticulture, hospitality, mathematics, nutrition and food science, pharmacy, political science, psychology, speech, veterinary medicine

Average tuition: individual courses—$49 per credit hour; master's—$9,000–$16,000

Length of program: 3 months–1 year per course; master's—2–5 years

Technologies: audiocassette and CD, CD-ROM, correspondence, Internet, teleconferencing, video

Accreditation: SACS, ABET, ADiA

Entrance requirements: individual courses—none; master's—bachelor's degree and GRE or GMAT score

Restrictions: Graduate students may be required to make 1 campus visit.

Special services: academic advising (graduate students only); online access to library resources

Aurora University

Certificate in Quality
School of Business and Professional Studies
Aurora University
347 S. Gladstone Ave.
Aurora, IL 60506-4892
1-800-PICK-AU1
Web: www.aurora.edu/qsm/
E-mail: certqual@aurora.edu
Programs: Certificate—Deming Management
Average tuition: $9,200
Length of program: 17 months
Technologies: Internet
Accreditation: NCACS
Entrance requirements: bachelor's degree and 3 years of acceptable supervisory, professional, or managerial work experience (an associate's degree and 5 years of work experience can be substituted)
Restrictions: none
Special services: none

Aviation and Electronic Schools of America

Silverton Business Park
7940 Silverton Ave.
Suite 101
San Diego, CA 92126
1-800-325-2742
Web: www.aesa.com
E-mail: sdinfo@aesa.com

Programs: License—FCC General Radiotelephone Operators License
Average tuition: $525
Length of program: 16 weeks
Technologies: correspondence, video
Accreditation: COE, DETC
Entrance requirements: none
Restrictions: Applicants must be at least 18 years old.
Special services: none

B

Bright Idea
Students must complete a technical orientation before registering for any online course at Baker College.

Baker College
Baker College Online
1050 W. Bristol Rd.
Flint, MI 48507-5508
1-800-469-4062
Web: www.baker.edu
Programs: Certificate—Financial Planning; ABA—General Business; BBA; MBA—Leadership Studies, Traditional; Certificate/MBA—Computer Information Systems, Healthcare Management, Human Resource Management, Industrial Management, Integrated Healthcare, International Business, Marketing; individual courses
Individual course subjects: Microsoft certification
Average tuition: $145 per credit hour
Length of program: 6 weeks per course
Technologies: Internet
Accreditation: NCACS
Entrance requirements: all programs—high school diploma or GED, or admission on the basis of test results; BBA—associate's degree or 90 quarter hours of college credit; MBA—bachelor's degree
Restrictions: none
Special services: virtual library

Ball State University
School of Continuing Education and Public Service
Ball State University
Muncie, IN 47306
1-800-872-0369
Web: www.bsu.edu/provost/distance/
E-mail: distance@wp.bsu.edu
Programs: Certificate—Public Relations and Corporate Communications; AA—General Arts, Business Administration; MA—Executive Development for Public Service; Master of Arts in Education—Educational Administration and Supervision, Elementary Education, Special Education; MBA; MS—Computer Science; BS/MS—Nursing; individual courses

Individual course subjects: accounting, anthropology, astronomy, business, criminal justice, economics, English, finance, geography, geology, health, history, insurance, journalism, management, mathematics, philosophy, physical education, physics, political science, psychology, religion, sociology, theatre

Average tuition: $120 per credit hour

Length of program: 9 months per course; AA—2 years; MS in Nursing—6 years

Technologies: audiocassette, correspondence, interactive TV, Internet, television, video

Accreditation: NCACS, NCATE, NLN

Entrance requirements: all programs—admission to the university; BS—registered nurse license and associate's degree or diploma in nursing; MS in Nursing—Registered Nurse license and bachelor's degree in nursing; master's—bachelor's degree; MBA—bachelor's degree and GMAT score

Restrictions: Master's programs (except for the MS in Nursing program) are open only to Indiana residents.

Special services: academic advising for degree candidates

Bellevue Community College

Distance Education
Room D261
3000 Landerholm Cr. SE
Bellevue, WA 98007-6484
425-641-2438
Web: online.bcc.ctc.edu
E-mail: landerso@bcc.ctc.edu
Programs: Certificate—Administrative Office Systems, Business Software Specialist; AAS; AA—General Studies; Certificate/AA—Media Communications and Technology, Web/Multimedia Authoring; individual courses

Individual course subjects: accounting, American studies, anthropology, art, astronomy, biology, business, chemistry, communications, computer science, economics, English, environmental studies, geography, geology, history, human development, information technology, mass communications, mathematics, oceanography, office technology, philosophy, political science, psychology, sociology, Spanish, speech, world studies

Average tuition: $54–$209 per credit (depending on residency)

Technologies: Internet, video

Accreditation: NASC

Entrance requirements: high school diploma or GED

Restrictions: Some courses require on-campus meetings.

Special services: academic advising; library services

Bellevue University

Online Admissions
1000 Galvin Rd. S
Bellevue, NE 68005
1-800-756-7920
Web: www.bellevue.edu/Framesets/online/educationfs.html
E-mail: online-u@scholars.bellevue.edu (undergraduate) or online-g@scholars.bellevue.edu (graduate)
Programs: BS—Business Information Systems, Criminal Justice Administration, Global Business Management, Management, Management Information Systems; MA—Leadership; MBA
Average tuition: BS—$9,250; MA/MBA—$10,175
Length of program: 12 weeks per course
Technologies: Internet
Accreditation: NCACS
Entrance requirements: BS—associate's degree, 60 transferable college credit hours, C grade average, 3 years of relevant work experience, and current employment; MA/MBA—bachelor's degree with a 2.5 GPA in the final 60 credit hours, a 3.0 GPA on prior graduate work, and 3 years of work or equivalent experience
Restrictions: none
Special services: academic advising; career services

Bemidji State University

Center for Extended Learning
333 Deputy Hall
1500 Birchmont Dr. NE
Bemidji, MN 56601-2699
1-800-475-2001, ext. 206
Web: cel.bemidji.msus.edu/cel/
E-mail: cel@vax1.bemidji.msus.edu
Programs: AA—Liberal Studies; AS/BS—Criminal Justice; individual courses
Individual course subjects: accounting, anthropology, biology, business, chemistry, criminal justice, economics, education, English, environmental studies, geography, geology, health, history, humanities, industrial technology, music, nursing, philosophy, physical education, physical science, political science, psychology, social work, sociology, Spanish
Average tuition: $199 per credit
Length of program: 18 weeks per course
Technologies: audiocassette, correspondence, interactive TV, Internet, video
Accreditation: NCACS
Entrance requirements: individual courses—none; AA/AS/BS—high school diploma or GED

Restrictions: Some programs and courses are restricted to Minnesota residents.

Special services: none

Berean University

1445 Boonville Ave.

Springfield, MO 65802

1-800-443-1083

Web: www.berean.edu

E-mail: berean@ag.org

Programs: Diploma—Bible and Doctrine, Specialized Ministries, Urban Bible Training; Diploma/AA—Church Ministries; BA—Bible/Christian Education, Bible/Missions, Bible/Pastoral Ministries; AA/BA—Bible/Theology; MA—Biblical Studies, Christian Counseling; Diploma/AA/MA—Ministerial Studies; individual courses

Individual course subjects: biblical studies, ministerial studies

Average tuition: $25–$387 per course

Length of program: 10 weeks–6 months per course; MA—5 years

Technologies: correspondence, Internet

Accreditation: DETC

Entrance requirements: diploma—none; AA/BA—high school diploma or GED; MA—bachelor's degree, 24 semester hours of undergraduate coursework in Bible and Theology, and an undergraduate GPA of 2.5

Restrictions: Students must be at least 20 years old.

Special services: e-mail forums for interaction with other students; student support services

Bright Idea
Berean University offers an all-Spanish curriculum for Spanish-speaking students wishing to pursue a diploma, associate's degree, or bachelor's degree.

Black Hills State University

BHSU Distance Education

Office of Extended Services

1200 University

USB 9508

Spearfish, SD 57799-9508

1-800-255-BHSU

Web: www.bhsu.edu/academics/distlrn/index.html

E-mail: vfish@mystic.bhsu.edu

Programs: individual courses

Individual course subjects: accounting, art, astronomy, biology, business, communications, computer information systems, computer science, criminal justice, economics, education, engineering, English, geography, geology, health, history, humanities, information technology, marketing, mass communications, mathematics, music, nursing, physical science, political science, psychology, sociology, Spanish, speech, statistics, theater

Average tuition: $125.45 per credit hour

Length of program: 15 weeks per course

Technologies: correspondence, Internet, television, video
Accreditation: NCACS
Entrance requirements: high school diploma with a 2.0 GPA
Restrictions: Some courses are limited to South Dakota residents.
Special services: none

Bladen Community College
7418 NC Hwy. 41 W
P.O. Box 266
Dublin, NC 28332
1-800-619-1406
Web: www.bcc.cc.nc.us/dstlrn/Default.html
E-mail: dperry@cis.bcc.cc.nc.us
Programs: AAS—Business Administration
Average tuition: $20 per semester hour (North Carolina residents); $163 per semester hour (out-of-state students)
Length of program: 2 years
Technologies: television, video
Accreditation: SACS
Entrance requirements: high school diploma or GED
Restrictions: Some courses require on-campus sessions.
Special services: academic advising; student counseling

Boise State University
Division of Continuing Education
1910 University Dr.
Boise, ID 83725
208-426-1709
Web: www.boisestate.edu/conted/
Programs: individual courses
Individual course subjects: accounting, chemistry, computer science, economics, education, engineering, English, geography, geology, health, history, management, marketing, mathematics, music, nursing, physics, political science, psychology, sociology, Spanish, theatre
Average tuition: $114.75 per credit
Technologies: CD-ROM, Internet, radio, television, video
Accreditation: NASC
Entrance requirements: high school diploma or GED
Restrictions: Some courses require on-campus meetings. Television courses require students to live within the broadcast area.
Special services: academic advising

Brevard Community College
1519 Clearlake Rd.
Cocoa, FL 32922
407-632-1111

Web: www.brevard.cc.fl.us/distlrn/

Programs: AA—General Studies; AS—Legal Assisting; individual courses

Individual course subjects: accounting, biology, business, communications, computer science, criminal justice, drafting and design, economics, hazardous materials, health, history, hospitality, humanities, legal assisting, mathematics, nutrition, office technology, physical education, physical science, psychology, speech

Average tuition: $50 per credit hour (Florida residents); $169 per credit hour (out-of-state students)

Length of program: 16 weeks per course

Technologies: correspondence, interactive TV, Internet, television, video

Accreditation: SACS

Entrance requirements: high school diploma or GED

Restrictions: Some courses or programs require on-campus sessions for orientation, discussion, and exams. Some courses may only be available to students in Brevard County, Florida.

Special services: academic advising; online library access

Brigham Young University

206 Harman Building

P.O. Box 21514

Provo, UT 84602-1514

1-800-914-8931

Web: coned.byu.edu/is/index.html

E-mail: indstudy@con2.byu.edu

Programs: Certificate—Family History, Organ Performance; individual courses

Individual course subjects: accounting, American studies, animal sciences, anthropology, art, astronomy, biology, botany, business, chemistry, communications, dance, economics, education, engineering, English, genealogy, geography, geology, German, health, Hebrew, high school subjects, history, horticulture, humanities, management information systems, mathematics, music, Near Eastern studies, nursing, nutrition and food science, philosophy, physical education, physical science, physics, political science, psychology, range science, religion, social work, sociology, Spanish, statistics, technology, theater, zoology

Average tuition: $84 per credit hour

Length of program: 1 year per course

Technologies: CD-ROM, correspondence, Internet

Accreditation: NASC

Entrance requirements: none

Restrictions: none

Special services: electronic report card; instantaneous online grading

Bright Idea
Brevard Community College's Online Demo Course introduces online learning and gives you an idea of what to expect in the "virtual" classroom.

Watch Out!
Enrollment in an individual independent study course or certificate program does not constitute admission to Brigham Young University.

Bucks County Community College

434 Swamp Rd.

Newtown, PA 18940

1-888-BUCKS77, ext. 8052

Web: www.bucks.edu/distance/index.html

E-mail: learning@bucks.edu

Programs: Certificate—Entrepreneurship; AA—Liberal Arts, Management and Marketing; ABA; individual courses

Individual course subjects: accounting, art, astronomy, biology, chemistry, communications, computer science, economics, education, English, health, history, hospitality, humanities, law, management, management information systems, marketing, mathematics, Microsoft certification, music, office management, philosophy, physical science, physics, political science, psychology, sociology

Average tuition: $71–$213 per credit hour (depending on residency)

Length of program: 17 weeks per course

Technologies: audiocassette, CD-ROM, correspondence, fax, Internet, video

Accreditation: MSACS

Entrance requirements: high school diploma or GED

Restrictions: Some courses require on-campus meetings.

Special services: academic advising; free Internet training; online library catalog; student counseling; tutoring services

Burlington College

95 North Ave.

Burlington, VT 05401

1-800-862-9616

Web: www.burlcol.edu/distance.htm

Programs: BA—Cinema Studies, Fine Arts, Individualized Major, Psychology, Transpersonal Psychology, Writing and Literature

Average tuition: $2,000 (half-time)–$3,400 (full-time) per semester

Length of program: 2–3 semesters (average)

Technologies: correspondence, fax, Internet

Accreditation: NEASC

Entrance requirements: completion of a minimum of 45 acceptable college credits with a C- grade average, and documentation of strong writing skills and an ability to work independently

Restrictions: All programs require a 4-day weekend of residency at the college before each semester. Students must enroll at least half-time (6–9 credits per semester).

Special services: individualized degree plans

Burlington County College

Office of Distance Learning
Route 530
Pemberton, NJ 08068
609-894-9311, ext. 7582
Web: www.bcc.edu/distance/index.htm
E-mail: sespensh@bcc.edu
Programs: AA—Liberal Studies; AS—Business Administration; individual courses
Individual course subjects: anthropology, art, biology, business, communications, computer science, economics, education, English, fashion design, film studies, French, geology, German, history, mathematics, music, nutrition and food science, political science, psychology, sociology, Spanish, theater
Average tuition: $60–$140 per credit (depending on residency)
Technologies: CD-ROM, Internet, radio, television, video
Accreditation: MSACS
Entrance requirements: high school diploma or GED
Restrictions: Many courses require some on-campus meetings. Some courses are only open to New Jersey residents.
Special services: none

C

Caldwell College

9 Ryerson Ave.
Caldwell, NJ 07006
973-618-3000
Web: www.caldwell.edu/academics/external.html
Programs: BA—Art, Communication Arts, Criminal Justice, English, History, Political Science, Psychology, Religious Studies, Social Studies, Sociology; BS—Accounting, Business Administration, Computer Science, International Business, Management, Marketing; individual courses
Individual course subjects: accounting, business, international business, management, marketing
Average tuition: $319 per credit
Length of program: 15 weeks per course
Technologies: audiocassette, correspondence, Internet, teleconferencing, video
Accreditation: MSACS
Entrance requirements: individual courses—students must enroll as visiting students and be enrolled in a distance-education degree program at another institution; BA/BS—high school GPA of 2.5 or more and at least 12 credits of prior college study

Money Saver
Caldwell College will
assist financially
needy adult students
with partial grants.

Restrictions: All students must be at least 23 years old and must attend the External Degree weekend on campus at the beginning of each semester. Some on-campus coursework is required for Art and Computer Science majors.

Special services: academic advising; access to the on-campus library; computing center; counseling office; learning center; and career development center

California College for Health Sciences

222 W. 24th St.

National City, CA 91950

619-477-4800

Web: www.cchs.edu

E-mail: cchsinfo@cchs.edu

Programs: Certificate—Business Essentials, Community Health Education, Gerontology, Healthcare Ethics, Health Psychology, Polysomnography; Diploma—Dental Assisting, EKG Technology, Home Health Aide, Medical Assisting, Pharmacy Technology, Physical Therapy Aide, Respiratory Care Assisting; AS—Allied Health, Early Childhood Education, EEG Technology, Medical Transcription, Respiratory Technology, Respiratory Therapy; AS/BS—Business; MBA—Healthcare; MS—Healthcare Administration, Public Health; BS/MS—Health Services

Average tuition: Certificate/AS/BS/MBA/MS—$100 per semester credit; Diplomas—$749

Length of program: 2 months per semester credit

Technologies: correspondence

Accreditation: ACCSCT, DETC

Entrance requirements: certificates—none; diplomas/AS—high school diploma or GED; BS—associate's degree or completion of 60 lower-division semester credits, including 21 credits of general education; MBA/MS—bachelor's degree

Restrictions: none

Special services: tuition payment plan

California Institute of Integral Studies

1453 Mission St.

San Francisco, CA 94103

415-575-6100

Web: www.ciis.edu/online/index.html

E-mail: info@ciis.edu

Programs: MA—Cultural Anthropology and Social Transformation; PhD—Humanities

Average tuition: MA—$24,820 per year; PhD—$27,670 per year

Length of program: 16 weeks per course

Technologies: Internet

Accreditation: WASC

Entrance requirements: MA—bachelor's degree; PhD—MA in Cultural Anthropology and Social Transformation or a closely related field with a GPA of 3.0 or higher.

Restrictions: All programs require 2 week-long, on-campus, residential seminars.

Special services: academic advising

California National University for Advanced Studies

16909 Parthenia St.

North Hills, CA 91343

1-800-782-2422

Web: www.cnuas.edu

E-mail: cnuadms@mail.cnuas.edu

Programs: BS—Business Administration, Computer Science, Quality Assurance Science; BS/MS—Engineering; MBA; Master of Human Resource Management

Average tuition: BS—$195 per unit; master's—$210 per unit

Length of program: 15 weeks per course

Technologies: correspondence, fax, Internet

Accreditation: DETC

Entrance requirements: Contact the school directly for entrance requirements.

Restrictions: none

Special services: academic advising; one-on-one instruction

California State University—Bakersfield

CSUB Extended University

9001 Stockdale Hwy.

Bakersfield, CA 93311-1099

661-664-2427

Web: www.csubak.edu/ExtUniversity/

E-mail: njohnson@csub.edu

Programs: Certificate—Geographic Information Systems; Certificate/BS—Environmental Resource Management; individual courses

Individual course subjects: business, computer science, criminal justice, economics, English, environmental resources management, finance, management, marketing, mathematics, nursing, political science, sociology

Average tuition: $90 per quarter unit

Technologies: interactive TV, Internet

Accreditation: WASC

Entrance requirements: individual courses—apply as a student (requires a high school diploma and minimum academic standards) or through the Open University (no requirements); Certificate in Environmental Resources Management—bachelor's degree; BS—2 years of previous college work or the equivalent

Time Saver
If you plan to take only one or two courses, apply through the Open University—you won't have to bother with submitting transcripts or filling out lengthy applications.

Restrictions: Some programs and courses may require students to reside near the university and/or attend on-campus meetings.

Special services: online access to library databases; technical support

California State University—Chico

Chico Distributed Campus
400 W. First St.
Chico, CA 95929
530-898-6105
Web: www.csuchico.edu/cdc/

Programs: Certificate—Alternative Dispute Resolution, Career Planning and Development, Cross-Cultural Language and Academic Development (CLAD), Paralegal Studies, Resource Specialist; BA—Liberal Studies, Political Science, Social Science, Sociology; BS—Nursing; MS—Telecommunications; BS/MS—Computer Science; individual courses

Individual course subjects: Asian studies, education, geography, history, management, marketing, mathematics, nursing, philosophy, physical education, physics, political science, psychology, religion, social sciences, social work, sociology, special education

Technologies: interactive TV, Internet, television, video

Accreditation: WASC, CSAB, NLN

Entrance requirements: individual courses—admission to the university; BA/BS—completion of a significant amount of college-level coursework; MS—bachelor's degree with an undergraduate GPA of 2.75 in the last 60 units and relevant background preparation. Note: Individual certificate programs have specific entrance requirements.

Restrictions: Many programs and courses are restricted to California residents, and some programs are only available to employees of participating companies. Many programs require students to take a number of on-campus courses or to attend labs and seminars at specified locations.

Special services: academic advising for certificate and degree candidates; technical support

California State University—Dominguez Hills

1000 E. Victoria St.
Carson, CA 90747
310-243-3741
Web: www.csudh.edu/dominguezonline/
E-mail: midl@csudh.edu

Programs: Certificate—Production and Inventory Control, Purchasing; BA—Interdisciplinary Studies; BS—Nursing; MA—Behavioral Science, Humanities; MBA; MS—Quality Assurance; individual courses

Individual course subjects: accounting, business, education, high school subjects, management, marketing, psychology, quality management, recreation

Average tuition: $135–$170 per unit
Length of program: 10–15 weeks per course; master's—2–2^1/2 years
Technologies: correspondence, Internet, television, videoconferencing
Accreditation: WASC, NLN
Entrance requirements: individual courses—apply for admission to the university or to Open University; BA/BS—completion of a significant amount of transferable, college-level coursework with a GPA of 2.0 or better; MA/MBA/MS—bachelor's degree with an undergraduate GPA of 2.5–3.0 (depending on the program) and relevant background preparation; MBA—also requires a GMAT score of 450 or higher
Restrictions: Television courses are restricted to students living in the local viewing area. Some courses require students to attend occasional on-campus meetings.
Special services: online library resources; online tutoring

California State University—Los Angeles

Distance Learning Unit
Office of Continuing Education
5151 State University Dr.
Los Angeles, CA 90032-8619
323-343-4916
Web: www.calstatela.edu/cont_ed/distance/
Programs: individual courses
Individual course subjects: business, education, educational technology, engineering, English as a second language, fire protection, library science, political science, small business management
Average tuition: $125 per quarter unit
Technologies: Internet, television, video, videoconferencing
Accreditation: WASC
Entrance requirements: admission to the university (high school diploma or GED required) or enrollment in the Open University (no requirements)
Restrictions: Television courses require students to live within the viewing area. Some courses may require on-campus meetings.
Special services: none

California State University—Northridge

College of Extended Learning
18111 Nordhoff St.
Northridge, CA 91330-8343
1-800-882-0128
Web: www.csun.edu/exl/distance/
Programs: MS—Communication Disorders; individual courses
Individual course subjects: engineering
Average tuition: $150–$237 per unit; MS—$18,074
Length of program: 16 weeks per course; MS—2–3 years

Technologies: Internet, teleconferencing, television, videoconferencing
Accreditation: WASC, ASHA
Entrance requirements: individual courses—admission to the university or to the Open University; MS—California residency, employment by a California school district, and either a bachelor's degree in Communication Disorders or appropriate prerequisite courses
Restrictions: Some courses require on-campus meetings. Students taking television course must live within the broadcast area.
Special services: academic advising (master's only)

California State University—Sacramento

6000 J St.
Sacramento, CA 95819
916-278-7948
Web: www.csus.edu/distance/
E-mail: siegfriedm@csus.edu
Programs: individual courses
Individual course subjects: accounting, anthropology, communications, computer science, criminal justice, economics, education, engineering, French, geography, geology, health, history, management information systems, nursing, philosophy, political science, psychology, Russian, sociology, statistics
Technologies: fax, Internet, television, video
Accreditation: WASC
Entrance requirements: admission to the university or enrollment through the continuing education program
Restrictions: Students taking televised courses must live in the broadcast area. Some courses require on-campus meetings.
Special services: free e-mail and Internet account

California State University—San Marcos

Office of Extended Studies
333 S. Twin Oaks Valley Rd.
San Marcos, CA 92096-0001
1-800-500-9377
Web: ww2.csusm.edu/es/online/online.html
E-mail: bre@mailhost1.csusm.edu
Programs: Certificate—Paralegal Studies; individual courses
Individual course subjects: education, history, sociology
Average tuition: $315 per course
Length of program: certificate—14 weeks
Technologies: Internet
Accreditation: WASC
Entrance requirements: none
Restrictions: Some courses require on-campus orientation sessions.
Special services: technical support

Cambrian College

Distance Education
Sudbury
Ontario P3A 3V8
Canada
705-566-8101
Web: homepages.cambrianc.on.ca/distance/default.htm
Programs: Certificate—Business Administration, Diabetes Education and Care, Early Childhood Education, General Insurance, Gerontology, Municipal Administration, Occupational Health and Safety, Registered Nurse Critical Care, Registered Nurse Occupational Health Nursing, Teachers of Adults, Working with the Aged; individual courses
Individual course subjects: biology, English, nursing, psychology
Average tuition: $71.37–$326.40 (Canadian) per course
Length of program: 8–15 weeks per course
Technologies: correspondence, Internet, teleconferencing
Accreditation: Canadian government
Entrance requirements: high school diploma or mature student status; some programs require professional experience and current employment in the field
Restrictions: Teleconferencing programs are only available in northern Ontario.
Special services: none

Canadian School of Management

Suite 1120
335 Bay St.
Toronto
Ontario, M5H 2R3
Canada
1-888-508-7642
Web: www.c-s-m.org
E-mail: csm@c-s-m.org
Programs: Certificate—Office Administration, Organization and Management, Travel Counseling and Tourism; Associate of Health Services Administration; Diploma—Business Administration, Facilities and Estate Management, Marketing Management; Certificate/Diploma—Front-Line Management; BS—Long-Term Care Administration; Diploma/BS— Management, Tourism and Hospitality Management; Executive Diploma— Enterprise Development, Knowledge Management, Organizational Science, Quality Management; Advanced Diploma—Management Action Learning, Marketing Professional Services; ABA; MBA—General, International Management; Certificate/Diploma/BS/MS—Health Services Administration
Average tuition: $230–$1,560 (Canadian) per course

Length of program: 2–3 years

Technologies: correspondence, Internet

Accreditation: DETC

Entrance requirements: certificates/diplomas/associate's/BS—high school diploma; MBA/MS—bachelor's degree. Note: Many programs require completion of prerequisite general education college-level courses or degrees, relevant work experience, or certified membership in the appropriate professional association.

Restrictions: none

Special services: personal tutoring; virtual library access

Capella University

330 2nd Ave. S

Suite 550

Minneapolis, MN 55401

1-888-CAPELLA

Web: www.capellauniversity.edu

Programs: Certificate—Addiction Disorder Treatment, Clinical Supervision, Communications Technology Management, Forensic Psychology, General Management, Geriatric Care, Mental Health Care Utilization and Management, Psycho-Neurological Testing, School Psychology, Teaching/Training Online; MBA—Finance; Certificate/MBA—E-Business, Information Technology, Leadership; Certificate/MS—Training and Development; MS/PhD—Addiction Psychology, Clinical Psychology, Communications Technology, Educational Psychology, General Education, Health Psychology, Human Services, Organization and Management, Organizational Psychology; Certificate/MS/PhD—Adult Education, Distance Education, Educational Administration, Healthcare Administration, Instructional Design, Marriage and Family Services, Professional Counseling, Social and Community Services, Sports Psychology; individual courses

Individual course subjects: business, education, psychology, social services

Average tuition: individual courses, certificates, and some master's programs—$895–$1,475 per course; directed study master's programs—$1,995 per quarter; PhD—$2,985 per quarter

Length of program: 12 weeks per course; master's/PhD—1–3 years

Technologies: Internet

Accreditation: NCACS

Entrance requirements: individual courses/certificates—none; MBA/MS—bachelor's degree; PhD—master's degree

Restrictions: Some programs require minimal residencies, typically through attendance of seminars lasting 3 days–2 weeks.

Special services: access to the University of Alabama at Huntsville's online library; one-on-one instruction via directed study courses

Capitol College

11301 Springfield Rd.

Laurel, MD 20708

1-800-950-1992

Web: www.capitol-college.edu/academics/dl/default.htm

Programs: BS—Software and Internet Applications; MS—Electronic Commerce Management, Information and Telecommunications Systems Management

Average tuition: $954 per course

Length of program: 7 years

Technologies: Internet

Accreditation: MSACS

Entrance requirements: BS—high school diploma; MS—bachelor's degree

Restrictions: none

Special services: academic advising; student counseling

Carnegie Mellon University

5000 Forbes Ave.

Pittsburgh, PA 15213

412-268-2000

Web: www.cmu.edu/home/education/education_distance.html

E-mail: dist-ed@cs.cmu.edu

Programs: Certificate—Information Resource Management, Software Engineering; individual courses

Individual course subjects: software engineering

Average tuition: graduate—$3,684 per course; continuing education—$2,200 per course; Certificate in Information Resource Management—$2,640 per course

Length of program: graduate—17 weeks per course; continuing education—6 months per course; Certificate in Information Resource Management—1–2 years; Certificate in Software Engineering—2–5 years

Technologies: CD-ROM, Internet, video

Accreditation: MSACS, ABET

Entrance requirements: graduate courses and Certificate in Software Engineering—2 years work experience in a software development project, undergraduate coursework in discrete mathematics, algorithms, and data structures, programming experience, and a bachelor's degree in a related field; continuing education courses—employment in the software development field; Certificate in Information Resource Management—3 years work experience and a bachelor's degree

Restrictions: The Certificate in Information Resource Management requires a 1-day session in New York City.

Special services: none

The Catholic Distance University

120 E. Colonial Hwy.
Hamilton, VA 20158-9012
1-888-254-4CDU
Web: www.cdu.edu
E-mail: CDU@CDU.EDU
Programs: Certificate—Catechetical Diploma; MA—Religious Studies; Master of Religious Studies; individual courses
Individual course subjects: religion
Average tuition: $200 per credit hour
Length of program: 9 months per course; master's—7–8 years
Technologies: correspondence, fax, Internet
Accreditation: DETC
Entrance requirements: individual courses—none; master's—bachelor's degree
Restrictions: none
Special services: tuition payment plan

Central Carolina Community College

1105 Kelly Dr.
Sanford, NC 27330
1-800-682-8353, ext. 284
Web: www.ccarolina.cc.nc.us/Academic%20Departments/
Distance%20Education/Index.htm
E-mail: jstrother@gw.ccarolina.cc.nc.us
Programs: AAS—Business Administration; AA—General Studies; individual courses
Individual course subjects: accounting, biology, business, economics, English, history, marketing, mathematics, philosophy, physical education, psychology, sociology, Spanish
Average tuition: $46.75 per semester credit hour (North Carolina residents); $189.75 per semester credit hour (out-of-state students)
Length of program: 13 weeks per course
Technologies: correspondence, Internet, television, video
Accreditation: SACS
Entrance requirements: high school diploma or GED
Restrictions: All courses require on-campus meetings. Students taking television courses must live in the broadcast area.
Special services: none

Central Michigan University

Distance and Distributed Learning
College of Extended Learning
Mount Pleasant, MI 48859
1-800-688-4268

Web: www.ddl.cmich.edu
E-mail: celinfo@mail.cel.cmich.edu
Programs: AuD; individual courses
Individual course subjects: accounting, astronomy, communication disorders, economics, English, finance, geography, health, journalism, management, management information systems, marketing, music, physics, political science, psychology, religion, sociology, Spanish, statistics
Average tuition: $165–$495 per course; AuD—$225–$315 per credit hour
Length of program: 12 weeks per course; AuD—2 years
Technologies: audiocassette, correspondence, Internet, television, video
Accreditation: NCACS, ASHA
Entrance requirements: individual courses—admission to the university; AuD—graduate degree in audiology, either the ASHA Certificate of Clinical Competence in Audiology or a valid state license, and 5 years of audiological work experience
Restrictions: none
Special services: academic advising; off-campus library services

Central State University

16801 Van Buren Blvd.
Building A
Riverside, CA 92504
1-888-600-8833
Web: www.university.edu
E-mail: csu@university.edu
Programs: BBA; MBA; DBA
Average tuition: BBA—$58 per unit; MBA/DBA—$87.50 per unit
Length of program: self-paced
Technologies: correspondence
Accreditation: NCACS
Entrance requirements: BBA—2 years of college education, including general education requirements, with a GPA of 2.0 or higher; MBA—bachelor's degree in a business-related major with a GPA of 3.0 or higher; DBA—MBA with a GPA of 3.0 or higher
Restrictions: none
Special services: academic advising

Central Texas College

Admissions
ATTN: Distance Learning Coordinator
P.O. Box 1800
Killeen, TX 76540
1-800-792-3348, ext. 1226
Web: www.ctcd.cc.tx.us/disted.htm
E-mail: distlrn1@ctcd.cc.tx.us

Bright Idea
The Central Texas College Web site has a sample course and a quiz to help you determine if you're a good candidate for distance learning.

Programs: individual courses

Individual course subjects: art, astronomy, aviation science, biology, business, communications, computer science, criminal justice, drafting and design, early childhood education, electronics, hospitality, humanities, industrial technology, mathematics, mental-health services, office management, social sciences, telecommunications

Average tuition: $60–$250 per semester hour (depending on residency)

Technologies: CD-ROM, correspondence, fax, Internet, television, video, videoconferencing

Accreditation: SACS

Entrance requirements: high school diploma or GED (applicants without a high school diploma may be admitted on the basis of test scores)

Restrictions: Some courses require on-campus meetings (Central Texas College has campus locations throughout the U.S. and around the world).

Special services: academic advising; online help desk; online library access

Central Wyoming College

2660 Peck Ave.
Riverton, WY 82501
307-855-2000
Web: webserve1.cwc.whecn.edu/academic/distance.htm
Programs: AAS—Surgical Technology; AA—General Studies; individual courses
Individual course subjects: art, broadcasting, business, English, geography, history, languages, nursing, physical education, political science, psychology, surgical technology, theater
Average tuition: $46–$138 per credit (depending on residency)
Length of program: 10–15 weeks per course
Technologies: CD-ROM, Internet, television, video
Accreditation: NCACS
Entrance requirements: high school diploma or GED
Restrictions: none
Special services: none

Cerro Coso Community College

3000 College Heights Blvd.
Ridgecrest, CA 93555-9571
1-888-537-6932
Web: www.cc.cc.ca.us/cconline/Default.htm
E-mail: mhightow@cc.cc.ca.us
Programs: AA—Business, Comparative Literature, English, History, Humanities, Liberal Arts/General Studies, Social Sciences; AS—Administration of Justice, Business Administration, Business Management, Computer Information Systems, Economics
Average tuition: $11 per unit (California residents); $133 per unit (out-of-state students)

Length of program: 8–16 weeks per course
Technologies: Internet
Accreditation: WASC
Entrance requirements: high school diploma, California High School Proficiency Exam (CHSPE) certificate, or GED
Restrictions: none
Special services: online access to library facilities; student counseling

Champlain College

Champlain College Online
163 S. Willard St.
Burlington, VT 05401-0670
1-888-545-3459
Web: www.champlain.edu/OLDE/index.html
E-mail: online@champlain.edu
Programs: AS—Web Site Development and Management; Certificate/AS—Accounting; Certificate/AS/BS—Business, Computer Programming, Hotel-Restaurant Management, Management, Telecommunications
Average tuition: $318 per credit
Length of program: 2 years
Technologies: Internet
Accreditation: NEASC
Entrance requirements: all programs—high school diploma or GED; BS—completion of 3 semesters of college-level coursework
Restrictions: none
Special services: academic advising; career planning and placement; online library services; tuition payment plan; tutoring

Charles County Community College

Information Center
P.O. Box 910
La Plata, MD 20646-0910
301-934-7765
Web: www.charles.cc.md.us/distance/index.htm
E-mail: info@charles.cc.md.us
Programs: AAS—Information Services Technology, Management Development; AA—General Studies; individual courses
Individual course subjects: accounting, art, astronomy, biology, business, computer science, economics, education, English, environmental studies, geology, health, history, mathematics, office technology, philosophy, political science, psychology, sociology, Spanish
Average tuition: $70–$180 per credit (depending on residency)
Length of program: 8–15 weeks per course
Technologies: CD-ROM, Internet, television, video
Accreditation: MSACS

Bright Idea
You can sample a Cerro Coso Community College online course at the school's Web site.

Unofficially...
Students who complete an associate's degree at Champlain College and maintain a 2.5 GPA are guaranteed admission to bachelor's degree programs.

Entrance requirements: high school diploma or GED

Restrictions: All courses require 1 or more on-campus meetings. AAS degrees are currently only partially available at a distance.

Special services: online academic advising; online library services

Charter Oak State College

Admissions Office

55 Paul Manafort Dr.

New Britain, CT 06053

860-832-3800

Web: www.cosc.edu

E-mail: info@mail.cosc.edu

Programs: AA/AS/BA/BS—General Studies; individual courses

Individual course subjects: anthropology, art, biology, business, communications, critical thinking, economics, English, film studies, geography, history, mathematics, philosophy, social sciences, sociology

Average tuition: $68–$135 per credit (depending on type of course and residency)

Length of program: degree programs—1–2 years

Technologies: correspondence, Internet, video

Accreditation: NEASC

Entrance requirements: 9 college-level credits from any acceptable source (regardless of level of formal education)

Restrictions: Applicants must be at least 16 years old.

Special services: academic advising; tuition payment plan

Chemeketa Community College

P.O. Box 14007

4000 Lancaster Dr. NE

Salem, OR 97309

503-399-7873

Web: www.chemek.cc.or.us/academics/distance/c_online/

Programs: AAS—Fire Protection Technology; AA—General Studies; AGS; individual courses

Individual course subjects: anthropology, biology, business, chemistry, computer science, drafting, economics, education, emergency services, English, English as a second language, fire protection, health, health services, history, hospitality, human development, humanities, mathematics, music, nutrition, philosophy, physical education, physics, psychology, science, writing

Average tuition: $36 per credit hour

Length of program: 11 weeks per course; AAS/AA/AGS—2 years

Technologies: correspondence, interactive TV, Internet, television, video

Accreditation: NASC

Entrance requirements: high school diploma or GED

Restrictions: Some courses require on-campus meetings. Students taking television courses must live within the broadcast area.

Special services: academic advising

Choice 2000 Charter School

155 E. 4th St.

Suite 100

Perris, CA 92570

909-940-5700

Web: www.choice2000.org

Programs: high school diploma (grades 7–12)

Average tuition: free (in-state residents); $175 per class (out-of-state residents)

Length of program: 9 weeks per course

Technologies: Internet

Accreditation: WASC

Entrance requirements: none

Restrictions: Students must visit the school office at least 3 times per year (other arrangements can be made for out-of-state students).

Special services: Parent Teacher Student Association (PTSA); school-sponsored social activities

Christopher Newport University

1 University Place

Newport News, VA 23606

1-800-333-4CNU

Web: www.cnuonline.cnu.edu

E-mail: online@cnu.edu

Programs: BA—Philosophy and Religious Studies; BS—Governmental Administration; individual courses

Individual course subjects: accounting, business, computer science, economics, education, electronic commerce, English, health, history, mathematics, philosophy, physics, political science, religion, sociology, Spanish

Average tuition: $145 per credit hour (Virginia residents); $351 per credit hour (out-of-state students)

Length of program: 15 weeks per course

Technologies: Internet

Accreditation: SACS

Entrance requirements: individual courses—none; BA/BS—high school diploma or GED

Restrictions: none

Special services: help line

Bright Idea
Although aimed at high school-age students, Choice 2000 Charter School also provides a way for adults to earn a high school diploma through distance learning.

Citizens' High School

P.O. Box 1929
Orange Park, FL 32067-1929
1-800-736-GRAD
Web: www.citizenschool.com
E-mail: citizenschool@schoolmail.com
Programs: high school diploma; individual courses
Individual course subjects: high school subjects
Average tuition: $105 per course; diploma—$395–$995 (depending on the number of grade levels needed to be completed)
Length of program: 1 year per course; diploma—4 months–3 years (depending on the number of grade levels needed to be completed)
Technologies: audiocassette, correspondence
Accreditation: DETC
Entrance requirements: none
Restrictions: none
Special services: academic advising; tuition payment plan

City University

335 116th Ave. SE
Bellevue, WA 98004
1-800-426-5596
Web: www.cityu.edu
E-mail: info@cityu.edu
Programs: individual courses
Individual course subjects: business, computer science, critical thinking, English, law, management
Length of program: 10 weeks per course
Technologies: CD-ROM, correspondence, Internet, video
Accreditation: NASC
Entrance requirements: high school diploma or GED
Restrictions: none
Special services: academic advising; electronic library services; tutoring services via facilitated distance-learning classes

Cleveland Institute of Electronics

1776 E. 17th St.
Cleveland, OH 44114
1-800-CIE-OHIO
Web: www.cie-wc.edu
E-mail: ciewc@cie-wc.edu
Programs: AAS—Electronics
Length of program: up to 4 years
Technologies: correspondence
Accreditation: DETC
Entrance requirements: high school diploma or GED

Restrictions: none
Special services: none

Coastal Carolina University

Division of Extended Learning and Public Services
P.O. Box 261954
Conway, SC 29528-6054
843-349-2666
Web: www.coastal.edu/learn/
E-mail: jshinabe@coastal.edu
Programs: Certificate—Basic Supervision, Creative Writing, Customer Service, Project Management Principles; BA/BS—Interdisciplinary Studies; individual courses
Individual course subjects: business, computer science, criminal justice, education, English, finance, genealogy, health, industrial technology, management, mathematics, music, political science, psychology, religion, science, small business management, sociology, speech, technical writing, test preparation, writing
Average tuition: $85–$115 per course
Length of program: 5–7 weeks per course
Technologies: correspondence, Internet
Accreditation: SACS
Entrance requirements: individual courses/certificates—none; BA/BS—prior college coursework
Restrictions: Some courses require on-campus meetings. Bachelor's programs may require taking some on-campus courses.
Special services: none

Cochise College

4190 W. Hwy. 80
Douglas, AZ 85607
1-800-966-7943
Web: xwing.cochise.cc.az.us/online-campus/
E-mail: admissions@cochise.cc.az.us
Programs: Certificate—International Business, UNIX; individual courses
Individual course subjects: biology, business, computer information systems, criminal justice, economics, education, English, mathematics, philosophy, political science, psychology, sociology
Average tuition: $52 per unit
Length of program: 16 weeks per course
Technologies: Internet
Accreditation: NCACS
Entrance requirements: none
Restrictions: none
Special services: academic advising

College for Financial Planning

6161 S. Syracuse Way
Greenwood Village, CO 80111-4707
1-800-237-9990
Web: www.fp.edu/programs/masters/overview.htm
Programs: MS—Financial Planning
Average tuition: $510 per course
Length of program: 5 years
Technologies: correspondence, fax, Internet
Accreditation: NCACS, DETC
Entrance requirements: bachelor's degree with a GPA of 2.5 or graduate degree, and previous college or professional work in financial planning
Restrictions: none
Special services: academic advising; access to the University of Phoenix's Learning Resource Center; student counseling

College of DuPage

Center for Independent Learning at Glen Ellyn
Instructional Center
Room 200
425 22nd St.
Glen Ellyn, IL 60137-6599
630-942-2130
Web: www.cod.edu/dept/CIL/CIL_home.htm
E-mail: schiesz@cdnet.cod.edu
Programs: individual courses
Individual course subjects: accounting, adult education, anthropology, biology, business, chemistry, childcare training, communications, computer information systems, criminal justice, economics, education, English, French, GED, health, history, humanities, law, management, marketing, mathematics, music, philosophy, physical science, physics, political science, psychology, social services, sociology, Spanish, speech
Average tuition: $32–$149 per credit hour (depending on residency)
Technologies: audiocassette, CD-ROM, correspondence, Internet, radio, television, video
Accreditation: NCACS
Entrance requirements: high school diploma
Restrictions: Some courses require on-campus meetings. Students who take radio and television courses must live in the broadcast area.
Special services: academic advising; student counseling

College of St. Scholastica

1200 Kenwood Ave.
Duluth, MN 55811
1-800-888-8796
Web: www.css.edu/depts/edu/grad/distant.html

E-mail: MEDL@css.edu
Programs: MEd
Average tuition: $512 per semester credit
Technologies: correspondence, fax, Internet, video
Accreditation: NCACS
Entrance requirements: bachelor's degree with a GPA of 2.8 and 2 years of professional experience in an educational setting
Restrictions: Requires 2 on-campus, 2-day seminars.
Special services: none

Colorado Electronic Community College

9075 E. Lowry Blvd.
Denver, CO 80230
1-800-801-5040
Web: www.cecc.cccoes.edu
E-mail: Darlene.Marshall@cecc.cccoes.edu
Programs: AA—General Studies; individual courses
Individual course subjects: agribusiness, anthropology, astronomy, chemistry, communications, economics, education, English, geography, geology, history, journalism, mathematics, music, philosophy, psychology, sociology, speech
Average tuition: $115 per semester hour
Length of program: 17 weeks per course
Technologies: audiocassette, correspondence, Internet, television, video
Accreditation: NCACS
Entrance requirements: none
Restrictions: Students must be at least 16 years old.
Special services: academic advising; career assessment

Colorado State University

Division of Educational Outreach
Fort Collins, CO 80523
1-800-525-4950
Web: www.csun.colostate.edu
E-mail: info@learn.colostate.edu
Programs: MBA; MEd—Education and Human Resource Studies; Master of Electrical Engineering; MS—Business Administration, Civil Engineering, Electronic Engineering, Statistics; BS/MS—Computer Science; Master of Agriculture; PhD—Electrical Engineering; MS/PhD—Bioresource and Agricultural Engineering, Chemical Engineering, Mechanical Engineering; individual courses
Individual course subjects: agriculture, anatomy, animal sciences, art, biology, computer science, construction, economics, education, environmental resources management, environmental studies, family and consumer sciences, fashion design and merchandising, history, horticulture, human development, industrial technology, marketing, mathematics, nutrition and

Unofficially...
Colorado Electronic Community College enables distance learners to earn degrees by taking classes from 12 of Colorado's community colleges. Students actually receive their degrees from Arapahoe Community College.

food science, occupational therapy, philosophy, psychology, range science, sociology, soil science, wildlife and fish science

Average tuition: individual courses—$120–$600 per course; degree programs—$416 per semester credit

Length of program: up to 1 year per course

Technologies: CD-ROM, correspondence, fax, Internet, television, video, videoconferencing

Accreditation: NCACS, ABET, NCATE

Entrance requirements: individual courses—none; BS—first bachelor's degree in a technical subject; master's—bachelor's degree in a related subject with a GPA of 3.0, GRE or GMAT score, and professional experience; PhD—master's degree with a GPA of 3.5 and GRE score

Restrictions: Degree programs are available only in the U.S. and Canada and at APO and FPO addresses.

Special services: academic advising; help center; library services; online tutorials

Columbia Union College

External Degree Program
7600 Flower Ave.
Takoma Park, MD 20912-7796
301-891-4124
Web: www.cuc.edu/ntp.html
Programs: BA—Psychology, Religion, Theology; BS—Business Administration, Information Systems, Respiratory Care; AA/AS/BA/BS—General Studies
Average tuition: $495 per semester hour
Length of program: 2–4 years
Technologies: correspondence, Internet
Accreditation: MSACS, NLN
Entrance requirements: AA/AS—high school diploma or GED; BA/BS—minimum 60 hours of previous college-level coursework with a cumulative GPA of 2.0
Restrictions: The BS in Respiratory Care requires 2 two-week, on-campus sessions.
Special services: none

Columbia University

Columbia Video Network
540 Mudd Building
500 W. 120th St.
Mailcode 4719
New York, NY 10027
212-854-6447
Web: www.cvn.columbia.edu
E-mail: cvn@cvn.columbia.edu

Programs: Certificate/MS—Earth and Environmental Engineering, Engineering and Management Systems, Materials Science; Certificate/MS/Professional Degree—Computer Science, Electrical Engineering, Mechanical Engineering
Average tuition: $951 per credit hour
Length of program: up to 5 years
Technologies: Internet, video, videoconferencing
Accreditation: MSACS, ABET
Entrance requirements: bachelor's degree in applied science, engineering, or mathematics
Restrictions: none
Special services: academic advising

Columbus State Community College

550 E. Spring St.
Columbus, OH 43215
1-800-621-5407
Web: global.cscc.edu
E-mail: global@cscc.edu
Programs: AA—General Studies; Associate of Business Management; individual courses
Individual course subjects: accounting, aviation maintenance, biological sciences, biology, chemistry, communications, computer programming, economics, education, English, finance, French, health, health information administration, hospitality, human resource management, humanities, legal assisting, management, marketing, mathematics, microcomputer technology, multimedia authoring, nursing, office management, physics, psychology, social sciences, Spanish
Average tuition: $61–$162 per credit hour (depending on residency)
Technologies: Internet, television, video
Accreditation: SACS
Entrance requirements: high school diploma or GED
Restrictions: none
Special services: academic advising; help desk; library services

Commonwealth International University

CIU Online
123 Camino de la Reina
Suite 200
San Diego, CA 92108
303-614-6666
Web: ciuonline.edu
Programs: MA—Human Behavior
Average tuition: $300 per credit hour
Length of program: 15 weeks per course

Money Saver
Commonwealth International University offers a special scholarship to online degree students.

Technologies: Internet
Accreditation: ACICS
Entrance requirements: bachelor's degree with a 2.5 GPA and college or professional experience in human behavior
Restrictions: none
Special services: none

Community College of Denver

Guided Independent Study
1391 N. Speer Blvd.
Suite 200-A
Denver, CO 80204-2552
303-620-4433, ext. 322
Web: ccdweb.ccd.cccoes.edu/ntlp/
Programs: individual courses
Individual course subjects: accounting, anthropology, art, biology, business, computer science, economics, English, geography, geology, gerontology, history, humanities, mathematics, nutrition, philosophy, political science, psychology, sociology
Average tuition: $56.30–$266.80 per credit hour (depending on residency)
Length of program: 15 weeks per course
Technologies: correspondence, Internet, television
Accreditation: NCACS
Entrance requirements: none
Restrictions: Some courses require on-campus sessions. Students taking television courses must live in the broadcast area.
Special services: none

Covenant Theological Seminary

12330 Conway Rd.
St. Louis, MO 63141-8914
1-800-264-8064
Web: www.covenantseminary.edu/ExternalStudy/Index.html
Programs: Certificate—Biblical and Theological Studies, Christianity and Contemporary Culture, Church History, General Studies, Theological Studies; Graduate Certificate/MA—General Theological Studies; MDiv
Average tuition: $232 per credit hour
Length of program: 3–4 years
Technologies: audiocassette, video
Accreditation: NCACS, ATS
Entrance requirements: certificates—none; graduate certificate/MA/MDiv—bachelor's degree
Restrictions: Only up to 30 semester hours of the MDiv degree can be completed at a distance.
Special services: personal mentoring

D

Dakota State University

Office of Distance Education
201-A Karl E. Mundt Library
Madison, SD 57042
1-800-641-4309
Web: courses.dsu.edu/disted/
E-mail: dsuinfo@pluto.dsu.edu
Programs: individual courses
Individual course subjects: business, computer science, English, health information administration, management information systems, mathematics, music, psychology, sociology
Average tuition: $125.45–$161.25 per credit hour
Length of program: 17 weeks per course
Technologies: Internet
Accreditation: NCACS
Entrance requirements: none
Restrictions: none
Special services: electronic library services; online student advising; online writing lab

Dallas TeleCollege

9596 Walnut St.
Dallas, TX 75243
1-888-468-4268
Web: ollie.dcccd.edu
E-mail: kle8852@dcccd.edu
Programs: AA/AS—General Studies; individual courses
Individual course subjects: astronomy, biology, business, communications, computer science, drafting and design, economics, education, English, history, human resource management, humanities, management, marketing, mathematics, Microsoft certification, multimedia authoring, music, nutrition, office technology, philosophy, physical education, political science, psychology, sociology, Spanish, speech
Average tuition: $25–$200 per semester credit hour (depending on residency)
Length of program: 16 weeks per course
Technologies: correspondence, Internet, television, video
Accreditation: SACS
Entrance requirements: high school diploma or GED
Restrictions: none
Special services: academic advising; career planning; disability services; technical support; virtual learning center

Unofficially...
Dallas TeleCollege is the distance-learning program of the seven Dallas County community colleges.

Daytona Beach Community College

Admissions Office
P.O. Box 2811
Daytona Beach, FL 32120-2811
904-254-4415
Web: www.dbcc.cc.fl.us/dbcc/htm/de/deindex.htm
E-mail: DISTANCE@dbcc.cc.fl.us
Programs: AA—Political Science/Economics, Social and Human Sciences; individual courses
Individual course subjects: anatomy, anthropology, art, astronomy, atmospheric sciences, business, child development, criminal justice, economics, education, English, French, geography, health, history, law, management, marketing, mass communications, mathematics, nutrition, office technology, philosophy, political science, psychology, sociology, Spanish, statistics
Length of program: 16 weeks per course
Technologies: interactive TV, Internet, television, video
Accreditation: SACS
Entrance requirements: high school diploma or GED
Restrictions: Some courses require on-campus meetings.
Special services: academic advising

Defiance College

701 N. Clinton St.
Defiance, OH 43512
419-783-2465
Web: www.globaltown.com/dfl/
Programs: Certificate—Church Education; AA/BA/BS—Religious Education
Length of program: 2–4 years
Technologies: correspondence
Accreditation: NCACS
Entrance requirements: Contact the college for entrance requirements.
Restrictions: none
Special services: academic mentoring; optional summer workshops

Drew University

The Theological School
Madison, NJ 07940
973-408-3111
Web: www.cyber-academy.com/drewlogon/
E-mail: drewlogon@yahoo.com
Programs: Certificate—Church Leadership, Funding Ministry, Gospel and Culture, Ministry with Men, Preaching Ministry, Searching for Dynamic Spirituality; DMin
Average tuition: certificates—$500; DMin—$9,000
Length of program: 3 years

Technologies: correspondence, Internet

Accreditation: MSACS

Entrance requirements: certificates—none; DMin—Master of Divinity degree or its equivalent with a cumulative GPA of 3.0, 3 years of full-time professional experience, and employment in a recognized ministerial position

Restrictions: The DMin program requires a 2-day retreat at the beginning of the program and a 3-week summer residency on campus.

Special services: none

Drexel University

3141 Chestnut St.

Philadelphia, PA 19104

1-800-2-DREXEL

Web: www.drexel.edu/distance/

Programs: Certificate—Competitive Intelligence; MBA; MS—Engineering Management, Information Systems

Average tuition: certificates—$6,825; MBA/MS—$437–$565 per credit hour

Length of program: 10 weeks per course; MBA/MS—up to 7 years

Technologies: Internet

Accreditation: MSACS, ABET

Entrance requirements: certificates—bachelor's degree and professional experience; MBA/MS—bachelor's degree in related field (or with related work experience) with a 3.0 GPA in the last 2 years of undergraduate study; MBA—also requires a GMAT score

Restrictions: none

Special services: academic advising; online student center

Duke University

The Fuqua School of Business

Executive MBA Programs

Towerview Dr.

Durham, NC 27708-0127

919-660-7804

Web: www.fuqua.duke.edu/admin/gemba/

E-mail: fuqua-gemba@mail.duke.edu

Programs: Executive MBA—Global

Average tuition: $89,700

Length of program: 19 months

Technologies: Internet

Accreditation: SACS

Entrance requirements: bachelor's degree, company sponsorship, and 10 years of professional experience with current international managerial responsibilities

Money Saver
The Global Executive MBA program provides each student with an IBM ThinkPad, all the program software, and technical support, all included in the tuition.

Restrictions: Requires 11 weeks total of international residencies.
Special services: none

Duquesne University

600 Forbes Ave.
Pittsburgh, PA 15282
1-800-456-0590
Web: www.duq.edu/distancelearning/index.html
Programs: MA—Leadership and Liberal Studies; Master of Music—Music Education; PharmD; PhD—Nursing
Average tuition: $425 per credit
Length of program: 2–5 years
Technologies: Internet
Accreditation: MSACS, ACPE, NLN
Entrance requirements: MA—bachelor's degree; Master of Music—bachelor's degree in music with a GPA of 2.5 overall and 3.0 in music courses; PharmD—BS in Pharmacy and current pharmacist license and registration; PhD—BS in Nursing, master's degree in nursing with a 3.5 GPA, GRE score of 1,500, evidence of scholarly work in nursing, and current license as a professional nurse
Restrictions: All programs require on-campus residencies.
Special services: academic advising; library services

Durham University

Business School
Mill Hill Lane
Durham City DH1 3LB
United Kingdom
+44(0)-191-374-2216
Web: www.dur.ac.uk/dubs/degree/dlmba.htm
E-mail: mbadl.eng@durham.ac.uk
Programs: MBA
Average tuition: 7,000 pounds
Length of program: 3–4 years
Technologies: correspondence
Accreditation: United Kingdom government
Entrance requirements: bachelor's degree or approved equivalent professional qualification and 2 years of relevant work experience
Restrictions: none
Special services: none

E

East Carolina University

Division of Continuing Studies
Erwin Building

Greenville, NC 27858

1-800-398-9275

Web: www.dcs.ecu.edu/DL/

E-mail: ludwickm@mail.ecu.edu

Programs: BS/MS—Industrial Technology; individual courses

Individual course subjects: adult education, biology, economics, education, electronics, finance, history, industrial technology, library science, mathematics, nutrition, physical science, psychology

Average tuition: $33–$278 per semester hour (depending on residency)

Length of program: 15 weeks per course

Technologies: interactive TV, Internet, video

Accreditation: SACS

Entrance requirements: individual courses—admission as a degree-seeking or nondegree student; BS—associate's degree in a technical area; MS—bachelor's degree and MAT or GRE score

Restrictions: none

Special services: academic advising

Eastern Oregon University

Division of Extended Programs

1410 "L" Ave.

La Grande, OR 97850

541-962-3378

Web: www.eou.edu/dep/

E-mail: dep@eou.edu

Programs: AS—Office Administration; BS—Fire Services Administration, Physical Education and Health; BA/BS—Business/Economics, Liberal Studies, Philosophy, Politics and Economics; Master of Teacher Education; individual courses

Individual course subjects: anthropology, biology, business, economics, English, health, history, humanities, library science, mathematics, multimedia authoring, music, office management, physical education, political science, psychology, science, sociology, writing

Average tuition: $85–$425 per course

Length of program: 11 weeks per course

Technologies: audiocassette, CD-ROM, computer conferencing, correspondence, interactive TV, Internet, video

Accreditation: NCACS

Entrance requirements: individual courses—none; AS—at least a junior in high school; BA/BS—high school diploma with a 3.0 GPA in certain subjects; master's—bachelor's degree with a 3.0 GPA in the last 2 years of undergraduate study and prior work experience

Restrictions: Courses and degrees are not offered outside North America, except to military personnel stationed abroad. Students taking interactive TV courses must live in the 10-county broadcast region in eastern Oregon.

Some science courses require on-campus labs. The AS program is only available to students in the eastern Oregon service region. Liberal Studies programs require attendance at an 8-hour workshop in eastern Oregon. The BS in Fire Services Administration requires on-campus meetings. The Master's program requires in-state class meetings.

Special services: academic advising for degree programs; external degree orientation sessions and planning workshops held throughout the eastern Oregon region

Watch Out!
This degree program is limited to a very small number of qualified students.

Eckerd College

Program for Experienced Learners

4200 54th Ave. S

St. Petersburg, FL 33711

727-864-8226

Web: www.eckerd.edu/pel/extcampus.html

E-mail: pel@eckerd.edu

Programs: BA—Business Management, Human Development, Organizational Studies

Average tuition: $655 per course

Length of program: 16 weeks per course

Technologies: correspondence

Accreditation: SACS

Entrance requirements: high school diploma and at least 30 semester hours of undergraduate study with grades of C or better, plus demonstrated writing proficiency

Restrictions: Students must be at least 25 years old and must attend an orientation session on-campus.

Special services: admission counseling

Elizabethtown College

Center for Continuing Education

One Alpha Dr.

Elizabethtown, PA 17022-2298

1-800-877-2694

Web: courses.etown.edu

E-mail: maronebr@etown.edu

Programs: Diploma—Accounting

Length of program: 13 weeks per course

Technologies: Internet

Accreditation: MSACS

Entrance requirements: bachelor's or graduate degree

Restrictions: none

Special services: technical support

Embry-Riddle Aeronautical University

Center for Distance Learning

Extended Campus

600 S. Clyde Morris Blvd.

Daytona Beach, FL 32114-3900

1-800-522-6787

Web: www.ec.erau.edu/cdl/index.htm

E-mail: indstudy@cts.db.erau.edu

Programs: AS—Aviation Business Administration; BS—Management of Technical Operations; AS/BS—Professional Aeronautics; Master of Aeronautical Science

Average tuition: $141 per credit hour

Length of program: up to 15 weeks per course

Technologies: audiocassette, correspondence, Internet, video

Accreditation: SACS

Entrance requirements: AS/BS—high school diploma or GED and 12 or more undergraduate credits; master's—bachelor's degree with a 2.0 GPA

Restrictions: none

Special services: library services; research assistance

Emporia State University

Office of Lifelong Learning

Box 4052

1200 Commercial

Emporia, KS 66801

316-341-5385

Web: www.emporia.edu/lifelong/bgs/bgs.htm

E-mail: achleits@emporia.edu

Programs: BGS; individual courses

Individual course subjects: business, communications, computer science, education, educational technology, English, health, instructional design, management, management information systems, music, physical science, psychology, social sciences, sociology

Average tuition: $91 per credit hour

Length of program: 1–2^1/2 years

Technologies: Internet

Accreditation: NCACS

Entrance requirements: individual courses—none; BGS—minimum of 60 undergraduate semester credit hours

Restrictions: none

Special services: academic advising; career placement services; library services; optional weekend orientation session on-campus; tuition payment plan

Endicott College

Endicott College-TIES Program
The Institute for Educational Studies
8115 McCormick Ave.
Oakland, CA 94605
510-638-2300
Web: www.tmn.com/ties/tieshome.htm
E-mail: ties@endicott.edu
Programs: MEd—Integrative Learning
Average tuition: $4,210 per semester
Length of program: $1^{1}/_{2}$ years
Technologies: Internet
Accreditation: NEASC
Entrance requirements: bachelor's degree
Restrictions: requires 2 residential colloquia
Special services: mentoring

F

Fairleigh Dickinson University

School of Engineering and Engineering Technology
1000 River Rd.
Teaneck, NJ 07666
201-692-2347
Web: alpha.fdu.edu/~dobrow/webbased.html
E-mail: tan@fdusvrt1.fdu.edu
Programs: MS—Electrical Engineering
Average tuition: $550 per credit
Length of program: 15 weeks per course
Technologies: Internet
Accreditation: MSACS, ABET
Entrance requirements: bachelor's degree in the sciences or engineering, completion of prerequisite undergraduate course requirements, and GRE score
Restrictions: none
Special services: none

The Fielding Institute

2112 Santa Barbara St.
Santa Barbara, CA 93105
1-800-340-1099
Web: www.fielding.edu
E-mail: admissions@fielding.edu
Programs: MA—Organizational Design and Effectiveness; EdD—Educational Leadership and Change; PhD—Clinical Psychology, Human and Organizational Systems, Human Development

Average tuition: MA—$12,750 per year; EdD—$12,000 per year; PhD—$12,750 per year

Length of program: MA—20 months; EdD/PhD—4–8 years

Technologies: Internet

Accreditation: WASC, APA

Entrance requirements: MA—bachelor's degree; EdD/PhD—master's degree

Restrictions: The MA requires 2 four-day, on-campus meetings. Doctoral programs require attendance at an orientation and planning session and an on-campus residency. Only students living in the continental U.S. and Canada may apply.

Special services: academic advising; library resources

Financial Times Management

CATT Department

128 Long Acre

London WC2E 9AN

United Kingdom

0171-447-2023

Web: www.ftmanagement.com

E-mail: catt@ftmanagement.com

Programs: Certificate—First-Level Management, Team Leadership; Diploma—Company Direction; Postgraduate Certificate/Postgraduate Diploma—Management, Quality; MA—Corporate Direction, Customer Service Management, Total Quality; MBA; MS—Information Management, Quality Engineering

Length of program: certificates—3–12 months; diplomas—2 years; MA/MBA/MS—3–4 years

Technologies: CD-ROM, correspondence, video

Accreditation: DETC (Note: Most programs are offered through government-recognized UK universities.)

Entrance requirements: certificates—none; diplomas—certificate or professional qualification in a related field; MA/MBA/MS—first degree or successful completion of the first module in the program

Restrictions: none

Special services: technical support; tutoring

Florida Gulf Coast University

10501 FGCU Blvd. S

Fort Myers, FL 33965-6565

1-800-590-FGCU

Web: www.fgcu.edu/DL/index.html

E-mail: tdugas@fgcu.edu

Programs: BS—Criminal Justice, Health Sciences; MBA; Master of Curriculum and Instruction—Educational Technology; Master of Health Science; MPA; individual courses

Individual course subjects: accounting, anthropology, Asian studies, computer science, criminal justice, education, gerontology, health, history, humanities, interdisciplinary studies, management, management information systems, nursing, psychology, social services, speech

Average tuition: undergraduate—$66.36–$299.32 per credit hour (depending on residency); graduate—$139.17–$499.91 per credit hour (depending on residency)

Length of program: degree programs—3–4 years

Technologies: interactive TV, Internet, television, video

Accreditation: SACS

Entrance requirements: individual courses—enrollment as a nondegree-seeking student or admission to the university (requires a high school diploma or GED); BS—significant amount of lower-division college coursework; master's—bachelor's degree

Restrictions: Some courses require on-campus meetings.

Special services: academic advising; library services; tutoring

Florida Institute of Technology

Extended Graduate Studies

150 W. University Blvd.

Melbourne, FL 32901-6975

407-674-8000

Web: www.segs.fit.edu/distance.html

Programs: MBA; MS—Management

Average tuition: $810–$942 per course

Technologies: Internet

Accreditation: SACS

Entrance requirements: bachelor's degree and satisfactory GMAT score

Restrictions: none

Special services: academic advising

Florida State University

Office of Distance Learning

P.O. Box 2550

Tallahassee, FL 32306-2550

877-FLSTATE

Web: www.fsu.edu/~distance/

E-mail: students@oddl.fsu.edu

Programs: BS—Computer Science, Information Studies, Nursing, Software Engineering; MEd—Math Education, Science Education; MS—Criminal Justice, Engineering, Information Studies, Instructional Systems Design

Average tuition: BS—$98.25 per credit hour; MEd/MS—$146.01–$506.74 per credit hour (depending on residency)

Length of program: 2–4 years

Technologies: CD-ROM, correspondence, Internet, video

Accreditation: SACS, CSAB, NLN, NCATE

Entrance requirements: BS—AA degree or higher; BS in Nursing—also requires Florida registered nurse license; MEd/MS—bachelor's degree with a 3.0 GPA on the last 2 undergraduate years and a GRE score of 1,000; MEd—applicants must also be practicing elementary or middle-school teachers

Restrictions: Students enrolling in the MS in Nursing program must live near St. Petersburg Junior College (Florida). MEd programs require 4-week resident summer sessions in Miami. Only Dade County public school teachers can apply for the MEd in Science Education program.

Special services: academic advising; library services at a participating Florida community college; online orientation; trained mentors

Floyd College

Continuing Education
415 E. Third Ave.
Rome, GA 30161
706-295-6324
Web: www.ed2go.com/floyd/
E-mail: lhaney@mail.fc.peachnet.edu
Programs: Certificate—Basic Supervision, Customer Service, Paralegal, Production and Inventory Management, Project Management, Purchasing, Total Quality; individual courses
Individual course subjects: business, computer science, finance, fire protection, grant writing, information technology, nursing, small business management, test preparation, writing
Average tuition: $39–$189 per course
Length of program: 6 weeks per course
Technologies: Internet
Accreditation: SACS
Entrance requirements: none
Restrictions: none
Special services: none

Watch Out!
None of these courses can be used for college credit, although they can be used to earn Continuing Education Units at Floyd College.

Foothill College

12345 El Monte Rd.
Los Altos Hills, CA 94022-4599
650-949-7614
Web: www.foothill.fhda.edu/fga/index.html
E-mail: turmelle@admin.fhda.edu
Programs: AA—General Studies/Social Science; individual courses
Individual course subjects: accounting, anthropology, art, broadcasting, business, computer information systems, economics, English, geography, history, humanities, management information systems, mathematics, music, philosophy, political science, psychology, sociology, theater
Average tuition: $50–$494 per course (depending on residency)
Technologies: Internet, television

Accreditation: WASC

Entrance requirements: high school diploma or GED

Restrictions: Television courses require an on-campus orientation. Degree candidates must take 1 lab course on campus.

Special services: none

Fort Hays State University

Virtual College

Sheridan Hal 304

600 Park St.

Hays, KS 67601

785-628-4291

Web: www.fhsu.edu/virtual_college/

Programs: BGS; Master of Liberal Studies; individual courses

Individual course subjects: agriculture, art, biology, communication disorders, communications, computer information systems, criminal justice, education, English, geosciences, history, information technology, interdisciplinary studies, languages, management, marketing, mathematics, music, nursing, philosophy, political science, psychology, social work, sociology, telecommunications

Average tuition: $65–$510 per course

Technologies: audiocassette, CD-ROM, interactive TV, Internet, video, videoconferencing

Accreditation: NCACS

Entrance requirements: individual courses—none; BGS—previous college coursework or associate's degree; master's—contact the graduate school directly for admissions information

Restrictions: Some courses require on-campus meetings. Some courses are only open to Kansas residents.

Special services: academic advising for degree candidates; career services; international student advising; library services; technical support

Fox Valley Technical College

Distance Education Services

P.O. Box 2277

1825 N. Bluemound Dr.

Appleton, WI 54913-2277

920-735-4871

Web: its.foxvalley.tec.wi.us/iss/disted/default.htm

Programs: AS—Security and Loss Prevention; individual courses

Individual course subjects: business, criminal justice, economics, education, marketing, mathematics, psychology, security services, sociology, writing

Average tuition: $75 per credit

Length of program: AS—2 years

Technologies: correspondence, interactive TV, Internet, television, video

Accreditation: NCACS

Entrance requirements: high school diploma or the equivalent

Restrictions: Interactive TV courses must be taken at a regional center.

Special services: library services

Franciscan University of Steubenville

Distance Learning

1235 University Blvd.

Steubenville, OH 43952

1-800-466-8336

Web: www2.franuniv.edu/disted/

E-mail: lcampana@franuniv.edu

Programs: MA—Theology and Christian Ministry; individual courses

Individual course subjects: philosophy, theology

Average tuition: $525 per course

Length of program: 6 months per course

Technologies: audiocassette, Internet

Accreditation: NCACS

Entrance requirements: individual courses—high school diploma or GED; MA—bachelor's degree in theology or religious studies, preferably from a Catholic college, with a 3.0 GPA

Restrictions: The MA requires 2 three-week, on-campus, summer sessions.

Special services: faculty facilitator

Franklin University

201 S. Grant Ave.

Columbus, OH 43215

1-888-341-6237

Web: www.alliance.franklin.edu

E-mail: alliance@franklin.edu

Programs: BS—Business Administration, Computer Science, Health Services Administration, Management Information Systems, Technical Administration

Average tuition: $212–$258 per credit hour

Length of program: 2 years

Technologies: audiocassette, fax, Internet, video

Accreditation: NCACS

Entrance requirements: associate's degree or 60 semester college credit hours with a cumulative GPA of 2.5

Restrictions: The associate's degree or lower-division college coursework must have been completed at a participating community college in Colorado, Illinois, Indiana, Ohio, Michigan, or Wisconsin.

Special services: dial-in library access; technical support; tuition payment plan; tutoring

Money Saver
If you take a Franciscan University distance-learning course for noncredit, you only have to pay for course materials and you don't have to turn in assignments or exams. But you can't transfer credit for the course to another college or apply it against a degree.

Bright Idea
Franklin University offers a one-hour credit course called Advanced Online Learning Strategies that participants in the degree program can take to learn how to use the Internet and understand online courses.

Front Range Community College

Distance Learning

4616 S. Shields St.

P.O. Box 270490

Fort Collins, CO 80527

970-204-8250

Web: frcc.cc.co.us/programs/distance/intro.html

Programs: individual courses

Individual course subjects: anthropology, art, biology, business, chemistry, computer science, economics, English, geography, geology, history, hospitality, humanities, management, marketing, mathematics, music, nutrition, paralegal studies, philosophy, physics, political science, psychology, sociology, Spanish, speech

Average tuition: $56.30 per credit hour (Colorado residents); $266.80 per credit hour (out-of-state students)

Technologies: Internet, television, video

Accreditation: NCACS

Entrance requirements: admission to the college

Restrictions: Students must be at least 16 years old. Some courses require on-campus meetings. Students taking television courses must live in the broadcast area.

Special services: academic advising; technical support

Money Saver
Students who don't want to earn academic credit may purchase course materials for distance-learning classes at Fuller Theological Seminary for only $87.95 per course.

Fuller Theological Seminary

Center for Lifelong Learning

ATTN: IDL

135 N. Oakland Ave.

Pasadena, CA 91182

1-800-999-9578, ext. 5266

Web: www.fuller.edu/cee/html/idl.html

E-mail: IDL@fuller.edu

Programs: Certificate—Christian Studies, Youth Ministry; MA—Cross-Cultural Studies, Theology; MA/ThM—Intercultural Studies; MDiv

Average tuition: $768 per course

Length of program: 10 weeks to 6 months per course

Technologies: audiocassette, correspondence, Internet, video

Accreditation: WASC, ATS

Entrance requirements: bachelor's degree with a 2.5 GPA

Restrictions: Only a third of the Certificate in Youth Studies, MA, and MDiv programs can be completed through distance learning; on-campus coursework may be completed at the main campus or extension sites in Washington, California, Arizona, and Colorado.

Special services: academic advising; international student services; library services; technical support

G

Gemological Institute of America

Robert Mouawad Campus

MS#34

5345 Armada Dr.

Carlsbad, CA 92008

1-800-421-7250, ext. 4001

Web: www.giaonline.gia.edu/public/deindex.htm

E-mail: deweb@gia.edu

Programs: Diploma—Accredited Jewelry Professional (AJP), Colored Stones Graduate, Diamonds Graduate, Graduate Gemologist (GG)

Average tuition: $1,047–$3,750

Technologies: audiocassette, correspondence, Internet

Accreditation: ACCSCT, DETC

Entrance requirements: none

Restrictions: The Graduate Gemologist Diploma requires students to take 3 extension classes, which are offered in several cities.

Special services: career services; traveling student labs; tuition payment plan

George Brown College

P.O. Box 1015

Station B

Toronto

Ontario M5T 2T9

Canada

1-888-553-5333

Web: www.gbrownc.on.ca/GBCWEB/disted.html

E-mail: online_learning@gbrownc.on.ca

Programs: Certificate—Camp Nursing, Dental Assistant Level II Upgrade, Electronics Technician, Hearing Instrument Specialist, Perinatal Intensive Care; Diploma—Court Reporting; BA—Industrial Technology; individual courses

Individual course subjects: business, communications, computer science, health, humanities, science

Average tuition: $50–$516 (Canadian) per course

Length of program: all courses are self-paced; diploma—2 years; BA—1 year

Technologies: audiocassette, CD-ROM, correspondence, Internet, video, videoconferencing

Accreditation: Canadian government

Entrance requirements: all programs and courses—high school diploma or mature student status; Dental Assistant Certificate—Certified Dental Assistant, CPR certificate, and current employment in a dental office; Hearing Instrument Specialist Certificate—graduation from a Hearing

Dispenser program; Nursing Certificates—registered nurse license, various health services certificates, and recent nursing experience; BA—3-year diploma in Science and Technology

Restrictions: Dental Assistant and Nursing Certificates have an on-site component. The diploma requires access to a court-reporting machine. The BA requires on-site videoconferencing sessions once a month.

Special services: technical support

Unofficially...
These programs are intended for Forest Service employees and other public land managers.

George Mason University

Distance Learning Program
10900 University Blvd.
Room 312
Manassas, VA 20110
703-993-8301
Web: dlp.gmu.edu
Programs: Certificate—National Forest Lands Management, Natural Resource Recreation Management
Average tuition: $145–$605 per course
Length of program: 6 months per course
Technologies: correspondence, Internet
Accreditation: SACS
Entrance requirements: none
Restrictions: none
Special services: none

The George Washington University

Office of Recruitment and Admissions
2300 "Eye" St. NW
Suite 719
Washington, DC 20037
202-994-2807
Web: www.gwu.edu/~distance/
Programs: Certificate—Advanced Family Nurse Practitioner, Clinical Research Administration, Event Management, International Public Health, Paramedic, Records Management; MA—Education and Human Development; MS—Project Management; BS/MS—Health Sciences
Average tuition: $295–$680 per credit hour
Length of program: certificates—1–2 years; BS—2–4 years
Technologies: CD-ROM, correspondence, Internet, television, video
Accreditation: MSACS, NAACLS, NCATE
Entrance requirements: Nurse Practitioner Certificate—registered nurse license and Adult Nurse Practitioner certification; Certificate in Event Management—high school diploma; Certificate in International Public Health—graduate degree or bachelor's degree with a minimum GPA of 3.0 and GRE score, and current employment in a healthcare services field; Paramedic Certificate—30 credit hours of college-level coursework and a

valid EMT certificate; Certificate in Clinical Research Administration and BS—associate's degree in health sciences and current employment in a health field; MA—bachelor's degree with a 2.75 GPA and GRE or MAT scores in the top 50th percentile; MS in Health Sciences—Physician Assistant certification; MS in Project Management—bachelor's degree with at least a B average

Restrictions: The Certificate in International Public Health requires a 10-day on-site workshop. The MS in Project Management requires a 2-day orientation session on-campus.

Special services: career services available for some programs

Georgia Institute of Technology

Center for Distance Learning
620 Cherry St.
Atlanta, GA 30332-0240
404-894-3378
Web: www.conted.gatech.edu/distance/index.html
E-mail: cmbi@conted.gatech.edu
Programs: MS—Electrical and Computer Engineering, Environmental Engineering, Health Physics, Industrial Engineering, Mechanical Engineering, Operations Research
Average tuition: $510 per semester hour
Length of program: 3–5 years
Technologies: Internet, video
Accreditation: SACS, ABET
Entrance requirements: bachelor's degree in engineering, mathematics, computer science, or science with a 3.0 GPA and GRE score (Note: All programs have strict prerequisite requirements.)
Restrictions: none
Special services: academic advising

Goddard College

123 Pitkin Rd.
Plainfield, VT 05667
802-454-8311
Web: www.goddard.edu/indexoffcampus.htm
E-mail: Admissions@earth.goddard.edu
Programs: BA/MA—Health Arts and Sciences, Individualized Studies, Social Ecology, Teacher Education; MA—Psychology and Counseling, School Guidance; MFA—Creative Writing, Interdisciplinary Arts
Length of program: BA—minimum 1 year; MA/MFA—$1^1/_2$–$2^1/_2$ years
Technologies: correspondence, Internet
Accreditation: NEASC
Entrance requirements: BA—high school diploma and typically at least 2 years of prior college credit; MA/MFA—bachelor's degree and background experience in a related field

Unofficially...
Distance-learning degree programs offered by Goddard College are based on individualized programs of study, rather than a preset curriculum.

Restrictions: All programs require a 7-day residency before each semester.

Special services: academic advising; library services

Watch Out!
This program requires access to a theological library adequate to support the academic work.

Golden Gate Baptist Theological Seminary

201 Seminary Dr.

Mill Valley, CA 94941-3197

1-888-442-8701

Web: www.ggbts.edu

E-mail: admissions@ggbts.edu

Programs: ThM

Average tuition: $1,500 per year

Length of program: 3–5 years

Technologies: Internet

Accreditation: WASC, ATS

Entrance requirements: BA and MDiv with a 2.7 GPA

Restrictions: Requires a 2-week, on-campus, summer seminar at the beginning of each year of the program.

Special services: academic advising

Golden Gate University

536 Mission St.

San Francisco, CA 94105-2968

1-888-874-CYBER

Web: cybercampus.ggu.edu

E-mail: cybercampus@ggu.edu

Programs: Undergraduate Certificate—Technology Management; Bachelor of Public Administration; Graduate Certificate—Accounting, Arts Administration, Healthcare Administration, Personal Financial Planning; MBA; Master of Healthcare Administration; Executive MPA; MS— Telecommunications Management; Undergraduate Certificate/Graduate Certificate/MS—Finance; Graduate Certificate/MS—Taxation

Average tuition: $1,060-$1,566 per course

Technologies: Internet

Accreditation: WASC

Entrance requirements: undergraduate programs—prior completion of required lower-division college coursework with a 2.0 cumulative GPA; graduate programs—bachelor's degree with a 2.5 GPA; MBA—also requires a GMAT score

Restrictions: none

Special services: academic advising

Goucher College

Center for Graduate and Continuing Studies

1021 Dulaney Valley Rd.

Baltimore, MD 21204-2794

410-337-6000

Web: www.goucher.edu

Programs: MA—Arts Administration, Historic Preservation, Women's Studies; MFA—Creative Nonfiction

Average tuition: MA—$485–$510 per credit hour; MFA—$4,590 per semester

Length of program: MA—up to 5 years; MFA—2 years

Technologies: correspondence, Internet, teleconferencing

Accreditation: MSACS

Entrance requirements: bachelor's degree

Restrictions: Students must spend 2 weeks each summer on campus.

Special services: tuition payment plan

Governors State University

University Park, IL 60466-0975

708-534-4092

Web: www.govst.edu/users/gsubog/bog/

E-mail: gsubog@govst.edu

Programs: BA—General Studies

Average tuition: $306 per course

Length of program: $7^1/_2$–15 weeks per course

Technologies: audiocassette, correspondence, Internet, telephone, television, video

Accreditation: NCACS

Entrance requirements: 60 or more semester credit hours of college coursework with a 2.0 GPA

Restrictions: Requires on-campus orientations for students residing within 50 miles of campus.

Special services: academic advising

Grantham College of Engineering

34641 Grantham College Rd.

Slidell, LA 70460

1-888-423-4242

Web: www.grantham.edu

E-mail: gce@grantham.edu

Programs: AS/BS—Computer Engineering Technology, Computer Science, Electronics Engineering Technology

Average tuition: $2,600 per semester

Length of program: 4–6 years

Technologies: correspondence, Internet

Accreditation: DETC

Entrance requirements: high school diploma or the equivalent

Restrictions: none

Special services: tuition payment plan

H

The Hadley School for the Blind

700 Elm St.
Winnetka, IL 60093-0299
1-800-323-4238
Web: www.hadley-school.org
E-mail: info@hadley-school.org
Programs: high school diploma; individual courses
Individual course subjects: abacus, biblical studies, Braille, business, career development, communications, computer science, high school subjects, human development, independent living, languages, music, recreation, typing
Average tuition: none
Length of program: up to 1 year per course
Technologies: audiocassette, correspondence, Internet
Accreditation: NCACS, DETC
Entrance requirements: none
Restrictions: Students in General Education courses must be at least 14 years old and be legally blind. Students in the high school diploma program must be US citizens. Students in parent/family courses must be the parent or grandparent of a blind or severely visually impaired child, or be the spouse, parent, adult child, or adult sibling of a blind or severely visually impaired adult. Students in the professional program must be professionals working in the blindness field.
Special services: academic advising

Hamilton College

HC Online
1801 E Kimberly Rd.
Suite #2
Davenport, IA 52807
1-800-747-1035
Web: www.hamiltonia.edu/hconline/
E-mail: sbaker@aicedu.com
Programs: AS—Applied Management, Interdisciplinary Studies
Average tuition: $1,500–$2,800 per trimester (depending on the number of credit hours)
Length of program: 18 months
Technologies: Internet
Accreditation: NCACS, ACICS
Entrance requirements: high school diploma or GED
Restrictions: none
Special services: enrollment advising; technical support; virtual library

Henley Management College

Greenlands

Henley-on-Thames

Oxfordshire RG9 3AU

United Kingdom

+44 (0) 1491-418803

Web: www.henleymc.ac.uk/HenleyMC.nsf/pages/TheHenleyMBA

E-mail: mba@henleymc.ac.uk

Programs: Diploma—Management; MBA

Length of program: 3–4 years

Technologies: audiocassette, correspondence, groupware, video

Accreditation: United Kingdom government

Entrance requirements: bachelor's degree and 3 years of relevant work experience

Restrictions: Students must be at least 27 years old.

Special services: evening access to the college library and support systems; intake coordinators; monthly open-house facility; optional face-to-face learning opportunities worldwide

Unofficially...
The school strongly recommends attending a starter residency and short weekend residencies every 6 months at the college, but they are not required.

Heriot-Watt University

Electronic University Network

ATTN: Heriot-Watt University Admissions

1977 Colestin Rd.

Hornbrook, CA 96044

1-800-225-3276

Web: www.wcc-eun.com/heriotwatt/index.html

E-mail: EUNSignUp@aol.com

Programs: MBA

Average tuition: $935–$995 per course

Length of program: $1–1^{1}/_{2}$ years

Technologies: correspondence, software

Accreditation: United Kingdom government

Entrance requirements: bachelor's degree and professional experience

Restrictions: none

Special services: online student conference area

Bright Idea
In this program, you can choose between an independent study option, for courses whose subject matter you already have experience with, and an instructor-guided study option (at a slightly higher fee), for those subjects with which you need more guidance.

Herkimer County Community College

Admissions Office

100 Reservoir Rd.

Herkimer, NY 13350

1-800-GO-4-HCCC

Web: hccc.ntcnet.com/IA/frames_ia.html

E-mail: Admissions@hccc.suny.edu

Programs: AAS—Business Accounting, Security, Travel and Tourism; AA—General Studies, Humanities, Social Science; AAS/AS—Business Administration, Criminal Justice; individual courses

Individual course subjects: business, criminal justice, English, health, hospitality, humanities, management information systems, mathematics, science, social sciences

Average tuition: $80–$175 per credit hour (depending on residency)

Length of program: 2 years

Technologies: Internet

Accreditation: MSACS

Entrance requirements: high school diploma or GED; SAT or ACT score strongly recommended

Restrictions: none

Special services: academic advising; career services; online library access; online student meeting place; tutoring

Unofficially...
The Home Study International K–12 programs offer parents a way to homeschool their children using an accredited, Maryland-approved curriculum.

Home Study International

P.O. Box 4437

Silver Spring, MD 20914-4437

301-680-6570

Web: www.hsi.edu

E-mail: contact@hsi.edu

Programs: high school diploma; individual courses

Individual course subjects: art, biology, business, communications, education, English, geography, health, high school subjects, history, K–12 subjects, languages, mathematics, nutrition, political science, psychology, religion, sociology, theology

Average tuition: preschool—$53; elementary school—$120-$360 (depending on grade); junior high—$68 per semester; high school—$290 per unit; undergraduate—$165 per semester credit hour

Length of program: K–12—1 year per grade; college-level—1 year per course

Technologies: audiocassette, correspondence

Accreditation: DETC

Entrance requirements: none

Restrictions: Students taking college-level courses must be at least 18 years old.

Special services: tuition payment plan

Hope International University

2500 E. Nutwood Ave.

Fullerton, CA 92831

714-879-3901, ext. 1251

Web: www.hiu.edu/html/dl.html

E-mail: palexander@hiu.edu

Programs: BS—Human Development; MA—Ministry; MBA—International Development; MS—Management; individual courses

Individual course subjects: biblical studies, counseling, ethnic studies, history, theology

Technologies: Internet, video

Accreditation: WASC

Entrance requirements: BS—high school diploma and a minimum of 45 transferable college semester units with a 2.0 GPA; MA/MBA/MS—bachelor's degree

Restrictions: Applicants must be at least 25 years old. Students live abroad while taking the MBA and MS programs.

Special services: local mentor (MA program)

Hospitality Training Center

220 N. Main St.

Hudson, OH 44236

800-231-3803

Web: www.htcfuturecareers.com

E-mail: info@htcfuturecareers.com

Programs: individual courses

Individual course subjects: flight attendant, hospitality, medical office management, paralegal studies, pharmacy technician

Length of program: 6 months

Technologies: correspondence

Accreditation: DETC

Entrance requirements: none

Restrictions: none

Special services: academic advising; career placement services; online job center

Houston Community College

Distance Education

4310 Dunlavy Room 215G

Houston, TX 77006

713-718-5275

Web: distance.hccs.cc.tx.us

Programs: individual courses

Individual course subjects: accounting, anthropology, art, business, computer science, criminal justice, drafting and design, economics, education, English, geography, geology, history, human resource management, management, mapping, marketing, mathematics, mental health services, philosophy, photography, political science, psychology, real estate, sociology, Spanish

Average tuition: $107–$366 (depending on residency)

Length of program: 16 weeks per course

Technologies: correspondence, Internet, television, video

Accreditation: SACS

Unofficially...
Hospitality Training Center offers training programs to prepare students for specific careers. It does not award certificates, diplomas, or degrees.

Entrance requirements: none

Restrictions: All courses require on-campus orientation meetings and exams.

Special services: career placement; student counseling

Hypnosis Motivation Institute

18607 Ventura Blvd.

Suite 310

Tarzana, CA 91356

1-800-682-4464

Web: www.hypnosismotivation.com/tutorial.html

E-mail: info@hypnosismotivation.com

Programs: Certificate—Hypnotherapy

Average tuition: $4,455

Length of program: 9–18 months

Technologies: video

Accreditation: DETC

Entrance requirements: none

Restrictions: none

Special services: private tutoring; tuition payment plan

I

ICI University

6300 N. Belt Line Rd.

Irving, TX 75063

972-751-1111

Web: www.ici.edu

E-mail: info@ici.edu

Programs: Advanced Certificate—Bible Message, Christian Communicator, Christian Counseling, Christian Doctrine, Christian Education, Christian Message, Christian Mission, Church Ministry, New Testament Interpretation, Old Testament Interpretation, The Pentecostal Message, Work of the Church; Diploma—Ministry, Theology; AA—Religious Studies; BA—Bible and Theology, Missions, Religious Education; MA—Biblical Studies, Ministerial Studies

Average tuition: $75 per credit hour

Length of program: 4–6 months per course

Technologies: audiocassette, CD-ROM, correspondence, Internet, video

Accreditation: DETC

Entrance requirements: certificates/diplomas—none; AA/BA—high school diploma or GED; MA—bachelor's degree

Restrictions: none

Special services: online library resources; technical support

ICS Learning Systems

925 Oak St.
Scranton, PA 18540-9887
1-800-275-4409
Web: www.icslearn.com/ICS/
E-mail: info@icslearn.com
Programs: high school diploma; Certificate—A+ Certification, COBOL, Home Health Aide, Modeling, PC Fundamentals; Diploma—Air Conditioning and Refrigeration, Animal Science, Appliance Repair, Art, Auto Body Repair, Auto Detailing, Auto Mechanics, Basic Electronics, Beauty Salon Management, Bookkeeping and Accounting, Carpentry, Catering and Gourmet Cooking, Child Day Care Management, Computer-Assisted Bookkeeping, Computer Graphic Art, Court Reporting, Dental Assisting, Desktop Publishing and Design, Diesel Mechanics, Drafting with AutoCAD, Dressmaking and Design, Drywall Installation and Finishing, Electrician, Electronics Technician, Fashion Merchandising, Fitness and Nutrition, Floral Design, Freelance Writing, General Drafting, Gunsmith, Home Inspection, Home Remodeling and Repair, Hotel/Restaurant Management, Interior Decoration, Internet Web Page Design, Java Programming, Jewelry Repair, Legal Assisting, Legal Secretary, Masonry, Medical Insurance Clerk, Medical Office Assisting, Medical Transcription, Motorcycle Repair, PC Repair, PC Specialist, Pet Grooming, Pharmacy Technician, Photography, Plumbing, Private Investigation, Professional Bartending, Professional Bridal Consulting, Professional Landscaping, Professional Locksmith, Professional Secretary, Programming in BASIC, Small Business Management, Small Engine Repair, Surveying and Mapping, Teacher Aide, Travel, TV/VCR Repair, Visual Basic Programming, Visual C++ Programming, Wildlife and Forestry Conservation; Associate of Specialized Business—Accounting, Applied Computer Science, Business Management, Finance, Hospitality Management, Marketing; Associate of Specialized Technology—Civil Engineering Technology, Electrical Engineering Technology, Electronics Technology, Industrial Engineering Technology, Mechanical Engineering Technology
Length of program: 2 months–2 years
Technologies: audiocassette, CD-ROM, computer disk, correspondence, Internet, slides, video
Accreditation: DETC
Entrance requirements: most certificates and diplomas—none; Court Reporting, Drafting with AutoCAD, Java Programming, Legal Assisting, Medical Insurance Clerk, Medical Transcription, and degree programs—high school diploma or GED
Restrictions: The Applied Computer Science degree and all Associate of Specialized Technology degrees require a 2-week resident laboratory.
Special services: Dial-A-Question hotline

Illinois Institute of Technology

IITV
10 W. 31st St.
Room 226SB
Chicago, IL 60616-3793
312-567-3460
Web: www.dlt.iit.edu/internet/index.html
E-mail: ia_pryor@vax1.ais.iit.edu
Programs: MS—Analytical Chemistry, Health Physics, Materials and Chemical Synthesis; individual courses
Individual course subjects: chemistry, computer science, engineering, physics, psychology
Average tuition: $575 per credit hour
Length of program: $2^1/2$ years
Technologies: Internet
Accreditation: NCACS, ABET
Entrance requirements: bachelor's degree in a related field with a 4.0 GPA and a GRE score of 1,200
Restrictions: none
Special services: courier services; library services

Indiana Institute of Technology

Extended Studies Division
1600 E. Washington Blvd.
Fort Wayne, IN 46803
1-800-288-1766, ext. 2278
Web: www.indtech.edu
E-mail: Stahl@indtech.edu
Programs: AS/BS—Business Administration
Length of program: 6 months per course
Technologies: correspondence
Accreditation: NCACS
Entrance requirements: high school diploma or GED
Restrictions: none
Special services: professor mentors

Indiana State University

Distance Education
Terre Haute, IN 47809
1-888-237-8080
Web: web.indstate.edu/disted/
E-mail: aafpetro@amber.indstate.edu
Programs: BS—Business Administration, Criminology, Electronics Technology, General Industrial Technology, Human Resource Development, Industrial Supervision, Insurance, Nursing, Vocational Trade-Industrial-Technical; individual courses

Individual course subjects: aerospace studies, art, athletic training, business, communications, computer science, construction, criminal justice, economics, education, electronics, English, finance, geography, geology, history, industrial technology, insurance, life sciences, mathematics, nursing, political science, psychology, sociology

Average tuition: $123 per credit hour

Length of program: 1 year per course; BS—2 years

Technologies: audiocassette, correspondence, interactive TV, Internet, video

Accreditation: NCACS, NLN

Entrance requirements: associate's degree or a significant amount of lower-division college credits

Restrictions: BS programs are only open to residents of Indiana. Interactive TV courses must be taken at one of the receive sites within Indiana.

Special services: academic advising; career counseling; computer support services; library services; student service coordinators

Indiana University

Office of Distance Learning
620 Union Dr.
Suite 129
Indianapolis, IN 46202-5167
317-274-4178
Web: www.indiana.edu/~iude/
E-mail: iude@indiana.edu

Programs: high school diploma; Certificate—Distance Education, Public Library, School Library/Media and Information Technology; AGS; BGS; Certificate/AS/BS—Labor Studies; Master of Recreation and Park Administration; MS—Adult Education, Language Education, Nursing, Therapeutic Recreation; individual courses

Individual course subjects: accounting, adult education, African-American studies, American studies, anatomy, anthropology, art, Asian languages, Asian studies, astronomy, biology, business, chemistry, classics, communications, comparative literature, computer science, criminal justice, economics, education, engineering, English, environmental studies, ethnic studies, French, geography, geology, German, health, high school subjects, history, Italian, journalism, labor studies, library science, linguistics, mathematics, mechanical engineering, music, nursing, pharmacology, philosophy, physical education, physics, political science, psychology, public affairs, recreation, religion, sociology, Spanish, speech, supervision, technology, telecommunications, women's studies

Average tuition: high school—$43 per course; undergraduate—$96.25 per credit hour; graduate—$157.60 per credit hour

Technologies: audiocassette, CD-ROM, correspondence, interactive TV, Internet, software, television, video

Money Saver
If you don't have a computer or Internet connection at home, you may still be able to take Internet courses through this program. All program participants get free access to Learning Centers located throughout the state that provide Internet-connected computers.

Watch Out!
Enrollment in individual courses does not constitute admission to Indiana University.

Accreditation: NCACS, ALA, NCATE

Entrance requirements: high school diploma/courses—permission from a high school principal or guidance counselor; certificates—bachelor's degree; undergraduate programs/courses—high school diploma or GED; MS—bachelor's degree with a 2.75 GPA and a GRE score above 1,500; MS in Nursing—bachelor's degree in nursing with a cumulative GPA of 3.0, a score of 400 or better on 2 sections of the GRE, and a current Indiana registered nurse license

Restrictions: Some courses and programs are only open to Indiana residents.

Special services: academic advising

Indiana Wesleyan University

Adult and Professional Studies
4301 S. Washington St.
Marion, IN 46953-5279
1-800-621-8667
Web: www.indwes.edu/aps/online/
Programs: MBA; individual courses
Individual course subjects: biblical studies, computer science, earth science, English, information technology, music, philosophy
Average tuition: $175 per credit hour
Length of program: 3–5 weeks per course
Technologies: Internet
Accreditation: NCACS
Entrance requirements: individual courses—none; MBA—bachelor's degree with a 2.5 GPA and 3 years of significant, full-time, work experience
Restrictions: The MBA requires 1 three-day, on-site course.
Special services: technical support

Institute of Transpersonal Psychology

744 San Antonio Rd.
Palo Alto, CA 94303
650-493-4430
Web: www.itp.edu/programs/global.html
E-mail: itpinfo@itp.edu
Programs: Certificate—Creative Expression, Spiritual Psychology, Wellness Counseling and Bodymind Consciousness, Women's Spiritual Development; Certificate/MA—Transpersonal Studies; Master of Transpersonal Psychology
Average tuition: certificates—$2,083 per quarter; MA—$1,669 per quarter; Master of Transpersonal Psychology—$2,304 per quarter
Length of program: 1 year
Technologies: computer conferencing, correspondence, Internet
Accreditation: WASC

Entrance requirements: certificates—none (psychology background is preferred); master's—bachelor's degree, preferably in psychology or the social sciences, with a 3.0 GPA in the major field of study and satisfactory completion of a certificate program

Restrictions: Certificates require 4-day, on-site seminars taught at various sites around the world.

Special services: faculty mentors

International Aviation and Travel Academy

Arlington Airport
4846 S. Collins St.
Arlington, TX 76018
1-800-678-0700
Web: www.iatac.com
Programs: individual courses
Individual course subjects: aircraft sales, hospitality
Length of program: self-paced
Technologies: correspondence
Accreditation: DETC
Entrance requirements: none
Restrictions: none
Special services: none

International Management Centres

Multinational Registry
Marriott
Castle St.
Buckingham MK18 1BP
United Kingdom
+44 (0) 1280-817-222
Web: www.imc.org.uk/imc/
E-mail: imc@imc.org.uk
Programs: Certificate/Diploma—Administration, Management Action Learning, Management Styles, Quality Management; Bachelor of Management; Bachelor of Professional Studies; MBA; Master of Philosophy (MPhil); MS; DBA; Doctor of Letters (DLitt); Doctor of Philosophy (DPhil)
Average tuition: certificates—3,985 pounds; diplomas—5,985 pounds; bachelor's—6,985 pounds; master's—8,985–11,985 pounds; DBA/DLitt/DPhil—12,985 pounds
Length of program: certificates—16 months; diplomas—1 year; bachelor's—1–2 years; master's—2 years; DBA/DLitt/DPhil—2–4 years
Technologies: correspondence, Internet
Accreditation: DETC
Entrance requirements: certificates—none; diplomas and bachelor's—3 years work experience; master's—4 years of experience at middle or senior

management level; DBA/DLitt/DPhil—MBA or master's degree in management and 6–12 years of managerial experience

Restrictions: Bachelor's program candidates must be at least 22 years old.

Special services: none

Iowa State University

Extended and Continuing Education

102 Scheman Bldg.

Ames, IA 50011-1112

515-294-6222

Web: www.lifelearner.iastate.edu

E-mail: lifelearner@iastate.edu

Programs: Certificate—Family Worker, Public Management, School Superintendent; Bachelor of Liberal Studies; BS—Professional Agriculture; Master of Agriculture; MBA; MEd—Educational Leadership, Higher Education; Master of Engineering—Systems Engineering; Master of Family and Consumer Sciences; MPA; Master of School Mathematics; MS—Agronomy, Computer Engineering, Mechanical Engineering, Microbiology, Statistics; BS/MS—Electrical Engineering; individual courses

Individual course subjects: accounting, agriculture, agronomy, animal sciences, atmospheric sciences, biology, computer science, economics, education, engineering, English, environmental studies, family and consumer sciences, finance, history, horticulture, human development, linguistics, management, marketing, mathematics, nutrition and food science, philosophy, political science, science, sociology, speech, statistics

Average tuition: undergraduate—$117 per credit; graduate—$184 per credit

Technologies: interactive TV, Internet, video

Accreditation: NCACS, AAFCS, ABET, NASPA

Entrance requirements: individual courses—none; BS—2 years of previous college coursework; certificates and master's—vary by department

Restrictions: Some programs are restricted to residents of Iowa or greater Des Moines. All others are restricted to residents of the U.S. and Canada.

Special services: academic advising; tuition payment plan

Watch Out!
Iowa Western
Community College's
distance-learning
courses and certificates cannot be used
for college credit.

Iowa Western Community College

Continuing Education

2700 College Rd.

Council Bluffs, IA 51503

712-325-3415

Web: www.ed2go.com/iwcc/

E-mail: bortmann@iwcc.cc.ia.us

Programs: Certificate—Basic Supervision, Customer Service, Paralegal, Production and Inventory Management, Project Management, Purchasing, Total Quality; individual courses

Individual course subjects: business, computer science, finance, fire protection, grant writing, information technology, logistics, management, paralegal studies, small business management, test preparation, writing

Average tuition: $55–$195 per course

Length of program: 6 weeks per course

Technologies: Internet

Accreditation: NCACS

Entrance requirements: none

Restrictions: none

Special services: none

ISIM University

Admissions Office

501 S. Cherry St.

Room #350

Denver, CO 80246

1-800-441-ISIM

Web: www.isimu.edu

E-mail: admissions@isimu.edu

Programs: Certificate—Business Management, Finance, Information Systems, Project Management; MBA; MS—Information Management; individual courses

Individual course subjects: business, finance, management, management information systems, technology, telecommunications

Average tuition: individual courses/certificate—$1,350 per course; master's—$415 per credit unit

Length of program: individual courses/certificates—8 weeks per course; MBA/MS—2–3 years

Technologies: correspondence, Internet

Accreditation: DETC

Entrance requirements: bachelor's degree and/or professional experience

Restrictions: none

Special services: tuition payment plan; virtual student union

Bright Idea
ISIM University's degree programs are offered either in online interactive format or guided self-study (correspondence) format, letting you choose the way you work best.

J

J. Sargeant Reynolds Community College

Division of Instructional Technologies and Distance Education

P.O. Box 85622

Richmond, VA 23285-5622

804-371-3612

Web: www.jsr.cc.va.us/itde/

Programs: Certificate—Dental Laboratory Technology, Opticians Apprentice; Certificate/AAS—Respiratory Therapy; individual courses

Individual course subjects: accounting, administrative assistance, biology, business, chemistry, computer science, dentistry, economics, English, finance, French, health, history, hospitality, management information systems, mathematics, opticianry, political science, psychology, respiratory therapy, sociology

Average tuition: $37.12 per credit hour (Virginia residents); $164.82 per credit hour (out-of-state students)

Technologies: audiographics, correspondence, Internet, television, video

Accreditation: SACS, COA

Entrance requirements: all courses and programs—high school diploma or the equivalent; Certificate in Dental Laboratory Technology—current employment in a dental laboratory; Opticians Apprentice Certificate—registration as an apprentice optician with the Virginia Department of Labor; Certificate in Respiratory Therapy—Certified Respiratory Therapy Technician or eligible for such certification

Restrictions: Students are required to attend some on-campus sessions.

Special services: none

Jamestown Community College

SUNY Learning Network
State University of New York
SUNY Plaza T-10
Albany, NY 12246
1-800-875-6269
Web: www.sunyjcc.edu/college-wide/offerings/online.html
Programs: AS—Computer Science
Average tuition: $92 per credit hour (New York residents); $162 per credit hour (out-of-state students)
Length of program: 16 weeks per course
Technologies: Internet
Accreditation: MSACS
Entrance requirements: high school diploma or the equivalent
Restrictions: none
Special services: none

Bright Idea
John Tracy Clinic's distance-education courses are available in both English and Spanish.

John Tracy Clinic

806 W. Adams Blvd.
Los Angeles, CA 90007
1-800-522-4582
Web: www.johntracyclinic.org
E-mail: mmartindale@johntracyclinic.org
Programs: individual courses
Individual course subjects: preschool subjects
Average tuition: free
Technologies: video

Accreditation: DETC

Entrance requirements: none

Restrictions: Enrollment is only open to parents, foster parents, and legal guardians of deaf children under the age of 5.

Special services: none

John Tracy Clinic Academy for Professional Studies

806 W. Adams Blvd.

Los Angeles, CA 90007

213-748-5481

Web: www.johntracyclinic.org/ProDistEd.htm

E-mail: gragusa@johntracyclinic.org

Programs: Certificate—Deaf and Hard-of-Hearing Early Childhood

Length of program: 1 year

Technologies: audiocassette, correspondence, Internet, video

Accreditation: DETC

Entrance requirements: bachelor's degree

Restrictions: none

Special services: none

Johns Hopkins University

Distance Education Division

School of Hygiene and Public Health

111 Market Place

Suite 850

Baltimore, MD 21202

410-223-1830

Web: distance.jhsph.edu

E-mail: distance@jhsph.edu

Programs: Graduate Certificate—Public Health; Master of Public Health

Average tuition: $493 per credit

Length of program: certificate—18 months; master's—3 years

Technologies: Internet

Accreditation: MSACS

Entrance requirements: bachelor's degree in nursing, engineering, or the natural or social sciences; GRE, MCAT or LSAT score; and 2 years of experience in the fields of health or human services, or graduate of a professional program

Restrictions: The certificate requires approximately 8 weeks of on-site sessions taken throughout the course of the program. The master's requires 20 credits to be earned in a face-to-face environment on campus or at one of the regional institutes scheduled periodically throughout the world.

Special services: academic advising; technology advising; virtual student lounge

Johnson Bible College

Distance Learning Office
Knoxville, TN 37998
1-800-669-7889
Web: ashley.jbc.edu/mastersnt/distance_learning.htm
E-mail: mketchen@jbc.edu
Programs: MA—New Testament
Average tuition: $150 per hour
Technologies: correspondence, fax, video
Accreditation: SACS, AABC
Entrance requirements: bachelor's degree with a 2.5 GPA, completion of Bible and Greek prerequisites, and scores from the AABC Bible Test and the GRE
Restrictions: 3 short on-campus sessions are required.
Special services: none

Johnson State College

External Degree Program
337 College Hill
Johnson, VT 05656
1-800-635-2356
Web: www.jsc.vsc.edu/academics/edp.html
E-mail: edpapply@badger.jsc.vsc.edu
Programs: BA—Anthropology/Sociology, Art, Biology, Business Management, Elementary Education, English, Health Sciences, History, Hospitality and Tourism Management, Journalism, Liberal Arts, Local Public Management, Mathematics, Music, Outdoor Education, Performing Arts, Political Science, Psychology, Teacher Education; BFA—Creative Writing, Performing Arts/Theater, Studio Arts; BS—Biology, Environmental Science, General Studies
Average tuition: $164 per credit (Vermont residents); $383 per credit (out-of-state students)
Technologies: correspondence, Internet
Accreditation: NEASC
Entrance requirements: at least 60 college-level credits with a grade of C- or better
Restrictions: Only residents of Vermont or near the Vermont borders of New Hampshire, Massachusetts, and New York may apply.
Special services: individual degree plans; local mentoring

Jones International University

967 E Mineral Ave.
Englewood, CO 80112
1-800-811-JONES

Web: www.jonesinternational.edu
E-mail: info@international.edu
Programs: Certificate—Advanced Public Relations for the Wired World, Applied Fundamentals for Telecommunications in Business, Communication Management for the Global Marketplace, Cyber Marketing, Essential Oral and Written Communication Skills for Managers, Human Resource Management for Changing Environments, Leaderships and Influence Through the Spoken and Written Word, Management Skills with a Human Directive, Marketing Fundamentals in Today's Electronic Business Environment, New Business Solutions Through Communications Technology, Practical Communication Technology Tools for Managers, Productive Organization Communication Skills for Management, Public Relations Fundamentals for the New Media Manager, Team Strategies for the Effective Manager, Telecommunications Applications for Managers, Using Human Communication Skills to Motivate Performance, Using the Internet in K–12 Education, Using the Internet in Higher Education; BA/MA—Business Communication; individual courses
Individual course subjects: business communications
Average tuition: Certificates/BA—$600 per course; MA—$700 per course
Length of program: 8 weeks per course; Certificates—24–32 weeks; BA—up to 7 years; MA—2–3 years
Technologies: Internet
Accreditation: NCACS
Entrance requirements: individual courses/certificates—none; BA—60 credit hours of undergraduate coursework or an associate's degree with a 2.5 GPA; MA—bachelor's degree
Restrictions: none
Special services: academic advising; Web-based library services; Web-based orientation at the beginning of each term

K

Kansas State University
Division of Continuing Education
13 College Court Bldg.
Manhattan, KS 66506-6001
1-800-622-2KSU
Web: www.dce.ksu.edu/distance.html
E-mail: info@dce.ksu.edu
Programs: Certificate—Food Science; BS—Animal Sciences and Industry, General Business, Interdisciplinary Social Science; Master of Agribusiness; Master of Engineering Management; MS—Chemical Engineering, Civil Engineering, Electrical Engineering; Master of Software Engineering; individual courses

Individual course subjects: agribusiness, agriculture, agronomy, animal sciences, computer information systems, counseling, dietetics, education, educational psychology, engineering, finance, history, horticulture, hospitality, human development, management, nutrition and food science, political science, psychology, social services, sociology, statistics, water resources, women's studies

Average tuition: undergraduate—$91.65 per credit; graduate—$134.40 per credit; Master of Agribusiness—$12,000

Length of program: 8–17 weeks per course; Master of Agribusiness—$2^1/_2$ years

Technologies: audiocassette, CD-ROM, computer conferencing, correspondence, Internet, video, videoconferencing

Accreditation: NCACS, ABET, ADiA

Entrance requirements: BS—2 years of previous college coursework with an overall GPA of 2.0; Master of Agribusiness—bachelor's degree with a 3.0 GPA in the last 2 years or a GMAT/GRE score and 2 years of professional experience; Engineering master's programs—bachelor's degree in a related field with a 3.0 GPA or a GRE score meeting minimum standards

Restrictions: The Master in Agribusiness requires 3 short, on-campus sessions. Videoconferencing courses are offered only in Kansas.

Special services: library services; technical support

Kaplan College

1801 Clint Moore Rd.
Suite 215
Boca Raton, FL 33487
1-800-669-2555
Web: www.kaplancollege.com
E-mail: info@kaplancollege.com

Programs: Diploma/Specialized Associate—Legal Nurse Consultant; Diploma/Specialized Associate/BS—Criminal Justice, Paralegal Studies

Average tuition: $4497.50–$19,995.00 (depending on the number of credits needed)

Length of program: diplomas—12 months; associate's—18 months; BS—36 months

Technologies: Internet

Accreditation: DETC

Entrance requirements: Legal Nurse Consultant Diploma—Registered Nurse licensure, nursing degree, or comparable medical credential; other diploma and degree programs—high school diploma or GED

Restrictions: Students must be at least 18 years old to enter the Criminal Justice program.

Special services: career guidance; online student chat room; tuition financing; tutoring

Keller Graduate School of Management

Online Educational Center
One Tower Lane
11th Floor
Oak Brook Terrace, IL 60181
1-800-225-8000
Web: online.keller.edu
E-mail: admissions@online.keller.edu
Programs: Certificate—Business Administration, Health Services Management, Human Resource Management, Information Systems Management, Project Management, Telecommunications Management; Master of Accounting and Financial Management; MBA; Master of Human Resource Management; Master of Information System Management; Master of Project Management; Master of Telecommunications Management
Average tuition: $1,440 per course
Length of program: 10 weeks per course
Technologies: Internet
Accreditation: NCACS
Entrance requirements: bachelor's degree and acceptable score on the GMAT, GRE, or Keller's alternative admission test
Restrictions: none
Special services: academic advising; career services; technical support

Kennesaw State University

Continuing Education
1000 Chastain Rd.
Kennesaw, GA 30144-5591
770-499-3355
Web: www.kennesaw.edu/coned/conedonline/online.shtml
E-mail: jgrine@kennesaw.edu
Programs: Certificate—Creative Writing, Technical Writing; individual courses
Individual course subjects: business communications, computer science, electronic commerce, Web site development
Average tuition: $164–$224 per course
Length of program: 5–6 weeks per course
Technologies: Internet
Accreditation: SACS
Entrance requirements: none
Restrictions: none
Special services: none

Watch Out!
None of the courses or certificates offered through Kennesaw's distance-learning program can be used for college credit.

Keystone National High School

School House Station
420 W. 5th St.
Bloomsburg, PA 17815-1564
1-800-255-4937
Web: www.keystonehighschool.com
Programs: high school diploma; individual courses
Individual course subjects: high school subjects
Average tuition: $165–$299 per course
Length of program: 8 weeks–1 year per course
Technologies: correspondence, Internet
Accreditation: NASC, DETC
Entrance requirements: completion of the 8th grade
Restrictions: none
Special services: advisory teaching service; helpdesk; online library services; tuition payment plan

King's College

Director of Distance Learning
133 N. River St.
Wilkes-Barre, PA 18711
570-208-5960
Web: www.kings.edu/~dstlrng/
E-mail: wpkeatin@kings.edu
Programs: MEd—Reading
Average tuition: $1,380 per course
Technologies: interactive TV, Internet
Accreditation: MSACS
Entrance requirements: bachelor's degree and GRE score
Restrictions: Students must complete at least 6 credits on campus and must have access to a location where the school provides television transmissions.
Special services: academic advising

Money Saver
A scholarship incentive program covering half of tuition costs is available for all certified teachers and students actively pursuing certification who participate in this program.

L

Lakehead University

Department of Part-Time Studies
955 Oliver Rd.
Thunder Bay
Ontario P7B 5E1
Canada
807-346-7730
Web: www.lakeheadu.ca/~disedwww/
E-mail: parttime@lakeheadu.ca
Programs: Certificate—Environmental Assessment; BA—General Studies; BS—Nursing; Master of Forestry; individual courses

Individual course subjects: biology, education, environmental studies, history, kinesiology, nursing, philosophy, political science, psychology, social work, sociology

Average tuition: $380–$760 (Canadian) per course

Length of program: certificate—2 years; BA—3 years; BS in Nursing—5–8 years

Technologies: audiocassette, audiographics, CD-ROM, computer conferencing, correspondence, Internet, teleconferencing, television, video, videoconferencing

Accreditation: Canadian government

Entrance requirements: all programs—high school diploma or the equivalent; BS in Nursing—nursing diploma, registered nurse license, and Basic Cardiac Life Support certification; master's—4 years honors bachelor's degree in forestry or a related field with a B average

Restrictions: The BS in Nursing is limited to residents of Ontario. The Master of Forestry requires a minimum on-campus residency of 1 full term.

Special services: counseling; learning assistance center

Lakeland College

Lakeland Online
P.O. Box 359
Sheboygan, WI 53082-0359
414-565-1217
Web: 199.170.23.12/Lakeland/online/online.asp
E-mail: online@Lakeland.edu
Programs: BA—Accounting, Business Administration, Computer Science, Marketing
Average tuition: $171.25 per credit hour
Length of program: 14 weeks per course
Technologies: Internet
Accreditation: NCACS
Entrance requirements: high school diploma or GED
Restrictions: none
Special services: online student forum; personal counseling; tuition payment plan

Lane Community College

Distance Learning
400 E. 30th Ave.
Eugene, OR 97405
541-726-2260
Web: lanecc.edu/distance/distance.htm
E-mail: leathersc@lanecc.edu
Programs: AA—General Studies; individual courses

Watch Out!
Quoted tuition and admission requirements are for Canadian students only. International students may have to pay more and meet more stringent entrance requirements. Contact the school directly for more information.

Bright Idea
You can take up to 3 courses before officially applying to the Lakeland College distance-learning degree program. This gives you a chance to discover if the program is right for you before committing.

Individual course subjects: anthropology, art, astronomy, biology, business, chemistry, computer science, economics, geography, health, history, humanities, psychology, sociology, Spanish, writing

Average tuition: $36 per credit hour (Oregon residents); $123 per credit hour (out-of-state students)

Technologies: Internet, television, video

Accreditation: NASC

Entrance requirements: none

Restrictions: Most courses require some on-campus sessions.

Special services: academic advising

Laurentian University

Centre for Continuing Education

935 Ramsey Lake Rd.

Sudbury

Ontario P3E 2C6

Canada

705-673-6569

Web: www.laurentian.ca/www/cce/index.htm

E-mail: cce_l@nickel.laurentian.ca

Programs: Certificate—Family Life Studies and Human Sexuality, Gerontology; BA—Native Studies, Psychology, Religious Studies, Sociology, Women's Studies; Bachelor of Liberal Science; BS—Nursing; Bachelor of Social Work; individual courses

Individual course subjects: anthropology, biology, chemistry, classics, economics, English, geography, geology, gerontology, history, international business, law, mathematics, music, native studies, nurse-midwife, nursing, philosophy, physical education, physics, political science, psychology, religion, social work, sociology, women's studies

Average tuition: $376.50–$2259.00 Canadian (depending on the number of credits taken)

Length of program: up to 8 years

Technologies: CD-ROM, correspondence, Internet, teleconferencing, television, video

Accreditation: Canadian government

Entrance requirements: high school diploma or the equivalent; BS in Nursing—Certificate of Registration from the College of Nurses of Ontario or eligibility for such certification

Restrictions: All programs are only available in Canada and the U.S.

Special services: counseling

Lee University

External Studies

100 Eighth St. NE

Cleveland, TN 37311

1-800-256-5916

Web: www.leeuniversity.edu/externalstudies/
E-mail: externalstudy@leeuniversity.edu
Programs: BA—Christian Ministry
Average tuition: $90 per credit hour
Length of program: 16 weeks per course
Technologies: correspondence, Internet
Accreditation: SACS
Entrance requirements: high school diploma or GED
Restrictions: none
Special services: academic advising; library services; mentoring

Lehigh University

Office of Distance Education
205 Johnson Hall
36 University Dr.
Bethlehem, PA 18015
610-758-6210
Web: www.distance.lehigh.edu/index.htm
E-mail: mak5@lehigh.edu
Programs: MBA; Master of Engineering—Chemical Engineering; MS—Chemistry, Molecular Biology, Pharmaceutical Chemistry, Polymer Science and Engineering, Quality Engineering; individual courses
Individual course subjects: engineering
Technologies: Internet, satellite
Accreditation: MSACS, ABET
Entrance requirements: bachelor's degree, professional experience, and current employment in the field
Restrictions: Satellite-based programs, including all master's degree programs, are only available to employees of participating corporate sites.
Special services: none

Leicester University

Higher Degrees Office
University Rd.
Leicester
LE1 7RH
United Kingdom
+44 (0) 116-252-2293
Web: www.le.ac.uk/cwis/distance.html
E-mail: higherdegrees@le.ac.uk
Programs: Certificate—Social Security Law; Certificate/Diploma—Management; MA—Mass Communications; Certificate/MA—Applied Linguistics and TESOL; Diploma/MA—Archaeology and Heritage, European Union Law, Law and Employment Relations, Primary Education; MBA—Business Administration; Certificate/MBA—Education Management;

MS—Criminal Justice Studies, Finance, Marketing; Diploma/MS—Forensic and Legal Psychology, Risk Crisis and Disaster Management, Sociology of Sport, Study of Security Management; MA/MS—Museum Studies

Length of program: certificates—1 year; diplomas—16–18 months; MA/MBA/MS—2 years

Technologies: correspondence

Accreditation: United Kingdom government

Entrance requirements: bachelor's degree in a related subject

Restrictions: Some programs require short on-campus residencies.

Special services: optional residential sessions; personal tutoring

Leicester University Centre for Labour Market Studies

7–9 Salisbury Rd.

Leicester

LE1 7QR

United Kingdom

+44 (0) 116-252-5951

Web: www.clms.le.ac.uk/WWW/HTML%20Pages/courses/courses/index.html

E-mail: clms1@leicester.ac.uk

Programs: Certificate—Training Practice; Diploma—Human Resource Management, Training and Development; MS—Training, Training and Human Resource Management, Training and Performance Management

Length of program: certificate—40 weeks; diplomas—1 year; MS—2 years

Technologies: correspondence, video

Accreditation: DETC, United Kingdom government

Entrance requirements: certificate—completion of general education; diploma—completion of general education and 3 years of relevant work experience; MS—bachelor's degree, acceptable professional experience, and successful completion of a Diploma program

Restrictions: Applicants should be at least 21 years old. The certificate is currently available in a limited number of countries.

Special services: local support in some areas; optional residential weekends; personal tutoring; regional study groups

Unofficially... Successfully completing a diploma through this program ensures a place in one of the master's programs.

Lesley College

29 Everett St.

Cambridge, MA 02138-2790

617-868-9600

Web: www.lesley.edu/online_courses.html

E-mail: online@mail.lesley.edu

Programs: Master of Technology in Education

Average tuition: $395 per credit

Length of program: less than 2 years

Technologies: Internet

Accreditation: NEASC

Entrance requirements: bachelor's degree

Restrictions: none

Special services: off-campus library services; tuition payment plan

Liberty University

Distance Learning Office

1971 University Blvd.

Lynchburg, VA 24502

1-800-424-9595

Web: www.liberty.edu/admissions/distance/index.htm

E-mail: wcpenn@liberty.edu

Programs: AA—General Studies; BS—Business, Multidisciplinary Studies, Psychology; MA—Counseling, Professional Counseling; MBA; MDiv; MEd; AA/BS/MS—Religion; EdD

Average tuition: AA/BS—$180 per semester hour; MA/MDiv/MEd/MS/EdD—$195 per semester hour; MBA—$330 per semester hour

Technologies: video

Accreditation: SACS, TRACS

Entrance requirements: AA/BS—high school diploma or GED; MA/MDiv/MEd/MS/EdD—bachelor's degree with a 3.0 GPA; MBA—GMAT score

Restrictions: Students must be at least 25 years old. Some programs may require on-campus sessions.

Special services: tuition payment plan

Life Bible College

School of Distance Learning

1100 Covina Blvd.

San Dimas, CA 91773

1-800-356-0001

Web: www.lifebible.edu/distance.htm

E-mail: correspo@lifebible.edu

Programs: AA—Biblical Studies; individual courses

Individual course subjects: biblical languages, biblical studies, ministry, theology

Average tuition: $165–$315 per course

Technologies: correspondence

Accreditation: AABC

Entrance requirements: high school diploma or the equivalent

Restrictions: none

Special services: none

Lifetime Career Schools

101 Harrison St.

Archbald, PA 18403

1-800-326-9221

Web: www.lifetime-career.com

E-mail: lcslearn@aol.com

Programs: Certificate—Computers; Diploma—Bookkeeping, Cooking, Doll Repair, Flower Arranging and Floristry, Landscaping, Secretarial, Sewing/Dressmaking, Small Business Management

Length of program: 8 months

Technologies: correspondence

Accreditation: DETC

Entrance requirements: certificate—high school diploma or the equivalent; diplomas—at least 2 years of high school education

Restrictions: Students must be at least 18 years old.

Special services: none

Louisiana State University

Office of Independent Study

E106 Pleasant Hall

Baton Rouge, LA 70803-1508

1-800-234-2256

Web: is.lsu.edu

Watch Out!
Enrolling in an LSU correspondence course does not constitute admission to the university.

Programs: high school diploma; individual courses

Individual course subjects: accounting, anthropology, astronomy, biological sciences, business education, Civil War studies, classical languages, classics, dairy science, economics, education, English, environmental studies, finance, French, geography, geology, German, high school subjects, history, kinesiology, library science, management, management information systems, marketing, mass communications, mathematics, mechanical engineering, music, office technology, philosophy, physical science, physics, political science, psychology, real estate, sociology, Spanish, speech, statistics, theater, vocational education, women's studies

Average tuition: high school—$70 per course; undergraduate—$60 per semester hour

Length of program: 9 months per course

Technologies: correspondence, Internet

Accreditation: SACS

Entrance requirements: individual courses—none; high school diploma—some high school coursework

Restrictions: none

Special services: none

M

Maharishi University of Management

Fairfield, IA 52557

1-800-369-6480

Web: www.mum.edu/SBPA/distance/

E-mail: admissions@mum.edu

Programs: MBA

Length of program: $1^1/2$–3 years

Technologies: Internet, satellite television

Accreditation: NCACS

Entrance requirements: bachelor's degree and GMAT score

Restrictions: none

Special services: academic advising; library services; school intranet

Marylhurst University

17600 Pacific Hwy.

P.O. Box 261

Marylhurst, OR 97036-0261

1-800-634-9982

Web: www.marylhurst.edu/online/index.html

E-mail: learning@marylhurst.edu

Programs: BA—Organizational Communication; BS—Management; MBA

Average tuition: BA/BS—$235–$312 per credit hour; MBA—$276–$337 per credit hour

Technologies: Internet

Accreditation: NASC

Entrance requirements: associate's degree or at least 90 hours of previous college coursework; a 3.0 GPA on previous college coursework and at least 2 years of full-time employment are preferred

Restrictions: none

Special services: academic advising; library services

Marywood University

School of Continuing Education

Office of Distance Education

2300 Adams Ave.

Scranton, PA 18509

1-800-836-6940

Web: www.marywood.edu/disted/

E-mail: disted_adm@ac.marywood.edu

Programs: Certificate—Certified Public Accountant, Comprehensive Business Skills, Office Administration, Professional Communications; BS—Accounting, Business Administration/Financial Planning, Business

Administration/Management, Business Administration/Marketing; individual courses

Individual course subjects: business, economics

Length of program: 2 months per course

Technologies: correspondence

Accreditation: MSACS

Entrance requirements: all programs—high school diploma or the equivalent; CPA certificate—bachelor's degree

Restrictions: none

Special services: academic advising; career services; library services; personalized advanced standing advising

McGill University

845 Sherbrooke St. W

Montreal

Quebec H3A 2T5

Canada

514-398-4455

Web: www.mcgill.ca/programs/distance.htm

Programs: Certificate—Educational Technology, Teaching English as a Second Language; MS—Occupational Health Sciences; individual courses

Individual course subjects: education, occupational health studies

Average tuition: $166.83–$826.83 (Canadian) per course (depending on residency)

Length of program: certificates—1 year; MS—3 years

Technologies: audiocassette, correspondence, fax, Internet, video

Accreditation: Canadian government

Entrance requirements: certificates—bachelor's degree and teacher permit issued by a provincial Department of Education or the equivalent; MS—bachelor's degree

Restrictions: The MS program requires 6 on-campus practica.

Special services: none

Memorial University of Newfoundland

School of Continuing Education

St. John's Newfoundland A1C 5S7

Canada

709-737-8000

Web: www.det.mun.ca/credit/credit.html

Programs: Certificate—Criminology, Library Studies, Municipal Administration, Newfoundland Studies, Public Administration, Records and Information; Certificate/Diploma—Business Administration; BBA; Bachelor of Commerce; Bachelor of Social Work; Bachelor of Technology; individual courses

Individual course subjects: anthropology, biology, business, classics, computer science, criminal justice, economics, education, engineering, English,

Accreditation: NASC

Entrance requirements: all programs and courses—high school diploma or GED; BS—significant amount of previous college coursework

Restrictions: none

Special services: academic advising; career services; library resources; online coordinator; online technology tutorials; technical support

Montana State University—Bozeman

Extended Studies

204 Culbertson Hall

P.O. Box 172200

Bozeman, MT 59717-2200

406-994-6683

Web: btc.montana.edu/distance/index2.html

E-mail: btc@montana.edu

Programs: BS—Nursing; MEd—Curriculum Instruction, Elementary School Administration, Secondary School Administration; Master of Nursing; MS—Mathematics Education, Science Education; individual courses

Individual course subjects: agriculture, biology, education, engineering, environmental studies, health, languages, mathematics, nursing, physics

Average tuition: $171.80–$429.50 per credit (depending on residency)

Length of program: BS—4 years; master's—2–3 years

Technologies: interactive TV, Internet, videoconferencing

Accreditation: NASC, NCATE

Entrance requirements: individual courses—none; BS—high school diploma with a 2.5 GPA or rank in the top half of graduating class; master's—bachelor's degree in related field with a 3.0 GPA and GRE score; MS—also require certification to teach grades 6–8 or 9–12, and at least 2 years of teaching experience

Restrictions: Interactive TV and videoconferencing courses are only open to Montana residents. Nursing programs require on-campus residencies. MS programs require on-campus summer sessions.

Special services: career services; library services; tuition payment plan

Moody Bible Institute

Independent Studies

820 N. LaSalle Blvd.

Chicago, IL 60610

1-800-955-1123

Web: www.moody.edu/ED/XS/Independent/Welcome.htm

E-mail: xstudies@moody.edu

Programs: Certificate—Adult Bible Studies; Associate of Biblical Studies; BS—Biblical Studies; individual courses

Individual course subjects: biblical studies, ministry

Average tuition: undergraduate—$120 per semester hour; certificate—$30 per course

Length of program: 1 year per course; associate's/BS—up to 10 years

Technologies: correspondence

Accreditation: NCACS, AABC

Entrance requirements: individual courses/certificate—none; associate's/ BS—high school diploma or GED

Restrictions: Students must be at least 17 years old, Christian, and members of an evangelical Protestant church.

Special services: academic counseling; tuition payment plan

Mortgage Bankers Association of America

1125 15th St. NW

Washington, DC 20005

1-800-793-MBAA

Web: www.mbaa.org/train_edu/

E-mail: education@mbaa.org

Programs: individual courses

Individual course subjects: finance

Average tuition: $125–$285 per course (MBAA members); $185-$410 per course (nonmembers)

Length of program: 3–8 months per course

Technologies: correspondence, Internet

Accreditation: DETC

Entrance requirements: These courses are intended for mortgage-banking professionals.

Restrictions: none

Special services: none

Mott Community College

Distance Learning Office

1401 E. Court St.

Flint, MI 48503

810-762-0282

Web: distance.mcc.edu

E-mail: zerbinos@edtech.mcc.edu

Programs: AAS—Computer Occupations Technology, General Business; AGS; AA/AS—General Studies; individual courses

Individual course subjects: computer science, education, health, humanities, mathematics, science, social sciences, technology

Average tuition: $450 per course

Length of program: 15 weeks per course; AAS/AA/AGS/AS—4 years

Technologies: audiocassette, correspondence, interactive TV, Internet, television, video

Accreditation: NCACS

Bright Idea
Mott Community College operates a College in the Workplace program, which enables employees of participating manufacturing companies throughout Michigan and the Midwest to take classes and complete degrees without ever coming to campus.

Entrance requirements: high school diploma or GED
Restrictions: Most courses require on-campus meetings.
Special services: academic advising; library services

N

National American University
321 Kansas City St.
Rapid City, SD 57701
1-800-843-8892
Web: www.national.edu/online/OnlineCampus.html
E-mail: sluckhur@national.edu
Programs: BS—Applied Management, Business Administration, Computer Information Systems; individual courses
Individual course subjects: accounting, computer science, economics, finance, law, management, mathematics
Average tuition: $900 per course
Length of program: 7–11 weeks per course
Technologies: Internet
Accreditation: NCACS
Entrance requirements: high school diploma or GED
Restrictions: none
Special services: academic advising; career services; library services; online learning resource center; online orientation; technical support

National Association Medical Staff Services Institute
P.O. Box 140647
Austin, TX 78714-0647
512-454-7928
Web: www.namss.org
Programs: Certificate—Medical Staff Organization Management
Average tuition: $1,050 (members of NAMSS); $1,550 (nonmembers)
Length of program: 15 months
Technologies: correspondence
Accreditation: DETC
Entrance requirements: high school diploma or GED
Restrictions: none
Special services: none

National Distance Education Center
500 N. Kimball Ave.
Suite 105
P.O. Box 92577
Southlake, TX 76092
1-800-774-5112

Money Saver
National American University offers a scholarship to active-duty military personnel who take distance-learning courses through the school.

Web: www.dilearn.com/ndec.htm
E-mail: ndecinfo@dilearn.com
Programs: individual courses
Individual course subjects: administrative assistance, bookkeeping, legal secretary, medical transcription, paralegal studies, pharmacy technician
Technologies: correspondence
Accreditation: DETC
Entrance requirements: none
Restrictions: none
Special services: none

National Genealogical Society

NGS Education Department
4527 17th St. N
Arlington, VA 22207-2399
1-800-473-0060, ext. 223
Web: www.ngsgenealogy.org/education/body_frame.html
E-mail: education@ngsgenealogy.org
Programs: individual courses
Individual course subjects: geneaology
Average tuition: American Genealogy course—$295 (NGS members) and $375 (nonmembers); Introduction to Genealogy course—$60 (NGS members) and $75 (nonmembers)
Length of program: 18 months
Technologies: correspondence, Internet
Accreditation: DETC
Entrance requirements: none
Restrictions: none
Special services: tuition payment plan

National-Louis University

122 S. Michigan Ave.
Chicago, IL 60603
1-800-443-5522
Web: www.nl.edu/nlu_programs/online.html
E-mail:
Programs: BS—Management; Master of Adult Education; individual courses
Individual course subjects: adult education, business, computer information systems, educational administration, mathematics, philosophy, psychology, science, social sciences, social services
Average tuition: $140–$700 per course
Length of program: 8 weeks per course; BS—2 years; master's—1 year
Technologies: interactive TV, Internet
Accreditation: NCACS

Entrance requirements: BS—2 years of previous college coursework; master's—bachelor's degree with a 3.0 GPA on the last 2 years of undergraduate coursework

Restrictions: The Master of Adult Education requires 2 residential workshops.

Special services: tuition payment plan

National Tax Training School

P.O. Box 382

Monsey, NY 10952

1-800-914-8138

Web: www.nattax.com

E-mail: about@nattax.com

Programs: Certificate—Tax Consultant; individual courses

Individual course subjects: taxation

Average tuition: $39.50–$115 per course; certificate—$263.75–$274.75

Length of program: up to 1 year per course

Technologies: correspondence

Accreditation: DETC

Entrance requirements: at least 2 years of high school education

Restrictions: none

Special services: tuition payment plan

National Technological University

700 Centre Dr.

Fort Collins, CO 80526

1-800-582-9976

Web: www.ntu.edu

Programs: MBA—International Business; MS—Chemical Engineering, Computer Engineering, Computer Science, Electrical Engineering, Engineering Management, Environmental Systems Management, Hazardous Waste Management, Health Physics, Management of Technology, Manufacturing Systems Engineering, Materials Science and Engineering, Software Engineering, Transportation Systems Engineering

Average tuition: $263 per credit

Technologies: Internet, satellite television

Accreditation: NCACS, ABET

Entrance requirements: MBA—bachelor's degree with a 2.9 GPA and 2 years of work experience in a managerial position; MS—BS degree in a related field with a cumulative 2.9 GPA

Restrictions: Degree programs are only open to employees of member organizations and companies.

Special services: none

Unofficially...
National Technological University is an alliance of more than 50 leading engineering schools, which provide the courses taught through the university.

National Truck Drivers School

188 College Dr.
P.O. Box 1899
Orange Park, FL 32067
1-800-488-SEMI
Web: www.truckschool.com
Programs: License—Commercial Drivers License (CDL) Preparation, CDL Prepared Independent Trucker's Program
Average tuition: license preparation—$3,795; CDL trucker's program—$5,095
Length of program: 1 month or more
Technologies: correspondence
Accreditation: DETC
Entrance requirements: none
Restrictions: All programs require resident training, which can be completed either as a 3-week block or in the course of 5 weekends.
Special services: job placement assistance

National University

11255 N. Torrey Pines Rd.
La Jolla, CA 92037-1011
1-800-NAT-UNIV
Web: online.nu.edu
Programs: Certificate—Cross-Cultural Language and Academic Development (CLAD); BA—Global Studies; BS—Nursing; MBA—Global
Average tuition: certificate/BA/BS—$165 per quarter unit; MBA—$185 per quarter unit
Length of program: 4–8 weeks per course
Technologies: CD-ROM, Internet, videoconferencing
Accreditation: WASC, NLN
Entrance requirements: certificate/BA—high school diploma or GED and 5 years of successful work experience; BS—associate's degree in nursing with a 2.75 GPA, current registered nurse license, and proof of registration in a professional liability program; MBA—bachelor's degree or higher with an overall GPA of 2.5
Restrictions: none
Special services: academic advising; library services; online help desk

Nazarene Bible College

111 Academy Park Loop
Colorado Springs, CO 80910
1-800-873-3873
Web: www.nbc.edu/online/online_main_page.htm
E-mail: admissions@nbc.edu
Programs: AA—Biblical Studies, Christian Education, Lay Ministries; Bachelor of Biblical Studies; Bachelor of Christian Education

Average tuition: $110 per credit hour
Length of program: 6 weeks per course
Technologies: Internet
Accreditation: AABC
Entrance requirements: high school diploma or GED
Restrictions: none
Special services: counseling; library services; technical support

New College of California

50 Fell St.
San Francisco, CA 94102
1-888-437-3460
Web: www.newcollege.edu/mediastudies/
E-mail: admissions@ncgate.newcollege.edu
Programs: MA—Media Studies
Average tuition: $2,700 per course
Length of program: 1–2 years
Technologies: Internet
Accreditation: WASC
Entrance requirements: bachelor's degree
Restrictions: none
Special services: mentoring

New Jersey Institute of Technology

Office of Distance Learning
Guttenberg Information Technologies Center
Suite 5600
University Heights
Newark, NJ 07102-1982
1-800-624-9850
Web: www.njit.edu/DL/
E-mail: dl@njit.edu
Programs: Certificate—Electronic Media Design, Information Systems Design and Development, Internet Applications Development, Managing Human Resources, Object-Oriented Design, Programming Environment Tools, Project Management, Telecommunications Networking, WebMaster; BS—Computer Science; MS—Engineering Management; BA/MS—Information Systems; individual courses
Individual course subjects: chemical engineering, chemistry, computer information science, economics, engineering management, English, environmental studies, human resource management, humanities, industrial engineering, management, management information systems, marketing, mathematics, physics, social sciences
Average tuition: BS—$206–$424 per credit (depending on residency); certificates/MS—$388–$534 per credit (depending on residency); WebMaster certificate—$2,495

Bright Idea
You can try out NJIT's distance-learning program at its Web site, which offers a demo video, a sample syllabus, and sample course notes.

Technologies: CD-ROM, fax, Internet, teleconferencing, video
Accreditation: MSACS, ABET, CSAB
Entrance requirements: individual courses/certificates—application as a nonmatriculated student; BS—high school diploma; MS—bachelor's degree with a 2.8 GPA and GRE score
Restrictions: Required classes that involve labs are not available via distance learning, but students can take them through local colleges.
Special services: academic advising; mentoring; virtual library

New River Community College

Independent and Distance Learning
P.O. Box 1127
Dublin, VA 24084
540-674-3600
Web: www.nr.cc.va.us/nrcc2/~idl/index.HTM
Programs: Associate of Arts and Sciences—Education, General Studies; individual courses
Individual course subjects: biology, business, childcare training, criminal justice, economics, English, finance, geology, health, history, information technology, languages, marketing, mathematics, music, political science, psychology, sign language, sociology, speech, study skills, word processing
Average tuition: $46.65 per credit hour (Virginia residents); $160.35 per credit hour (out-of-state students)
Technologies: audiocassette, computer software, interactive TV, Internet, television, video
Accreditation: SACS
Entrance requirements: high school diploma or GED
Restrictions: Some courses require on-campus meetings.
Special services: academic advising; library resources

New School University

Distance-Learning Office
68 Fifth Ave.
New York, NY 10011
212-229-5880
Web: www.dialnsa.edu
E-mail: admissions@dialnsa.edu
Programs: Certificate—English Language Teaching, Group Practice Management, Media Management, World Wide Web Page Design; BA—Liberal Studies; MA—Media Studies; individual courses
Individual course subjects: art, biological sciences, business, communications, computer art, computer science, culinary arts, English language, ethnic studies, fashion design, food-service management, graphic design, health services, human resource management, humanities, interior design, languages, mass communications, mathematics, music, nonprofit management, photography, social sciences, theater, writing

Average tuition: undergraduate—$528–$602 per credit; graduate—$650 per credit

Length of program: 9 weeks per course

Technologies: Internet

Accreditation: MSACS

Entrance requirements: individual courses—none; BA—60 credits of previous college-level coursework; certificate in World Wide Web Page Design—strong computing knowledge; other certificates and MA—bachelor's degree

Restrictions: The Certificate in Media Management requires 4 short, on-site sessions.

Special services: academic advising; online orientation; online student lounge; technical support

New York University

School of Continuing and Professional Studies

7 E. 12th St.

11th Floor

New York, NY 10003-4475

212-998-7088

Web: www.scps.nyu.edu/dyncon/virt/

E-mail: advice.scps@nyu.edu

Programs: Certificate—Electronic Commerce, English to Spanish Translation, Information Technology, Internet Technologies, Object-Oriented Programming, UNIX Systems Management; MS—Management and Systems; individual courses

Individual course subjects: accounting, business, career development, construction, health, hospitality, information technology, international relations, languages, organization, psychology, real estate, sociology, taxation, world studies, writing

Average tuition: $2,480 per course

Length of program: certificates—4 years; MS—2–3 years

Technologies: Internet

Accreditation: MSACS

Entrance requirements: individual courses/certificates—none (background experience is recommended for certificates); MS—bachelor's degree and GMAT or GRE score

Restrictions: none

Special services: library services

NHRAW Home Study Institute

P.O. Box 16790

Columbus, OH 43216-6790

614-488-1835

Web: www.nhraw.org

Money Saver
If you are not a North American Heating, Refrigeration, and Airconditioning Wholesalers Association (NHRAW) member but are sponsored by a wholesaler who is, you can enroll in the association's correspondence courses at the lower member fee.

E-mail: nhrawmail@nhraw.org
Programs: individual courses
Individual course subjects: air conditioning/heating/refrigeration
Average tuition: $64 per course (NHRAW members); $120 per course (non-members)
Length of program: 3 months per course
Technologies: computer disk, correspondence
Accreditation: DETC
Entrance requirements: employment in the HVACR industry
Restrictions: none
Special services: instructional support

Niagara College

Distance Learning
P.O. Box 1005
Woodlawn Rd.
Welland
Ontario L3B 5S2
Canada
905-735-2211, ext. 7511
Web: www.niagarac.on.ca/student/programs/distlear/index.htm
E-mail: distance@niagarac.on.ca
Programs: Certificate—American Hotel/Motel Association Training; Diploma—General Arts and Science; individual courses
Individual course subjects: accounting, biology, business, computer science, economics, education, electronics, English, health, hospitality, human resources management, industrial operations, languages, law, marketing, multimedia authoring, psychology, sociology
Average tuition: $106.50–$435.00 (Canadian) per course
Technologies: audiocassette, CD-ROM, computer disk, correspondence, Internet, video
Accreditation: Canadian government
Entrance requirements: none
Restrictions: Some courses require on-campus sessions.
Special services: none

North Carolina Central University

1801 Fayetteville St.
Durham, NC 27707
919-560-6100
Web: www.nccu.edu/univcoll/facdev/index.html
Programs: individual courses
Individual course subjects: accounting, biology, chemistry, computer information systems, computer science, counseling, criminal justice, economics,

economics, English, geography, health, history, library science, mathematics, philosophy, physical education, plastics, political science, psychology, sociology

Length of program: 16 weeks per course

Technologies: Internet, television, video

Accreditation: MSACS

Entrance requirements: individual courses—none; diplomas/AA—high school diploma or GED

Restrictions: Some courses require on-campus meetings. Students taking television courses must live in the broadcast area.

Special services: academic advising; library services

Northeastern University

Distance Education On-Line
360 Huntington Ave.
Suite 328-CP
Boston, MA 02115
617-373-5618
Web: www.nuol.edu
E-mail: NUOL@neu.edu
Programs: Certificate—Advanced Web Design, Data Communications, Internet Technologies, Technical Writing, Webmaster Technology
Average tuition: $630–$830 per course
Length of program: 9 months
Technologies: Internet
Accreditation: NEASC
Entrance requirements: none
Restrictions: none
Special services: career services; technical support

Northeastern Arizona University

NAU Online
Flagstaff, AZ 86011
520-523-0111
Web: nauonline.nau.edu
E-mail: nauonline@nau.edu
Programs: Certificate—International Tourism Management, Parks and Recreation Management, Professional Communication, Restaurant Management; individual courses
Individual course subjects: anthropology, art, biology, business, chemistry, communication disorders, communications, criminal justice, dental hygiene, education, engineering, English, geography, history, hospitality, humanities, liberal arts, mathematics, music, nursing, parks and recreation, political science, public affairs, sociology
Average tuition: $115 per credit hour (Arizona residents); $346 per credit hour (out-of-state students)

Technologies: Internet
Accreditation: NCACS
Entrance requirements: none
Restrictions: none
Special services: career services; library services; technical support

Northern State University

Office of Continuing Education
Spafford Hall
Room 106
Aberdeen, SD 57401
605-626-2486
Web: www.northern.edu/extension/index.htm
Programs: individual courses
Individual course subjects: accounting, art education, art history, biology, business, communication disorders, computer information systems, criminal justice, economics, education, engineering, English, geography, geology, health services, history, humanities, information technology, marketing, mass communications, mathematics, nursing, political science, psychology, sociology, Spanish, statistics, theater
Average tuition: $125.45 per credit hour
Technologies: correspondence, Internet, television, video
Accreditation: NCACS
Entrance requirements: high school diploma or GED
Restrictions: Some courses are only open to South Dakota residents.
Special services: none

Northern Virginia Community College

Extended Learning Institute
8333 Little River Turnpike
Annandale, VA 22003-3796
1-800-627-5443
Web: eli.nv.cc.va.us/vc/
Programs: AAS—Business Management, Information Systems Technology; AS—Business Administration, Engineering, General Studies; individual courses
Individual course subjects: accounting, administrative assistance, art, biological sciences, biology, business, chemistry, criminal justice, economics, engineering, English, finance, French, geography, health information technology, history, humanities, information technology, library science, management, marketing, mathematics, philosophy, physical education, physics, political science, psychology, sociology, Spanish, speech, theater
Average tuition: $38.97–$166.67 per credit (depending on residency)
Length of program: 16 weeks per course

Technologies: audiocassette, Internet, television, video, videoconferencing
Accreditation: SACS
Entrance requirements: high school diploma or the equivalent
Restrictions: Some courses require on-campus meetings.
Special services: academic advising; career planning; counseling; tutoring

Northwest Missouri State University

800 University Dr.
Maryville, MO 64468-6001
660-562-1562
Web: www.NorthwestOnline.org
E-mail: admissions@mail.nwmissouri.edu
Programs: BS—Business Management; individual courses
Individual course subjects: American studies, computer science, humanities, industrial operations, labor studies, management information systems, music, philosophy, production and inventory management, world studies
Average tuition: $102.25 per credit hour (Missouri residents); $173.25 per credit hour (out-of-state students)
Length of program: 4 months per course; BS—4 years
Technologies: Internet
Accreditation: NCACS
Entrance requirements: individual courses—none; BS—AAS degree or the equivalent
Restrictions: none
Special services: academic advising; career advising; library services

Northwestern College (Minnesota)

Center for Distance Education
3003 Snelling Ave. N
Saint Paul, MN 55113-1598
1-800-308-5495
Web: www.nwc.edu/disted/de_home.htm
E-mail: distance.ed.dpt@nwc.edu
Programs: Certificate—Bible; BA—Intercultural Ministries; individual courses
Individual course subjects: biblical studies, Greek, history, mathematics, philosophy, psychology, religious education, science
Average tuition: $180 per credit
Length of program: 16 weeks per course; BA—2 years
Technologies: audiocassette, correspondence, Internet, video
Accreditation: NCACS
Entrance requirements: individual courses/certificate—high school diploma or GED; BA—2 years of previous college coursework
Restrictions: none
Special services: none

Bright Idea
Try out Northwestern College's distance-learning program and get a feel for what distance learning is like by taking a free, 2-week course designed to teach you how distance learning works and improve your Internet skills. Go to www2.nc.edu/virtcol/ for details.

Northwestern College (Ohio)

Virtual College
1441 N. Cable Rd.
Lima, OH 45805
419-227-3141
Web: www2.nc.edu/virtcol/
E-mail: info@nc.edu
Programs: AS—Administrative Assistant, Agribusiness Marketing/Management Technology, Automotive Management, Computer Technology, Legal Assisting, Legal Secretarial, Marketing, Medical Office Assistant Technology, Medical Secretarial, Pharmacy Assistant Technology, Travel Management, Word Processing Administrative Support; BS—Healthcare Management; AS/BS—Accounting, Business Administration; individual courses
Individual course subjects: accounting, administrative assistance, agribusiness, business, data processing, finance, health services, hospitality, legal secretarial, management, marketing, mathematics, medical office management, medical secretarial, paralegal studies, pharmacy technician, science, typing, word processing
Average tuition: $126 per credit hour
Length of program: 10 weeks per course
Technologies: Internet
Accreditation: NCACS
Entrance requirements: high school diploma or GED
Restrictions: Students must be at least 22 years old.
Special services: online library

Nova Southeastern University

3301 College Ave.
Ft. Lauderdale, FL 33314
1-800-541-6682
Web: www.nova.edu
Programs: Certificate—Charter Schools Administration, Computer Applications for Education, Early Childhood Education, Middle Grades Education, Online Teaching and Learning; BS—Professional Management; MBA; MS—Management Information Systems; PhD—Dispute Resolution, Information Science, Information Systems; MS/EdS—Curriculum Instruction and Technology, Education, Educational Technology; MS/EdD—Instructional Technology and Distance Education; MS/PhD—Computer Information Systems, Computer Science; MS/EdD/PhD—Computing Technology in Education
Average tuition: Certificates/EdS—$265 per credit; BS—$230 per credit; MBA—$489 per credit; MS—$265-$370 per credit; EdD/PhD—$4,150 per term; PhD in Dispute Resolution—$560 per credit

Length of program: 6–12 weeks per course; MBA/MS/EdS—12–21 months; EdD/PhD—3–7 years

Technologies: Internet

Accreditation: SACS

Entrance requirements: certificates—bachelor's degree; BS—associate's degree or the equivalent number of college credits; MBA/MS/EdS—bachelor's degree in a related field with a 2.5 GPA or a GMAT score of 450 or a GRE score of 1,000 or significant professional experience; EdD/PhD—master's degree in a related field with a 3.25 GPA and relevant professional experience

Restrictions: The MBA requires a 1-week residency. The MS in Instructional Technology and Distance Education requires 3 short on-campus residencies. PhD programs require several short on-campus residencies.

Special services: academic advising; academic mentoring; electronic library system; help desk; student advising

O

Ohio University

Office of Independent Studies

Tupper Hall 302

Ohio University

Athens, OH 45701

1-800-444-2910

Web: www.ohiou.edu/adultlearning/

E-mail: independent.study@ohio.edu

Programs: AA—Arts and Humanities, Social Sciences; Associate of Individualized Studies; AS—Sciences; Bachelor of Specialized Studies; MBA; individual courses

Individual course subjects: accounting, anthropology, aviation, biological sciences, business, business communications, business statistics, chemistry, communications, criminal justice, economics, English language, English literature, family and consumer sciences, finance, geography, health, history, human resource management, humanities, industrial operations, journalism, languages, law, management, management information systems, marketing, mathematics, music, philosophy, physical education, physical science, physics, political science, psychology, security services, social sciences, social services, sociology, sport sciences, study skills, theater, women's studies

Average tuition: $75 per quarter hour; MBA—$32,000

Length of program: self-paced; MBA—2 years

Technologies: audiocassette, computer disk, correspondence, Internet, video

Accreditation: NCACS

Watch Out!
Enrollment in an
individual course
does not constitute
admission to Ohio
University.

Entrance requirements: individual courses—none; AA/AS/bachelor's—high school diploma or the equivalent; MBA—bachelor's degree and support from your current employer

Restrictions: The MBA requires 3 one-week residencies and 3 weekend residencies.

Special services: academic advising

Oklahoma State University

Distance Learning
University Extension
Stillwater, OK 74078-6046
405-744-6700
Web: www.okstate.edu/outreach/distance/
Programs: MBA; Master of Political Science—Fire and Emergency Management; MS—Chemical Engineering, Computer Science, Electrical Engineering, Engineering and Technology Management, Environmental Sciences, Mechanical Engineering, Telecommunications Management; individual courses
Individual course subjects: accounting, animal sciences, anthropology, art, broadcasting, business, business communications, computer science, economics, education, electronics, engineering, English, environmental studies, finance, fire protection, French, geography, German, health, high school subjects, history, horticulture, human development, human resource management, journalism, management, management information systems, marketing, mathematics, nutrition, philosophy, political science, psychology, sociology, Spanish, statistics, technology, telecommunications
Average tuition: $70–$254.50 per credit hour
Length of program: up to 1 year per course; master's—$1^1/_2$–5 years
Technologies: audiocassette, correspondence, interactive TV, Internet, television, video
Accreditation: NCACS, ABET
Entrance requirements: individual courses—none; MBA—bachelor's degree and GMAT score; Master of Political Science—bachelor's degree in a fire and emergency management-related discipline or significant practical experience in a fire and emergency management career; MS in Engineering and Technology Management—bachelor's degree in engineering, mathematics, or the physical sciences with a 3.0 GPA and 3 years employment; MS in Environmental Studies—bachelor's degree with a 3.0 GPA and GRE score; MS in Telecommunications Management—bachelor's degree and GRE score of 1,610 or GMAT score of 510; other MS—bachelor's degree with a B average in the last 2 years of undergraduate studies and background experience in the field

Restrictions: master's programs (and interactive TV courses) are only available at participating companies or at participating public sites in Oklahoma.
Special services: academic advising; job placement services

Oral Roberts University

Adult Learning Service Center
7777 S. Lewis Ave.
Tulsa, OK 74171
1-888-900-4678
Web: www.oru.edu/university/departments/ALSCweb/htmlpages/
welcome-slle.htm
E-mail: alsc@oru.edu
Programs: BS—Business Administration, Christian Care and Counseling, Church Ministries, Elementary Christian School Education, Liberal Studies; MA—Education; MDiv; Master of Management; EdD
Length of program: 4 months per course
Technologies: correspondence, Internet
Accreditation: SACS, ATS
Entrance requirements: BS—high school diploma or GED; Master's—bachelor's degree; EdD—master's degree in education
Restrictions: Master's and EdD programs require several residencies.
Special services: academic advising

Oregon State University

Distance and Continuing Education
4943 The Valley Library
Corvallis, OR 97331-4504
1-800-235-6559
Web: osu.orst.edu/dept/osustate/
Programs: MS—Nutrition and Food Management; individual courses
Individual course subjects: agriculture, agriculture and resource economics, art, atmospheric sciences, business, economics, education, forestry, geosciences, history, mathematics, nutrition and food science, philosophy, political science, psychology, public health, range science, sociology, soil science, statistics, wildlife and fish science, women's studies, writing
Average tuition: individual courses—$125–$240 per credit; MS—$290 per quarter credit
Technologies: correspondence, interactive TV, Internet, teleconferencing, television, video
Accreditation: NASC, ADiA
Entrance requirements: individual courses—none; MS—bachelor's degree with a 3.0 GPA and Registered Dietitian license
Restrictions: Interactive TV courses are only available at Oregon locations.
Special services: academic advising

Unofficially...
In addition to the distance-learning programs profiled here, OSU offers a variety of undergraduate and graduate degrees throughout the state. Students must attend classes at a partner community college or state university to participate, however.

P

Pacific Oaks College

Office of Admissions
5 Westmoreland Place
Pasadena, CA 91103
1-800-684-0900
Web: www.pacificoaks.edu/programs/distance.html
Programs: Certificate/BA/MA—Human Development
Average tuition: $500 per semester unit
Length of program: 2+ years
Technologies: Internet
Accreditation: WASC
Entrance requirements: certificate—MA degree; BA—completion of 60 semester units of undergraduate coursework with a C grade average; MA—bachelor's degree
Restrictions: All students must take at least 2 classes on-site, in the form of 1-week intensive sessions, weekend classes, or summer sessions.
Special services: academic advising

Palm Beach Community College

Central Campus
4200 Congress Ave.
Lake Worth, FL 33461-4796
561-439-8114
Web: www.pbcc.cc.fl.us/dl/
Programs: AA—General Studies; individual courses
Individual course subjects: art history, astronomy, biological sciences, business, chemistry, computer science, creative writing, economics, education, English, geology, health, mathematics, political science, psychology, Spanish, statistics
Average tuition: $46.14 per semester hour (Florida residents); $170.49 per semester hour (out-of-state students)
Technologies: interactive TV, Internet, television, video, videoconferencing
Accreditation: SACS
Entrance requirements: high school diploma or GED
Restrictions: Students taking interactive TV classes must go to a local receive site. Some courses require on-campus meetings.
Special services: academic advising; career center; library services; virtual-learning assistants

Parkland College

Distance and Virtual Learning Department
2400 W. Bradley Ave.
Champaign, IL 61821
217-351-2542

Web: online.parkland.cc.il.us

E-mail: courseinfo@online.parkland.cc.il.us

Programs: AAS—Business Management; AA—Mass Communications/ Journalism, Mass Communications/Public Relations, Psychology; AGS; AS—Business Administration, Business Education; individual courses

Individual course subjects: agribusiness, anthropology, biology, business, chemistry, communications, computer information systems, computer science, economics, English, history, mathematics, music, nursing, office management, physical education, political science, psychology, sociology, speech

Average tuition: $49–$89 per credit hour (depending on residency)

Technologies: Internet, television

Accreditation: NCACS

Entrance requirements: high school diploma or the equivalent

Restrictions: Some courses may require a limited number of on-campus sessions.

Special services: registration advising; technical support

Pennsylvania State University

Department of Distance Education/World Campus

207 Mitchell Building

University Park, PA 16802-3601

1-800-252-3592

Web: www.outreach.psu.edu/DE/

E-mail: psude@cde.psu.edu

Programs: Certificate—Adult Development and Aging Services, Advanced Business Management, Basic Supervisory Leadership, Business Management, Chemical Dependency Counselor Education, Children Youth and Family Services, Customer Relationship Management, Dietetics and Aging, Educational Technology Integration, General Business, Geographic Information Systems, Human Resources, Legal Issues for Business Professionals, Legal Issues for Those Dealing with the Elderly, Logistics and Supply Chain Management, Marketing Management, Noise Control Engineering, Paralegal, Retail Management, Senior Retail Management, Small Business Management, Turfgrass Management, Writing Social Commentary; ABA; Associate of Dietetic Food Systems Management; Associate of Hotel, Restaurant, and Institutional Management; Associate of Human Development and Family Studies; Associate of Letters, Arts, and Sciences; MEd—Adult Education; individual courses

Individual course subjects: accounting, acoustics, African-American studies, African studies, agricultural economics, agronomy, American studies, animal sciences, anthropology, architectural design, architectural engineering, art, art history, astronomy, atmospheric sciences, biological sciences, biology, business, chemistry, civil engineering, classics, communications, comparative literature, computer science, counseling, criminal justice, dairy science, dietetics, earth sciences, economics, education, educational psychology, electrical engineering, engineering, English, entomology, finance, forestry, French, geography, geosciences, German, health, health services, history, horticulture, hospitality, human development, instructional design, kinesiology, labor studies, law, logistics, management, management information systems, marketing, mathematics, mechanical engineering, music, nuclear engineering, nursing, nutrition and food science, philosophy, physics, plant pathology, political science, poultry science, psychology, religion, sociology, Spanish, speech, statistics, theater, turf management, Web site development

Average tuition: Certificates in Chemical Dependency Counselor Education, Logistics and Supply Chain Management, and Turfgrass Management—$720 per course; Certificate in Geographic Information Systems—$595–$1,295 per course; Certificate in Educational Technology Integration and MEd—$798 per course; all other programs—$103–$240 per semester hour

Length of program: 6 weeks–8 months per course

Technologies: audiocassette, correspondence, Internet, teleconferencing, video, videoconferencing

Accreditation: MSACS, ADiA

Entrance requirements: individual courses/certificates/associate's—high school diploma or GED; Certificates in Chemical Dependency Counselor Education and Educational Technology Integration—also requires 60 credits of undergraduate coursework; Certificate in Noise Control Engineering—also requires a bachelor's degree in engineering, math, or science; Associate of Dietetic Food Systems Management and Associate of Hotel, Restaurant, and Institutional Management—also requires employment in a food/hospitality service facility; MEd—bachelor's degree and GRE or MAT score

Restrictions: none

Special services: academic advising; library services

Phoenix Special Programs and Academies

1717 W. Northern Ave.
Suite 104
Phoenix, AZ 85021-5469
1-800-426-4952
Web: www.phoenixacademies.org/main/dl/index.html
E-mail: e-mail@phoenixacademies.org
Programs: high school diploma; individual courses
Individual course subjects: high school subjects, K–12 subjects
Average tuition: $89–$350 per course
Length of program: 6–12 months per course
Technologies: correspondence, Internet
Accreditation: NCACS

Entrance requirements: completion of 7th grade

Restrictions: none

Special services: academic advising; helpline

Piedmont Technical College

Distance Learning

P.O. Box 1467

Greenwood, SC 29648-1467

864-941-8644

Web: www.piedmont.tec.sc.us/dl/

E-mail: koenig@ped.tec.sc.us

Programs: AA—General Studies; individual courses

Individual course subjects: art, astronomy, biological sciences, business, chemistry, criminal justice, economics, English, health services, history, management, mathematics, mortuary science, nursing, philosophy, political science, psychology, sociology, Spanish, speech

Average tuition: $51–$150 per credit hour (depending on residency)

Length of program: 17 weeks per course

Technologies: Internet, television, video

Accreditation: SACS

Entrance requirements: high school diploma or GED

Restrictions: Some courses can only be taken at specific locations.

Special services: academic advising; library support

Portland Community College

705 N. Killingsworth St.

Portland, OR 97217

503-977-4730

Web: www.distance.pcc.edu

E-mail: admissions@pcc.edu

Programs: Certificate—Medical Assisting; AAS—Management and Supervisory Development; AA—General Studies; AGS; individual courses

Individual course subjects: anthropology, biology, business, career development, computer information systems, computer science, construction, consumer studies, criminal justice, dental hygiene, economics, education, electronics, English, English as a second language, fire protection, GED, geography, health, health education, health information technology, history, humanities, management, mathematics, medical assisting, music, nursing, nutrition and food science, office technology, political science, psychology, radiologic science, real estate, science, small business management, sociology, Spanish, speech, veterinary technology, writing

Average tuition: $38–$140 per credit (depending on residency)

Length of program: 8–12 weeks per course

Technologies: interactive TV, Internet, television, video

Accreditation: NASC

Bright Idea
If you want to find
out what Internet
courses are like
before signing up,
take a multimedia
tour of an Internet
course at Portland
Community College's
Web site.

Entrance requirements: none

Restrictions: Some courses require on-campus meetings. Interactive TV courses can only be taken at selected campus and work sites in Oregon.

Special services: academic advising; career services center; online library services; women's resource center

Portland State University

Office of Independent Study

P.O. Box 1491

Portland, OR 97207-1491

1-800-547-8887, ext. 4865

Web: extended.pdx.edu/distance_frm.htm

E-mail: xsis@ses.pdx.edu

Programs: individual courses

Individual course subjects: art, atmospheric sciences, business, chemistry, criminal justice, economics, English, geography, geology, high school subjects, history, mathematics, nutrition, psychology, religion, sociology, statistics

Average tuition: high school—$100 per course; college—$75 per credit

Length of program: 12 months per course

Technologies: correspondence, Internet

Accreditation: NASC

Entrance requirements: none

Restrictions: none

Special services: disability services

Unofficially...
Portland State
University offers
several bachelor's
and master's degree
programs at various
sites around the
state. Check the Web
site or contact the
address listed to
find out if a degree
program is available
at a site near you.

Prairie Bible Institute

Box 4000

Three Hills

Alberta T0M 2N0

Canada

1-800-785-4226

Web: www.pbi.ab.ca

E-mail: DistanceEd@pbi.ab.ca

Programs: Certificate—Basic Bible, Basic Counseling, Bible, Christian Ministry, Missions, Theological Studies; AA—Religious Studies; Bachelor of Ministry; individual courses

Individual course subjects: biblical studies, counseling, history, ministry, missionary studies, theology

Average tuition: undergraduate—$119 (Canadian) per credit; graduate—$139 (Canadian) per credit

Length of program: 9–12 months per course

Technologies: correspondence

Accreditation: Canadian government, AABC

Entrance requirements: undergraduate courses/programs—high school diploma or the equivalent; graduate courses/programs—bachelor's degree

Restrictions: none

Special services: library services; local mentoring (bachelor's program)

Prescott College

Adult Degree Program

220 Grove Ave.

Prescott, AZ 86301

520-776-7116

Web: www.prescott.edu/adp/adp.html

E-mail: adpadmissions@prescott.edu

Programs: BA—Environmental Studies, Human Services, Management, Sustainable Community Development, Teacher Education/Certification

Average tuition: $205 per credit hour

Length of program: 12 weeks per course

Technologies: correspondence

Accreditation: NCACS

Entrance requirements: at least 30 semester credits of prior college-level coursework

Restrictions: Students must attend an orientation weekend and liberal arts seminar on campus.

Special services: academic advising; independent mentored studies; internships

Unofficially... Prescott College's distance-learning program enables students to individualize their degrees to meet specific career or personal goals. The program relies heavily on credit for life experience and independent study rather than a preset curriculum.

Professional Career Development Institute

430 Technology Pkwy.

Norcross, GA 30092

1-800-223-4542

Web: www.pcdi.com

Programs: high school diploma; Diploma—Animal Science, Auto Mechanics, Bookkeeping and Accounting, Bridal Consulting, Carpentry, Child Day Care, Computer Programming, Computer Repair, Conservation, Electrician, Electronics Specialist, Fashion Merchandising, Fitness, Floral Design, Gunsmithing, Home Inspection, Hotel/Restaurant Management, Interior Decorating, Landscape Design, Legal Transcription, Locksmithing, Medical and Dental Assisting, Medical Billing, Medical Transcription, Motorcycle Repair, Paralegal, Personal-Computer Training, Pharmacy Technician, Plumbing, Private Investigator, Property Management, Real Estate Appraisal, Small-Business Management, Tax Preparation, Teacher Assistant, Travel, VCR Repair, Writing Children's Literature

Length of program: 6–12 months

Technologies: audiocassette, correspondence

Accreditation: DETC, SACS (high school diploma program only)

Entrance requirements: Diplomas in Computer Programming and Computer Repair—1 year of computing experience; Diplomas in Private Investigator and Teacher Assistant—high school diploma; all other programs—none

Restrictions: none
Special services: none

Purdue University

The Office of Distance Learning
1137 Engineering Administration Building
Room 301
West Lafayette, IN 47907-1137
765-496-3337
Web: www.purdue.edu/DISTANCE/
E-mail: distlearn@evpaa.purdue.edu
Programs: MBA—Food and Agricultural Business; MS—Management; PhD—Educational Administration
Average tuition: MBA—$37,500; MS—$39,000
Length of program: MBA/MS—2 years; PhD—3 years
Technologies: computer conferencing, interactive TV, Internet
Accreditation: NCACS
Entrance requirements: MBA/MS—bachelor's degree with a 3.0 GPA, GMAT score in the 60th percentile, 5 years of work experience, and current position of significant responsibility; PhD—master's degree in educational administration
Restrictions: The MBA requires 4 residency sessions, including 1 international residency. The MS requires 6 residency sessions, including 1 international residency. The PhD requires attendance of on-site sessions.
Special services: technical support

R

Unofficially...
Distance courses may be combined with one of the seminary's extension programs in Memphis, Greensboro, Atlanta, Washington, DC, and other areas.

Reformed Theological Seminary

Virtual Campus
2101 Carmel Rd.
Charlotte, NC 28226
1-800-227-2013
Web: www.rts.edu/distance-education/
E-mail: distance.education@rts.edu
Programs: Certificate—Biblical Studies, General Studies, Historical Studies, Missions, Theological Studies; MA—Religion; individual courses
Individual course subjects: biblical studies, Christian studies, counseling, interdisciplinary studies, missionary studies, theology
Average tuition: $220 per credit hour
Length of program: 6 months per course
Technologies: audiocassette, correspondence, Internet
Accreditation: SACS, ATS
Entrance requirements: certificates—none; individual courses/MA—bachelor's degree

Restrictions: The MA requires 2 one-week, on-campus seminars.
Special services: academic advising; career advising; library services; local mentoring

Regent University
Distance Education
1000 Regent Dr.
Virginia Beach, VA 23464
757-226-4180
Web: www.regent.edu/distance/
E-mail: admissions@regent.edu
Programs: MA—Biblical Studies, Entertainment and Arts Management, Journalism, Political Management, Practical Theology, Public Policy; MBA; MEd; Master of Law—International Taxation; MPA; MA/PhD—Communication, Organizational Leadership
Average tuition: $340–$400 per semester credit hour
Length of program: MBA—32 months; master's and PhD—1–5 years
Technologies: audiocassette, correspondence, Internet, video
Accreditation: SACS, ABA, ATS
Entrance requirements: Master of Law—law degree; other master's—bachelor's degree with a 2.75 GPA; PhD in Communication—master's degree in communication or a closely related field with a 3.0 GPA and GRE score; PhD in Organizational Leadership—master's degree and 3 years of relevant professional experience
Restrictions: Most programs require short residencies.
Special services: academic advising; faculty mentors; library services; online study resources; personalized degree plans

Regents College
7 Columbia Circle
Albany, NY 12203-5159
1-888-647-2388
Web: www.regents.edu
E-mail: admissions@regents.edu
Programs: Certificate—Healthcare Informatics, Home Healthcare Nursing; AAS—Administrative/Management Studies, Aviation Studies, Technical Studies; AS—Business, Computer Software, Electronics Technology, Nuclear Technology; Associate of Occupational Studies—Aviation; AA/AS/BA/BS—Liberal Arts; BS—Accounting, Computer Information Systems, Computer Technology, Electronics Engineering Technology, Finance, General Business, International Business, Management Information Systems, Management of Human Resources, Marketing, Nuclear Engineering Technology, Operations Management; AAS/BS—Technology; MA—Liberal Studies; AAS/AS/MS—Nursing
Average tuition: certificates/MS—$300 per credit; AAS/Associate of Occupational Studies—$365 enrollment fee and $290 per year; AA/AS—

$685 enrollment fee and $325 per year; BA/BS—$800 enrollment fee and $350 per year; MA—$5,175

Length of program: Certificate in Healthcare Informatics—up to 5 years; Certificate in Home Healthcare Nursing—6 months; undergraduate programs—self-paced; MA/MS—up to 7 years

Technologies: correspondence, Internet

Accreditation: MSACS, ABET, NLN

Entrance requirements: Certificate in Healthcare Informatics—bachelor's degree in a healthcare discipline; Certificate in Home Healthcare Nursing—registered nurse license, cardiopulmonary resuscitation certification, and personal malpractice insurance coverage; AAS/AS in Nursing—completion of at least half of a nursing program, registered nurse license, or license in a medical field; other undergraduate programs—high school diploma or the equivalent; MA—bachelor's degree; MS—bachelor's degree in nursing, registered nurse license, and satisfactory GRE or MAT score

Restrictions: none

Special services: Electronic Peer Network; team advising; tuition payment plan

Rensselaer Polytechnic Institute

Professional and Distance Education

CII Suite 4011

110 8th St.

Troy, NY 12180-3590

518-276-7787

Web: www.pde.rpi.edu

E-mail: rsvp@rpi.edu

Programs: Certificate—Bioinformatics, Computer Graphics and Data Visualization, Computer Networks, Database Systems Design, Graphical User Interfaces, Human Computer Interaction, Management and Technology, Manufacturing Systems Engineering, Microelectronics Manufacturing Engineering, Microelectronics Technology and Design, Quality and Reliability, Service Systems, Software Engineering; MBA; Master of Engineering—Computer and Systems Engineering, Industrial and Management Engineering; Certificate/Master of Engineering—Mechanical Engineering; MS—Engineering Science, Information Technology, Management, Technical Communication; Certificate/MS—Computer Science; Master of Engineering/MS—Electric Power Engineering, Electrical Engineering; individual courses

Individual course subjects: biology, communications, computer science, engineering, engineering systems, management

Average tuition: $665 per credit

Length of program: certificates—1 year; master's—2–5 years

Technologies: Internet, television, videoconferencing, video

Accreditation: MSACS, ABET

Entrance requirements: MBA—bachelor's degree with a 3.0 QPA, GMAT score of 600, and technical background; certificates/Master of Engineering/MS—bachelor's degree in engineering, science, or related field with a 3.0 QPA

Restrictions: Television, videoconferencing, and video programs are only open to employees of participating corporations.

Special services: academic advising

Rhodec International

35 East St.
Brighton BN1 1HL
United Kingdom
+44 (0) 1273-327476
Web: www.rhodec.com
E-mail: contact@rhodec.com
Programs: Associate Diploma/Diploma/BA—Interior Design
Average tuition: associate diploma—325–495 pounds (depending on method of delivery); diploma—855 pounds
Length of program: associate diploma—1 year; diploma—2–3 years; BA—4 years
Technologies: correspondence, Internet
Accreditation: DETC
Entrance requirements: none
Restrictions: none
Special services: personal tutoring; tuition payment plan

Richard Milburn High School

WISE Internet High School
14416 Jefferson Davis Hwy.
Suite 8
Woodbridge, VA 22191
703-494-0147
Web: www.rmhs.org/page4.html
Programs: high school diploma; individual courses
Individual course subjects: high school subjects
Average tuition: $500 per course
Length of program: 4 weeks or more per course
Technologies: Internet
Accreditation: SACS, DETC
Entrance requirements: none
Restrictions: none
Special services: student counseling

Unofficially...
Richard Milburn High School can even award American high school diplomas to students living outside the United States.

Rio Salado College

2323 W. 14th St.
Tempe, AZ 85281
480-517-8000

Web: www.rio.maricopa.edu/distance_learning/
Programs: individual courses
Individual course subjects: accounting, anthropology, art, biology, business, chemical-dependency studies, communications, computer science, counseling, economics, education, English, geography, geology, health, history, human development, humanities, management, mathematics, medical terminology, nutrition and food science, office technology, philosophy, political science, psychology, quality management, sociology, Spanish, supermarket management, theater, water resources, waste management
Average tuition: $40–$65 per credit hour (depending on residency)
Length of program: 14 weeks per course
Technologies: audiocassette, CD-ROM, correspondence, Internet, teleconferencing, video
Accreditation: NCACS
Entrance requirements: none
Restrictions: Some courses require on-campus meetings.
Special services: academic advising; career counseling; disability services; library services; technical support; tutoring

Rochester Institute of Technology

Distance Learning
91 Lomb Memorial Dr.
Rochester, NY 14623
1-800-CALL-RIT
Web: www.distancelearning.rit.edu
E-mail: DISTED@rit.edu
Programs: Undergraduate Certificate—Basic Quality Management, Basic Technical Communication, Data Communications, Digital Imaging and Publishing, Emergency Management, Environmental Management Science, Industrial Environmental Management, Telecommunications Network Management, Voice Communications; Graduate Certificate—Health Systems Finance, Integrated Health Systems, Statistical Quality; BS—Applied Arts and Science, Electrical/Mechanical Engineering Technology, Environmental Management and Technology; MS—Applied Statistics, Cross-Disciplinary Professional Studies, Environmental Health and Safety Management, Information Technology, Software Development and Management; Undergraduate Certificate/MS—Health Systems Administration; individual courses
Individual course subjects: applied science, business, engineering, graphic design, liberal arts, science, technology
Average tuition: undergraduate—$249–$273 per credit hour; graduate—$546 per credit hour
Length of program: 11 weeks per course
Technologies: audiocassette, Internet, video
Accreditation: MSACS, ABET

Entrance requirements: individual courses/undergraduate certificates—none; health graduate certificates—bachelor's degree in a related field and 3 years of work experience; Certificate in Statistical Quality—bachelor's degree; BS—prior college-level coursework or associate's degree; MS in Cross-Disciplinary Professional Studies—bachelor's degree with a 3.0 GPA and 3 years of management experience; MS in Health Systems Administration—bachelor's degree with a 3.0 GPA and 3 years of experience in a health-related organization as either a clinician or manager; other MS—bachelor's degree with a 3.0 GPA

Restrictions: The BS in Electrical/Mechanical Engineering Technology requires some resident lab experience.

Special services: academic advising; disability services; library services; tuition payment plan

Roger Williams University

University College
Distance Program
One Old Ferry Rd.
Bristol, RI 02809-2921
401-254-3530
Web: www.rwu.edu/programs/uvc/distance.html
Programs: BS—Business Management, Criminal Justice, Industrial Technology, Public Administration
Technologies: audiocassette, correspondence, Internet, video
Accreditation: NEASC
Entrance requirements: high school diploma or GED and prior college coursework or creditable employment experience
Restrictions: Most students are required to meet with advisers and complete a variety of activities on campus (this requirement can be waived with the permission of a faculty adviser).
Special services: academic advising

Rogers State University

1701 W. Will Rogers Blvd.
Claremore, OK 74017
918-343-7548
Web: www.ruonline.edu
E-mail: online@rsu.edu
Programs: AA—Business Administration, Liberal Arts; AS—Computer Science; individual courses
Individual course subjects: accounting, business, computer science, economics, English, geography, history, mathematics, music, physics, political science, psychology, sociology, Spanish
Average tuition: $95.78 per credit hour (Oklahoma residents); $174.83 per credit hour (out-of-state students)

Money Saver
Rogers State University offers a scholarship to Oklahoma residents who enter the distance-learning program. To qualify, you must enroll in 12 credit hours and maintain a 2.5 GPA. Contact the admissions office for more information.

Length of program: 16 weeks per course
Technologies: Internet, video
Accreditation: NCACS
Entrance requirements: high school diploma or GED
Restrictions: none
Special services: academic advising; help desk

Rutgers University

SCILS
4 Huntington St.
New Brunswick, NJ 08903
732-932-7969
Web: www.rutgers.edu
E-mail: kvander@scils.rutgers.edu
Programs: Certificate—Communication Management, Youth Literature and Technology; individual courses
Individual course subjects: communications, library science
Average tuition: $267.60 per credit (New Jersey residents); $395 per credit (out-of-state students)
Length of program: Certificates—3 years
Technologies: Internet, video
Accreditation: MSACS, ALA
Entrance requirements: individual courses/Certificate in Communication Management—bachelor's or master's degree in any discipline; Certificate in Youth Literature and Technology—bachelor's or master's degree in librarianship, education, or a related field and experience in youth literature
Restrictions: Some courses may require on-campus meetings.
Special services: online library

S

Saint Joseph's College of Maine

Continuing and Professional Studies
278 Whites Bridge Rd.
Standish, ME 04084
1-800-343-5498
Web: www.sjcme.edu/cps/
E-mail: admiss@sjcme.edu
Programs: Certificate—American Studies, Christian Tradition, Graduate Healthcare Finance, Graduate Medical/Dental Administration, Healthcare, Home Schooling, Professional Studies, Project Management, Secondary Education, Women's Studies; AS—Management; BA—Criminal Justice, Education, Liberal Arts; BS—Healthcare Administration, Professional Arts, Radiologic Science, Respiratory Care; Certificate/BS—Business

Administration, Long-Term Care Administration; MA—Pastoral Studies; Master of Health Services Administration; MS—Nursing

Average tuition: Certificate in Project Management—$550 per course; certificates/AS/BA/BS—$190 per credit hour; graduate certificates/master's—$230 per credit hour

Technologies: correspondence, Internet

Accreditation: NEASC

Entrance requirements: Graduate, Home Schooling, and Secondary Education Certificates—bachelor's degree; BS in Radiologic Science—certificate or associate's degree in radiologic science and national certification; BS in Respiratory Care—certificate or associate's degree in respiratory therapy and registration with the National Board for Respiratory Care; other undergraduate degrees—high school diploma or the equivalent; MA—bachelor's degree; Master of Health Services Administration—bachelor's degree and 2 years of health-related experience; MS—bachelor's degree in nursing with a 3.0 GPA and 2 years of experience as a Registered Nurse

Restrictions: All degree programs require a 2-week summer residency.

Special services: academic advising; tuition payment plan

Saint Leo University

P.O. Box 6665
Saint Leo, FL 33544
1-800-404-7355
Web: www.saintleo.com
Programs: BA—Accounting, Business Administration; BS—Computer Information Systems
Length of program: 8 weeks per course
Technologies: Internet
Accreditation: SACS
Entrance requirements: previous college-level coursework or college credits earned through examinations or professional experience
Restrictions: none
Special services: none

Saint Louis University

School of Nursing
3525 Carolina
St. Louis, MO 63104-1099
314-577-8970
Web: www.slu.edu/colleges/NR/programs/online/
E-mail: ruchalpl@slu.edu
Programs: MS—Nursing
Length of program: 5 years
Technologies: Internet

Accreditation: NCACS, NLN

Entrance requirements: bachelor's degree in nursing with a 3.0 GPA, GRE score, registered nurse license, and 1 year of nursing practice experience

Restrictions: Requires 2 one-week residencies

Special services: none

Saint Mary-of-the-Woods College

Women's External Degree Program
Saint Mary-of-the-Woods, IN 47876-0068
1-800-926-SMWC
Web: www.smwc.edu/wed/wed.html
E-mail: ADM-SMWC@smwc.edu
Programs: AA—Early Childhood Education; AS—General Business; BA—English, Human Services, Journalism, Philosophy, Psychology, Teacher Education; Certificate/BA—Theology; Certificate/AA/BA—Gerontology, Paralegal Studies; AA/BA—Humanities; BS—Accounting, Business Administration, Human Resource Management, Marketing, Mathematics, Science; Certificate/BS—Computer Information Systems
Technologies: correspondence
Accreditation: NCACS, NCATE
Entrance requirements: high school diploma or GED
Restrictions: All programs are only open to women. Students must attend a $2^1/_2$-day orientation and spend 1 day on campus each semester. Education field experience and student teaching must be completed within 200 miles of the school.
Special services: academic advising

Salve Regina University

Graduate Extension Study
100 Ochre Point Ave.
Newport, RI 02840-4192
1-800-637-0002
Web: www.salve.edu/geshome.html
E-mail: frankel@salve.edu
Programs: MA—Human Development, International Relations; MBA; MS—Management
Average tuition: $350 per credit hour
Length of program: 5 years
Technologies: correspondence, Internet
Accreditation: NEASC
Entrance requirements: bachelor's degree and MAT, GRE, or GMAT score
Restrictions: All programs require an on-campus residency, which can be fulfilled through the 4-day Graduate Extension Study Institute.
Special services: one-on-one instruction

San Diego State University

College of Extended Studies
5250 Campanile Dr.
San Diego, CA 92182
619-594-5821
Web: www-rohan.sdsu.edu/~dl/
E-mail: extended.std@sdsu.edu
Programs: Certificate—Instructional Technology; Master of Rehabilitation Counseling; individual courses
Individual course subjects: accounting, biological sciences, education, exercise studies, history, life sciences, music, nutrition, social sciences
Average tuition: $250 per credit
Technologies: interactive TV, Internet, television
Accreditation: WASC, CORE
Entrance requirements: individual courses—none; certificate/master's—bachelor's degree with a 2.75 GPA in the last 60 semester units
Restrictions: Interactive TV and television courses are only available to local students.
Special services: none

San Jose State University

Continuing Education
Administration Building 103
One Washington Sq.
San Jose, CA 95192-0135
408-924-2670
Web: disted.sjsu.edu/menu/
E-mail: de@cE-mail.sjsu.edu
Programs: Certificate—Marketing Communications Management; individual courses
Individual course subjects: atmospheric sciences, business, communications, economics, education, educational technology, English, geography, mechanical engineering, nursing, occupational therapy, political sciences, psychology
Average tuition: $155 per unit
Length of program: individual courses—14 weeks per course; certificate—4–5 weeks per course
Technologies: Internet
Accreditation: WASC
Entrance requirements: none
Restrictions: Some courses may require on-campus meetings or field trips.
Special services: none

Schoolcraft College/Madonna University

OMNIBUS
18600 Haggerty Rd.
Livonia, MI 48152
734-462-4599
Web: www.schoolcraft.cc.mi.us
E-mail: omnibus@cca.munet.edu
Programs: AS—General Studies; BS—Business; MS—Business Administration
Length of program: 4 years
Technologies: audiocassette, Internet, television, video
Accreditation: NCACS
Entrance requirements: Contact the program directly.
Restrictions: Requires 5 on-campus visits.
Special services: none

Seminary Extension Independent Study Institute

901 Commerce St.
Suite 500
Nashville, TN 37203-3631
615-242-2453
Web: www.seminaryextension.com
E-mail: seminaryext@mindspring.com
Programs: Certificate—Biblical Backgrounds, Church Leadership, Pastoral Training; Diploma—Biblical Studies, Educational Ministries, Pastoral Ministries; individual courses
Individual course subjects: biblical studies, Christian studies, pastoral ministries, theology
Length of program: self-paced
Technologies: audiocassette, correspondence, Internet, video
Accreditation: DETC
Entrance requirements: individual courses/certificates—none; diplomas—high school diploma or the equivalent
Restrictions: none
Special services: none

Seton Hall University

Seton Worldwide
400 S. Orange Ave.
South Orange, NJ 07079
1-888-SETON-WW
Web: www.setonworldwide.net/
E-mail: setonworldwide@shu.edu
Programs: Certificate—Work-Life Ministry; MA—Counseling, Strategic Communication and Leadership; Master of Arts in Education—Catholic School Leadership, Educational Administration and Supervision, Human

Resources Training and Development, Law Enforcement Leadership; MEd—Higher Education; Master of Healthcare Administration

Average tuition: certificate—$10,200; master's—$24,500–$29,500

Length of program: master's—21–24 months

Technologies: Internet

Accreditation: MSACS

Entrance requirements: Master of Arts in Education—bachelor's degree with a 3.0 GPA, GRE or MAT score, and 5 years of related experience; Master of Healthcare Administration—bachelor's degree with a 3.0 GPA, GRE, GMAT or LSAT score, and 5 years of managerial-level experience; Certificate/MA/MEd—BA degree and GRE or MAT score

Restrictions: All programs require short residencies.

Special services: access to experts in the field; after-hours support; library services; mentoring; tuition payment plan

> **Money Saver**
> Significant scholarships are available for priests who enroll in the MA in Counseling program and for Catholic educators who work in New Jersey and who enroll in the Master of Arts in Education—Catholic School Leadership program.

Simon Fraser University

Centre for Distance Education

8888 University Dr.

Burnaby

British Columbia V5A 1S6

Canada

604-291-3524

Web: www.sfu.ca/cde/

E-mail: cde@sfu.ca

Programs: Certificate—Health and Fitness Studies, Liberal Arts, Literacy Instruction; BA—Criminology and Psychology; Certificate/Diploma/BA—Criminology; Bachelor of General Studies; individual courses

Individual course subjects: anthropology, archaeology, biological sciences, business, Canadian studies, communications, computer science, criminal justice, economics, education, English, French, geography, gerontology, history, humanities, Japanese, kinesiology, liberal arts, linguistics, mathematics, Native American studies, philosophy, political science, psychology, publishing, sociology, statistics, women's studies

Technologies: correspondence

Accreditation: Canadian government

Entrance requirements: individual courses/certificates/BA—high school diploma; diploma—bachelor's degree with a 2.4 GPA

Restrictions: none

Special services: academic advising

Sinclair Community College

Distance Learning Division

444 W. Third St.

Dayton, OH 45402-1460

1-888-226-2457

Web: www.sinclair.edu/distance/index.html

E-mail: distance@sinclair.edu

Programs: AA—Liberal Arts and Sciences; AS—Business Administration; individual courses

Individual course subjects: accounting, art, automotive mechanics, biology, business, chemistry, communications, computer information systems, dietetics, drafting, economics, electronics, English, health, history, Japanese, law, management, marketing, mathematics, music, office technology, physics, plastics, psychology, purchasing, sociology

Average tuition: $31–$83 per credit hour (depending on residency)

Length of program: 11 weeks per course

Technologies: audiocassette, CD-ROM, correspondence, interactive TV, Internet, video

Accreditation: NCACS

Entrance requirements: high school diploma or GED

Restrictions: Interactive TV courses must be taken at a participating off-campus site.

Special services: academic advising; disability services; library services; tutoring

Skidmore College

University Without Walls

Saratoga Springs, NY 12866-1632

518-580-5450

Web: www.skidmore.edu/administration/uww/Skidmore/index.html

E-mail: mmonigan@Skidmore.edu

Programs: BA/BS—Individualized Studies; MA—Liberal Studies

Average tuition: $4,500 annual enrollment fee; $550 per course taken through the school

Length of program: self-paced

Technologies: correspondence, Internet

Accreditation: MSACS

Entrance requirements: BA/BS—high school diploma; MA—bachelor's degree

Restrictions: BA/BS students are required to attend 3 on-campus meetings. MA students must attend 2 on-campus residencies.

Special services: academic advising; personalized degree plans

Southern Christian University

1200 Taylor Rd.

Montgomery, AL 36117

1-800-351-4040

Web: www.southernchristian.edu

E-mail: admissions@southernchristian.edu

Programs: MDiv; MS—Clinical Counseling, Pastoral Counseling; MS/ DMin—Marriage and Family Therapy, Ministry; BA/BS/MA/DMin— Biblical Studies
Average tuition: $315 per semester hour
Length of program: 16 weeks per course; graduate programs—3 years
Technologies: video
Accreditation: SACS
Entrance requirements: BA/BS—AA degree or the equivalent; MA/MS— bachelor's degree with a 2.0 GPA and GRE or MAT score; DMin—MDiv degree or the equivalent with a 3.0 cumulative GPA
Restrictions: DMin students must attend a 2-week seminar on campus.
Special services: academic advising; library services

Southwest Missouri State University
College of Continuing Education and the Extended University
901 S. National Ave.
Springfield, MO 85804
1-888-767-8444
Web: smsuonline.smsu.edu
E-mail: dlit@mail.smsu.edu
Programs: MS—Administrative Studies, Computer Information Systems; individual courses
Individual course subjects: accounting, communications, computer information systems, management, political science, psychology, religion
Average tuition: $101–$345 per credit hour
Length of program: 16 weeks per course; MS—2 years
Technologies: Internet
Accreditation: NCACS
Entrance requirements: individual courses—permission of the instructor; MS—bachelor's degree with a 2.75 GPA, combined GRE score of 1,300 (or the equivalent GMAT score), and 3 years of relevant work experience
Restrictions: The MS in Computer Information Systems requires some on-campus instruction time.
Special services: academic advising; help desk; library access; tuition payment plan

Southwestern Adventist University
Adult Degree Office
Keene, TX 76059
1-800-433-2240, ext. 204
Web: www.swau.edu/adp/
E-mail: mizherj@swau.edu
Programs: AS—Health Fitness, Office Technology; BA—Broadcasting, Business Administration, English, History, International Affairs, Music,

Religion, Theology; AS/BA—Computer Information Systems; BBA; BS—Broadcasting, Computer Science, Corporate Communication, Criminal Justice, Elementary Education, Management, Music, Office Systems Administration, Psychology; BA/BS—Journalism, Mathematics, Social Science

Average tuition: $299 per credit hour

Length of program: 6 months per course

Technologies: correspondence

Accreditation: SACS

Entrance requirements: high school diploma or GED, or associate's degree

Restrictions: All programs require an initial 6-day seminar.

Special services: none

Southwestern Assemblies of God University

School of Distance Education

3295 N. Hwy. 77

Waxahachie, TX 75165-5735

1-888-937-7248, ext. 2422

Web: www.sagu.edu/sde/

E-mail: info@sagu.edu

Programs: BA—Church Ministries, Education; BS—Business; MS—Practical Theology

Average tuition: $2,660 for 14–16 semester hours

Length of program: 3 months per course; MS—2 years

Technologies: audiocassette, Internet, video

Accreditation: SACS, AABC

Entrance requirements: BA/BS—high school diploma or GED; MS—bachelor's degree

Restrictions: An initial 2-day orientation seminar is required; students also have to return to campus at the beginning of each semester for registration and course opening seminars.

Special services: academic advising; library services; online chapel; tuition payment plan

Spertus Institute of Jewish Studies

618 S. Michigan Ave.

Chicago, IL 60605

1-888-322-1769

Web: www.spertus.edu/College/MJS/index.html

E-mail: college@spertus.edu

Programs: MS—Jewish Studies; Doctor of Jewish Studies

Average tuition: MS—$180 per quarter hour; doctor—$220 per quarter hour

Length of program: 1 year per course

Time Saver
Contact the school directly to learn about specific degrees you can earn through this program.

Strayer University

Strayer Online
1025 15th St. NW
Washington DC 20005
202-408-2400
Web: www.strayer.edu/online/frtr.htm
E-mail: jct@strayer.edu
Programs: AA—General Studies, Marketing; BS—Computer Networking, International Business; AA/BS—Accounting, Economics; Diploma/AA/BS—Computer Information Systems; MS—Information Systems, Professional Accounting; AA/BS/MS—Business Administration; individual courses
Individual course subjects: accounting, business, computer information systems, economics
Average tuition: individual courses/diploma/AA/BS—$200 per credit hour; MS—$260 per credit hour
Length of program: 11 weeks per course
Technologies: Internet
Accreditation: MSACS
Entrance requirements: individual courses/diploma/AA/BS—high school diploma or the equivalent; MS—bachelor's degree
Restrictions: none
Special services: academic advising; career development advising; online learning resources; technical support; tutoring

Suffolk University

Office of Graduate Admission
8 Ashburton Place
Boston, MA 02108-2770
617-573-8302
Web: www.suffolkemba.org
E-mail: admissions@SuffolkeMBA.org
Programs: MBA
Average tuition: $1,845 per course
Length of program: 14 weeks per course
Technologies: Internet
Accreditation: NEASC
Entrance requirements: bachelor's degree and GMAT score
Restrictions: none
Special services: academic advising; career services; electronic library databases; membership in MBA Association

Watch Out!
Students must successfully complete an online seminar prior to entering Strayer University's distance-learning program.

Syracuse University

Independent Study Degree Programs
700 University Ave.
Syracuse, NY 13244-2530
1-800-442-0501
Web: www.suce.syr.edu/DistanceEd/Index.html
E-mail: suisdp@uc.syr.edu
Programs: AA/BA—Liberal Studies; MA—Advertising Design and Illustration; MBA; MLS; MS—Communications Management, Engineering Management, Information Resources Management, Nursing, Telecommunications and Network Management; Master of Social Science; individual courses
Individual course subjects: architecture, engineering, English, fashion, geography, grant writing, information technology, management, philosophy, political science, psychology, sociology
Average tuition: undergraduate—$353 per credit; graduate—$583 per credit; noncredit—$249–$349 per course
Length of program: 16 weeks per course; degree programs—4–6 years
Technologies: correspondence, Internet
Accreditation: MSACS, ABET, ALA, NLN
Entrance requirements: individual courses—none; AA/BS—high school diploma; MBA/MLS/MS—bachelor's degree with a 3.0 GPA, sufficient GRE or GMAT score, and relevant professional experience
Restrictions: All degree programs require limited on-campus residencies.
Special services: academic advising; career services; tuition payment plan

T

Tarrant County College District

Distance Learning
TCC South Campus
5301 Campus Dr.
Fort Worth, TX 76119
817-515-4532
Web: dl.tccd.net/index.html
E-mail: info@dl.tccd.net
Programs: individual courses
Individual course subjects: accounting, anthropology, biology, business, computer science, criminal justice, economics, English, French, geology, health, history, management, mathematics, music, office administration, philosophy, physical education, political science, psychology, sociology, Spanish, speech, theater
Average tuition: $26–$140 per semester hour (depending on residency)
Technologies: Internet, television

Accreditation: SACS

Entrance requirements: high school diploma, GED, or individual approval

Restrictions: Many courses require 1 or more on-campus sessions. Students taking television courses must live within the broadcast area.

Special services: help desk

Taylor University

World Wide Campus

1025 W. Rudisill Blvd.

Fort Wayne, IN 46807-2197

1-800-845-3149

Web: wwcampus.tayloru.edu

E-mail: wwcampus@tayloru.edu

Programs: Certificate—Christian Worker, Justice and Ministry; AA—Biblical Studies, Justice Administration, Liberal Arts; individual courses

Individual course subjects: art, biblical languages, biblical studies, biological sciences, Christian studies, communications, criminal justice, education, English, ethnic studies, history, mathematics, missionary studies, pastoral ministries, philosophy, psychology, religious education, social sciences, theology

Average tuition: $119–$169 per credit hour

Length of program: 6–12 months per course

Technologies: correspondence, Internet

Accreditation: NCACS

Entrance requirements: individual courses/certificates—none; AA—high school diploma with a 2.5 GPA or GED composite score of 52

Restrictions: none

Special services: academic advising; career development; library support; learning support

Teikyo Post University

800 Country Club Rd.

P.O. Box 2540

Waterbury, CT 06723-2540

1-800-345-2562

Web: www.teikyopost.edu

E-mail: online@teikyopost.edu

Programs: Certificate—Child Development; BS—Integrated Business, Management Information Systems; AS/BS—Management; individual courses

Individual course subjects: biology, business, communications, criminal justice, economics, English, finance, history, legal assisting, management, management information systems, marketing, mathematics, political science, psychology, sociology

Average tuition: $870 per course

Bright Idea

Taylor University's Internet courses are offered in either an independent learning format, for students who work better on their own, or an online classroom format, for students who need a more structured format.

Technologies: Internet, teleconferencing, video, videoconferencing
Accreditation: NEASC
Entrance requirements: individual courses/AS/BS—high school diploma or the equivalent; certificate—employment at a childcare facility
Restrictions: Videoconferencing courses must be taken at a participating site.
Special services: academic advising; library resources

Tennessee Temple University

School of External Studies
1815 Union Ave.
Chattanooga, TN 37404
1-800-553-4050
Web: www.tntemple.edu/
E-mail: ttuinfo@temple.edu
Programs: AA/BS—Biblical Studies; individual courses
Individual course subjects: biblical languages, biblical studies, biology, Christian studies, English, history, humanities, languages, mathematics, missionary studies, pastoral ministries, philosophy, political science, psychology, religious education, social sciences, theology
Length of program: 120 days per course; AA—4 years; BS—8 years
Technologies: correspondence
Accreditation: AABC
Entrance requirements: high school diploma or the equivalent
Restrictions: none
Special services: none

Texas A&M University

Office of Distance Education
College Station, TX 77843-1478
409-845-4282
Web: www.tamu.edu/ode/
E-mail: distance-ed@tamu.edu
Programs: Master of Agriculture; MEd—Educational Technology; Master of Engineering—Petroleum Engineering; MS—Educational Human Resources Development, Engineering Systems Management; individual courses
Individual course subjects: agriculture, architecture, business, education, educational technology, geosciences, liberal arts, library science, life sciences, petroleum engineering, science, veterinary medicine
Average tuition: $272.92–$434.92 per credit hour (depending on residency)
Technologies: Internet, television, video, videoconferencing
Accreditation: SACS, ABET
Entrance requirements: individual courses—none; master's—bachelor's degree in engineering, science, computer science, mathematics, or business and 2 years of postundergraduate work or military experience

Restrictions: Videoconferencing courses, including all degree programs, must be taken at broadcast sites at locations throughout Texas.

Special services: library services; student counseling

Texas Tech University

Outreach and Extended Studies

Box 42191

Lubbock, TX 79413

1-800-MY-COURSE

Web: www.dce.ttu.edu

E-mail: distlearn@ttu.edu

Programs: high school diploma; Certificate—Effective Employee Supervision, Effective Human Resource Management, Medical Spanish for Healthcare Professionals; BBA—General Business; BGS; individual courses

Individual course subjects: accounting, agricultural economics, agriculture, anthropology, business, chemistry, childcare training, counseling, early childhood education, economics, education, educational psychology, educational technology, engineering, English, geography, high school subjects, history, hospitality, human development, K–12 subjects, languages, law, legal assistance, management, marketing, mass communications, mathematics, music, nutrition and food science, plant sciences, political science, psychology, real estate, social work, sociology, soil science

Average tuition: elementary school—$416 per semester; middle and high school—$79 per course; college—$63 per credit hour; continuing education—$40 per course; certificates—$585–$655

Length of program: 3–6 months per course

Technologies: correspondence, Internet

Accreditation: SACS

Entrance requirements: K–12—permission of a school administrator or parent/guardian (homeschooled students only); individual courses/certificates—none; BBA/BGS—30 hours of college credit with a cumulative GPA of 2.25

Restrictions: none

Special services: academic advising; online writing and learning center

Texas Woman's University

Office of Graduate Admission

P.O. Box 425649

Denton, TX 76204-5649

940-898-3073

Web: www.dl.twu.edu

E-mail: dl@twu.edu

Programs: MLS; MS—Speech/Language Pathology; individual courses

Individual course subjects: communication disorders, educational administration, English, health, library science, nursing, nutrition and food sciences,

Bright Idea
Homeschooled students can take a complete K–12 curriculum approved by the state of Texas through Texas Tech University's distance-learning program.

occupational therapy, performing arts, physical therapy, psychology, social work, sociology, women's studies

Average tuition: $77 per credit hour (Texas residents); $288 per hour (out-of-state students)

Technologies: Internet, videoconferencing

Accreditation: SACS, ALA, ASHA

Entrance requirements: individual courses—bachelor's degree with a B average; MLS—bachelor's degree with a B average and cumulative GRE score of 1,350; MS—bachelor's degree with a B average on the last 60 hours of undergraduate coursework, acceptable GRE score, and sponsorship by an educational entity

Restrictions: Master's programs and other videoconferencing courses are limited to participating sites in Texas.

Special services: academic advising; library services; online writing lab; technical support

Thomas Edison State College

101 W. State St.

Trenton, NJ 08608-1176

609-984-1150

Web: www.tesc.edu

E-mail: info@tesc.edu

Programs: Certificate—Computer-Aided Design, Electronics; AAS—Radiologic Services; AA—General Studies; BA—Anthropology, Art, Communications, English, Environmental Studies, Foreign Language, History, Humanities, Journalism, Liberal Studies, Music, Philosophy, Photography, Political Science, Religion, Social Sciences/History, Sociology, Theater Arts; AS—Civil and Construction Engineering Technology; BS—Advertising Management, Civil Engineering, Construction, Cytotechnology, Dental Hygiene, Economics, Gerontology, Health and Nutrition Counseling, Health Services, Health Services Administration, Health Services Education, Logistics, Medical Imaging, Mental Health and Rehabilitative Services, Natural Sciences/Mathematics, Nursing, Organizational Management, Perfusion Technology, Psychology, Social Services Administration; Certificate/BS—Labor Studies; AS/BS—Administration of Justice, Air Traffic Control, Architectural Design, Aviation Flight Technology, Aviation Maintenance Technology, Banking, Biology, Biomedical Electronics, Chemistry, Child Development Services, Clinical Laboratory Science, Community Services, Computer Science Technology, Electrical Technology, Electronics Engineering Technology, Emergency Disaster Management, Engineering Graphics, Environmental Sciences, Fire Protection Science, Forestry, General Management, Horticulture, Hospital Healthcare Administration, Hotel/Motel/Restaurant Management, Insurance, International Business, Laboratory Animal Science, Legal Services, Manufacturing Engineering Technology,

Marine Engineering Technology, Mathematics, Mechanical Engineering Technology, Nondestructive Testing Technology, Nuclear Engineering Technology, Nuclear Medicine Technology, Physics, Procurement, Purchasing and Materials Management, Radiation Protection, Radiation Therapy, Real Estate, Recreation Services, Respiratory Care, Retailing Management, Small Business Management/Entrepreneurship, Social Services, Social Services to Special Populations, Surveying, Transportation/ Distribution Management; Certificate/AS/BS—Accounting, Administrative Office Management, Computer Information Systems, Computer Science, Finance, Human Resources Management, Marketing, Operations Management, Public Administration; MS—Management

Average tuition: $585 annual enrollment fee (New Jersey residents); $1,040 annual enrollment fee (out-of-state students); additional fees vary depending on the methods used to complete degree requirements

Technologies: audiocassette, correspondence, Internet, television, video

Accreditation: MSACS, NLN

Entrance requirements: certificates/AAS/AA/AS/BA/BS—high school diploma or the equivalent; BS in Nursing—registered nurse license; MS— bachelor's degree, corporate or organizational sponsorship, and 5 years of supervisory experience

Restrictions: Students must be at least 21 years old. The BS in Nursing is only open to New Jersey residents. The MS requires 2 weekend residencies.

Special services: academic advising; mentoring

Tompkins Cortland Community College

170 N. St.

Dryden, NY 13053

1-888-567-8211

Web: www.sunytccc.edu/e-tc3/e-tc3.htm

E-mail: yavitsr@sunytccc.edu

Programs: Certificate—Basic Supervision, Materials Management; AAS— Chemical Dependency, Hotel and Restaurant Management, Paralegal; individual courses

Individual course subjects: accounting, business, computer science, English, health, hospitality, paralegal studies, psychology, sociology

Average tuition: certificate—$79–$129 per course; individual courses/ AAS—$98 per credit hour (New York residents) and $196 per credit hour (out-of-state students)

Length of program: 6–16 weeks per course

Technologies: Internet

Accreditation: MSACS

Entrance requirements: certificates—none; individual courses/AAS—high school diploma or the equivalent

Unofficially... Thomas Edison State University enables you to earn a degree by combining credit from testing, portfolios demonstrating knowledge, on-the-job and military training, previously earned licenses and certificates, and distance-learning courses.

Restrictions: none

Special services: academic advising; counseling and career services; learning assistance; library services

Touro University International

Unofficially...
Touro University International is an accredited branch campus of Touro College, located in New York.

10542 Calle Lee

Suite 102

Los Alamitos, CA 90720

714-816-0366

Web: www.tourouniversity.edu

E-mail: registration@tourouniversity.edu

Programs: MBA; BS/PhD—Business Administration

Average tuition: BS—$180 per semester credit; MBA—$312 per semester credit; PhD—$500 per semester credit

Length of program: BS—2 years; MBA/PhD—15 months

Technologies: Internet

Accreditation: MSACS

Entrance requirements: BS—60 semester credits of undergraduate liberal arts study with a 2.2 overall GPA; MBA—bachelor's degree with a 3.0 GPA on the last 60 semester hours; PhD—master's degree with a 3.2 GPA

Restrictions: none

Special services: academic advising; Cyber Library; technology support

Troy State University

Distance Learning Center

Third Floor

Wallace Hall

Troy, AL 36082

334-670-3976

Web: www.tsulearn.net

E-mail: tsulearn@trojan.troyst.edu

Programs: Bachelor of Applied Science—Resource Management; MPA; MS—Foundations of Education, Human Resources Management, International Relations

Average tuition: Bachelor of Applied Science—$170 per semester hour; MPA/MS—$250 per semester hour

Length of program: 8–16 weeks per course

Technologies: Internet, television, video

Accreditation: SACS, NCATE

Entrance requirements: Bachelor of Applied Science—high school diploma; MPA/MS—bachelor's degree with a 2.5 GPA and a GRE score of 850, MAT score of 33, or GMAT score of 450

Restrictions: none

Special services: none

Troy State University—Montgomery

External Degree Program
P.O. Drawer 4419
Montgomery, AL 36103
1-800-355-TSUM
Web: www.tsum.edu/DL/
E-mail: edp@tsum.edu
Programs: AS—General Education; BA/BS—Professional Studies; individual courses
Individual course subjects: accounting, art, biology, business, career development, communications, computer information systems, economics, English, finance, geography, history, law, management, marketing, mathematics, music, political science, psychology, quality management, religion, science, sociology, Spanish, speech
Average tuition: $61 per quarter hour (Alabama residents); $85 per quarter hour (out-of-state students)
Length of program: self-paced
Technologies: correspondence, Internet, television
Accreditation: SACS
Entrance requirements: high school diploma or GED
Restrictions: Television courses are only open to students living in the broadcast area and require a limited number of on-campus meetings. Alabama residents enrolling in a degree program must attend an on-campus orientation.
Special services: academic advising; personalized degree plans

Tulane University

School of Public Health and Tropical Medicine
Center for Applied Environmental Public Health
1430 Tulane Ave.
TW 43
New Orleans, LA 70112-2699
1-800-862-2122
Web: caeph.tulane.edu/mph_occupational_health.htm
E-mail: murphree@mailhost.tcs.tulane.edu
Programs: Master of Public Health—Occupational Health and Safety Management
Average tuition: $450 per credit hour
Length of program: 2 years
Technologies: Internet
Accreditation: SACS, CEPH
Entrance requirements: bachelor's degree with a 2.75 GPA and 40 semester hours in science, math, or engineering, and 3 years of experience in health and safety or occupational health programs
Restrictions: none
Special services: technical assistance

Unofficially...
With this program, you earn an associate's degree from Tulsa Community College and a bachelor's degree from Emporia State University. This program may require some meetings, including academic advising sessions, on Tulsa Community College's campus.

Tulsa Community College/Emporia State University

Office of Distance Learning
909 S. Boston Ave.
Tulsa, OK 74119-2095
1-888-822-2973
Web: www.tulsa.cc.ok.us/dl/
E-mail: jscott@tulsa.cc.ok.us
Programs: BGS; individual courses
Individual course subjects: accounting, art, Asian studies, biology, business, childcare training, computer information systems, computer science, economics, engineering, English, French, geography, geology, history, humanities, Italian, management, marketing, mathematics, music, occupational therapy, philosophy, political science, psychology, sociology, Spanish, speech
Average tuition: $32 per semester hour (Oklahoma residents); $101 per semester hour (out-of-state students)
Technologies: CD-ROM, interactive TV, Internet, television
Accreditation: NCACS
Entrance requirements: high school diploma or the equivalent
Restrictions: Some courses require on-campus meetings. Students taking television courses must live within the broadcast area. Interactive TV courses must be taken at one of the community college's campuses.
Special services: academic advising

U

Ulster County Community College

Stone Ridge, NY 12484
1-800-724-0833
Web: www.sunyulster.edu/distance/
E-mail: admissions@sunyulster.edu
Programs: AS—Individual Studies; individual courses
Individual course subjects: biology, business, communications, French, history, mathematics, psychology, sociology, Spanish
Average tuition: $89–$178 per credit hour (depending on residency)
Technologies: Internet, video
Accreditation: MSACS
Entrance requirements: high school diploma or the equivalent
Restrictions: none
Special services: academic advising

The Union Institute

Center for Distance Learning
440 E. McMillan St.
Cincinnati, OH 45206-1925
1-800-486-3116

Web: www.tui.edu/Programs/Undergrad/Distant.html
E-mail: dean-cdl@tui.edu
Programs: BA/BS—Individualized Majors
Average tuition: $262 per credit hour
Length of program: 16–20 months
Technologies: Internet
Accreditation: NCACS
Entrance requirements: evidence of ability to do college-level work and be a self-directed learner
Restrictions: requires a 4-day residential entrance colloquium and a 3-day residential seminar each semester.
Special services: academic advising; online academic research library; online conference and conversation center

United States Sports Academy
Student Services
One Academy Dr.
Daphne, AL 36526
334-626-3303
Web: WWW.sport.ussa.edu/programs/dl1.htm
Programs: Master of Sport Science—Sport Coaching, Sport Management, Sports Medicine and Fitness
Length of program: 15 weeks per course
Technologies: computer disk, correspondence, Internet
Accreditation: SACS
Entrance requirements: bachelor's degree with a 2.75 cumulative GPA and a GRE score of 800, MAT raw score of 27, or GMAT score of 400
Restrictions: none
Special services: library services

University College of Cape Breton
Distance Education
Extension and Community Affairs
P.O. Box 5300
Sydney
Nova Scotia B1P 6L2
Canada
1-888-959-9995
Web: www.uccb.ns.ca/distance/
E-mail: distance@uccb.ns.ca
Programs: Certificate—Canadian Institute of Management, Public Administration; Graduate Certificate—Educational Technology; Graduate Diploma—Education; BA—Community Studies; Bachelor of Technology—Environmental Studies; individual courses

Unofficially...
The Union Institute lets students design their own degree programs to meet their individual needs and goals. Through the school's distance-learning program, you can earn a degree in anthropology, business administration, communication, computer science, criminal justice, English, healthcare, marketing, psychology, social work, or many other areas of concentration.

Individual course subjects: business, economics, education, English, environmental engineering, political science, problem-centered studies, psychology, public administration

Length of program: 4–8 months per course

Technologies: audiographics, CD-ROM, correspondence, Internet

Accreditation: Canadian government

Entrance requirements: individual courses—letter of permission from your home institution; Bachelor of Technology—completion of a technology diploma in chemical, environmental, or civil engineering; all other programs—contact the school for entrance requirements

Restrictions: Some courses required for the Certificate in Public Administration and the Canadian Institute of Management are currently not available via distance learning.

Special services: career education and placement

Watch Out!
Enrollment in an individual course does not constitute admission to the University of Alabama.

University of Alabama

Distance Education

Box 870388

Tuscaloosa, AL 35487-0388

1-800-452-5971

Web: bama.disted.ua.edu

E-mail: disted@ccs.ua.edu

Programs: MS—Aerospace Engineering, Civil Engineering, Electrical Engineering, Engineering, Engineering Management, Environmental Engineering; BS/MS—Mechanical Engineering; individual courses

Individual course subjects: advertising, American studies, astronomy, biology, business, chemical engineering, classics, coaching, communications, computer science, counseling, criminal justice, economics, education, engineering, English, family and consumer sciences, film studies, finance, geography, German, health education, high school subjects, history, hospitality, human development, human environment, Japanese, journalism, law, library science, management, mass communications, materials science, mathematics, music, nursing, philosophy, physics, political science, psychology, public relations, rehabilitation services, religion, sociology, Spanish, statistics, telecommunications, theater

Average tuition: correspondence courses—$185–$355 per course; high school—$75 per course; undergraduate—$110 per semester hour; graduate—$165 per semester hour

Length of program: 6 weeks–1 year per course; BS/MS—6 years

Technologies: correspondence, interactive TV, Internet, video

Accreditation: SACS, ABET

Entrance requirements: high school courses—permission from the local high school; college courses/BS—high school diploma or GED; graduate school courses—bachelor's degree and permission of the department or program sponsoring the course; MS—bachelor's degree

Restrictions: Interactive TV courses must be taken at a participating site in Alabama. The BS is only open to residents of southeast Alabama. MS programs must be taking at a participating corporate or open site (contact the school about establishing a site).

Special services: academic advising (degree programs only); library services

University of Alaska—Fairbanks

Center for Distance Education
P.O. Box 756700
Fairbanks, AK 99775-6700
907-474-5353
Web: www.dist-ed.uaf.edu/default.html
E-mail: racde@uaf.edu
Programs: individual courses
Individual course subjects: anthropology, art, aviation science, biology, broadcasting, business, classical languages, computer information systems, computer science, drafting, economics, education, English, geography, Greek, health, history, journalism, languages, library science, linguistics, mathematics, music, Native American studies, philosophy, political science, psychology, sociology, statistics, theater, women's studies
Average tuition: $75–$167 per credit
Length of program: 3–12 months per course
Technologies: audiocassette, CD, CD-ROM, correspondence, Internet, video
Accreditation: NASC
Entrance requirements: none
Restrictions: none
Special services: none

Watch Out!
Enrollment in a distance-learning course does not constitute admission to the University of Alaska—Fairbanks.

University of Alaska—Southeast

Distance Education
11120 Glacier Hwy.
Juneau, AK 99801
1-800-478-9069
Web: www.jun.alaska.edu/uas/distance.html
E-mail: Distance.Ed@uas.alaska.edu
Programs: Certificate—Administrative Office Support, Computer Applications, Desktop Publishing and Graphics, Early Childhood Education, Elementary Education, Media Office Specialist, Networking Essentials, Web Publishing; AAS—Computer Information Office Systems, Environmental Technology, Health Information Management; AA—General Studies; AS—Child Development, Human Service Technology; BBA; Master of Early Childhood Education; MPA; individual courses
Individual course subjects: accounting, anthropology, art, biology, business, child development, communications, computer information systems, education, English, environmental studies, geography, geology, health information

administration, history, human development, law, mathematics, music, philosophy, political science, public administration, social work, sociology, statistics, technology, wildlife

Average tuition: $75–$300 per course

Length of program: 4–12 months per course; certificates—1 year; associate's/BBA—2 years; Master of Early Childhood Education—2–7 years; MPA—6 years

Technologies: audiocassette, computer software, correspondence, Internet, teleconferencing, television, video

Accreditation: NASC

Entrance requirements: college courses—none; graduate courses—bachelor's degree; certificates/associate's—high school diploma or GED; BBA—completion of general education prerequisites with a 2.0 GPA; Certificate/Master's in Early Childhood Education and Certificate in Elementary Education—bachelor's degree with a 2.5 GPA and support from the local school district; MPA—bachelor's degree with a 3.0 GPA

Restrictions: Most programs are not available outside Alaska. The Certificate and Master's in Early Childhood Education require 2 two-week summer residencies.

Special services: academic advising (degree programs); library services

University of Arizona

Extended University

888 N. Euclid Ave.

Tucson, AZ 85721

1-800-478-9508

Web: www.eu.arizona.edu/dist/

E-mail: distance@u.arizona.edu

Programs: MA—Information Resources and Library Science; individual courses

Individual course subjects: accounting, aerospace engineering, African-American studies, anthropology, art, Asian studies, astronomy, atmospheric sciences, automotive mechanics, cell biology, chemistry, civil engineering, college preparation, consumer studies, economics, education, electrical and computer engineering, engineering, English, English as a Second Language, entomology, environmental resources management, French, geography, geosciences, German, health education, history, industrial and systems engineering, library science, marketing, mathematics, mechanical engineering, museum studies, music, Native American studies, opticianry, pharmacology, physics, plant pathology, political science, psychology, quality engineering, real estate, Russian, Slavic languages, sociology, Spanish, writing

Average tuition: $115 per credit

Length of program: 3–9 months per course; MA—6 years

Technologies: audiocassette, correspondence, Internet, television, video

Accreditation: NCACS, ALA

Entrance requirements: individual courses—none; graduate courses—bachelor's degree; MA—bachelor's degree with a 3.0 GPA and competitive score on the GRE

Restrictions: The MA requires an on-campus residency.

Special services: none

University of Baltimore

1420 N. Charles St.

Baltimore, MD 21201

877-APPLY-UB

Web: ubonline.edu

E-mail: webinfo@ubmail.ubalt.edu

Programs: MBA

Average tuition: $264 per credit (Maryland residents); $393 per credit (out-of-state students)

Length of program: 2 years

Technologies: Internet

Accreditation: MSACS

Entrance requirements: bachelor's degree and GMAT score

Restrictions: none

Special services: career counseling; disability support services; Graduate Business Association; help desk; library services

University of California Extension

Center for Media and Independent Learning

2000 Center St.

Suite 400

Berkeley, CA 94704

510-642-4124

Web: www-cmil.unex.berkeley.edu/

Programs: Certificate—Business, Business Administration, Computer Information Systems, Hazardous Materials Management, Marketing, Project Management, Telecommunications Engineering; individual courses

Individual course subjects: accounting, anthropology, art, astronomy, biochemistry, biological sciences, biology, botany, chemistry, computer programming, computer science, economics, education, electronics, engineering, English, environmental studies, film studies, finance, genetics, geology, hazardous materials, health, health services, high school subjects, history, HIV/AIDS education, human resources management, information technology, interdisciplinary studies, international business, languages, law, library science, management, management information systems, marketing, mathematics, music, nutrition, pharmacology, philosophy, physics, political science, psychology, purchasing, radiologic science, real estate, religion, sociology, statistics, technical communication, telecommunications, writing

Unofficially...
University of
California Extension
is accredited
through the
University of
California—Berkeley.

Average tuition: $195–$595 per course

Length of program: 6–12 months per course

Technologies: America Online, correspondence, Internet

Accreditation: WASC

Entrance requirements: none

Restrictions: none

Special services: none

University of California—Los Angeles

UCLA Extension

P.O. Box 24901

Los Angeles, CA 90024-0901

310-825-9971

Web: www.onlinelearning.net

E-mail: learning@unex.ucla.edu

Programs: Certificate—College Counseling, Cross-Cultural Language and Academic Development (CLAD), General Business Studies, Online Teaching, Personal Financial Planning, Teaching English as a Foreign Language, Teaching English to Speakers of Other Languages, Technical Communication; individual courses

Individual course subjects: advertising, art, art history, broadcasting, business, communications, computer art, computer programming, computer science, creative writing, education, English, finance, graduate-school preparation, graphic design, history, international business, journalism, management, management information systems, marketing, mathematics, nonprofit management, philosophy, political science, public health, public relations, real estate, technical writing

Average tuition: $495–$575 per course

Length of program: 6–12 weeks per course; Certificates—up to 5 years

Technologies: Internet

Accreditation: WASC

Entrance requirements: none

Restrictions: none

Special services: technical support

University of Central Florida

Center for Distributed Learning

12424 Research Pkwy.

Suite 264

Orlando, FL 32826

407-207-4910

Web: pegasus.cc.ucf.edu/~distrib/studentinfo/home.html

E-mail: distrib@mail.ucf.edu

Programs: BS—Engineering Technology, Nursing, Vocational Education and Industry Training; BA/BS—Liberal Studies; individual courses

Individual course subjects: art, business, computer science, criminal justice, education, engineering, English, health, health services, international relations, management, nursing, paralegal studies, psychology, sociology
Average tuition: $73.40 per credit hour (Florida residents); $306.35 per credit hour (out-of-state students)
Technologies: interactive TV, Internet, video
Accreditation: SACS, ABET
Entrance requirements: high school diploma or GED
Restrictions: Some courses require on-campus meetings. Interactive TV courses must be taken at participating sites. The BS in Engineering Technology is restricted to designated centers throughout Florida.
Special services: none

University of Colorado—Boulder

Independent Learning Program
Division of Continuing Education
Campus Box 178
1505 University Ave.
Boulder, CO 80309-0178
1-800-331-2801
Web: www.Colorado.EDU/cewww/index.html
E-mail: cewww@colorado.edu
Programs: individual courses
Individual course subjects: anthropology, art, astronomy, business education, communication disorders, communications, computer science, economics, education, English, family and consumer science, geography, geology, health, high school subjects, history, journalism, kinesiology, mathematics, music, philosophy, political science, psychology, real estate, science, social sciences, sociology, study skills, writing
Average tuition: high school—$70 per course; college—$240–$400 per course
Length of program: 4–12 months per course
Technologies: correspondence, Internet
Accreditation: NCACS
Entrance requirements: high school courses—junior or senior in high school; college courses—none
Restrictions: none
Special services: academic advising; library services

University of Colorado—Denver

Graduate School of Public Affairs
Campus Box 142
P.O. Box 173364
Denver, CO 80217-3364
303-556-5970

Web: carbon.cudenver.edu/public/gspa/programs/c02.html
E-mail: pete.wolfe@cudenver.edu
Programs: MPA
Technologies: Internet
Accreditation: NCACS
Entrance requirements: bachelor's degree and GRE, GMAT, or LSAT score
Restrictions: Some electives must be taken in intensive format at a variety of locations around Colorado.
Special services: academic advising

University of Delaware
UD Online
210 John M. Clayton Hall
Newark, DE 19716-7410
1-800-UD-FOCUS
Web: www.udel.edu/ContEd/online.html
E-mail: continuing-ed@udel.edu
Programs: BS—Hotel Restaurant and Institutional Management, Nursing; individual courses
Individual course subjects: biological sciences, business, chemical engineering, chemistry, civil and environmental engineering, communications, comparative literature, consumer studies, dietetics, economics, education, electrical and computer engineering, engineering technology, English, health, history, hospitality, human development, human resource management, international relations, languages, mathematics, mechanical engineering, music, nursing, nutrition, operations research, philosophy, political science, sociology, statistics, urban studies
Average tuition: undergraduate—$177–$510 per credit hour (depending on residency); graduate—$236–$681 per credit hour (depending on residency)
Technologies: correspondence, interactive TV, Internet, video
Accreditation: MSACS, NLN
Entrance requirements: individual courses—none; BS—high school diploma or the equivalent; BS in Nursing—also requires registered nurse license
Restrictions: Interactive TV courses must be taken at selected sites throughout Delaware. The BS in Nursing requires 3 on-campus weekends.
Special services: academic advising; information technologies help center; library resources

University of Findlay
1000 N. Main St.
Findlay, OH 45840-3695
1-800-472-9502
Web: www.gcampus.org
Programs: BS—Business Management, Environmental Management; MBA
Average tuition: BS—$15,080 per year; MBA—$2,691 per semester

Technologies: Internet

Accreditation: NCACS

Entrance requirements: BS—at least 62 transferable undergraduate semester hours with a C- grade average; MBA—bachelor's degree and GMAT score

Restrictions: none

Special services: academic advising; counseling services; helpdesk; library resources; tuition payment plan

University of Florida

Florida Campus Direct

1012 Turlington Hall

Gainesville, FL 32611

352-392-3261

Web: www.fcd.ufl.edu

Programs: Certificate—Dietary Manager, Legal Assistant; BS—Electronic Engineering, Fire and Emergency Services; Master of Agriculture; MBA; Master of Health Administration; MS—Engineering; AuD; PharmD; individual courses

Individual course subjects: advertising, agriculture, anthropology, architecture, art, astronomy, business, chemistry, computer science, construction, criminal justice, economics, education, engineering, English, environmental resource management, environmental studies, fashion, geography, geology, German, health, high school subjects, history, human development, insurance, interdisciplinary studies, journalism, Latin American studies, liberal arts, library science, life sciences, linguistics, management, marketing, mass communications, mathematics, medicine, mental-health services, nursing, nutrition and food sciences, pharmacy, philosophy, physician assisting, political science, psychology, public administration, public relations, religion, social sciences, sociology, Spanish, special education, statistics, teaching English as a second language, waste management

Average tuition: high school—$110 per course; Dietary Manager Certificate—$310; Legal Assistant Certificate—$1,350; undergraduate—$71.38 per semester hour (Florida residents) and $304.33 per semester hour (out-of-state students); graduate—$144.20 per semester hour (Florida residents) and $504.93 per semester hour (out-of-state students); MBA—$29,500; AuD—$1,395 per course

Length of program: Legal Assistant Certificate/AuD—18 months; MBA—33 months; master's—24 months; PharmD—3 years

Technologies: correspondence, Internet, video, videoconferencing

Accreditation: SACS, ABET, ACEHSA, ACPE, ADiA, ASHA

Entrance requirements: high school courses—permission from a high school superintendent, principal, or counselor; individual courses—none; certificates—high school diploma or GED; BS in Engineering—high school diploma or GED with a C average in high school courses; BS in Fire and

Emergency Services—AA or the equivalent; master's—bachelor's degree with a 2.0 GPA on junior and senior undergraduate work and GRE or GMAT score; Master of Health Administration—bachelor's degree with a 3.0 GPA on junior and senior undergraduate work, GRE score of 1,000, and work experience; AuD/PharmD—contact the department directly

Restrictions: The MBA and Master of Health Administration require some on-campus sessions.

Special services: tuition payment plan

Watch Out!
Registration in an individual independent study course or certificate program does not constitute admission to the University of Georgia.

University of Georgia

Center for Continuing Education

1197 S. Lumpkin St.

Athens, GA 30602-3603

706-542-6741

Web: indy.gactr.uga.edu/dl.html

Programs: Certificate—Principles of Marketing Research, Principles of Turfgrass Management, Towing and Recovery; individual courses

Individual course subjects: accounting, agricultural economics, anthropology, art, astronomy, biology, classical languages, classics, counseling, economics, education, educational psychology, English, environmental studies, forestry, French, geography, geology, German, health education, history, horticulture, human development, journalism, management, marketing, mass communications, mathematics, nutrition and food science, philosophy, political science, psychology, recreation and leisure studies, religion, sociology, soil science, Spanish, speech, theater, veterinary medicine, women's studies

Average tuition: individual courses—$101 per semester hour; certificates—$249–$295

Length of program: 1 year per course/certificate

Technologies: correspondence, Internet

Accreditation: SACS

Entrance requirements: none

Restrictions: none

Special services: none

University of Hawaii

Distance Learning and Instructional Technology

2532 Correa Rd.

Bldg. 37

Honolulu, HI 96822

808-956-5023

Web: www.hawaii.edu/dl/

Programs: Certificate—Telecommunication and Information Resource Management; Diploma—Education; BA—Business Administration; MBA; MS—Nursing

University of Illinois—Chicago

University of Illinois Online
363 Henry Administration Bldg.
506 S. Wright St.
MC 353
Urbana, IL 61801
217-244-6465
Web: www.online.uillinois.edu
E-mail: uiol-info@uillinois.edu
Programs: Certificate—Advanced Practice Nurse, Designing and Implementing an Anticoagulation Clinic, Health Information Management, School Nurse; Master of Health Professions Education; PharmD
Average tuition: certificates/master's—$313–$5,294 per semester (depending on residency and the number of semester hours taken); PharmD—$638–$6,827 per semester (depending on residency and the number of semester hours taken)
Technologies: Internet
Accreditation: NCACS, ACPE
Entrance requirements: Advanced Practice Nurse and School Nurse certificates—bachelor's degree in nursing with a 4.0 GPA and license to practice as a professional nurse; Certificate in Health Information Management—master's degree; Master of Health Professions Education—bachelor's or advanced degree in a health professions discipline with a 3.75 GPA; Pharmacy Certificate and PharmD—bachelor's degree in pharmacy and valid pharmacy license
Restrictions: All programs are restricted to residents of Illinois. The Certificate in Health Information Management requires some on-campus meetings. The Master of Health Professions Education requires attendance at an annual on-campus conference. The PharmD requires a full-time, on-campus, 30-week commitment.
Special services: technical support

University of Illinois—Springfield

University of Illinois Online
363 Henry Administration Bldg.
506 S. Wright St.
MC 353
Urbana, IL 61801
217-244-6465
Web: http://www.online.uillinois.edu/
E-mail: uiol-info@uillinois.edu
Programs: BA—Liberal Studies; MS—Management Information Systems
Average tuition: BA—$93 per credit hour; MS—$104.50 per credit hour
Length of program: 16 weeks per course

Watch Out!
If you're concerned about your computer skills, you can enroll in a class called "Communicating Through the Internet" before entering the BA program. The course will count toward your degree completion as well as teach you how to maneuver on the Internet.

Technologies: Internet

Accreditation: NCACS

Entrance requirements: BA—AA or minimum of 45 lower-division college credits with a 2.0 GPA; MS—bachelor's degree with a 2.5 GPA and GRE or GMAT score

Restrictions: All programs are restricted to residents of Illinois.

Special services: academic advising

University of Illinois—Urbana-Champaign

University of Illinois Online

363 Henry Administration Bldg.

506 S. Wright St.

MC 353

Urbana, IL 61801

217-244-6465

Web: www.online.uillinois.edu

E-mail: uiol-info@uillinois.edu

Programs: Master of Computer Science; MEd—Curriculum Technology and Education Reform, Vocational and Technical Education; MS— Electrical Engineering, Library and Information Science, Theoretical and Applied Mechanics

Average tuition: $840 per course; MS in Library and Information Science— $6,120–$18,531 (depending on residency and how long it takes to complete the program)

Length of program: 2–3 years

Technologies: Internet, video

Accreditation: NCACS, ABET, ALA

Entrance requirements: MEd in Curriculum Technology and Education Reform—bachelor's degree and support from the school where the applicant is employed; MEd in Vocational and Technical Education—bachelor's degree with a 3.0 GPA on the last 60 hours of undergraduate coursework; other master's—bachelor's degree with a 3.0 GPA and GRE score

Restrictions: All programs are restricted to residents of Illinois. The MS in Library and Information Science requires several short on-campus residencies.

Special services: free access to electronic databases

University of Iowa

Division of Continuing Education

Center for Credit Programs

116 International Center

Iowa City, IA 52242-1802

1-800-272-6430

Web: www.uiowa.edu/~ccp/bls/blstxt.html

E-mail: credit-programs@uiowa.edu

Programs: Bachelor of Liberal Studies; individual courses

Individual course subjects: African-American studies, African studies, American studies, anthropology, art, art history, Asian languages, calligraphy, classics, communications, dance, economics, English, French, geography, German, gerontology, history, Italian, journalism, leisure studies, linguistics, mass communications, mathematics, Native American studies, physical education, political science, Portuguese, psychology, religion, social work, sociology, Spanish, speech, sports science, statistics, theater, women's studies, world studies

Average tuition: $88–$117 per semester hour

Length of program: up to 9 months per course

Technologies: correspondence, interactive TV, Internet, television

Accreditation: NCACS

Entrance requirements: individual courses—none; bachelor's—AA from an Iowa community college with a 2.0 GPA, or 62 semester hours of transferable college coursework with a 2.25 GPA

Restrictions: none

Special services: academic advising

University of London

The External Programme
The Information Centre
Senate House
Malet St.
London WC1E 7HU
United Kingdom
0171-862-8360
Web: www.lon.ac.uk/external/
E-mail: enquiries@external.lon.ac.uk
Programs: Diploma—Theology; Advanced Diploma—Education; BA— French, German, Italian, Jewish History, Spanish and Latin American Studies, Philosophy; Diploma/BA—English; Bachelor of Divinity; Bachelor of Laws; Bachelor of Music; BS—Accounting and Finance, Banking and Finance, Economics and Management, Information Systems and Management, Management, Management with Law, Mathematics Computing and Statistics; Diploma/BS—Computing and Information Systems, Economics; BA/MA—Geography; Postgraduate Diploma—Dental Diagnostic and Radiology, Environmental Assessment; Postgraduate Diploma/MA—Distance Education; MBA; Master of Clinical Dentistry; MS—Community Dental Practice, Dental Public Health, Dental Radiology, Development Finance, Financial Economics, Financial Management, Materials Science and Engineering, Occupational Psychology; Postgraduate Diploma/MS—Agricultural Development, Agricultural Economics, Applied Environmental Economics, Drugs and Alcohol Policy and Intervention, Economic Principles, Environment and Development, Environmental Management, Epidemiology, Food Industry and

Unofficially...
You can fulfill the requirements for this degree entirely through distance learning or by combining distance-learning courses with Saturday and evening classes or classes taken at other institutions.

Management, Health Systems Management, Infectious Diseases, Livestock Health and Production, Managing Rural Change, Organizational Behavior, Public Policy and Management, Sustainable Agriculture and Rural Development

Length of program: diplomas—2–5 years; bachelor's—3–8 years; master's—2–5 years

Technologies: correspondence, Internet

Accreditation: United Kingdom government

Entrance requirements: Contact the school for specific entrance requirements.

Restrictions: Students must be at least 17 years old. Computing, economics, and law programs require taking courses at an institution approved by the University of London. Except for the MS in Dental Public Health, all dental programs require taking an intensive course in the UK each year.

Special services: none

University of Maine

Division of Lifelong Learning
110 Chadbourne Hall
Orono, ME 04469
207-581-3143
Web: www.ume.maine.edu/ced/de/
Programs: Certificate—Child and Family Services, Classical Studies, Maine Studies; Bachelor of University Studies; MA—Liberal Studies
Technologies: Internet, video
Accreditation: NEASC
Entrance requirements: certificates/bachelor's—high school diploma or the equivalent; MA—bachelor's degree and GRE score
Restrictions: The Bachelor of University Studies may require taking some on-campus courses.
Special services: none

University of Manitoba

Distance Education Program
188 Continuing Education Complex
Winnipeg
Manitoba R3T 2N2
Canada
1-888-216-7011
Web: www.umanitoba.ca/faculties/con_ed/de/index.html
E-mail: stusvcs_ced@umanitoba.ca
Programs: Certificate—Curriculum and Instruction, Educational Administration and Foundations, Educational Psychology; BA—Canadian Studies, History, Political Studies, Psychology, Sociology; Bachelor of Nursing; Bachelor of Social Work; individual courses

Individual course subjects: anthropology, biology, classics, computer science, economics, education, English, French, geography, geology, history, interdisciplinary courses, mathematics, microbiology, Native American studies, nursing, philosophy, political science, psychology, recreation, religion, social work, sociology, statistics

Average tuition: $360.50–$721.00 (Canadian) per course

Length of program: 4–8 months per course; certificate—up to 9 years; bachelor's—2–7 years

Technologies: audiocassette, correspondence, Internet, teleconferencing, video

Accreditation: Canadian government

Entrance requirements: certificates—Bachelor of Education with a 2.0 GPA and a General Certificate, Limited Certificate, or Clinician's Certificate granted by Manitoba Education and Training (or the equivalent); individual courses/bachelor's—high school diploma or the equivalent; Bachelor of Nursing—also requires registered nurse license; Bachelor of Social Work—also requires 2 years of work experience in the social services

Restrictions: none

Special services: library services; one-on-one instructional support

University of Maryland—University College

University Blvd. at Delphi Rd.
College Park, MD 20742
301-985-7000
Web: www.umuc.edu/distance/index.html
E-mail: umucinfo@info.umuc.edu
Programs: BA—English, Humanities; BA/BS—Accounting, Behavioral and Social Sciences, Business and Management, Communication Studies, Computer and Information Science, Computer Studies, Fire Science, Information Systems, Management Studies, Paralegal Studies, Psychology; MBA; Master of Distance Education; Master of International Management; MS—Computer Systems Management, Technology Management, Telecommunications Management; BS/MS—Environmental Management, Management; Master of Software Engineering; individual courses

Individual course subjects: biology, computer science, economics, health services, history, journalism, mathematics, science, Spanish, speech, study skills

Average tuition: individual courses/BA/BS—$184 per semester hour (Maryland residents) and $236 per semester hour (out-of-state students); MBA—$20,250; Master of International Management—$5,900 per seminar; MS in Management/Technology Management—$4,950 per seminar; Master of Software Engineering—$272-$415 per course; other master's—$281 per semester hour (Maryland residents) and $382 per semester hour (out-of-state students)

Length of program: MBA—2 years; master's—2$^1/_2$ years or more

Watch Out!
The selection of majors for the BA is limited and may vary from year to year at the University of Manitoba. Contact the school directly for information on current programs.

Technologies: Internet, voice-mail conferencing

Accreditation: MSACS

Entrance requirements: individual courses/BA/BS—high school diploma or the equivalent; MS in Environmental Management—bachelor's degree in social science, physical science, biological science, or engineering and 1 year of experience in an environmental field; MS in Technology Management—bachelor's degree in social science, biological science, physical science or engineering, 5 years of management experience, and a current position as a mid- or senior-level manager; other master's—bachelor's degree with a 3.0 GPA; Master of International Management/MS in Management—also requires 5 years of managerial experience and a current position as a mid- or senior-level manager

Restrictions: none

Special services: academic advising; career planning; disabled student services; library assistance; resource teams (undergraduate only); technical assistance; tutoring

Bright Idea
The University of Massachusetts at Lowell's Web site has several free tutorials that will teach you how to navigate the Internet and take online courses. Be sure to complete the tutorials before signing up for a class.

University of Massachusetts—Lowell

Continuing Studies and Corporate Education

One University Ave.

Lowell, MA 01854

978-934-2467

Web: cybered.uml.edu

E-mail: cybered@uml.edu

Programs: Certificate—Fundamentals of Information Technology, Intranet Development, Online Communications Skills, Plastics Technology, UNIX; AS/BS—Information Systems; individual courses

Individual course subjects: computer science, criminal justice, economics, management, management information systems, mathematics, psychology, sociology, statistics, writing

Average tuition: $650 per course

Length of program: 14 weeks per course; AS/BS—4 years

Technologies: Internet

Accreditation: NEASC

Entrance requirements: individual courses/certificates—none; AS/BS—high school diploma or the equivalent

Restrictions: none

Special services: academic advising; technical support

University of Minnesota—Twin Cities

Distance Education

101 Wesbrook Hall

77 Pleasant St. SE

Minneapolis, MN 55455

1-800-234-6564

Web: www.cee.umn.edu/idl/

E-mail: indstudy@tc.umn.edu

Programs: Certificate—Liberal Arts, Science and Quantitative Methods; individual courses

Individual course subjects: accounting, African-American studies, agronomy, American studies, anthropology, art history, biology, business, cell biology, child development, classical languages, classics, computer science, creative writing, economics, educational psychology, English, English literature, environmental studies, finance, French, genetics, geography, geology, geosciences, German, history, humanities, journalism, management, marketing, mass communications, mathematics, mechanical engineering, music, Native American studies, nursing, nutrition and food science, philosophy, physical therapy, physics, political science, psychology, public health, rehabilitation services, Russian, Scandinavian languages, social sciences, social work, Spanish, speech, statistics, technical writing, theater, women's studies

Average tuition: $154.50 per credit

Length of program: 10 weeks–9 months per course

Technologies: audiocassette, CD-ROM, computer software, correspondence, Internet, video

Accreditation: NCACS

Entrance requirements: individual courses—none; certificates—completion of 12 college credits with a 2.2 GPA

Restrictions: none

Special services: academic advising; career services; disability services; library services

University of Missouri

Center for Distance and Independent Study

136 Clark Hall

Columbia, MO 652110-4200

1-800-609-3727

Web: cdis.missouri.edu

E-mail: cdis@missouri.edu

Programs: high school diploma; individual courses

Individual course subjects: accounting, African-American studies, animal sciences, anthropology, astronomy, atmospheric sciences, biological and agricultural engineering, biological sciences, classics, communications, computer science, economics, education, engineering, English, entomology, family and consumer sciences, geography, geology, German, health services, high school subjects, history, human development, K–12 subjects, languages, management, marketing, mathematics, military science, pest management, philosophy, physics, plant pathology, plant sciences, political science, psychology, recreation and park resources, Russian, social services, sociology, statistics, women's studies

☀ **Bright Idea**
The University of Missouri's accredited high school curriculum is a good choice for homeschooled students, students outside the U.S., and adult students who dropped out of high school.

Average tuition: elementary—$65 per part; high school—$90 per course; college—$132.60 per credit hour; graduate—$167.80 per credit hour
Length of program: 1–9 months per course
Technologies: correspondence, Internet
Accreditation: NCACS
Entrance requirements: none
Restrictions: none
Special services: academic advising (high school diploma program)

University of Montana

External Pharm. D. Program
Continuing Education
Missoula, MT 59812
406-243-6431
Web: www.umt.edu/ccesp/distance/pharmd/
E-mail: acobb@selway.umt.edu
Programs: PharmD
Average tuition: $187.45 per credit
Technologies: Internet, video
Accreditation: NASC, ACPE
Entrance requirements: bachelor's degree in pharmacy and eligibility for licensure to practice pharmacy in Montana
Restrictions: requires a 1-day meeting on campus each semester
Special services: academic advising; online library access

University of Nebraska—Lincoln

Department of Distance Education
Room 255
Clifford Hardin Nebraska Center for Continuing Education
33rd and Holdrege
Lincoln, NE 68583-9100
402-472-4321
Web: www.unl.edu/conted/disted/index.html
E-mail: unldde1@unl.edu
Programs: high school diploma; Certificate—Educational Technology; individual courses
Individual course subjects: accounting, adult education, agricultural economics, art, art history, astronomy, biological sciences, broadcasting, business, classics, dietetics, economics, English, family and consumer sciences, finance, geography, health, high school subjects, history, industrial and systems engineering, instructional design, journalism, management, marketing, mathematics, nursing, nutrition, philosophy, physics, political science, psychology, real estate, sociology, statistics
Average tuition: high school—$94 per course; undergraduate—$82.75 per credit; graduate—$109.50 per credit
Length of program: 5 weeks–1 year per course

Technologies: audiocassette, correspondence, Internet, video
Accreditation: NCACS
Entrance requirements: none
Restrictions: none
Special services: academic advising

University of Nevada—Reno

Independent Study by Correspondence
Division of Continuing Education
P.O. Box 14429
Reno, NV 89507
1-800-233-8928 ext. 4652
Web: www.dce.unr.edu/istudy/
E-mail: Istudy@scs.unr.edu
Programs: individual courses
Individual course subjects: accounting, anthropology, criminal justice, economics, education, educational administration, English, environmental studies, French, gaming management, geography, German, health, health services, high school subjects, history, hospitality, instructional design, Italian, journalism, management, mathematics, music, nutrition, political science, psychology, sociology, Spanish, Western European studies, women's studies
Average tuition: high school—$70 per course; undergraduate—$77 per credit; graduate—$99 per credit
Length of program: 4 weeks–1 year per course
Technologies: audiocassette, correspondence, Internet, video
Accreditation: NASC
Entrance requirements: none
Restrictions: none
Special services: academic counseling; on-campus library and computer lab privileges; tutoring

Watch Out!
Enrolling in an individual course does not constitute admission to the University of Nevada.

University of North Carolina—Chapel Hill

Division of Continuing Education
CB# 1020 The Friday Center
Chapel Hill, NC 27599-1020
1-800-862-5669
Web: www.fridaycenter.unc.edu
E-mail: pubpro@unc.edu
Programs: individual courses
Individual course subjects: accounting, African-American studies, African studies, anthropology, art, atmospheric sciences, biology, business, chemistry, classical languages, classics, communications, computer science, earth sciences, economics, education, English, environmental studies, French, geography, health services, history, hospitality, interdisciplinary studies, Italian, journalism, library sciences, marine sciences, mass communications,

Watch Out!
Taking an individual course does not constitute enrollment at any University of North Carolina institution.

mathematics, music, nursing, nutrition, philosophy, physics, political science, psychology, recreation and leisure studies, religion, sociology, Spanish, statistics, theater

Average tuition: $49–$147 per credit hour (North Carolina residents); $83–$390 per credit hour (out-of-state students)

Length of program: 17 weeks–9 months per course

Technologies: audiocassette, CD, correspondence, Internet, video

Accreditation: SACS

Entrance requirements: none

Restrictions: none

Special services: academic advising

Unofficially...
Participating companies in the distance-learning BS in Engineering programs include 3M, Hewlett-Packard, Lucent Technologies, Whirlpool, Polaris, and 30 others.

University of North Dakota

Continuing Education

P.O. Box 9021

Grand Forks, ND 58202-9021

1-800-342-8230

Web: www.und.edu

E-mail: linda_kilichowski@mail.und.nodak.edu

Programs: BS—Chemical Engineering, Electrical Engineering, Mechanical Engineering; MS—Space Studies; individual courses

Individual course subjects: accounting, anthropology, art, atmospheric sciences, business education, chemical engineering, dietetics, economics, English, French, geography, geology, history, humanities, management, mathematics, music, nutrition, occupational therapy, philosophy, psychology, real estate, religion, Scandinavian languages, sociology, Spanish, vocational education

Average tuition: individual courses/BS—$125–$395 per class; MS—$112.08–$299.25 per credit (depending on residency)

Technologies: correspondence, Internet, video

Accreditation: NCACS, ABET

Entrance requirements: individual courses—none; BS—high school diploma ranked in the top half of the graduating class or completion of 24 semester credits with a 2.0 GPA; MS—bachelor's degree in engineering, science, business, social science, communication or information systems with a 2.75 GPA, or 4 years of work experience in space-related activities

Restrictions: The BS is only open to employees of participating companies in the U.S. and Canada and requires on-campus summer labs.

Special services: academic advising

University of North Texas

Center for Studies in Aging

Department of Applied Gerontology

P.O. Box 310919

Denton, TX 76203-0919

940-565-3449

Web: www.unt.edu/aging/programs/dislearn.htm

E-mail: phyllis@scs.cmm.unt.edu

Programs: Certificate—Aging; MS—Administration of Aging Organizations, Administration of Long-Term Care and Retirement Facilities, Applied Gerontology

Average tuition: $425 per course (Texas residents); $1,050 per course (out-of-state students)

Length of program: 3 years

Technologies: Internet, video

Accreditation: SACS

Entrance requirements: certificate—bachelor's degree with a 2.8 GPA; master's—also requires a GRE score of 800

Restrictions: none

Special services: none

University of Northern Iowa

Continuing Education Credit Programs

132 SHC

Cedar Falls, IA 50614-0223

1-800-648-3864

Web: www.uni.edu/contined/cp/distance.html

E-mail: contined@uni.edu

Programs: Certificate—Superintendency; Bachelor of Liberal Studies; MA—Communication Education, Educational Technology, English, Library Science, Mathematics for the Middle Grades, Public Relations; Master of Arts in Education—Elementary Reading and Language Arts, Middle School Education, Principalship, Special Education-Inclusion; Master of Music—Music Education; individual courses

Individual course subjects: accounting, astronomy, communications, economics, education, English, family and consumer sciences, geography, geology, health, history, humanities, management, marketing, mathematics, music, political science, psychology, religion, social sciences, social work, sociology

Average tuition: undergraduate—$88–$117 per semester hour; graduate—$184 per semester hour

Length of program: 1 year per course; master's—2–3 years

Technologies: correspondence, interactive TV, Internet, television

Accreditation: NCACS

Entrance requirements: individual courses—none; bachelor's—AA or 62 transferable semester hours; master's—contact the school for entrance requirements

Restrictions: Certificate and master's programs require some on-campus instruction and are limited to Iowa residents.

Special services: academic advising

Watch Out!
Enrollment in an individual course does not constitute admission to a degree program.

University of Oklahoma

College of Continuing Education
Oklahoma Center for Continuing Education
1700 Asp Ave.
Norman, OK 73019
405-325-4414
Web: www.occe.ou.edu/dist_ed.html
E-mail: lhayes@ou.edu
Programs: Bachelor of Liberal Studies; individual courses
Individual course subjects: accounting, anthropology, art, astronomy, business, chemistry, Chinese, classical languages, classics, economics, education, engineering, English, finance, French, geography, geology, German, Greek, health, high school subjects, history, Japanese, journalism, languages, library science, linguistics, management, marketing, mass communications, mathematics, music, philosophy, political science, psychology, Russian, sociology, Spanish, sports sciences, theater
Average tuition: $68.50–$72.50 per credit (Oklahoma residents); $204.50–$225.50 per credit (out-of-state students)
Length of program: bachelor's—2–4 years
Technologies: correspondence, interactive TV, Internet, television
Accreditation: NCACS
Entrance requirements: individual courses—none; bachelor's—high school diploma, AA, or the equivalent
Restrictions: Interactive TV courses must be taken at participating sites. Students taking television courses must live within the broadcast area. The Bachelor of Liberal Studies requires attendance at 3–5 on-campus intensive seminars.
Special services: none

University of Phoenix

University of Phoenix Online
4605 E. Elwood St.
7th Floor
Phoenix, AZ 85040
1-800-765-4922
Web: online.uophx.edu
Programs: AA—General Studies; BS—Business/Administration, Business/Information Systems, Business/Management, Business/Marketing, Business/Project Management, Information Technology/Database Management, Information Technology/Networks and Telecommunications, Information Technology/Programming and Operating Systems, Information Technology/Systems and Analysis, Information Technology/Web Management; MA—Organizational Management; Master of Arts in Education; MBA—general, Global Management, Technology Management; MS—

Computer Information Systems; BS/MS—Nursing; Doctor of Management—Organizational Leadership

Average tuition: AA/BS—$330–$375 per credit hour; master's—$375–$470 per credit hour

Length of program: 2–5 years

Technologies: Internet

Accreditation: NCACS, NLN

Entrance requirements: AA—high school diploma or GED; BS—high school diploma or GED and current employment; BS in Nursing—associate's degree or diploma in nursing with a 2.0 GPA in all prior nursing courses and a valid registered nurse license; master's—bachelor's degree with a 2.5 GPA, current employment, and 3 years of related work experience; MS in Nursing—bachelor's degree in nursing with a 2.5 GPA, valid registered nurse license, 3 years of full-time nursing work experience, and current employment

Restrictions: Students must be at least 23 years old.

Special services: electronic library

University of Pittsburgh

Center for Instructional Development and Distance Education

3804 Forbes Ave.

Pittsburgh, PA 15260

412-624-7216

Web: www.pitt.edu/~ciddeweb/UESP/

E-mail: rwi+@pitt.edu

Programs: individual courses

Individual course subjects: anthropology, art history, astronomy, chemistry, classics, communication disorders, communications, criminal justice, economics, educational psychology, English, English literature, geology, German, health, history, instructional design, legal studies, management information systems, mathematics, music, nursing, philosophy, physical education, political science, psychology, public administration, religion, statistics, theater

Average tuition: undergraduate—$197 per credit; graduate—$425 per credit

Technologies: corrspondence

Accreditation: MSACS

Entrance requirements: high school diploma or the equivalent

Restrictions: Students generally attend 3 three-hour Saturday workshops per course.

Special services: academic counseling; tutoring

University of Saint Augustine for Health Sciences

1 University Blvd.

St. Augustine, FL 32086-5783

1-800-241-1027

Unofficially...
The MBA is offered in conjunction with ISIM University, also accredited by DETC (and reviewed in this book). ISIM University actually awards the degree.

Web: www.usa.edu
E-mail: info@usa.edu
Programs: MBA—Healthcare; MS—Physical Therapy; Doctor of Physical Therapy
Average tuition: MS—$15,320; MBA—$18,930; Doctor of Physical Therapy—$12,875–$15,875
Length of program: 15 weeks per course; Doctor of Physical Therapy—3–5 years
Technologies: correspondence
Accreditation: DETC
Entrance requirements: MBA/MS—graduate of an accredited physical therapy program; Doctor of Physical Therapy—master's degree in physical therapy
Restrictions: The MBA requires attendance at nationwide seminars. The MS requires attendance at a seminar (held throughout the country) and at least 3 on-campus residencies.
Special services: library resources center

University of Saint Francis

USF Online
500 Wilcox St.
Joliet, IL 60435
815-740-3360
Web: www.stfrancis.edu/lspace/index.htm
Programs: BS—Health Arts; MBA
Average tuition: BS—$880 per course; MBA—$380 per semester hour
Length of program: BS—2¹/₂ years; MBA—1 year
Technologies: Internet
Accreditation: NCACS
Entrance requirements: BS—open to licensed, qualified health professionals who have completed a hospital diploma program or associate's degree; MBA—bachelor's degree with a 2.75 GPA and 2 years of full-time employment in a management position or sufficient GMAT scores
Restrictions: none
Special services: academic advising; help desk; library research resources

University of Sarasota

5250 17th St.
Sarasota, FL 34235
1-800-331-5995
Web: www.sarasota.edu/distance.html
Programs: Certificate—Business, Finance, Healthcare Administration, Human Resources, International Trade, Marketing; MA—Guidance Counseling, Mental Health Counseling; MBA; DBA; EdS—School Counseling; EdD—Counseling Psychology, Curriculum and Instruction/ Higher Education, Organizational Leadership, Pastoral Community

Counseling; EdS/EdD—Curriculum and Instruction/K–12, Educational Leadership/K–12

Average tuition: $247–$371 per credit

Length of program: 16 weeks per course

Technologies: correspondence, Internet

Accreditation: SACS

Entrance requirements: certificates—bachelor's or master's degree; MA/MBA—bachelor's degree with a 3.0 GPA; DBA/EdS/EdD—master's degree with a 3.0 GPA

Restrictions: All degree programs require several 1- and 2-week in-residence courses.

Special services: academic advising; faculty mentor; library resources

University of South Alabama

Office of Admissions

182 Administration Bldg.

Mobile, AL 36688-0002

1-800-872-5247

Web: usaonline.southalabama.edu

E-mail: admiss@usamail.usouthal.edu

Programs: Certificate—Educational Administration; BS—Nursing; MBA; MS—Instructional Design and Development

Average tuition: BS—$219–$695 per course; certificate/MBA/MS—$245–$825 per course

Length of program: 15 weeks per course

Technologies: Internet

Accreditation: SACS, NLN

Entrance requirements: certificate—master's degree, Alabama Class A Professional Certificate in an approved teaching field or support area, and 2 years of teaching experience; BS—current registered nurse license, 2.5 GPA in all prerequisites, and evidence of CPR certification; MBA/MS—bachelor's degree

Restrictions: none

Special services: academic advising; career services; library resources

University of Southern California

University Park Campus

Los Angeles, CA 90089

213-740-2311

Web: www.usc.edu/dept/engineering/Distance_Learning/

Programs: MS—Aerospace Engineering, Computer Engineering, Computer Science; MS/Engineer—Electrical Engineering; individual courses

Individual course subjects: accounting, aerospace engineering, business, computer science, electrical engineering, engineering, industrial and systems

Unofficially...
Participating corporations in USC's program include NASA, Qualcomm, Lockheed, JPL, and Boeing, among others.

engineering, mechanical engineering, software engineering, technology, telecommunications

Average tuition: graduate courses/programs—$748–$768 per unit; non-credit courses—$50–$140 per course; video noncredit courses—$850 per course

Length of program: 14 weeks per course; MS/Engineer—up to 5 years

Technologies: interactive TV, Internet, video

Accreditation: WASC, ABET

Entrance requirements: graduate courses—permission of the department sponsoring the course; noncredit courses—none; master's—bachelor's degree in a related field and GRE; Engineer—MS in Electrical Engineering

Restrictions: All degree programs and interactive TV courses are only available to employees of participating corporations and at 4 public locations in California.

Special services: academic advising

Watch Out!
Enrolling in an individual course does not constitute admission to the University of Southern Colorado.

University of Southern Colorado

Division of Continuing Education

2200 Bonforte Blvd.

Pueblo, CO 81001-4901

1-800-388-6154

Web: www.uscolo.edu:80/coned/

E-mail: coned@uscolo.edu

Programs: Certificate—Basic Supervision, Customer Service, Paralegal; BS—Social Science; individual courses

Individual course subjects: anthropology, art, biology, business, chemistry, computer science, economics, education, English, geography, geology, grant writing, history, information technology, management, marketing, nursing, political science, psychology, small-business management, social sciences, sociology, women's studies

Average tuition: $59.00–$340.38 per course

Length of program: 6 weeks–1 year per course; certificates—15–30 weeks

Technologies: correspondence, Internet, television, video

Accreditation: NCACS

Entrance requirements: individual courses/certificates—none; BS—high school diploma or the equivalent

Restrictions: Students taking television courses must live in the broadcast area.

Special services: none

University of Southern Indiana

USI Learning Network

8600 University Blvd.

Evansville, IN 47712-3596

1-800-813-4238

Average tuition: MA—$25,200; MBA—$33,000

Length of program: MA—2 years and 3 months; MBA—3 years and 3 months

Technologies: Internet, teleconferencing, video

Accreditation: SACS

Entrance requirements: bachelor's degree with a B average in upper-division coursework and 7 years of relevant work experience or GMAT score

Restrictions: requires semiannual 3-day retreats and a 9-day international study tour

Special services: library resources

University of Texas—San Antonio

College of Business

6900 North Loop 1604 West

San Antonio, TX 78249

210-458-5372

Web: cobweb.utsa.edu/motprg/

E-mail: wflannery@utsa.edu

Programs: MS—Management of Technology

Average tuition: $110 per semester credit hour (Texas residents); $326 per semester credit hour (out-of-state students)

Technologies: videoconferencing

Accreditation: SACS

Entrance requirements: bachelor's degree in an engineering, scientific, or technical field with a 3.0 GPA and GMAT score of 500

Restrictions: none

Special services: academic advising

University of Texas System

UT TeleCampus

Office of Information Technology and Distance Education

201 W. Seventh St.

Austin, TX 78701-2981

1-888-TEXAS16

Web: www.uol.com/

E-mail: telecampus@utsystem.edu/telecampus/

Programs: MBA—General Management; MEd—Educational Technology

Average tuition: $580 per course (Texas residents); $1,222 per course (out-of-state studies)

Technologies: audiocassette, CD-ROM, Internet, video

Accreditation: SACS

Entrance requirements: MBA—bachelor's degree with 3.0 GPA and GMAT score; MEd—bachelor's degree and GRE score

Restrictions: none

Special services: digital library; technical support

Unofficially...
Students in the MBA program earn the degree from one of the eight participating UT schools where they decide to apply. The MEd is earned through UT—Brownsville.

University of Utah

Independent Study/Distance Education

Continuing Education

1901 E. South Campus Dr.

Room 2180

Salt Lake City, UT 84112-9364

1-800-INSTUDY

Web: www.dce.utah.edu/

E-mail: inthing@admin.dce.utah.edu/disted/

Programs: individual courses

Individual course subjects: anthropology, art, art history, atmospheric sciences, bioengineering, biology, chemistry, communication disorders, communications, economics, education, educational psychology, English, film studies, finance, geography, gerontology, health education, history, mathematics, music, nutrition and food science, performing arts, philosophy, physics, political science, psychology, recreation and park resources

Average tuition: $85 per semester credit hour

Length of program: up to 9 months per course

Technologies: correspondence, Internet, television, video

Accreditation: NASC

Entrance requirements: none

Restrictions: Students taking television courses must live in the broadcast area. Some courses require an on-campus meeting.

Special services: none

University of Waterloo

Distance Education Office

200 University Ave. W

Waterloo Ontario N2L 3G1

Canada

519-888-4050

Web: www.adm.uwaterloo.ca:80/infoded/de.html

E-mail: distance@uwaterloo.ca

Programs: Certificate—Classical Languages, General Social Work, Social Work-Child Abuse; BA—Canadian Studies, Economics, English, Geography, General, History, Medieval Studies, Philosophy, Psychology, Religious Studies, Social Development Studies, Sociology; Certificate/BA—Classical Studies, French; Bachelor of Environmental Studies; BS; Master of Applied Science—Management of Technology; individual courses

Individual course subjects: accounting, anthropology, applied mathematics, art, biology, Canadian studies, chemistry, classical languages, classics, computer science, conflict resolution, dance, earth sciences, economics, English, environmental studies, French, geography, German, Germanic languages, gerontology, Greek, health, history, kinesiology, mathematics, Native American studies, philosophy, physics, psychology, public affairs, religion, Russian, Scandinavian languages, science, Slavic languages, social sciences, social work, sociology, Spanish, statistics, women's studies

Average tuition: individual courses/certificate/bachelor's—$435 (Canadian) per course (Candian residents) or $1,217.40 (Canadian) per course (international students); MA—$25,000 (Canadian)

Length of program: 4 months per course; MA—3–5 years

Technologies: audiocassette, Internet, correspondence, video

Accreditation: Canadian government

Entrance requirements: individual courses/certificate/bachelor's—high school diploma or the equivalent or mature-student status and relevant background experience; master's—bachelor's degree with a B average

Restrictions: Only residents of Canada and the U.S. may apply.

Special services: none

University of Wisconsin Extension

432 N. Lake St.

Madison, WI 53706

608-262-3980

Web: www.uwex.edu/disted/catalog/

E-mail: info@uwex.edu

Programs: BS—Nursing; individual courses

Individual course subjects: African-American studies, African studies, agriculture, anthropology, art, art history, astronomy, atmospheric sciences, biology, botany, business, chemistry, classical languages, classics, communications, criminal justice, dance, economics, education, educational psychology, emergency services, engineering, English, forestry, French, geography, geology, German, Greek, health, health education, health services, Hebrew, high school subjects, history, interior design, Italian, journalism, Judaic studies, mass communications, mathematics, music, philosophy, physics, political science, Portuguese, production and inventory management, psychology, Russian, Scandinavian languages, social sciences, social work, sociology, Spanish, statistics, women's studies

Average tuition: $119 per credit hour

Length of program: 1 year per course

Technologies: correspondence, Internet, teleconferencing

Accreditation: NCACS, NLN

Entrance requirements: individual courses—none; BS—associate's degree or diploma in nursing and registered nurse license

Restrictions: Enrollment in the BS is limited to residents of Wisconsin.

Special services: academic advising

Unofficially...
The BS can be earned through one of the five sponsoring University of Wisconsin campuses.

University of Wisconsin—Green Bay

Extended Degree Office

ES 109

2420 Nicolet Dr.

Green Bay, WI 54311-7001

1-800-621-2313

Web: www.uwgb.edu/gbextdeg/

E-mail: gbextdeg@uwgb.edu

Programs: BA—Interdisciplinary Studies

Average tuition: $109 per credit hour

Technologies: audiocassette, Internet, teleconferencing, video

Accreditation: NCACS

Entrance requirements: high school diploma or the equivalent

Restrictions: BA students must attend at least 2 on-campus meetings. Enrollment is limited to Wisconsin residents.

Special services: academic advising

University of Wisconsin—Madison

University of Wisconsin—Extension

432 N. Lake St.

Madison, WI 53706

608-262-3980

Web: www.uwex.edu/disted/catalog/

E-mail: info@uwex.edu

Programs: Master of Administrative Medicine; Master of Engineering—Professional Practice, Technical Japanese

Average tuition: $1,050 per credit hour

Technologies: Internet, teleconferencing, television, videoconferencing

Accreditation: NCACS, ABET

Entrance requirements: bachelor's degree in a related field with a 3.0 GPA; Master of Administrative Medicine—also requires current employment as a clinician in the healthcare field; Master of Engineering in Professional Practice—also requires 4 years of professional experience

Restrictions: The Master of Administrative Medicine requires 2 seven-week on-campus sessions. The Master of Engineering in Professional Practice requires weeklong summer residencies.

Special services: academic advising; library services

University of Wisconsin—Platteville

Distance Learning Center

1 University Plaza

Platteville, WI 53818

608-342-1071

Web: vms.www.uwplatt.edu/~disted/

E-mail: disted@uwplatt.edu

Programs: BS—Business Administration; MS—Project Management; Diploma/MS—Criminal Justice

Average tuition: BS—$160 per credit hour (Wisconsin residents) and $340 per credit hour (out-of-state students); diploma/MS—$468 per credit hour (Wisconsin residents) and $608 per credit hour (out-of-state students)

Length of program: BS—self-paced; master's—up to 7 years

Technologies: correspondence, Internet, teleconferencing, video

Accreditation: NCACS

Entrance requirements: BS—high school diploma or the equivalent; diploma/MS—bachelor's degree with a 2.75 GPA

Restrictions: BS in Business Administration students must be at least 22 years old.

Special services: academic advising; library services; technical support

University of Wisconsin—Superior

Extended Degree Program
Erlanson 105
Belknap and Catlin
P.O. Box 2000
Superior, WI 54880
715-394-8487
Web: milo.uwsuper.edu
Programs: BA/BS—Individualized Major
Average tuition: $109–$395 per credit
Technologies: correspondence, Internet
Accreditation: NCACS
Entrance requirements: high school diploma or the equivalent
Restrictions: none
Special services: academic advising

University of Wisconsin—Whitewater

Online MBA
4033 Carlson Hall
College of Business and Economics
Whitewater, WI 53190
414-472-1945
Web: academics.uww.edu/BUSINESS/onlinemba/
E-mail: gradbus@uwwvax.uww.edu
Programs: MBA
Average tuition: $730.50–$2,125.50 per course
Length of program: 6–16 weeks per course
Technologies: Internet
Accreditation: NCACS
Entrance requirements: bachelor's degree with a 2.75 GPA and GMAT score
Restrictions: none
Special services: academic advising

Upper Iowa University

External Degree
P.O. Box 1861
Fayette, IA 52142
(888) 877-3742 (undergraduate) or

Online Program Office
PO Box 1857
Fayette, IA 52142
1-800-773-9298 (graduate)
Web: www.uiu.edu
E-mail: extdegree@uiu.edu (undergraduate) or online@uiu.edu (graduate)
Programs: AA—Liberal Arts; BS—Accounting, Business, Human Resources Management, Human Services, Management, Marketing, Public Administration, Social Science; MA—Business Leadership; individual courses
Individual course subjects: art, biology, business, communications, English, history, management information systems, mathematics, physical science, political science, psychology, public administration, sociology, Spanish
Average tuition: individual courses/AA/BS—$155 per semester hour; MA—$600–$800 per course
Length of program: 2–6 months per course
Technologies: correspondence, Internet, video
Accreditation: NCACS
Entrance requirements: individual courses/AA/BS—high school diploma or GED with a cumulative GPA of 2.0; MA—bachelor's degree with a 2.5 GPA or an acceptable GMAT or GRE score
Restrictions: none
Special services: academic advising; career counseling; library services

Utah Electronic Community College

800 W. University Pkwy.
Mailcode 219
Orem, UT 84058-5999
1-888-569-UECC
Web: www.utah-ecc.org
E-mail: UECC@uvsc.edu
Programs: individual courses
Individual course subjects: accounting, art, aviation science, biological sciences, building management, business, communications, computer science, criminal justice, economics, education, English, English as a second language, environmental studies, health, hospitality, human development, humanities, languages, law, legal studies, mathematics, philosophy, physical education, physical science, political science, railroad operations, social sciences, surveying

Average tuition: $61.50 per credit hour

Technologies: CD-ROM, correspondence, interactive TV, Internet, teleconferencing, television, video

Accreditation: NASC

Entrance requirements: high school diploma or the equivalent

Restrictions: Some courses have optional on-campus meetings.

Special services: academic advising

Utah State University

Independent and Distance Education

3080 Old Main Hill

Logan, UT 84322-3080

1-800-233-2137

Web: www.ext.usu.edu/distance/

Programs: Certificate—Administrative Supervisory Certificate in Education, Child Development Associate, Early Childhood Education, Mild/Moderate Education, School Library Media; BS—Accounting, Agribusiness, Business Administration; MEd—Educational Technology; MS—Human Environments; BS/MS—Business Information Systems, Computer Science, Psychology; Master of Social Sciences—Human Resources Management; Master of Technical Writing; individual courses

Individual course subjects: accounting, art, biology, business, business education, chemistry, economics, elementary education, English, geography, geology, health, history, human development, human resource management, landscaping, management, management information systems, mathematics, physical education, recreation, statistics, wildlife and fish science

Average tuition: $85–$298 per credit

Length of program: 15 weeks–1 year per course

Technologies: correspondence, interactive TV, Internet

Accreditation: NASC, APA, CSAB, NCATE

Entrance requirements: individual courses/certificates—high school diploma or the equivalent; Administrative Supervisory Certificate in Education—master's degree, Professional Teaching Certificate or the equivalent, 2 years of school-related experience, and MAT score of 43 or GRE score of 1,000; BS—associate's degree or completion of prespecialization requirements with a 2.5 GPA; master's—bachelor's degree in a related field with a 3.0 GPA and satisfactory GMAT, GRE, or MAT score

Restrictions: With the exception of the Master of Technical Writing, all degree programs must be taken at one of the receive sites in Utah. Not all programs are available at all sites.

Special services: academic advising; disability resources; library services; technical support

Unofficially...
The Utah Electronic Community College is a consortium of five accredited community colleges. You only have to submit one application to be admitted to all of the participating schools and take distance-learning courses from them (you will have to choose one school as your "home" school).

Utica College of Syracuse University

Continuing Education

Online Programs

1600 Burrstone Rd.

Utica, NY 13502

315-792-3253

Web: www.ucsu.edu/academic/contedu/gerontology/Gero_Home.html

E-mail: rlucchino@utica.ucsu.edu

Programs: Certificate—Studies in Gerontology

Average tuition: $1,050 per course

Technologies: Internet

Accreditation: MSACS

Entrance requirements: high school diploma, GED, or equivalent work experience

Restrictions: none

Special services: none

V

☼

Bright Idea
Vatterott College offers a 1-week introductory course designed to help new users understand distance learning concepts and how to use the Internet.

Vatterott College

Vatterott Global Online

3131 Frederick Ave.

St. Joseph, MO 64506

1-888-766-3601

Web: www.VatterottGlobal.com

E-mail: VGO@ccp.com

Programs: Diploma——Computer Programming and Systems Analysis; Associate of Computer Programming and Network Management; individual courses

Individual course subjects: Microsoft certification

Length of program: 10 weeks per course; diploma—60 weeks; associate's——80 weeks

Technologies: CD-ROM, Internet

Accreditation: ACCET, ACCSCT

Entrance requirements: none (high school diploma or the equivalent is highly recommended)

Restrictions: none

Special services: career services; online library

Virginia Tech

Institute for Distance and Distributed Learning

Blacksburg, VA 24061-0445

540-231-6664

Web: vto.vt.edu

E-mail: VTO@vt.edu

Programs: MA——Political Science; individual courses

Individual course subjects: computer science, English, entomology, human development, humanities, mathematics, philosophy, political science

Average tuition: individual courses——$145.85 per credit hour (Virginia residents) and $300.65 per credit hour (out-of-state students); MA—$2,061 per semester (Virginia residents) and $3,366 per semester (out-of-state students)

Technologies: Internet

Accreditation: SACS

Entrance requirements: individual courses—none; MA—bachelor's degree and GRE score

Restrictions: none

Special services: electronic tutoring environment; library services

W

Walden University

Office of Academic Affairs

155 Fifth Ave. S

Minneapolis, MN 55401

1-800-444-6795

Web: www.waldenu.edu

E-mail: info@waldenu.edu

Programs: Certificate/MS—Psychology; PhD—Applied Management and Decision Sciences, Health Services, Human Services, Professional Psychology; MS/PhD—Education

Average tuition: MS—$230–$305 per credit hour; PhD—$3,175 per quarter; PhD in Professional Psychology—$305 per quarter hour

Length of program: MS—2 years; PhD—3–4 years

Technologies: Internet

Accreditation: NCACS

Entrance requirements: certificate—doctoral degree in psychology or a related field; MS in Education—bachelor's degree and 2 years of related professional experience; MS in Psychology—bachelor's degree in psychology; PhD—master's degree and 3 years of related professional experience

Restrictions: Certificate and PhD programs require residencies at various locations around the U.S. The PhD in Psychology requires 1 year spent in residency on campus.

Special services: academic counseling; library services; online student union; writing center

Warren Wilson College

MFA Program for Writers

P.O. Box 9000

Asheville, NC 28815-9000

828-298-3325, ext. 380

Web: www.warren-wilson.edu/~mfa/index.shtml
E-mail: agrimm@warren-wilson.edu
Programs: MFA—Creative Writing
Length of program: 2 years
Technologies: correspondence
Accreditation: SACS
Entrance requirements: BA degree with undergraduate concentrations in literature and writing and application manuscript
Restrictions: Requires a 10-day residency at the beginning of each semester.
Special services: one-on-one instruction

Washington State University

Office of Extended Degree Programs
P.O. Box 645220
Pullman, WA 99164-5220
1-800-222-4850
Web: www.eus.wsu.edu/edp/
E-mail: edp@wsu.edu
Programs: Certificate—Professional Writing; BA—Business Administration, Criminal Justice, Human Development, Social Sciences; BS—Agriculture; PharmD
Average tuition: $178 per credit
Length of program: 15 weeks–1 year per course; PharmD—2–4 years
Technologies: CD-ROM, correspondence, interactive TV, Internet, video, videoconferencing
Accreditation: NASC, ACPE
Entrance requirements: certificate—bachelor's degree; BA/BS—completion of an AA or 27 semester hours or 40 quarter hours of transferable college credit with a GPA of 2.0; PharmD—bachelor's degree in pharmacy and license to practice pharmacy in Washington
Restrictions: Engineering courses require on-campus meetings. The PharmD requires weekend workshops, held in Washington.
Special services: academic advising; disability services; library services; online writing lab

Weber State University

Distance-Learning Office
4005 University Circle
Ogden, UT 84408-4005
1-800-848-7770, ext. 6785
Web: www.weber.edu/ce/dl/distance%20learning.htm
E-mail: wsuonline@weber.edu
Programs: Certificate—Production and Inventory Management; AS—Respiratory Therapy; BS—Advanced Respiratory Therapy, Clinical Laboratory Science, Health Information Management, Health Promotion, Health Services Administration, Radiologic Sciences; individual courses

Individual course subjects: accounting, anthropology, art, botany, business, business education, chemistry, clinical laboratory science, communications, construction, criminal justice, economics, engineering, English, finance, French, geography, geology, gerontology, graphic design, health, health information administration, health services, history, human development, industrial operations, information technology, interior design, library science, management, marketing, mathematics, music, nursing, nutrition, philosophy, physical education, political science, production and inventory management, psychology, radiologic science, respiratory therapy, sales and service technology, social work, sociology, Spanish, telecommunications, transportation and logistics, zoology

Average tuition: $187–$285 per course

Technologies: audiocassette, correspondence, Internet, video

Accreditation: NASC, NAACLS

Entrance requirements: high school diploma or the equivalent

Restrictions: none

Special services: academic advising; library services; tutoring; women's center; writing resources

Webster University

Enrollment Services Center
470 E. Lockwood Ave.
St. Louis, MO 63119-3194
314-968-7490
Web: online.webster.edu
E-mail: worldclassroom@webster.edu
Programs: MA—Teaching; MBA
Average tuition: MA—$326 per credit hour; MBA—$410 per credit hour
Length of program: 3 months per course
Technologies: Internet
Accreditation: NCACS
Entrance requirements: bachelor's degree
Restrictions: none
Special services: academic advising; career enter; online library; online writing center

West Virginia Wesleyan College

Distance Education
59 College Ave.
Buckhannon, WV 26201
304-473-8000
Web: www.wvwc.edu/aca/outreach/distant.htm
E-mail: outreach@wvwc.edu
Programs: Certificate—Business Principles; BS—Nursing; individual courses

Individual course subjects: art, business, computer science, economics, English, family and consumer sciences, health, history, mathematics, music, nursing, philosophy, physical education, physical science, political science, psychology, sociology
Average tuition: $301–$458 per course
Length of program: 9 months per course
Technologies: correspondence, video
Accreditation: NCACS, NLN
Entrance requirements: individual courses/certificate—none; BS—registered nurse license
Restrictions: none
Special services: none

Western Carolina University

Division of Continuing Education and Summer School
University Outreach Center
Cullowhee, NC 28723
1-800-928-4968
Web: cess.wcu.edu/conted/disted/disted.html
E-mail: mpm_online@wcu.edu
Programs: BS—Birth–Kindergarten; Master of Project Management
Average tuition: $53.25 per semester hour (North Carolina residents); $409.50 per semester hour (out-of-state students)
Length of program: 2 years
Technologies: Internet
Accreditation: SACS, NCATE
Entrance requirements: BS—associate's degree with a 2.5 GPA; master's—bachelor's degree, GMAT score of 400, and professional experience in project management
Restrictions: Some courses for the BS must be completed at one of the participating North Carolina community colleges, and some courses require on-campus lab sessions.
Special services: library services

Western Illinois University

Extended Learning
5 Horrabin Hall
1 University Circle
Macomb, IL 61455
309-298-2666
Web: www.wiu.edu/users/miebis/
E-mail: E-Learning@wiu.edu
Programs: BA—Individualized Studies; individual courses
Individual course subjects: agricultural economics, anthropology, biological sciences, communications, computer science, criminal justice, economics,

elementary education, engineering technology, English, family and consumer sciences, finance, geography, geology, history, journalism, languages, management, marketing, mathematics, philosophy, physical education, political science, psychology, recreation and park resources, religion, safety education, sociology, special education

Average tuition: $91 per semester hour

Length of program: 6 months per course

Technologies: audiocassette, computer conferencing, correspondence, Internet, television, video

Accreditation: NCACS

Entrance requirements: individual courses—high school diploma or GED; BS—high school diploma or GED and either significant full-time work experience or prior college coursework with a C average

Restrictions: Students enrolling in the program must have graduated from high school 5 or more years ago.

Special services: academic advising; student-designed learning

Western Michigan University

Division of Continuing Education
Department of Distance Education
A-103 Ellsworth Hall
Kalamazoo, MI 49008-5161
616-387-4216
Web: www.wmich.edu/conted/dde/index.html
E-mail: distance-education-info@wmich.edu
Programs: Certificate—Teaching Children Who Are Visually Impaired and in Orientation and Mobility; individual courses
Individual course subjects: African-American studies, anthropology, biological sciences, career development, chemical-dependency studies, chemistry, computer science, counseling, economics, education, English, family and consumer sciences, geography, geosciences, health services, history, industrial engineering, journalism, management information systems, manufacturing engineering, mathematics, medicine, music, occupational therapy, philosophy, physical education, political science, psychology, religion, social work, sociology, vocational education

Average tuition: $144.91 per credit hour

Length of program: 1 year per course

Technologies: audiocassette, correspondence, Internet, video

Accreditation: NCACS

Entrance requirements: individual courses—none; certificate—bachelor's degree with a 3.0 GPA and prior work or volunteer experience

Restrictions: none

Special services: none

Unofficially...
The BA program enables students to earn a bachelor's degree by combining credit from previous college coursework, life experience, completion of proficiency exams, and distance-learning courses to create a personalized program of study.

Western Oregon University

Division of Extended Programs
345 N. Monmouth Ave.
Monmouth, OR 97361
503-838-8483
Web: www.wou.edu/Provost/ExtendedAndSummerStudies/dist.html
E-mail: disted@wou.edu
Programs: Certificate/BA/BS—Fire Services Administration; individual courses
Individual course subjects: anthropology, criminal justice, education, English, fire protection, German, political science, psychology, special education, writing
Average tuition: $270–$510 per course
Length of program: 15 weeks per course
Technologies: correspondence, Internet, television, video
Accreditation: NASC
Entrance requirements: individual courses—none; certificate/BA/BS—completion of 24 hours of lower-division fire science coursework and Firefighter II designation or the equivalent
Restrictions: Students taking television courses must live within the broadcast area.
Special services: academic advising

Western Piedmont Community College

1001 Burkemont Ave.
Morganton, NC 28655-4511
828-438-6000
Web: www.wp.cc.nc.us/distance.html
Programs: AAS—Paralegal Technology; individual courses
Individual course subjects: accounting, art, business, computer information systems, economics, electronics, English, geography, legal studies, marketing, mathematics, office technology, psychology
Average tuition: $20 per semester hour (North Carolina residents); $163 per semester hour (out-of-state students)
Length of program: AAS—3 years
Technologies: Internet, television
Accreditation: SACS
Entrance requirements: high school diploma or GED
Restrictions: none
Special services: academic advising; career services; library resources

Westlawn School of Yacht Design

733 Summer St.
Stamford, CT 06901
203-359-0500

Web: www.westlawn.org
E-mail: westlawn@earthlink.net
Programs: individual courses
Individual course subjects: yacht design
Average tuition: $4,800
Technologies: correspondence, Internet
Accreditation: DETC
Entrance requirements: none
Restrictions: none
Special services: none

Wheaton College

Office of Distance Learning
Wheaton College Graduate School
Wheaton, IL 60187-5593
1-800-888-0141
Web: www.wheaton.edu/distancelearning/index.htm
E-mail: distance.learning@wheaton.edu
Programs: Certificate—Advanced Biblical Studies; MA—Biblical and Theological Studies, Missions and Intercultural Studies; individual courses
Individual course subjects: biblical studies, theology
Average tuition: individual courses—$190 per semester hour; certificate/MA—$380 per semester hour
Length of program: 1 year per course
Technologies: audiocassette, Internet
Accreditation: NCACS
Entrance requirements: individual courses—bachelor's degree; Certificate/MA—bachelor's degree with a GPA of 2.75 and GRE or MAT score
Restrictions: The MA requires 1 semester in residence and 2 weeklong intensive courses.
Special services: academic advising

Worcester Polytechnic Institute

ADLN Office
Fuller Labs
100 Institute Rd.
Worcester, MA 01609
508-831-5881
Web: www.wpi.edu/Academics/ADLN/
E-mail: adln@wpi.edu
Programs: Certificate—Management, Pollution Prevention, Waste Remediation Systems; MBA; MS—Civil and Environmental Engineering; Certificate/MS—Fire Protection Engineering
Average tuition: $661 per credit hour
Technologies: interactive TV, Internet, video

Accreditation: NEASC, ABET

Entrance requirements: certificates/MS—BS in engineering or related field; MBA—bachelor's degree

Restrictions: One-third of the required courses for the MS in Fire Protection Engineering must be completed on campus.

Special services: academic advising; library services

World College

Lake Shores Plaza

5193 Shore Dr.

Suite 105

Virginia Beach, VA 23455-2500

1-800-696-7532

Web: www.cie-wc.edu/World_College/world_college.html

Programs: Bachelor of Electronic Engineering Technology

Length of program: 8 years

Technologies: correspondence

Accreditation: DETC

Entrance requirements: none

Restrictions: none

Special services: instruction assistance

Index of Distance-Learning Programs by Location

Appendix A

United States

Alabama
Andrew Jackson University
Auburn University
Southern Christian University
Troy State University
Troy State University—
Montgomery
United States Sports Academy
The University of Alabama
University of South Alabama

Alaska
University of Alaska—Fairbanks
University of Alaska—Southeast

Arizona
Arizona State University
Cochise College
Northeastern Arizona University
Phoenix Special Programs and
Academies
Prescott College
Rio Salado College
University of Arizona
University of Phoenix

California
American Graduate University
Aviation and Electronic Schools of
America
California College for Health
Sciences
California Institute of Integral
Studies
California National University for
Advanced Studies
California State University—
Bakersfield
California State University—Chico
California State University—
Dominguez Hills
California State University—Los
Angeles

California State University—
Northridge
California State University—
Sacramento
California State University—San
Marcos
Central State University
Cerro Coso Community College
Choice 2000 Charter School
Commonwealth International
University
Endicott College—TIES Program
The Fielding Institute
Foothill College
Fuller Theological Seminary
Gemological Institute of America
Golden Gate Baptist Theological
Seminary
Golden Gate University
Hope International University
Hypnosis Motivation Institute
Institute of Transpersonal
Psychology
John Tracy Clinic
John Tracy Clinic Academy for
Professional Studies
Life Bible College
National University
New College of California
Pacific Oaks College
San Diego State University
San Jose State University
Touro University International
University of California Extension
University of California—Los
Angeles
University of Southern California

Colorado
Adams State College
Aims Community College
American Health Science
University
College for Financial Planning

Colorado Electronic Community
College
Colorado State University
Community College of Denver
Front Range Community College
ISIM University
Jones International University
National Technological University
Nazarene Bible College
University of Colorado—Boulder
University of Colorado—Denver
University of Southern Colorado

Connecticut
Charter Oak State College
Teikyo Post University
Westlawn School of Yacht Design

Delaware
University of Delaware

District of Columbia
The George Washington University
Mortgage Bankers Association of
America
Strayer University

Florida
Brevard Community College
Citizens' High School
Daytona Beach Community College
Eckerd College
Embry-Riddle Aeronautical
University
Florida Gulf Coast University
Florida Institute of Technology
Florida State University
Kaplan College
National Truck Drivers School
Nova Southeastern University
Palm Beach Community College
Saint Leo University
University of Central Florida
University of Florida
University of Saint Augustine for
Health Sciences
University of Sarasota

Georgia
Georgia Institute of Technology
Kennesaw State University
Professional Career Development
Institute
State University of West Georgia
University of Georgia

Hawaii
University of Hawaii

Idaho
Boise State University
University of Idaho

Illinois
American Institute for Paralegal
Studies
Aurora University
College of DuPage
Governors State University
The Hadley School for the Blind
Illinois Institute of Technology
Keller Graduate School of
Management
Moody Bible Institute
National-Louis University
Parkland College
Spertus Institute of Jewish Studies
University of Illinois—Chicago
University of Illinois—Springfield
University of Illinois—Urbana-
Champaign
University of Saint Francis
Western Illinois University
Wheaton College

Indiana
Anderson University
Ball State University
Indiana Institute of Technology
Indiana State University
Indiana University
Indiana Wesleyan University
Purdue University
Saint Mary-of-the-Woods College

Taylor University
University of Southern Indiana

Iowa
American Institute of Commerce
Hamilton College
Iowa State University
Iowa Western Community College
Maharishi University of Management
University of Iowa
University of Northern Iowa
Upper Iowa University

Kansas
Emporia State University
Fort Hays State University
Kansas State University

Louisiana
American College of Prehospital Medicine
Grantham College of Engineering
Louisiana State University
Tulane University

Maine
Saint Joseph's College of Maine
University of Maine

Maryland
Capitol College
Charles County Community College
Columbia Union College
Goucher College
Home Study International
Johns Hopkins University
University of Baltimore
University of Maryland University College

Massachusetts
Lesley College
Northeastern University
Suffolk University
University of Massachusetts—

Lowell
Worcester Polytechnic Institute

Michigan
Andrews University/Home Study International
Baker College
Central Michigan University
Michigan State University
Michigan Technological University
Mott Community College
Schoolcraft College/Madonna University
Western Michigan University

Minnesota
Art Instruction Schools
Bemidji State University
Capella University
College of St. Scholastica
Northwestern College
University of Minnesota—Twin Cities
Walden University

Mississippi
Mississippi State University

Missouri
Aquinas Institute of Theology
Berean University
Covenant Theological Seminary
Northwest Missouri State University
Saint Louis University
Southwest Missouri State University
Stephens College
University of Missouri
Vatterott College
Webster University

Montana
Montana State University—Billings
Montana State University—Bozeman
University of Montana

Nebraska

Bellevue University
University of Nebraska—Lincoln

Nevada

University of Nevada—Reno

New Jersey

Atlantic Cape Community College
Burlington County College
Caldwell College
Drew University
Fairleigh Dickinson University
New Jersey Institute of Technology
Rutgers University
Seton Hall University
Thomas Edison State College

New York

Columbia University
Herkimer County Community College
Jamestown Community College
Mercy College
Mohawk Valley Community College
Monroe Community College
National Tax Training School
New School University
New York University
Regents College
Rensselaer Polytechnic Institute
Rochester Institute of Technology
Skidmore College
State University of New York
State University of New York—Albany
State University of New York—Binghamton
State University of New York—Empire State College
State University of New York—Institute of Technology at Utica/Rome
Syracuse University
Tompkins Cortland Community College

Ulster County Community College
Utica College of Syracuse University

North Carolina

American Institute of Applied Science
Bladen Community College
Central Carolina Community College
Duke University
East Carolina University
North Carolina Central University
North Carolina State University
Reformed Theological Seminary
University of North Carolina—Chapel Hill
Warren Wilson College
Western Carolina University
Western Piedmont Community College

North Dakota

North Dakota Division of Independent Study
North Dakota State College of Science
University of North Dakota

Ohio

Cleveland Institute of Electronics
Columbus State Community College
Defiance College
Franciscan University of Steubenville
Franklin University
Hospitality Training Center
NHRAW Home Study Institute
Northwestern College
Ohio University
Sinclair Community College
The Union Institute
University of Findlay

Oklahoma

Oklahoma State University
Oral Roberts University
Rogers State University
Tulsa Community
College/Emporia State University
University of Oklahoma

Oregon

Chemeketa Community College
Eastern Oregon University
Lane Community College
Marylhurst University
Oregon State University
Portland Community College
Portland State University
Western Oregon University

Pennsylvania

The American College
Bucks County Community College
Carnegie Mellon University
Drexel University
Duquesne University
Elizabethtown College
ICS Learning Systems
Keystone National High School
King's College
Lehigh University
Lifetime Career Schools
Marywood University
Northampton Community College
The Pennsylvania State University

Rhode Island

Roger Williams University
Salve Regina University

South Carolina

Piedmont Technical College

South Dakota

Black Hills State University
Dakota State University
National American University
Northern State University

Tennessee

American Academy of Nutrition
Johnson Bible College
Lee University
Seminary Extension Independent
Study Institute
Tennessee Temple University
University of Tennessee—Knoxville

Texas

Amber University
Central Texas College
Dallas TeleCollege
Houston Community College
ICI University
International Aviation and Travel
Academy
Modern Gun School
National Association Medical Staff
Services Institute
National Distance Education
Center
Southwestern Adventist University
Southwestern Assembles of God
University
Texas A&M University
Texas Tech University
Texas Woman's University
University of Houston
University of North Texas
University of Texas—Austin
University of Texas—Dallas
University of Texas—San Antonio
University of Texas System

Utah

Brigham Young University
University of Utah
Utah Electronic Community
College
Utah State University
Weber State University

Vermont

Burlington College
Champlain College

Goddard College
Johnson State College

Virginia

American Military University
Atlantic University
The Catholic Distance University
Christopher Newport University
George Mason University
J. Sargeant Reynolds Community College
Liberty University
National Genealogical Society
New River Community College
Northern Virginia Community College
Regent University
Richard Milburn High School
Virginia Tech
World College

Washington

Bellevue Community College
City University
Washington State University

West Virginia

West Virginia Wesleyan College

Wisconsin

Fox Valley Technical College
Lakeland College
University of Wisconsin Extension
University of Wisconsin—Green Bay
University of Wisconsin—Madison
University of Wisconsin—Platteville
University of Wisconsin—Superior
University of Wisconsin—Whitewater

Wyoming

Central Wyoming College

Index of Distance-Learning Degree Programs by Subject

Note: This index refers only to complete certificate, diploma, degree, and other programs. See Appendix C for a list of distance-learning programs that offer individual courses in a variety of subjects.

A+ Certificate
ICS Learning Systems (Certificate)

Accounting and Bookkeeping
Athabasca University (Certificate)
Caldwell College (BS)
Champlain College (Certificate/AS)
Elizabethtown College (Diploma)
Golden Gate University (Graduate Certificate)
Herkimer County Community College (AAS)
ICS Learning Systems (Diploma/Associate's)
Keller Graduate School of Management (Master's)
Lakeland College (BA)
Lifetime Career Schools (Diploma)
Marywood University (Certificate/BS)
Northwestern College (Ohio) (AS/BS)
Professional Career Development Institute (Diploma)
Regents College (BS)
Saint Leo University (BA)
Saint Mary-of-the-Woods College (BS)
State University of New York—Empire State College (AS/BS)
State University of New York—Institute of Technology at Utica/Rome (MS)

Strayer University (AA/BS/MS)
Thomas Edison State College
(Certificate/AS/BS)
University of London (BS)
University of Maryland—University
College (BA/BS)
Upper Iowa University (BS)
Utah State University (BS)

Acquisition, Purchasing, and Contracts Management

American Graduate University
(Certificate/Master's)
California State University—
Dominguez Hills (Certificate)
Floyd College (Certificate)
Iowa Western Community College
(Certificate)
Thomas Edison State College
(AS/BS)

Actuarial Science
See Statistics

Addiction Studies
See Chemical Dependency Counseling

Administrative Assistance
ICS Learning Systems (Diploma)
Lifetime Career Schools (Diploma)
Northwestern College (Ohio) (AS)

Administrative Medicine
University of Wisconsin—Madison
(Master's)

Adult Education
Cambrian College (Certificate)
Capella University
(Certificate/MS/PhD)
Indiana University (MS)
National-Louis University
(Master's)

The Pennsylvania State University
(MEd)
Simon Fraser University
(Certificate)

Advertising
Thomas Edison State College (BS)

Advertising Design
See Graphic Design

Aeronautics and Aerospace Studies
Embry-Riddle Aeronautical
University (AS/BS/Master's)

Agribusiness
Kansas State University (Master's)
Northwestern College (Ohio) (AS)
Purdue University (MBA)
Utah State University (BS)

Agricultural Economics
University of London
(Postgraduate Diploma/MS)

Agriculture
Colorado State University
(Master's)
Iowa State University (BS/Master's)
Texas A&M University (Master's)
University of Florida (Master's)
University of London
(Postgraduate Diploma/MS)
Washington State University (BS)

Agronomy
Iowa State University (MS)

Air Conditioning, Heating, and Refrigeration
ICS Learning Systems (Diploma)

Air Traffic Control

Thomas Edison State College
(AS/BS)

Allied Health

See Health

American Studies

Saint Joseph's College of Maine
(Certificate)
University of Maine (Certificate)

Analytical Chemistry

Illinois Institute of Technology
(MS)

Animal Sciences

ICS Learning Systems (Diploma)
Kansas State University (BS)
Professional Career Development
Institute (Diploma)
Thomas Edison State College
(AS/BS)

Anthropology

Athabasca University (BA)
California Institute of Integral
Studies (MA)
Johnson State College (BA)
Thomas Edison State College (BA)

Appliance Repair

ICS Learning Systems (Diploma)

Applied Mathematics and Science

Athabasca University (BGS)
Bellevue Community College
(AAS)
Rochester Institute of Technology
(BS)
State University of New York—
Binghamton (MS)

Archaeology

Leicester University (Diploma/MA)

Architectural Design

Thomas Edison State College
(AS/BS)

Art Administration

Golden Gate University (Graduate
Certificate)
Goucher College (MA)

Art and Design

Burlington College (BA)
Caldwell College (BA)
ICS Learning Systems (Diploma)
Johnson State College (BA/BFA)
Thomas Edison State College (BA)

Arts and Entertainment Business

*See Music, Arts, and Entertainment
Business*

Arts and Sciences

See Liberal Arts

Athletic and Sports Administration

United States Sports Academy
(Master's)

Athletic Training and Sports Medicine

United States Sports Academy
(Master's)

Audiology

*See Communication Disorders and
Audiology*

Auto Body Repair, Painting, and Detailing

ICS Learning Systems (Diploma)

Automotive Mechanics

ICS Learning Systems (Diploma)
Northwestern College (Ohio) (AS)
Professional Career Development
Institute (Diploma)

Aviation Administration

Embry-Riddle Aeronautical
University (AS)

Aviation Maintenance

Thomas Edison State College
(AS/BS)

Aviation Science

Regents College (AAS/Associate's)
Thomas Edison State College
(AS/BS)

Banking

See Finance and Banking

Bartending

ICS Learning Systems (Diploma)

Beauty Salon Management

ICS Learning Systems (Diploma)

Behavioral Science

See Psychology

Biblical Studies

Berean University
(Diploma/AA/BA/MA)
Covenant Theological Seminary
(Certificate)

ICI University
(Certificate/BA/MA)
Johnson Bible College (MA)
Life Bible College (AA)
Moody Bible Institute
(Certificate/Associate's/BS)
Nazarene Bible College
(AA/Bachelor's)
Northwestern College (Minnesota)
(Certificate)
Prairie Bible Institute (Certificate)
Reformed Theological Seminary
(Certificate)
Regent University (MA)
Seminary Extension Independent
Study Institute
(Certificate/Diploma)
Southern Christian University
(BA/BS/MA/DMin)
Taylor University (AA)
Tennessee Temple University
(AA/BS)
Wheaton College (Certificate/MA)

Bioinformatics

Rensselaer Polytechnic Institute
(Certificate)

Biological and Physical Sciences

Ohio University (AS)
Saint Mary-of-the-Woods College
(BS)
Thomas Edison State College (BS)
University of Minnesota—Twin
Cities (Certificate)
University of Waterloo (BS)

Biology

Johnson State College (BS)
Thomas Edison State College
(AS/BS)

Biomedical Science and Technology

Aims Community College (AAS)
Thomas Edison State College
(AS/BS)

Blood Bank Technology

University of Illinois—Chicago
(Certificate)

Bookkeeping

See Accounting and Bookkeeping

Bridal Consulting

ICS Learning Systems (Diploma)
Professional Career Development
Institute (Diploma)

Broadband Communications

Aims Community College
(Certificate/AGS)

Broadcasting

Southwestern Adventist University
(BA)

Building

See Construction

Building Management

Canadian School of Management
(Diploma)
Michigan State University
(Certificate)
Professional Career Development
Institute (Diploma)

Business

Amber University (MBA)
Andrew Jackson University
(BS/MBA)

Athabasca University
(Certificate/MBA)
Atlantic Cape Community College
(AA)
Auburn University (MBA)
Baker College (ABA/BBA/MBA)
Ball State University (AA/MBA)
Bellevue University (MBA)
Bladen Community College (AAS)
Bucks County Community College
(ABA)
Burlington County College (AS)
Caldwell College (BS)
California College for Health
Sciences (Certificate/AS/BS)
California National University for
Advanced Studies (BS/MBA)
California State University—
Dominguez Hills (MBA)
Cambrian College (Certificate)
Canadian School of Management
(Diploma/ABA/MBA)
Central Carolina Community
College (AAS)
Central State University
(BBA/MBA/DBA)
Cerro Coso Community College
(AA/AS)
Champlain College
(Certificate/AS/BS)
Colorado State University
(MBA/MS)
Columbia Union College (BS)
Drexel University (MBA)
Durham University (MBA)
Eastern Oregon University
(BA/BS)
Financial Times Management
(Diploma/MA/MBA)
Florida Gulf Coast University
(MBA)
Florida Institute of Technology
(MBA)
Franklin University (BS)

Golden Gate University (MBA)

Henley Management College
(MBA)

Heriot-Watt University (MBA)

Herkimer County Community
College (AAS/AS)

Indiana Institute of Technology
(AS/BS)

Indiana State University (BS)

Indiana Wesleyan University (MBA)

International Management Centres
(Certificate/Diploma/MBA/DBA)

Iowa State University (MBA)

ISIM University (MBA)

Kansas State University (BS)

Keller Graduate School of
Management (Certificate/MBA)

Lakeland College (BA)

Lehigh University (MBA)

Leicester University (MBA)

Liberty University (BS/MBA)

Maharishi University of
Management (MBA)

Marylhurst University (MBA)

Marywood University
(Certificate/BS)

Memorial University of
Newfoundland
(Certificate/Diploma/BBA)

Mercy College (BS/MBA)

Mott Community College (AAS)

National American University (BS)

Northampton Community College
(AA)

Northern Virginia Community
College (AS)

Northwestern College (Ohio)
(AS/BS)

Nova Southeastern University
(MBA)

Ohio University (MBA)

Oklahoma State University (MBA)

Oral Roberts University (BS)

Parkland College (AS)

The Pennsylvania State University
(Certificate/ABA)

Regent University (MBA)

Regents College (AS/BS)

Rensselaer Polytechnic Institute
(MBA)

Rogers State University (AA)

Saint Joseph's College of Maine
(Certificate/BS)

Saint Leo University (BA)

Saint Mary-of-the-Woods College
(AS/BS)

Salve Regina University (MBA)

Schoolcraft College/Madonna
University (BS/MS)

Sinclair Community College (AS)

Southwest Missouri State University
(MS)

Southwestern Adventist University
(BA/BBA)

Southwestern Assemblies of God
University (BS)

State University of New York—
Empire State College
(AS/Bachelor's/BS)

Stephens College (BS/MBA)

Strayer University (AA/BS/MS)

Suffolk University (MBA)

Syracuse University (MBA)

Teikyo Post University (BS)

Texas Tech University (BBA)

Touro University International
(BS/MBA/PhD)

University of Alaska—Southeast
(BBA)

University of Baltimore (MBA)

University of California Extension
(Certificate)

University of California—Los
Angeles (Certificate)

University of Findlay (MBA)

University of Florida (MBA)

University of Hawaii (BA/MBA)

University of London (MBA)

University of Maryland University College (MBA)
University of Phoenix (BS/MBA)
University of Saint Francis (MBA)
University of Sarasota (Certificate/MBA/DBA)
University of South Alabama (MBA)
University of Tennessee—Knoxville (Physician Executive MBA)
University of Wisconsin—Platteville (BS)
University of Wisconsin—Whitewater (MBA)
Upper Iowa University (BS)
Utah State University (BS)
Washington State University (BA)
Webster University (MBA)
West Virginia Wesleyan College (Certificate)
Worcester Polytechnic Institute (MBA)

Business Communications
Ball State University (Certificate)
Jones International University (Certificate/BA/MA)
Marywood University (Certificate)
Northeastern Arizona University (Certificate)
Southwestern Adventist University (BS)

Business Education
Parkland College (AS)

Business Information Systems
See Management Information Systems

Business Writing
See Technical and Business Writing

Canadian Studies
Athabasca University (BA)
Memorial University of Newfoundland (Certificate)
University of Manitoba (BA)
University of Waterloo (BA)

Career and Professional Development
Amber University (BA/MA)
Athabasca University (Certificate)
California State University—Chico (Certificate)

Carpentry
ICS Learning Systems (Diploma)
Professional Career Development Institute (Diploma)

Cartography
See Surveying and Mapping

Chemical-Dependency Counseling
Capella University (Certificate/MS/PhD)
The Pennsylvania State University (Certificate)
Tompkins Cortland Community College (AAS)
University of London (Postgraduate Diploma/MS)

Chemistry
Illinois Institute of Technology (MS)
Lehigh University (MS)
Thomas Edison State College (AS/BS)

Child Development
Teikyo Post University (Certificate)
Thomas Edison State College (AS/BS)

University of Alaska—Southeast
(AS)
Utah State University (Certificate)

Childcare Training

ICS Learning Systems (Diploma)
Northampton Community College
(Diploma)
Professional Career Development
Institute (Diploma)

Christian Counseling

Berean University (MA)
ICI University (Advanced
Certificate)
Oral Roberts University (BS)
Prairie Bible Institute (Certificate)

Christian Studies

The Catholic Distance University
(Certificate)
Covenant Theological Seminary
(Certificate)
Drew University (Certificate)
Fuller Theological Seminary
(Certificate)
ICI University (Certificate)
Saint Joseph's College of Maine
(Certificate)
Taylor University (Certificate)

Church Administration

See Ministry

Classical Languages

University of Waterloo (Certificate)

Classics

University of Maine (Certificate)
University of Waterloo
(Certificate/BA)

Clinical Laboratory Science

California College for Health
Sciences (Diploma/AS)
The George Washington University
(Certificate)
Thomas Edison State College
(AS/BS)
Weber State University (BS)

Clinical Supervision

Capella University (Certificate)

Coaching

United States Sports Academy
(Master's)

Commerce

See International Business

Communication Disorders and Audiology

California State University—
Northridge (MS)
Central Michigan University (AuD)
Texas Woman's University (MS)
University of Florida (AuD)

Communications

Andrew Jackson University (BA)
Athabasca University (Bachelor's)
Caldwell College (BA)
Northeastern University
(Certificate)
Regent University (MA/PhD)
Rochester Institute of Technology
(Undergraduate Certificate)
Rutgers University (Certificate)
Syracuse University (MS)
Thomas Edison State College (BA)
University of Maryland—University
College (BA/BS)

University of Northern Iowa (MA)
University of Southern Indiana
(AS)

Communications Technology

Capella University
(Certificate/MS/PhD)
Jones International University
(Certificate)

Community Services

See Social Services/Social Work

Community Studies

University College of Cape Breton
(BA)

Comparative Literature

Cerro Coso Community College
(AA)

Competitive Intelligence

Drexel University (Certificate)

Computer-Aided Design

Michigan State University
(Certificate)
New Jersey Institute of Technology
(Certificate)
Thomas Edison State College
(Certificate)

Computer Art and Graphics

ICS Learning Systems (Diploma)
Rensselaer Polytechnic Institute
(Certificate)
Rochester Institute of Technology
(Undergraduate Certificate)

Computer Information Systems

Athabasca University
(Certificate/BS)
Baker College (Certificate/MBA)
Cerro Coso Community College
(AS)
National American University (BS)
New York University (Certificate)
Nova Southeastern University
(MS/PhD)
Regents College (BS)
Rensselaer Polytechnic Institute
(Certificate)
Saint Leo University (BS)
Saint Mary-of-the-Woods College
(Certificate/BS)
Southwest Missouri State University
(MS)
Southwestern Adventist University
(AS/BA)
Strayer University
(Diploma/AA/BS)
Thomas Edison State College
(Certificate/AS/BS)
University of Alaska—Southeast
(Certificate/AAS)
University of California Extension
(Certificate)
University of London
(Diploma/BS)
University of Maryland—University
College (BA/BS/MS)
University of Massachusetts—
Lowell (Certificate)
University of Phoenix (MS)
Vatterott College
(Diploma/Associate's)

Computer Programming

Champlain College
(Certificate/AS/BS)
Cochise College (Certificate)

ICS Learning Systems
(Certificate/Diploma)
New Jersey Institute of Technology
(Certificate)
New York University (Certificate)
Professional Career Development
Institute (Diploma)
University of Massachusetts—
Lowell (Certificate)
University of Phoenix (BS)
Vatterott College
(Diploma/Associate's)

Computer Repair

ICS Learning Systems (Diploma)
Professional Career Development
Institute (Diploma)

Computer Science

Ball State University (MS)
Caldwell College (BS)
California National University for
Advanced Studies (BS)
California State University—Chico
(BS/MS)
Colorado State University (BS/MS)
Columbia University
(Certificate/MS/Professional
Degree)
Florida State University (BS)
Franklin University (BS)
Grantham College of Engineering
(AS/BS)
ICS Learning Systems
(Certificate/Associate's)
Jamestown Community College
(AS)
Lakeland College (BA)
Lifetime Career Schools
(Certificate)
Mercy College (BS)
Mott Community College (AAS)
National Technological University
(MS)

New Jersey Institute of Technology
(BS)
Northwestern College (Ohio) (AS)
Nova Southeastern University
(MS/PhD)
Oklahoma State University (MS)
Professional Career Development
Institute (Diploma)
Regents College (BS)
Rensselaer Polytechnic Institute
(Certificate/MS)
Rogers State University (AS)
Southwestern Adventist University
(BS)
State University of New York—
Binghamton (MS)
Strayer University (BS)
Thomas Edison State College
(Certificate/AS/BS)
University of Alaska—Southeast
(Certificate)
University of Houston (MS)
University of Idaho (MS/PhD)
University of Illinois—Urbana-
Champaign (Master's)
University of Maryland—University
College (BA/BS)
University of Southern California
(MS)
Utah State University (BS/MS)

Conflict Resolution and Peace Studies

California State University—Chico
(Certificate)
Nova Southeastern University
(PhD)

Conservation and Wildlife

ICS Learning Systems (Diploma)
Professional Career Development
Institute (Diploma)

Construction

ICS Learning Systems (Diploma)
Thomas Edison State College (BS)

Contracts Management

*See Acquisition, Purchasing, and
Contracts Management*

Counseling

Athabasca University (Certificate)
Capella University
(Certificate/MS/PhD)
Goddard College (MA)
Institute of Transpersonal
Psychology (Certificate)
Liberty University (MA)
Mississippi State University (MS)
Seton Hall University (MA)
Southern Christian University (MS)
University of California—Los
Angeles (Certificate)
University of Sarasota
(MA/EdS/EdD)

Court Reporting

George Brown College (Diploma)
ICS Learning Systems (Diploma)

Creative Writing

Coastal Carolina University
(Certificate)
Goddard College (MFA)
Goucher College (MFA)
Institute of Transpersonal
Psychology (Certificate)
Johnson State College (BFA)
Kennesaw State University
(Certificate)
Professional Career Development
Institute (Diploma)
Warren Wilson College (MFA)

Criminal Justice

American Institute of Applied
Science (Diploma)
Andrew Jackson University
(BS/MS)
Athabasca University (Bachelor's)
Bellevue University (BS)
Bemidji State University (AS/BS)
Caldwell College (BA)
Cerro Coso Community College
(AS)
Florida Gulf Coast University (BS)
Florida State University (MS)
Herkimer County Community
College (AAS/AS)
Indiana State University (BS)
Kaplan College
(Diploma/Associate's/BS)
Leicester University (MS)
Memorial University of
Newfoundland (Certificate)
Michigan State University (MS)
Roger Williams University (BS)
Saint Joseph's College of Maine
(BA)
Seton Hall University (Master's)
Simon Fraser University
(Certificate/Diploma/BA)
Southwestern Adventist University
(BS)
State University of New York—
Empire State College (AS/BS)
Taylor University (AA)
Thomas Edison State College
(AS/BS)
University of Wisconsin—Platteville
(Diploma/MS)
Washington State University (BA)

Criminology

See Criminal Justice

Cross-Cultural, Language and Academic Development (CLAD)

California State University—Chico (Certificate)
National University (Certificate)
University of California—Los Angeles (Certificate)

Culinary Arts

ICS Learning Systems (Diploma)
Lifetime Career Schools (Diploma)

Cultural Studies

See Ethnic Studies

Customer Service Management

Coastal Carolina University (Certificate)
Financial Times Management (MA)
Floyd College (Certificate)
Iowa Western Community College (Certificate)
The Pennsylvania State University (Certificate)
University of Southern Colorado (Certificate)

Cytotechnology

Thomas Edison State College (BS)

Data Communications and Processing

Rochester Institute of Technology (Undergraduate Certificate)

Dental Assistance

California College for Health Sciences (Diploma)
George Brown College (Certificate)
ICS Learning Systems (Diploma)

Monroe Community College (Certificate)
Professional Career Development Institute (Diploma)

Dental Hygiene

Thomas Edison State College (BS)

Dental Laboratory Technology

J. Sargeant Reynolds Community College (Certificate)

Dental Radiology

University of London (Postgraduate Diploma/MS)

Dentistry

University of London (Master's/MS)

Desktop Publishing

ICS Learning Systems (Diploma)
University of Alaska—Southeast (Certificate)

Diesel Mechanics

ICS Learning Systems (Diploma)

Dietetics

The Pennsylvania State University (Certificate/Associate's)
University of Florida (Certificate)

Distance Education

Athabasca University (Advanced Graduate Diploma/Master's)
Capella University (Certificate/MS/PhD)
Indiana University (Certificate)
Nova Southeastern University (MS/EdD)
State University of West Georgia (Certificate)

University of London
(Postgraduate Diploma/MA)
University of Maryland University
College (Master's)

Doll Repair
Lifetime Career Schools (Diploma)

Drafting and Design
ICS Learning Systems (Diploma)

Drama
See Theater

Dressmaking
See Fashion Design and Merchandising

Early Childhood Education
California College for Health
Sciences (AS)
Cambrian College (Certificate)
Nova Southeastern University
(Certificate)
Saint Mary-of-the-Woods College
(AA)
University of Alaska—Southeast
(Certificate/Master's)
Utah State University (Certificate)
Western Carolina University (BS)

Earth and Space Sciences
University of Houston (BA)
University of North Dakota (MS)

Ecology
See Environmental Studies

Economics
Cerro Coso Community College
(AS)
Daytona Beach Community College
(AA)

Eastern Oregon University
(BA/BS)
Strayer University (AA/BS)
Thomas Edison State College (BS)
University of London
(Diploma/BS/MS)
University of Waterloo (BA)

Education
Capella University (MS/PhD)
College of St. Scholastica (MEd)
Colorado State University (MEd)
Eastern Oregon University
(Master's)
Endicott College (MEd)
The Fielding Institute (EdD)
The George Washington University
(MA)
Goddard College (BA/MA)
Johnson State College (BA)
King's College (MEd)
Leicester University (Diploma/MA)
Liberty University (MEd/EdD)
New River Community College
(Associate's)
Nova Southeastern University
(MS/EdS)
Oral Roberts University (MA/EdD)
Prescott College (BA)
Regent University (MEd)
Saint Joseph's College of Maine
(BA)
Saint Mary-of-the-Woods College
(BA)
Southwestern Assemblies of God
University (BA)
Stephens College (BA)
Troy State University (MS)
University College of Cape Breton
(Graduate Diploma)
University of Hawaii(Diploma)
University of Idaho (MEd)
University of London (Advanced
Diploma)

University of Phoenix (Master's)
Utah State University (Certificate)
Walden University (MS/PhD)
Webster University (MA)

Educational Administration

Ball State University (Master's)
Capella University
(Certificate/MS/PhD)
Iowa State University
(Certificate/MEd)
Leicester University
(Certificate/MBA)
Montana State University—
Bozeman (MEd)
Nova Southeastern University
(Certificate)
Purdue University (PhD)
Seton Hall University (Master's)
University of Manitoba
(Certificate)
University of Northern Iowa
(Certificate/Master's)
University of Sarasota (EdS/EdD)
University of South Alabama
(Certificate)
Utah State University (Certificate)

Educational Psychology

Capella University
(Certificate/MS/PhD)
University of Manitoba
(Certificate)

Educational Technology

Florida Gulf Coast University
(Master's)
Jones International University
(Certificate)
Lesley College (Master's)
McGill University (Certificate)
Mississippi State University (MS)
Nova Southeastern University
(Certificate/MS/EdS/EdD/PhD)

The Pennsylvania State University
(Certificate)
San Diego State University
(Certificate)
State University of New York—
Albany (MS)
Texas A&M University (MEd)
University College of Cape Breton
(Graduate Certificate)
University of California—Los
Angeles (Certificate)
University of Illinois—Urbana-
Champaign (MEd)
University of Nebraska—Lincoln
(Certificate)
University of Northern Iowa (MA)
University of Texas System (MEd)
Utah State University (MEd)

Electrical Technology

Thomas Edison State College
(AS/BS)

Electrician

ICS Learning Systems (Diploma)
Professional Career Development
Institute (Diploma)

Electronic Commerce

Capella University
(Certificate/MBA)
Capitol College (MS)
New York University (Certificate)

Electronic Media Design

New Jersey Institute of Technology
(Certificate)

Electronics

Cleveland Institute of Electronics
(AAS)
George Brown College
(Certificate)

ICS Learning Systems
(Diploma/Associate's)
Indiana State University (BS)
Professional Career Development
Institute (Diploma)
Regents College (AS)
Rensselaer Polytechnic Institute
(Certificate)
Thomas Edison State College
(Certificate)

Elementary and Secondary Education

Ball State University (Master's)
Johnson State College (BA)
Nova Southeastern University
(Certificate)
Saint Joseph's College of Maine
(Certificate)
Southwestern Adventist University
(BS)
University of Alaska—Southeast
(Certificate)
University of Northern Iowa
(Master's)
University of Sarasota (EdS/EdD)

Emergency Management

Leicester University (Diploma/MS)
Oklahoma State University
(Master's)
Rochester Institute of Technology
(Undergraduate Certificate)
Thomas Edison State College
(AS/BS)

Emergency Medical Technician

American College of Prehospital
Medicine (AS/BS)
The George Washington University
(Certificate)

Engineering

Auburn University (Master's)
California National University for
Advanced Studies (BS/MS)
Florida State University (MS)
Michigan Technological University
(BS)
North Carolina State University
(Master's)
Northern Virginia Community
College (AS)
State University of New York—
Binghamton (Master's)
University of Alabama (MS)
University of Florida (MS)
University of Wisconsin—Madison
(Master's)

Engineering—Aerospace

University of Alabama (MS)
University of Southern California
(MS)

Engineering—Biological and Agricultural

Colorado State University
(MS/PhD)
University of Idaho (Master's/MS)

Engineering—Bioresource

Colorado State University
(MS/PhD)

Engineering—Chemical

Colorado State University
(MS/PhD)
Kansas State University (MS)
Lehigh University (Master's)
National Technological University
(MS)
Oklahoma State University (MS)
University of North Dakota (BS)

Engineering—Civil

Colorado State University (MS)
ICS Learning Systems (Associate's)
Kansas State University (MS)
Thomas Edison State College (BS)
University of Alabama (MS)
University of Idaho (Master's/MS)

Engineering—Civil and Construction

Thomas Edison State College (AS)

Engineering—Civil and Environmental

Worcester Polytechnic Institute
(MS)

Engineering—Computer

Grantham College of Engineering
(AS/BS)
Iowa State University (MS)
National Technological University
(MS)
University of Idaho (Master's/MS)
University of Southern California
(MS)

Engineering—Computer Systems

Rensselaer Polytechnic Institute
(Master's)

Engineering—Electric Power

Rensselaer Polytechnic Institute
(Master's/MS)
University of Idaho (Certificate)

Engineering—Electrical

Colorado State University
(Master's/PhD)
Columbia University

(Certificate/MS/Professional
Degree)
Fairleigh Dickinson University
(MS)
ICS Learning Systems (Associate's)
Iowa State University (BS/MS)
Kansas State University (MS)
National Technological University
(MS)
Oklahoma State University (MS)
Rensselaer Polytechnic Institute
(Master's/MS)
Rochester Institute of Technology
(BS)
State University of New York at
Binghamton (MS)
University of Alabama (MS)
University of Houston (MS)
University of Idaho
(Master's/MS/PhD)
University of Illinois—Urbana-
Champaign (MS)
University of North Dakota (BS)
University of Southern California
(MS/Engineer)

Engineering—Electrical and Computer Science

Georgia Institute of Technology
(MS)

Engineering—Electronics

Colorado State University (MS)
Grantham College of Engineering
(AS/BS)
Regents College (BS)
Thomas Edison State College
(AS/BS)
University of Florida (BS)

Engineering—Environmental

Columbia University
(Certificate/MS)

Georgia Institute of Technology
(MS)
University of Alabama (MS)

Engineering—Geological

University of Idaho (MS)

Engineering—Graphics

Thomas Edison State College
(AS/BS)

Engineering—Industrial

Georgia Institute of Technology
(MS)
ICS Learning Systems (Associate's)
State University of New York—
Binghamton (MS)

Engineering—Industrial and Management

Rensselaer Polytechnic Institute
(Master's)

Engineering—Management

Columbia University
(Certificate/MS)
Drexel University (MS)
Kansas State University (Master's)
National Technological University
(MS)
New Jersey Institute of Technology
(MS)
Oklahoma State University (MS)
Syracuse University (MS)
University of Alabama (MS)
University of Houston (MS)
University of Idaho (Master's)

Engineering—Manufacturing

Thomas Edison State College
(AS/BS)

Engineering—Manufacturing Systems

National Technological University
(MS)
Rensselaer Polytechnic Institute
(Certificate)

Engineering—Marine

Thomas Edison State College
(AS/BS)

Engineering—Materials Science and Engineering

National Technological University
(MS)
University of London (MS)

Engineering—Mechanical

Colorado State University
(MS/PhD)
Columbia University
(Certificate/MS/Professional
Degree)
Georgia Institute of Technology
(MS)
ICS Learning Systems (Associate's)
Iowa State University (MS)
Michigan Technological University
(MS/PhD)
Oklahoma State University (MS)
Rensselaer Polytechnic Institute
(Certificate/Master's)
Rochester Institute of Technology
(BS)
Thomas Edison State College
(AS/BS)
University of Alabama (BS/MS)
University of Idaho (Master's)
University of North Dakota (BS)

Engineering—Metallurgical

University of Idaho (MS)

Engineering—Microelectronic

Rensselaer Polytechnic Institute
(Certificate)

Engineering—Mining

University of Idaho (MS)

Engineering—Noise Control

The Pennsylvania State University
(Certificate)

Engineering—Nuclear

Regents College (BS)
Thomas Edison State College
(AS/BS)

Engineering—Petroleum

Texas A&M University (Master's)

Engineering—Quality

Financial Times Management (MS)
Lehigh University (MS)

Engineering Sciences

Rensselaer Polytechnic Institute
(MS)

Engineering—Software

Carnegie Mellon University
(Certificate)
Florida State University (BS)
Kansas State University (Master's)
National Technological University
(MS)
Rensselaer Polytechnic Institute
(Certificate)
University of Maryland University
College (Master's)

Engineering—Systems

Iowa State University (Master's)
Texas A&M University (MS)

Engineering—Systems Science

State University of New York at
Binghamton (MS)

Engineering Technology

University of Central Florida (BS)

Engineering—Textile

North Carolina State University
(Certificate)

Engineering—Transportation Systems

National Technological University
(MS)

English

Athabasca University (BA)
Burlington College (BA)
Caldwell College (BA)
Cerro Coso Community College
(AA)
Johnson State College (BA)
Saint Mary-of-the-Woods College
(BA)
Southwestern Adventist University
(BA)
Stephens College (BA)
Thomas Edison State College (BA)
University of Houston (BA)
University of London
(Diploma/BA)
University of Maryland—University
College (BA)
University of Northern Iowa (MA)
University of Waterloo (BA)

English Language

Athabasca University (Certificate)

Enterprise Development

Canadian School of Management
(Executive Diploma)

Entrepreneurship

See Small Business Management

Environmental and Natural Resources Management

California State University—Bakersfield (Certificate/BS)
California State University—Chico (Certificate)
George Mason University (Certificate)
National Technological University (MS)
Rochester Institute of Technology (Undergraduate Certificate/BS)
University of Findlay (BS)
University of Maryland—University College (BS/MS)

Environmental Studies

Goddard College (BA/MA)
Johnson State College (BS)
Lakehead University (Certificate)
Oklahoma State University (MS)
Prescott College (BA)
Thomas Edison State College (AS/BA/BS)
University College of Cape Breton (Bachelor's)
University of Alaska—Southeast (AAS)
University of London (Postgraduate Diploma/MS)
University of Waterloo (Bachelor's)

Epidemiology

University of London (Postgraduate Diploma/MS)

Ethnic Studies

Fuller Theological Seminary (MA/ThM)

Event Management

The George Washington University (Certificate)

Facilities Management

See Building Management

Family and Consumer Sciences

Iowa State University (Master's)

Family Services

See Marriage and Family Services

Family Studies

See Human Development

Farm Management

See Agribusiness

Fashion Design and Merchandising

ICS Learning Systems (Diploma)
Lifetime Career Schools (Diploma)
North Carolina State University (Certificate/Master's)
Professional Career Development Institute (Diploma)

Film Studies

Burlington College (BA)

Finance and Banking

Aims Community College (AA)
The American College (Certificate/MS)
American Graduate University (Certificate)
Baker College (Certificate)
Capella University (MBA)
College for Financial Planning (MS)

Golden Gate University
(Undergraduate
Certificate/Graduate Certificate/
MS)
ICS Learning Systems (Associate's)
ISIM University (Certificate)
Keller Graduate School of
Management (Master's)
Leicester University (MS)
Marywood University (BS)
Mercy College (MS)
Regents College (BS)
Thomas Edison State College
(Certificate/AS/BS)
University of California—Los
Angeles (Certificate)
University of London (BS/MS)
University of Sarasota (Certificate)

Fine Arts

See Art and Design

Fire Protection and Security Services

Chemeketa Community College
(AAS)
Eastern Oregon University (BS)
Fox Valley Technical College (AS)
Herkimer County Community
College (AAS)
Leicester University (Diploma/MS)
State University of New York—
Empire State College
(Bachelor's/BS)
Thomas Edison State College
(AS/BS)
University of Florida (BS)
University of Maryland—University
College (BA/BS)
Western Oregon University
(Certificate/BA/BS)
Worcester Polytechnic Institute
(Certificate/MS)

Floral Design

ICS Learning Systems (Diploma)
Lifetime Career Schools (Diploma)
Professional Career Development
Institute (Diploma)

Food Science

See Nutrition and Food Science

Food Service Management

University of London
(Postgraduate Diploma/MS)

Forensic Psychology

Capella University (Certificate)
Leicester University (Diploma/MS)

Forensic Science

See Criminal Justice

Forestry

Lakehead University (Master's)
Thomas Edison State College
(AS/BS)

Freelance Writing

See Journalism

French

Athabasca University
(Certificate/BA)
University of London (BA)
University of Waterloo
(Certificate/BA)

Genealogy

Brigham Young University
(Certificate)

General Studies

See Liberal Arts

Geographic Information Systems

California State University—Bakersfield (Certificate)
The Pennsylvania State University (Certificate)

Geography

University of London (BA/MA)
University of Waterloo (BA)

German

University of London (BA)

Gerontology and Geriatrics

California College for Health Sciences (Certificate)
Cambrian College (Certificate)
Capella University (Certificate)
Laurentian University (Certificate)
The Pennsylvania State University (Certificate)
Saint Mary-of-the-Woods College (Certificate/AA/BA)
Thomas Edison State College (BS)
University of North Texas (Certificate/MS)
Utica College of Syracuse University (Certificate)

Global Studies

See World Studies

Government

See Political Science

Graphic Design

Mohawk Valley Community College (AAS)
Syracuse University (MA)

Guidance

See Counseling

Gunsmithing

ICS Learning Systems (Diploma)
Professional Career Development Institute (Diploma)

Hazardous Materials

See Waste Management

Health

Anglia Polytechnic University (BS)
Athabasca University (Master's)
California College for Health Sciences (Certificate/AS)
Capella University (MS/PhD)
Florida Gulf Coast University (BS/Master's)
The George Washington University (BS/MS)
Goddard College (BA/MA)
Johnson State College (BA)
University of Saint Francis (BS)

Health and Fitness

See Physical Education

Health Education

California College for Health Sciences (Certificate)
Cambrian College (Certificate)
Thomas Edison State College (BS)
University of Illinois—Chicago (Master's)
Weber State University (BS)

Health Information Administration

The George Washington University (Certificate)
Regents College (Certificate)
Stephens College (Certificate/BS)

University of Alaska—Southeast
(AAS)
University of Illinois—Chicago
(Certificate)
Weber State University (BS)

Health Physics

Georgia Institute of Technology
(MS)
Illinois Institute of Technology
(MS)
National Technological University
(MS)

Health Services Administration

Athabasca University
(Certificate/Bachelor's)
Baker College (Certificate/MBA)
California College for Health
Sciences (BS/MBA/MS)
Canadian School of Management
(Certificate/Diploma/Associate's/
BS/MS)
Capella University
(Certificate/MS/PhD)
Franklin University (BS)
Golden Gate University (Graduate
Certificate/Master's)
Keller Graduate School of
Management (Certificate)
New School University (Certificate)
Northwestern College Ohio) (BS)
Rochester Institute of Technology
(Undergraduate Certificate/
Graduate Certificate/MS)
Saint Joseph's College of Maine
(Certificate/BS/Master's)
Seton Hall University (Master's)
State University of New York—
Empire State College
(AS/Bachelor's/BS)
Thomas Edison State College (BS)

University of Florida (Master's)
University of London
(Postgraduate Diploma/MS)
University of Saint Augustine for
Health Sciences (MBA)
University of Sarasota (Certificate)
University of Southern Indiana
(BS)
Walden University (PhD)
Weber State University (BS)

Hearing Instrument Specialist

George Brown College
(Certificate)

High School Diploma

Choice 2000 Charter School
Citizens' High School
The Hadley School for the Blind
ICS Learning Systems
Indiana University
Keystone National High School
Louisiana State University
Phoenix Special Programs and
Academies
Professional Career Development
Institute
Richard Milburn High School
Texas Tech University
University of Missouri
University of Nebraska—Lincoln
University of Texas—Austin

Higher Education

Iowa State University (MEd)
Seton Hall University (MEd)
University of Sarasota (EdD)

Historic Preservation

Goucher College (MA)

History

Athabasca University (BA)
Atlantic Cape Community College
(AA)
Caldwell College (BA)
Cerro Coso Community College
(AA)
Johnson State College (BA)
Reformed Theological Seminary
(Certificate)
Southwestern Adventist University
(BA)
Thomas Edison State College (BA)
University of Houston (BA)
University of Manitoba (BA)
University of Waterloo (BA)

Home Economics

See Family and Consumer Sciences

Home Health Nursing/Aide

Athabasca University (Certificate)
California College for Health
Sciences (Diploma)
ICS Learning Systems (Certificate)
Regents College (Certificate)

Home Inspection

ICS Learning Systems (Diploma)
Professional Career Development
Institute (Diploma)

Home Schooling

Saint Joseph's College of Maine
(Certificate)

Horticulture

Thomas Edison State College
(AS/BS)

Hospital Administration

Thomas Edison State College
(AS/BS)

Hospitality

Canadian School of Management
(Certificate/Diploma/BS)
Champlain College
(Certificate/AS/BS)
Herkimer County Community
College (AAS)
ICS Learning Systems
(Diploma/Associate's)
Johnson State College (BA)
Niagara College (Certificate)
Northeastern Arizona University
(Certificate)
Northwestern College (Ohio) (AS)
The Pennsylvania State University
(Associate's)
Professional Career Development
Institute (Diploma)
Thomas Edison State College
(AS/BS)
Tompkins Cortland Community
College (AAS)
University of Delaware (BS)
University of Houston
(BS/Master's)

Hotel, Restaurant, and Institutional Management

See Hospitality

Human Development

Eckerd College (BA)
The Fielding Institute (PhD)
The George Washington University
(MA)
Hope International University (BS)
Laurentian University (Certificate)
Pacific Oaks College
(Certificate/BA/MA)
The Pennsylvania State University
(Associate's)
Salve Regina University (MA)
Washington State University (BA)

Human Environments

Utah State University (MS)

Human Resource Management

The American College (Certificate)
Baker College (Certificate/MBA)
California National University for Advanced Studies (Master's)
Indiana State University (BS)
Jones International University (Certificate)
Keller Graduate School of Management (Certificate/Master's)
Leicester University Centre for Labour Market Studies (Diploma/MS)
New Jersey Institute of Technology (Certificate)
The Pennsylvania State University (Certificate)
Regents College (BS)
Saint Mary-of-the-Woods College (BS)
Seton Hall University (Master's)
Texas A&M University (MS)
Texas Tech University (Certificate)
Thomas Edison State College (Certificate/AS/BS)
Troy State University (MS)
University of Sarasota (Certificate)
Upper Iowa University (BS)
Utah State University (Master's)

Human Sciences

See Social Sciences

Human Services

See Social Services/Social Work

Humanities

Athabasca University (BA)
California Institute of Integral Studies (PhD)

California State University—Dominguez Hills (MA)
Cerro Coso Community College (AA)
Herkimer County Community College (AA)
Saint Mary-of-the-Woods College (AA/BA)
Thomas Edison State College (BA)
University of Maryland—University College (BA)

Hypnotherapy

Hypnosis Motivation Institute (Certificate)

Inclusive Education

Athabasca University (Diploma)

Individualized Studies

Burlington College (BA)
Goddard College (BA/MA)
Ohio University (Associate's)
Skidmore College (BA/BS)
Stephens College (BA)
Ulster County Community College (AS)
The Union Institute (BA/BS)
University of Wisconsin—Superior (BA/BS)
Western Illinois University (BA)

Industrial Operations

Baker College (Certificate/MBA)
Indiana State University (BS)
Regents College (BS)
Rochester Institute of Technology (Undergraduate Certificate)
Thomas Edison State College (Certificate/AS/BS)
University of Houston (BS)

Industrial Relations

See Labor Studies

Industrial Technology
East Carolina University (BS/MS)
George Brown College (BA)
Indiana State University (BS)
Roger Williams University (BS)

Infectious Diseases
University of London
(Postgraduate Diploma/MS)

Information Management and Sciences
See Management Information Systems

Information Technology
Aims Community College
(Certificate)
Capella University
(Certificate/MBA)
Capitol College (BS)
Charles County Community
College (AAS)
Indiana University (Certificate)
New Jersey Institute of Technology
(Certificate)
New York University (Certificate)
Northeastern University
(Certificate)
Northern Virginia Community
College (AAS)
Rensselaer Polytechnic Institute
(MS)
Rochester Institute of Technology
(MS)
University of Massachusetts—
Lowell (Certificate)
University of Phoenix (BS)

Instructional Design
Capella University
(Certificate/MS/PhD)
Florida State University (MS)
Montana State University—
Bozeman (MEd)

University of Manitoba
(Certificate)
University of South Alabama (MS)

Insurance
The American College (Certificate)
Cambrian College (Certificate)
Indiana State University (BS)
Thomas Edison State College
(AS/BS)

Interdisciplinary Studies
California State University—
Dominguez Hills (BA)
Coastal Carolina University
(BA/BS)
Goddard College (MFA)
Hamilton College (AS)
Liberty University (BS)
Rochester Institute of Technology
(MS)
State University of New York—
Empire State College (AS/BS)
University of Wisconsin—Green
Bay (BA)

Interior Decorating
ICS Learning Systems (Diploma)
Professional Career Development
Institute (Diploma)

Interior Design
Rhodec International (Associate
Diploma/Diploma/BA)

International Affairs
Salve Regina University (MA)
Southwestern Adventist University
(BA)
Troy State University (MS)

International Business
Athabasca University (Bachelor's)
Baker College (Certificate/MBA)

Bellevue University (BS)
Caldwell College (BS)
Canadian School of Management
(MBA)
Cochise College (Certificate)
Duke University (Executive MBA)
Hope International University
(MBA)
Memorial University of
Newfoundland (Bachelor's)
National Technological University
(MBA)
National University (MBA)
Regents College (BS)
Strayer University (BS)
Thomas Edison State College
(AS/BS)
University of Maryland—University
College (Master's)
University of Phoenix (MBA)
University of Sarasota (Certificate)
University of Texas—Dallas
(MA/Executive MBA)

Internet

See Information Technology

Interpreter

New York University (Certificate)

Italian

University of London (BA)

Japanese

University of Wisconsin——Madison
(Master's)

Jewelry

Gemological Institute of America
(Diploma)
ICS Learning Systems (Diploma)

Journalism

ICS Learning Systems (Diploma)
Johnson State College (BA)
Parkland College (AA)
Regent University (MA)
Saint Mary-of-the-Woods College
(BA)
Southwestern Adventist University
(BA/BS)
Thomas Edison State College (BA)

Judaic Studies

Spertus Institute of Jewish Studies
(MS/Doctor)
University of London (BA)

Knowledge Management

See Management Information Systems

Labor Studies

Amber University (BS/MS)
Athabasca University
(Certificate/Bachelor of
Administration/BA)
Indiana University
(Certificate/AS/BS)
State University of New York—
Empire State College (AS/BS)
Thomas Edison State College
(Certificate/BS)

Landscaping

ICS Learning Systems (Diploma)
Lifetime Career Schools (Diploma)
Professional Career Development
Institute (Diploma)

Language Education

Indiana University (MS)

Languages

Thomas Edison State College (BA)

Latin American Studies
University of London (BA)

Law
Leicester University
(Certificate/Diploma/MA)

Law Enforcement
See Criminal Justice

Leadership
Amber University (MBA)
The American College (Certificate)
Baker College (MBA)
Bellevue University (MA)
Capella University
(Certificate/MBA)
Duquesne University (MA)
Financial Times Management
(Certificate)
Jones International University
(Certificate)
The Pennsylvania State University
(Certificate)
Regent University (MA/PhD)
Seton Hall University (MA)
University of Sarasota (EdD)
Upper Iowa University (MA)

Legal Assistance/ Paralegal Studies
American Institute for Paralegal
Studies (Certificate)
Brevard Community College (AS)
California State University—Chico
(Certificate)
California State University—San
Marcos (Certificate)
ICS Learning Systems (Diploma)
Iowa Western Community College
(Certificate)
Floyd College (Certificate)

Northwestern College –(Ohio)
(AS)
Kaplan College
(Diploma/Associate's/BS)
Pennsylvania State University
(Certificate)
Professional Career Development
Institute (Diploma)
Saint Mary-of-the-Woods College
(Certificate/AA/BA)
Thomas Edison State College
(AS/BS)
Tompkins Cortland Community
College (AAS)
University of Florida (Certificate)
University of Maryland—University
College (BA/BS)
University of Southern Colorado
(Certificate)
Western Piedmont Community
College (AAS)

Legal Nurse Consultant
Kaplan College
(Diploma/Associate's)

Legal Secretary
ICS Learning Systems (Diploma)
Northwestern College (Ohio) (AS)
Professional Career Development
Institute (Diploma)

Leisure Studies
*See Recreation, Park Resources, and
Leisure Studies*

Liberal Arts
Andrews University/Home Study
International (AA/BA/BS)
Athabasca University
(Diploma/BA/BGS)
Atlantic Cape Community College
(AA/AS)

Ball State University (AA)

Bellevue Community College (AA)

Bemidji State University (AA)

Brevard Community College (AA)

Bucks County Community College
(AA)

Burlington County College (AA)

California State University—Chico
(BA)

Central Carolina Community
College (AA)

Central Wyoming College (AA)

Cerro Coso Community College
(AA)

Charles County Community
College (AA)

Charter Oak State College
(AA/AS/BA/BS)

Chemeketa Community College
(AA/AGS)

Colorado Electronic Community
College (AA)

Columbia Union College
(AA/AS/BA/BS)

Columbus State Community
College (AA)

Covenant Theological Seminary
(Certificate)

Dallas TeleCollege (AA/AS)

Duquesne University (MA)

Eastern Oregon University
(BA/BS)

Emporia State University (BGS)

Foothill College (AA)

Fort Hays State University
(BGS/Master's)

Governors State University (BA)

Herkimer County Community
College (AA)

Indiana University (AGS/BGS)

International Management Centers
(MS/DLitt)

Iowa State University (Bachelor's)

Johnson State College (BA/BS)

Lakehead University (BA)

Lane Community College (AA)

Laurentian University (Bachelor's)

Liberty University (AA)

Mercy College (AA/AS)

Montana State University—
Billings (BS)

Mott Community College
(AA/AGS/AS)

New River Community College
(Associate's)

New School University (BA)

Niagara College (Diploma)

Northampton Community College
(AA)

Northern Virginia Community
College (AS)

Ohio University (AA)

Oral Roberts University (BS)

Palm Beach Community College
(AA)

Parkland College (AGS)

Pennsylvania State University
(Associate's)

Piedmont Technical College (AA)

Portland Community College
(AA/AGS)

Reformed Theological Seminary
(Certificate)

Regents College
(AA/AS/BA/BS/MA)

Rogers State University (AA)

Saint Joseph's College of Maine
(BA)

Schoolcraft College/Madonna
University (AS)

Simon Fraser University
(Certificate/Bachelor's)

Sinclair Community College (AA)

Skidmore College (MA)

Strayer University (AA)

Syracuse University (AA/BA)

Taylor University (AA)

Texas Tech University (BGS)

Thomas Edison State College
(AA/BA)
Troy State University—Montgomery
(AS)
Tulsa Community College/
Emporia State University (BGS)
University of Alaska—Southeast
(AA)
University of Central Florida
(BA/BS)
University of Illinois—Springfield
(BA)
University of Iowa (Bachelor's)
University of Maine
(Bachelor's/MA)
University of Minnesota—Twin
Cities (Certificate)
University of Northern Iowa
(Bachelor's)
University of Oklahoma
(Bachelor's)
University of Phoenix (AA)
University of Waterloo (BA)

Library Science

Indiana University (Certificate)
Memorial University of
Newfoundland (Certificate)
Northampton Community College
(Diploma)
Rutgers University (Certificate)
Syracuse University (MLS)
Texas Woman's University (MLS)
University of Arizona (MA)
University of Illinois—Urbana-
Champaign (MS)
University of Northern Iowa (MA)
Upper Iowa University (AA)
Utah State University (Certificate)

Linguistics

Leicester University
(Certificate/MA)

Livestock Science

University of London
(Postgraduate Diploma/MS)

Locksmithing

ICS Learning Systems (Diploma)
Professional Career Development
Institute (Diploma)

Logistics

*See Transportation, Logistics, and
Supply Chain Management*

Long-Term Care Administration

Canadian School of Management
(BS)
Saint Joseph's College of Maine
(Certificate/BS)
University of North Texas (MS)

Management

Amber University (MBA)
American Graduate University
(Certificate)
Athabasca University
(Bachelor's/Advanced Graduate
Diploma)
Aurora University (Certificate)
Bellevue University (BS)
Bucks County Community College
(AA)
Caldwell College (BS)
Canadian School of Management
(Certificate/Diploma/BS/
Advanced Diploma)
Capella University (Certificate)
Cerro Coso Community College
(AS)
Champlain College
(Certificate/AS/BS)
Charles County Community
College (AAS)

Columbus State Community
College (Associate's)

Eckerd College (BA)

Financial Times Management
(Certificate/Postgraduate
Certificate/Postgraduate
Diploma)

Florida Institute of Technology
(MS)

Hamilton College (AS)

Henley Management College
(Diploma)

Hope International University
(MS)

ICS Learning Systems (Associate's)

International Management Centres
(Certificate/Diploma/Bachelor's)

ISIM University (Certificate)

Johnson State College (BA)

Jones International University
(Certificate)

Leicester University
(Certificate/Diploma)

Leicester University Centre for
Labour Market Studies (MS)

Marylhurst University (MS)

Marywood University (BS)

National American University (BS)

National-Louis University (BS)

Northern Virginia Community
College (AAS)

Northwest Missouri State University
(BS)

Nova Southeastern University (BS)

Oral Roberts University (Master's)

Parkland College (AAS)

Pennsylvania State University
(Certificate)

Portland Community College
(AAS)

Prescott College (BA)

Purdue University (MS)

Regents College (AAS)

Rensselaer Polytechnic Institute
(MS)

Roger Williams University (BS)

Saint Joseph's College of Maine
(AS)

Salve Regina University (MS)

Southwestern Adventist University
(BS)

State University of New York—
Empire State College
(Bachelor's/BS)

Teikyo Post University (AS/BS)

Thomas Edison State College
(AS/BS/MS)

University College of Cape Breton
(Certificate)

University of Findlay (BS)

University of London (BS)

University of Maryland—University
College (BA/BS/MS)

University of Phoenix (BS)

University of Texas System (MBA)

Upper Iowa University (BS)

Walden University (PhD)

Worcester Polytechnic Institute
(Certificate)

Management Information Systems

Amber University (BS)

Athabasca University
(Certificate/BA)

Bellevue University (BS)

Canadian School of Management
(Executive Diploma)

Capitol College (MS)

Carnegie Mellon University
(Certificate)

Columbia Union College (BS)

Drexel University (MS)

Financial Times Management (MS)

Florida State University (BS/MS)

Franklin University (BS)

ISIM University (Certificate/MS)

Keller Graduate School of
Management (Certificate/Master's)

Memorial University of
Newfoundland (Certificate)
Mississippi State University (MS)
New Jersey Institute of Technology
(Certificate/BA/MS)
New York University (MS)
Nova Southeastern University
(MS/PhD)
Regents College (BS)
Rensselaer Polytechnic Institute
(Certificate)
Strayer University (MS)
Syracuse University (MS)
Teikyo Post University (BS)
University of Hawaii (Certificate)
University of Illinois—Springfield
(MS)
University of London (BS)
University of Maryland—University
College (BA/BS)
University of Massachusetts—
Lowell (AS/BS)
University of Phoenix (BS)
University of Tennessee—Knoxville
(MS)
University of Texas—San Antonio
(MS)
Utah State University (BS/MS)

Manufacturing

See Industrial Technology

Marketing

Baker College (Certificate/MBA)
Bucks County Community College
(AA)
Caldwell College (BS)
Canadian School of Management
(Diploma/Advanced Diploma)
ICS Learning Systems (Associate's)
Jones International University
(Certificate)
Lakeland College (BA)

Leicester University (MS)
Marywood University (BS)
Mercy College (MS)
Northwestern College (Ohio) (AS)
Pennsylvania State University
(Certificate)
Regents College (BS)
Saint Mary-of-the-Woods College
(BS)
San Jose State University
(Certificate)
State University of New York—
Empire State College
(Bachelor's/BS)
Strayer University (AA)
Thomas Edison State College
(Certificate/AS/BS)
University of California Extension
(Certificate)
University of Phoenix (BS)
University of Sarasota (Certificate)
Upper Iowa University (BS)

Marriage and Family Services

Capella University
(Certificate/MS/PhD)
Pennsylvania State University
(Certificate)
Southern Christian University
(MS/DMin)
University of Maine (Certificate)

Masonry

ICS Learning Systems (Diploma)

Mass Communications

Bellevue Community College
(Certificate/AA)
Leicester University (MA)
New College of California (MA)
New School University (MA)
Parkland College (AA)

Materials Management

*See Production and Inventory
Management*

Materials Science

Columbia University
(Certificate/MS)

Mathematics

Johnson State College (BA)
Saint Mary-of-the-Woods College
(BS)
Southwestern Adventist University
(BA/BS)
Thomas Edison State College
(AS/BS)
University of London (BS)

Mathematics Education

Florida State University (MEd)
Iowa State University (Master's)
Montana State University—
Bozeman (MS)
University of Idaho (MA)
University of Northern Iowa (MA)

Mechanics

University of Houston (BS)
University of Illinois—Urbana-
Champaign (MS)

Media Studies

See Mass Communications

Medical Assistance

California College for Health
Sciences (Diploma)
Portland Community College
(Certificate)
Professional Career Development
Institute (Diploma)

Medical Imaging

Anglia Polytechnic University (MS)
Thomas Edison State College (BS)

Medical Office Management

ICS Learning Systems (Diploma)
National Association Medical Staff
Services Institute (Certificate)
Northwestern College (Ohio) (AS)
Professional Career Development
Institute (Diploma)

Medical Record Administration

See Health Information Administration

Medical Secretary

Northwestern College (Ohio) (AS)

Medical Spanish for Healthcare Professionals

Texas Tech University (Certificate)

Medical Technology

See Clinical Laboratory Science

Medical Transcription

California College for Health
Sciences (AS)
ICS Learning Systems (Diploma)
Professional Career Development
Institute (Diploma)

Medieval Studies

University of Waterloo (BA)

Mental Health Services

Capella University (Certificate)
Thomas Edison State College (BS)
University of Sarasota (MA)

Microbiology

Iowa State University (MS)

Military Studies

American Military University
(BA/MA)

Ministry

Aquinas Institute of Theology
(DMin)
Berean University
(Diploma/AA/MA)
Drew University
(Certificate/DMin)
Franciscan University of
Steubenville (MA)
Fuller Theological Seminary
(Certificate)
Hope International University
(MA)
ICI University (Advanced
Certificate/Diploma/MA)
Lee University (BA)
Nazarene Bible College (AA)
Northwestern College (Minnesota)
(BA)
Oral Roberts University (BS)
Prairie Bible Institute
(Certificate/Bachelor's)
Seminary Extension Independent
Study Institute (Diploma)
Seton Hall University (Certificate)
Southern Christian University
(MS/DMin)
Southwestern Assembles of God
University (BA)
Taylor University (Certificate)

Missionary Studies

Berean University (BA)
ICI University (Advanced
Certificate/BA)
Prairie Bible Institute (Certificate)

Reformed Theological Seminary
(Certificate)
Wheaton College (MA)

Modeling

ICS Learning Systems (Certificate)

Molecular Biology

Lehigh University (MS)

Motorcycle Repair

ICS Learning Systems (Diploma)
Professional Career Development
Institute (Diploma)

Multimedia Authoring

*See Web Site Development/Multimedia
Authoring*

Museum Studies

Leicester University (MA/MS)

Music

Johnson State College (BA)
Southwestern Adventist University
(BA)
Thomas Edison State College (BA)
University of London (Bachelor's)

Music, Arts, and Entertainment Business

New School University (Certificate)
Regent University (MA)

Music Education

Duquesne University (Master's)
University of Northern Iowa
(Master's)

Native American Studies

Laurentian University (BA)

Natural Resources

See Environmental and Natural Resources Management

Natural Sciences

See Biological and Physical Sciences

Nondestructive Testing Technology

Thomas Edison State College (AS/BS)

Nuclear Medicine Technology

Thomas Edison State College (AS/BS)

Nuclear Technology

Regents College (AS)

Nurse Practitioner

The George Washington University (Certificate)

Nursing

Athabasca University (Bachelor's/Advanced Graduate Diploma)
Ball State University (BS/MS)
California State University—Chico (BS)
California State University—Dominguez Hills (BS)
Cambrian College (Certificate)
Duquesne University (PhD)
Florida State University (BS)
George Brown College (Certificate)
Indiana State University (BS)
Indiana University (MS)
Lakehead University (BS)
Laurentian University (BS)

Montana State University—Bozeman (BS/Master's)
National University (BS)
Regents College (AAS/AS/MS)
Saint Joseph's College of Maine (MS)
Saint Louis University (MS)
Syracuse University (MS)
Thomas Edison State College (BS)
University of Delaware (BS)
University of Hawaii (MS)
University of Illinois—Chicago (Certificate)
University of Manitoba (Bachelor's)
University of Phoenix (BS/MS)
University of South Alabama (BS)
University of Southern Indiana (BS)
University of Wisconsin Extension (BS)
West Virginia Wesleyan College (BS)

Nutrition and Food Science

American Academy of Nutrition (AS)
American Health Science University (Certificate)
Auburn University (MS)
ICS Learning Systems (Diploma)
Kansas State University (Certificate)
Oregon State University (MS)
Thomas Edison State College (BS)

Occupational Safety and Health

Cambrian College (Certificate)
McGill University (MS)
Rochester Institute of Technology (MS)
Tulane University (Master's)

Office Management and Technology

Bellevue Community College
(Certificate)
Canadian School of Management
(Certificate)
Eastern Oregon University (AS)
Marywood University (Certificate)
Southwestern Adventist University
(AS/BS)
Thomas Edison State College
(Certificate/AS/BS)
University of Alaska—Southeast
(Certificate)

Operations Research

Georgia Institute of Technology
(MS)

Opticianry

J. Sargeant Reynolds Community
College (Certificate)

Organization

Athabasca University (Bachelor's)
Canadian School of Management
(Certificate/Executive Diploma)
Capella University (MS/PhD)
Eckerd College (BA)
The Fielding Institute (MA/PhD)
Marylhurst University (BA)
Thomas Edison State College (BS)
University of London
(Postgraduate Diploma/MS)
University of Phoenix
(MA/Doctor)

Outdoor Education

Johnson State College (BA)

Paralegal Studies

See Legal Assistance/Paralegal Studies

Paramedic

See Emergency Medical Technician

Parks and Recreation

*See Recreation, Park Resources, and
Leisure Studies*

Pastoral Ministries and Counseling

Berean University (BA)
Saint Joseph's College of Maine
(MA)
Seminary Extension Independent
Study Institute
(Certificate/Diploma)
Southern Christian University (MS)
University of Sarasota (EdD)

Peace Studies

*See Conflict Resolution and Peace
Studies*

Performing Arts

Johnson State College (BA/BFA)

Perfusionist

Thomas Edison State College (BS)

Perinatal Intensive Care

George Brown College
(Certificate)

Pet Grooming

ICS Learning Systems (Diploma)

Pharmacology

Lehigh University (MS)

Pharmacy

Duquesne University (PharmD)
University of Florida (PharmD)
University of Illinois—Chicago
(PharmD)

University of Montana (PharmD)
Washington State University
(PharmD)

Pharmacy Technology
California College for Health
Sciences (Diploma)
ICS Learning Systems (Diploma)
Northwestern College (Ohio) (AS)
Professional Career Development
Institute (Diploma)

Philosophy
Christopher Newport University
(BA)
Eastern Oregon University
(BA/BS)
International Management Centres
(Master's/DPhil)
Saint Mary-of-the-Woods College
(BA)
Stephens College (BA)
Thomas Edison State College (BA)
University of London (BA)
University of Waterloo (BA)

Photography
ICS Learning Systems (Diploma)
Thomas Edison State College (BA)

Physical Education
Eastern Oregon University (BS)
ICS Learning Systems (Diploma)
Mississippi State University (MS)
Professional Career Development
Institute (Diploma)
Simon Fraser University (Certificate)
Southwestern Adventist University
(AS)

Physical Therapist Assistance
California College for Health
Sciences (Diploma)

Physical Therapy
University of Saint Augustine for
Health Sciences (MS/Doctor)

Physics
Michigan State University
(MS/PhD)
Thomas Edison State College
(AS/BS)

Piano and Organ
Brigham Young University
(Certificate)

Plastics
Lehigh University (MS)
University of Massachusetts—
Lowell (Certificate)

Plumbing
ICS Learning Systems (Diploma)
Professional Career Development
Institute (Diploma)

Political Science
Ball State University (MA)
Caldwell College (BA)
California State University—Chico
(BA)
Daytona Beach Community College
(AA)
Eastern Oregon University
(BA/BS)
Johnson State College (BA)
Regent University (MA)
Thomas Edison State College (BA)
University of Manitoba (BA)
Virginia Tech (MA)

Pollution Prevention
Worcester Polytechnic Institute
(Certificate)

Polysomnography

California College for Health
Sciences (Certificate)

Private Investigation

ICS Learning Systems (Diploma)
Professional Career Development
Institute (Diploma)

Procurement

Thomas Edison State College
(AS/BS)

Production and Inventory Management

California State University—
Dominguez Hills (Certificate)
Floyd College (Certificate)
Iowa Western Community College
(Certificate)
Thomas Edison State College
(AS/BS)
Tompkins Cortland Community
College (Certificate)
Weber State University (Certificate)

Professional Studies

International Management Centres
(Bachelor's)
Saint Joseph's College of Maine
(Certificate/BS)
Troy State University—
Montgomery (BA/BS)

Project Management

American Graduate University
(Certificate/Master's)
Coastal Carolina University
(Certificate)
Floyd College (Certificate)
The George Washington University
(MS)
Iowa Western Community College
(Certificate)

ISIM University (Certificate)
Keller Graduate School of
Management (Certificate/Master's)
New Jersey Institute of Technology
(Certificate)
Saint Joseph's College of Maine
(Certificate)
University of California Extension
(Certificate)
University of Phoenix (BS)
University of Wisconsin—Platteville
(MS)
Western Carolina University
(Master's)

Property Management

See Building Management

Psycho-Neurological Testing

Capella University (Certificate)

Psychology

Athabasca University (BA)
Burlington College (BA)
Caldwell College (BA)
California State University—
Dominguez Hills (MA)
Capella University (MS/PhD)
Columbia Union College (BA)
Commonwealth International
University (MA)
The Fielding Institute (PhD)
Goddard College (MA)
Johnson State College (BA)
Laurentian University (BA)
Liberty University (BS)
Mercy College (BA/BS)
Saint Mary-of-the-Woods College
(BA)
Simon Fraser University (BA)
Southwestern Adventist University
(BS)
Stephens College (BA)

Thomas Edison State College (BS)
University of Houston (BA/BS)
University of Idaho (MS)
University of Manitoba (BA)
University of Maryland—University
College (BA/BS)
University of Waterloo (BA)
Utah State University (BS/MS)
Walden University
(Certificate/MS/PhD)

Public Administration/ Public Affairs

Andrew Jackson University (MPA)
Athabasca University
(Certificate/Bachelor's)
Cambrian College (Certificate)
Christopher Newport University
(BS)
Florida Gulf Coast University
(MPA)
Golden Gate University
(Bachelor's/Executive MPA)
Iowa State University
(Certificate/MPA)
Johnson State College (BA)
Memorial University of
Newfoundland (Certificate)
Regent University (MA/MPA)
Roger Williams University (BS)
State University of New York—
Empire State College (AS/BS)
Thomas Edison State College
(Certificate/AS/BS)
Troy State University (MPA)
University College of Cape Breton
(Certificate)
University of Alaska—Southeast
(MPA)
University of Colorado—Denver
(MPA)
University of London
(Postgraduate Diploma/MS)
Upper Iowa University (BS)

Public Health

California College for Health
Sciences (MS)
The George Washington University
(Certificate)
Johns Hopkins University
(Graduate Certificate/Master's)

Public Relations

Ball State University (Certificate)
Jones International University
(Certificate)
Parkland College (AA)
University of Northern Iowa (MA)

Purchasing

*See Acquisition, Purchasing, and
Contracts Management*

Quality Management/Quality Assurance

California National University for
Advanced Studies (BS)
California State University—
Dominguez Hills (MS)
Canadian School of Management
(Executive Diploma)
Financial Times Management
(Postgraduate
Certificate/Postgraduate
Diploma/MA)
Floyd College (Certificate)
International Management Centres
(Certificate/Diploma)
Iowa Western Community College
(Certificate)
Rensselaer Polytechnic Institute
(Certificate)
Rochester Institute of Technology
(Undergraduate Certificate)

Radiation Protection and Therapy

Thomas Edison State College
(AS/BS)

Radio/Television/Motion Pictures

See Broadcasting

Radiography

Anglia Polytechnic University (MS)

Radiologic Science

Saint Joseph's College of Maine
(BS)
Thomas Edison State College
(AAS)
Weber State University (BS)

Radiotelephone Operator

Aviation and Electronic Schools of
America (License)

Ranch Management

See Agribusiness

Real Estate

Professional Career Development
Institute (Diploma)
Thomas Edison State College
(AS/BS)

Recreation, Park Resources, and Leisure Studies

George Mason University
(Certificate)
Indiana University (Master's)
Northeastern Arizona University
(Certificate)
Thomas Edison State College
(AS/BS)

Rehabilitation Services

Athabasca University (Certificate)
San Diego State University
(Master's)

Religion

Andrews University/Home Study
International (BA)
Caldwell College (BA)
The Catholic Distance University
(MA/Master's)
Christopher Newport University
(BA)
Columbia Union College (BA)
ICI University (AA)
Laurentian University (BA)
Liberty University (AA/BS/MS)
Prairie Bible Institute (AA)
Reformed Theological Seminary
(MA)
Southwestern Adventist University
(BA)
Thomas Edison State College (BA)
University of Waterloo (BA)

Religious Education

Berean University (BA)
Defiance College
(Certificate/AA/BA/BS)
ICI University (Advanced
Certificate/BA)
Nazarene Bible College
(AA/Bachelor's)
Oral Roberts University (BS)

Resource Management

Troy State University (Bachelor's)

Respiratory Therapy

California College for Health
Sciences (AS)
Columbia Union College (BS)
J. Sargeant Reynolds Community
College (Certificate/AAS)

Saint Joseph's College of Maine
(BS)
Thomas Edison State College
(AS/BS)
Weber State University (AS/BS)

Respiratory Therapy Technician

California College for Health
Sciences (AS)

Retailing

Pennsylvania State University
(Certificate)
Thomas Edison State College
(AS/BS)

Science

See Biological and Physical Sciences

Science Education

Florida State University (MEd)
Montana State University—
Bozeman (MS)

Secondary Education

*See Elementary and Secondary
Education*

Secretarial

See Administrative Assistance

Security Services

See Fire Protection and Security Services

Service Systems

Rensselaer Polytechnic Institute
(Certificate)

Small Business Management

Bucks County Community College
(Certificate)

ICS Learning Systems (Diploma)
Lifetime Career Schools (Diploma)
The Pennsylvania State University
(Certificate)
Professional Career Development
Institute (Diploma)
Thomas Edison State College
(AS/BS)

Social Commentary

The Pennsylvania State University
(Certificate)

Social Sciences

Athabasca University (BS)
Caldwell College (BA)
California State University—Chico
(BA)
Cerro Coso Community College
(AA)
Daytona Beach Community College
(AA)
Foothill College (AA)
Herkimer County Community
College (AA)
Kansas State University (BS)
Ohio University (AA)
Southwestern Adventist University
(BA/BS)
Syracuse University (Master's)
Thomas Edison State College (BA)
University of Maryland—University
College (BA/BS)
University of Southern Colorado
(BS)
University of Waterloo (BA)
Upper Iowa University (BS)
Washington State University (BA)

Social Services/ Social Work

Capella University
(Certificate/MS/PhD)
Iowa State University (Certificate)

Laurentian University (Bachelor's)
Memorial University of
Newfoundland (Bachelor's)
Prescott College (BA)
Saint Mary-of-the-Woods College
(BA)
State University of New York—
Empire State College (AS/BS)
Thomas Edison State College
(AS/BS)
University of Alaska—Southeast
(AS)
University of Manitoba
(Bachelor's)
University of Waterloo (Certificate)
Upper Iowa University (BS)
Walden University (PhD)

Sociology

Athabasca University (BA)
Caldwell College (BA)
California State University—Chico
(BA)
Johnson State College (BA)
Laurentian University (BA)
Thomas Edison State College (BA)
University of Manitoba (BA)
University of Waterloo (BA)

Software Development and Management

Capitol College (BS)
Regents College (AS)
Rochester Institute of Technology
(MS)

Space Sciences

See Earth and Space Sciences

Spanish

University of London (BA)

Special Education

Ball State University (Master's)
University of Northern Iowa
(Master's)

Specialized Studies

Ohio University (Bachelor's)

Speech and Language Pathology

*See Communication Disorders and
Audiology*

Spiritual Development and Psychology

Institute of Transpersonal
Psychology (Certificate)

Sports and Exercise Studies

Capella University
(Certificate/MS/PhD)
Leicester University (Diploma/MS)

Sports Management

See Athletic and Sports Administration

Sports Medicine

*See Athletic Training and Sports
Medicine*

Statistics

Colorado State University (MS)
Iowa State University (MS)
Rochester Institute of Technology
(Graduate Certificate/MS)
University of Tennessee—Knoxville
(Certificate)

Studio Arts

See Art and Design

Supervision

Coastal Carolina Community
College (Certificate)
Floyd College (Certificate)
Iowa Western Community College
(Certificate)
Texas Tech University (Certificate)
Tompkins Cortland Community
College (Certificate)
University of Southern Colorado
(Certificate)

Surgical Technology

Central Wyoming College (AAS)

Surveying and Mapping

ICS Learning Systems (Diploma)
Michigan Technological University
(BS)
Thomas Edison State College
(AS/BS)

Sustainable Development

Prescott College (BA)
University of London
(Postgraduate Diploma/MS)

Taxation and Tax Preparation

Golden Gate University (Graduate
Certificate/MS)
National Tax Training School
(Certificate)
Professional Career Development
Institute (Diploma)
Regent University (Master's)

Teacher Education

See Education

Teacher's Aide

ICS Learning Systems (Diploma)
Professional Career Development
Institute (Diploma)

Teaching—Deaf and Hearing Impaired

John Tracy Clinic Academy for
Professional Studies (Certificate)

Teaching—English as a Second Language

Leicester University
(Certificate/MA)
McGill University (Certificate)
New School University (Certificate)
University of California—Los
Angeles (Certificate)

Teaching—Visually Disadvantaged

Western Michigan University
(Certificate)

Technical Administration

Embry-Riddle Aeronautical
University (BS)
Franklin University (BS)
Regents College (AAS)

Technical and Business Writing

Kennesaw State University
(Certificate)
Northeastern University
(Certificate)
Utah State University (Master's)
Washington State University
(Certificate)

Technical Communication

Rensselaer Polytechnic Institute
(MS)
Rochester Institute of Technology
(Undergraduate Certificate)
University of California—Los
Angeles (Certificate)

Technology

Memorial University of
Newfoundland (Bachelor's)
Regents College (AAS/BS)
University of Houston (MS)

Technology Management

Golden Gate University
(Undergraduate Certificate)
National Technological University
(MS)
Oklahoma State University (MS)
University of Maryland—University
College (MS)
University of Phoenix (MBA)
University of Waterloo (Master's)

Telecommunications

Aims Community College
(Certificate/AA)
California State University—Chico
(MS)
Champlain College
(Certificate/AS/BS)
Jones International University
(Certificate)
New Jersey Institute of Technology
(Certificate)
University of California Extension
(Certificate)
University of Phoenix (BS)

Telecommunications Management

Capitol College (MS)
Golden Gate University (MS)
Keller Graduate School of
Management (Certificate/Master's)
Oklahoma State University (MS)
Rochester Institute of Technology
(Undergraduate Certificate)
Syracuse University (MS)
University of Hawaii (Certificate)
University of Maryland—University
College (MS)

Textiles

See Fashion Design and Merchandising

Theater

Johnson State College (BFA)
Thomas Edison State College (BA)

Theology

Anderson University (Certificate)
Berean University (AA/BA)
Columbia Union College (BA)
Covenant Theological Seminary
(Certificate/Graduate
Certificate/MA/MDiv)
Franciscan University of
Steubenville (MA)
Fuller Theological Seminary
(MA/MDiv)
Golden Gate Baptist Theological
Seminary (ThM)
ICI University (Diploma/BA)
Liberty University (MDiv)
Oral Roberts University (MDiv)
Prairie Bible Institute (Certificate)
Reformed Theological Seminary
(Certificate)
Regent University (MA)
Saint Mary-of-the-Woods College
(Certificate/BA)
Southern Christian University
(MDiv)
Southwestern Adventist University
(BA)
Southwestern Assembles of God
University (MS)
University of London (Diploma)
Wheaton College (MA)

Therapeutic Recreation

Indiana University (MS)

Trade

See International Business

Training and Development

Capella University (Certificate/MS)
Leicester University Centre for Labour Market Studies (Certificate/ Diploma/MS)
North Carolina State University (Certificate)

Transpersonal Studies

Atlantic University (MA)
Burlington College (BA)
Institute of Transpersonal Psychology (Certificate/MA/Master's)

Transportation, Logistics, and Supply Chain Management

Pennsylvania State University (Certificate)
Thomas Edison State College (AS/BS)

Travel and Tourism

See Hospitality

Truck Driving

National Truck Drivers School (License)

Turf Management

Pennsylvania State University (Certificate)

TV/VCR Repair

ICS Learning Systems (Diploma)
Professional Career Development Institute (Diploma)

Vocational Education

Mississippi State University (Certificate)

University of Central Florida (BS)
University of Illinois—Urbana-Champaign (MEd)

Vocational Studies

Indiana State University (BS)

Waste Management

National Technological University (MS)
University of California Extension (Certificate)
Worcester Polytechnic Institute (Certificate)

Web Site Development/ Multimedia Authoring

Bellevue Community College (Certificate/AA)
Champlain College (AS)
ICS Learning Systems (Diploma)
New Jersey Institute of Technology (Certificate)
New School University (Certificate)
Northeastern University (Certificate)
University of Alaska—Southeast (Certificate)
University of Phoenix (BS)

Women's Studies

Athabasca University (BA)
Goucher College (MA)
Laurentian University (BA)
Saint Joseph's College of Maine (Certificate)

Word Processing

Northwestern College (Ohio) (AS)

World Studies

National University (BA)

Index of Distance-Learning Individual Course Programs by Subject

Note: This index refers only to distance-learning programs that offer individual courses for K–12 credit, college credit, graduate school credit, continuing education, and professional development. See Appendix B for an index of degree, diploma, and certificate programs, organized by subject.

Abacus
Hadley School for Blind

Accounting and Bookkeeping
Athabasca University
Atlantic Cape Community College
Ball State University
Bellevue Community College
Bemidji State University
Black Hills State University
Boise State University
Brevard Community College
Brigham Young University
Bucks County Community College
Caldwell College
California State University—Dominguez Hills
California State University—Sacramento
Central Carolina Community College
Central Michigan University
Charles County Community College

Christopher Newport University
College of DuPage
Columbus State Community
College
Community College of Denver
Florida Gulf Coast University
Foothill College
Houston Community College
Indiana University
Iowa State University
J. Sargeant Reynolds Community
College
Louisiana State University
Mississippi State University
National American University
National Distance Education
Center
New York University
Niagara College
North Carolina Central University
North Carolina State University
Northampton Community College
Northern State University
Northern Virginia Community
College
Northwestern College (Ohio)
Ohio University
Oklahoma State University
Pennsylvania State University
Rio Salado College
Rogers State University
San Diego State University
Sinclair Community College
Southwest Missouri State University
State University of New York
State University of New York—
Empire State College
Strayer University
Tarrant County College District
Texas Tech University
Tompkins Cortland Community
College
Troy State University—
Montgomery

Tulsa Community College/
Emporia State University
University of Alaska—Southeast
University of Arizona
University of California Extension
University of Georgia
University of Idaho
University of Minnesota—
Twin Cities
University of Missouri
University of Nebraska—Lincoln
University of Nevada—Reno
University of North Carolina—
Chapel Hill
University of North Dakota
University of Northern Iowa
University of Oklahoma
University of Southern California
University of Tennessee—Knoxville
University of Waterloo
Utah Electronic Community
College
Utah State University
Weber State University
Western Piedmont Community
College

Acoustics
Pennsylvania State University

Addiction Studies
See Chemical Dependency Studies

Administrative Assistance
J. Sargeant Reynolds Community
College
National Distance Education
Center
Northern Virginia Community
College
Northwestern College (Ohio)

Adult Education
College of DuPage
East Carolina University

Indiana University
National-Louis University
University of Idaho
University of Nebraska—Lincoln

Advertising

State University of New York
University of Alabama
University of California—
Los Angeles
University of Florida

Aeronautics and Aerospace Studies

Indiana State University

African American Studies

Indiana University
Pennsylvania State University
University of Arizona
University of Iowa
University of Minnesota—
Twin Cities
University of Missouri
University of North Carolina—
Chapel Hill
University of Wisconsin Extension
Western Michigan University

African Studies

Pennsylvania State University
University of Iowa
University of North Carolina—
Chapel Hill
University of Wisconsin Extension

Agribusiness

Colorado Electronic Community
College
Kansas State University
Northwestern College (Ohio)
Parkland College

Agricultural Economics

North Carolina State University
Pennsylvania State University
Texas Tech University
University of Georgia
University of Idaho
University of Nebraska—Lincoln
University of Tennessee—Knoxville
Western Illinois University

Agriculture

Colorado State University
Fort Hays State University
Iowa State University
Kansas State University
Montana State University—
Bozeman
North Carolina State University
Oregon State University
Texas A&M University
Texas Tech University
University of Florida
University of Wisconsin Extension

Agriculture and Resource Economics

Oregon State University

Agronomy

Iowa State University
Kansas State University
Pennsylvania State University
University of Minnesota—
Twin Cities

Air Conditioning, Heating, and Refrigeration

NHRAW Home Study Institute
North Dakota State College of
Science

Aircraft Sales

International Aviation and Travel
Academy

Allied Health

See Health

American Studies

Bellevue Community College
Brigham Young University
Indiana University
Northwest Missouri State University
Pennsylvania State University
University of Alabama
University of Iowa
University of Minnesota—Twin
Cities

Anatomy

Colorado State University
Daytona Beach Community College
Indiana University

Animal Sciences

Brigham Young University
Colorado State University
Iowa State University
Kansas State University
North Carolina State University
Oklahoma State University
Pennsylvania State University
University of Missouri

Anthropology

Athabasca University
Atlantic Cape Community College
Ball State University
Bellevue Community College
Bemidji State University
Brigham Young University
Burlington County College
California State University—
Sacramento

Charter Oak State College
Chemeketa Community College
College of DuPage
Colorado Electronic Community
College
Community College of Denver
Daytona Beach Community College
Eastern Oregon University
Florida Gulf Coast University
Foothill College
Front Range Community College
Houston Community College
Indiana University
Lane Community College
Laurentian University
Louisiana State University
Memorial University of
Newfoundland
North Carolina State University
Northeastern Arizona University
Ohio University
Oklahoma State University
Parkland College
Pennsylvania State University
Portland Community College
Rio Salado College
Simon Fraser University
State University of New York
State University of New York—
Empire State College
State University of West Georgia
Tarrant County College District
Texas Tech University
University of Alaska—Fairbanks
University of Alaska—Southeast
University of Arizona
University of California Extension
University of Colorado—Boulder
University of Florida
University of Georgia
University of Idaho
University of Iowa
University of Manitoba
University of Minnesota—Twin
Cities

University of Missouri
University of Nevada—Reno
University of North Carolina—
Chapel Hill
University of North Dakota
University of Oklahoma
University of Pittsburgh
University of Southern Colorado
University of Tennessee—Knoxville
University of Texas—Austin
University of Utah
University of Waterloo
University of Wisconsin Extension
Weber State University
Western Illinois University
Western Michigan University
Western Oregon University

Applied Science and Mathematics
Rochester Institute of Technology
University of Waterloo

Archaeology
Simon Fraser University

Architectural Design
Pennsylvania State University

Architecture
Syracuse University
Texas A&M University
University of Florida

Art and Design
Arizona State University
Art Instruction Schools
Atlantic Cape Community College
Bellevue Community College
Black Hills State University
Brigham Young University
Bucks County Community College
Burlington County College

Central Texas College
Central Wyoming College
Charles County Community
College
Charter Oak State College
Colorado State University
Community College of Denver
Daytona Beach Community
College
Foothill College
Fort Hays State University
Front Range Community College
Home Study International
Houston Community College
Indiana State University
Indiana University
Lane Community College
New School University
Northampton Community College
Northeastern Arizona University
Northern Virginia Community
College
Oklahoma State University
Oregon State University
Pennsylvania State University
Piedmont Technical College
Portland State University
Rio Salado College
Sinclair Community College
State University of New York
State University of New York—
Empire State College
Taylor University
Troy State University—
Montgomery—Montgomery
Tulsa Community
College/Emporia State University
University of Alaska—Fairbanks
University of Alaska—Southeast
University of Arizona
University of California Extension
University of California—Los
Angeles
University of Central Florida

University of Colorado——Boulder
University of Florida
University of Georgia
University of Iowa
University of Nebraska—Lincoln
University of North Carolina—
Chapel Hill
University of North Dakota
University of Oklahoma
University of Southern Colorado
University of Texas—Austin
University of Utah
University of Waterloo
University of Wisconsin Extension
Upper Iowa University
Utah Electronic Community
College
Utah State University
Weber State University
West Virginia Wesleyan College
Western Piedmont Community
College

Art Education
Northern State University

Art History
Athabasca University
Northern State University
Palm Beach Community College
Pennsylvania State University
University of California—Los
Angeles
University of Iowa
University of Minnesota—Twin
Cities
University of Nebraska—Lincoln
University of Pittsburgh
University of Texas—Austin
University of Utah
University of Wisconsin Extension

Asian Languages
Indiana University
University of Iowa

Asian Studies
California State University—Chico
Florida Gulf Coast University
Indiana University
Tulsa Community
College/Emporia State University
University of Arizona

Astronomy
Athabasca University
Ball State University
Bellevue Community College
Black Hills State University
Brigham Young University
Bucks County Community College
Central Michigan University
Central Texas College
Charles County Community
College
Colorado Electronic Community
College
Dallas TeleCollege
Daytona Beach Community College
Indiana University
Lane Community College
Louisiana State University
Palm Beach Community College
Pennsylvania State University
Piedmont Technical College
State University of New York
University of Alabama
University of Arizona
University of California Extension
University of Colorado—Boulder
University of Florida
University of Georgia
University of Missouri
University of Nebraska—Lincoln
University of Northern Iowa
University of Oklahoma
University of Pittsburgh
University of Texas—Austin
University of Wisconsin Extension

Athletic Training and Sports Medicine

Indiana State University

Atmospheric Sciences

Daytona Beach Community College
Iowa State University
Oregon State University
Pennsylvania State University
Portland State University
San Jose State University
University of Arizona
University of Missouri
University of North Carolina—Chapel Hill
University of North Dakota
University of Utah
University of Wisconsin Extension

Audiology

See Communication Disorders

Automotive Mechanics

North Dakota State College of Science
Sinclair Community College
University of Arizona

Aviation Science

Central Texas College
University of Alaska—Fairbanks
Utah Electronic Community College

Aviation Maintenance

Columbus State Community College

Banking

See Finance

Behavioral Science

See Psychology

Biblical Languages

Life Bible College
Taylor University
Tennessee Temple University

Biblical Studies

Berean University
The Hadley School for the Blind
Hope International University
Indiana Wesleyan University
Life Bible College
Moody Bible Institute
Northwestern College (Minnesota)
Prairie Bible Institute
Reformed Theological Seminary
Seminary Extension Independent Study Institute
Taylor University
Tennessee Temple University
Wheaton College

Biochemistry and Biophysics

University of California Extension

Biological Sciences

Columbus State Community College
Louisiana State University
Mercy College
New School University
Northampton Community College
Northern Virginia Community College
Ohio University
Palm Beach Community College
Pennsylvania State University
Piedmont Technical College
San Diego State University
Simon Fraser University

State University of West Georgia
Taylor University
University of California Extension
University of Delaware
University of Missouri
University of Nebraska—Lincoln
Utah Electronic Community
College
Western Illinois University
Western Michigan University

Biology

Athabasca University
Atlantic Cape Community College
Auburn University
Bellevue Community College
Bemidji State University
Black Hills State University
Brevard Community College
Brigham Young University
Bucks County Community College
Burlington County College
Cambrian College
Central Carolina Community
College
Central Texas College
Charles County Community
College
Charter Oak State College
Chemeketa Community College
Cochise College
College of DuPage
Colorado State University
Columbus State Community
College
Community College of Denver
Dallas TeleCollege
East Carolina University
Eastern Oregon University
Fort Hays State University
Front Range Community College
Home Study International
Indiana University
Iowa State University

J. Sargeant Reynolds Community
College
Lakehead University
Lane Community College
Laurentian University
Memorial University of
Newfoundland
Montana State University—
Bozeman
New River Community College
Niagara College
North Carolina Central University
North Carolina State University
Northeastern Arizona University
Northern State University
Northern Virginia Community
College
Parkland College
Pennsylvania State University
Portland Community College
Rensselaer Polytechnic Institute
Rio Salado College
Sinclair Community College
State University of New York
Tarrant County College District
Teikyo Post University
Tennessee Temple University
Troy State University—
Montgomery
Tulsa Community
College/Emporia State University
Ulster County Community College
University of Alabama
University of Alaska—Fairbanks
University of Alaska—Southeast
University of California Extension
University of Georgia
University of Idaho
University of Manitoba
University of Maryland—
University College
University of Minnesota—
Twin Cities
University of North Carolina—
Chapel Hill

University of Southern Colorado
University of Utah
University of Waterloo
University of Wisconsin Extension
Upper Iowa University
Utah State University

Biostatistics

State University of New York

Botany

Brigham Young University
University of California Extension
University of Wisconsin Extension
Weber State University

Braille

The Hadley School for the Blind

Broadcasting

Central Wyoming College
Foothill College
Oklahoma State University
University of Alaska—Fairbanks
University of California—
Los Angeles
University of Nebraska—Lincoln
University of Texas—Austin

Building

See Construction

Building Management

Utah Electronic Community
College

Business

Adams State College
Arizona State University
Athabasca University
Atlantic Cape Community College
Ball State University
Bellevue Community College

Bemidji State University
Black Hills State University
Brevard Community College
Brigham Young University
Burlington County College
Caldwell College
California State University—
Bakersfield
California State University—
Dominguez Hills
California State University—Los
Angeles
Capella University
Central Carolina Community
College
Central Texas College
Central Wyoming College
Charles County Community
College
Charter Oak State College
Chemeketa Community College
Christopher Newport University
City University
Coastal Carolina University
Cochise College
College of DuPage
Community College of Denver
Dakota State University
Dallas TeleCollege
Daytona Beach Community
College
Eastern Oregon University
Emporia State University
Floyd College
Foothill College
Fox Valley Technical College
Front Range Community College
George Brown College
The Hadley School for the Blind
Herkimer County Community
College
Home Study International
Houston Community College
Indiana State University

Indiana University
Iowa Western Community College
ISIM University
J. Sargeant Reynolds Community College
Kennesaw State University
Lane Community College
Marywood University
Memorial University of Newfoundland
Mercy College
Mohawk Valley Community College
National-Louis University
New River Community College
New School University
New York University
Niagara College
North Carolina State University
North Dakota State College of Science
Northampton Community College
Northeastern Arizona University
Northern State University
Northern Virginia Community College
Northwestern College (Ohio)
Ohio University
Oklahoma State University
Oregon State University
Palm Beach Community College
Parkland College
Pennsylvania State University
Piedmont Technical College
Portland Community College
Portland State University
Rio Salado College
Rochester Institute of Technology
Rogers State University
San Jose State University
Simon Fraser University
Sinclair Community College
State University of New York
State University of New York—Empire State College
State University of West Georgia

Strayer University
Tarrant County College District
Teikyo Post University
Texas A&M University
Texas Tech University
Tompkins Cortland Community College
Troy State University—Montgomery
Tulsa Community College/Emporia State University
Ulster County Community College
University College of Cape Breton
University of Alabama
University of Alaska—Fairbanks
University of Alaska—Southeast
University of California—Los Angeles
University of Central Florida
University of Delaware
University of Florida
University of Idaho
University of Minnesota—Twin Cities
University of Nebraska—Lincoln
University of North Carolina—Chapel Hill
University of Oklahoma
University of Southern California
University of Southern Colorado
University of Southern Indiana
University of Wisconsin Extension
Upper Iowa University
Utah Electronic Community College
Utah State University
Weber State University
West Virginia Wesleyan College
Western Piedmont Community College

Business Communications

Jones International University
Ohio University
Oklahoma State University

Business Education

Louisiana State University
University of Colorado—Boulder
University of Idaho
University of North Dakota
Utah State University
Weber State University

Business Information Systems

See Management Information Systems

Business Statistics

Ohio University

Business Writing

See Technical Writing

Calligraphy

University of Iowa

Canadian Studies

Simon Fraser University
University of Waterloo

Career Development

Athabasca University
The Hadley School for the Blind
New York University
Portland Community College
State University of New York
Troy State University—
Montgomery
University of Tennessee—Knoxville
Western Michigan University

Carpentry

North Dakota State College of
Science

Cartography

See Surveying and Mapping

Cartooning

University of Tennessee—Knoxville

Cell Biology

University of Arizona
University of Minnesota—
Twin Cities

Ceramics

State University of New York

Chemical Dependency Studies

Rio Salado College
Western Michigan University

Chemistry

Athabasca University
Bellevue Community College
Bemidji State University
Boise State University
Brigham Young University
Bucks County Community College
Chemeketa Community College
College of DuPage
Colorado Electronic Community
College
Columbus State Community
College
Front Range Community College
Illinois Institute of Technology
Indiana University
J. Sargeant Reynolds Community
College
Lane Community College
Laurentian University
Michigan State University
New Jersey Institute of Technology
North Carolina Central University
North Carolina State University
Northeastern Arizona University
Northern Virginia Community
College

Ohio University
Palm Beach Community College
Parkland College
Pennsylvania State University
Piedmont Technical College
Portland State University
Sinclair Community College
State University of New York
Texas Tech University
University of Arizona
University of California Extension
University of Delaware
University of Florida
University of North Carolina—
Chapel Hill
University of Oklahoma
University of Pittsburgh
University of Southern Colorado
University of Tennessee—Knoxville
University of Utah
University of Waterloo
University of Wisconsin Extension
Utah State University
Weber State University
Western Michigan University

Child Development
Daytona Beach Community College
University of Alaska—Southeast
University of Minnesota—
Twin Cities

Childcare Training
College of DuPage
New River Community College
Texas Tech University
Tulsa Community
College/Emporia State University

Chinese
University of Oklahoma

Christian Studies
Reformed Theological Seminary
Seminary Extension Independent
Study Institute
Taylor University
Tennessee Temple University

Church Administration
See Ministry

Civil War Studies
Louisiana State University

Classical Languages
Louisiana State University
University of Alaska—Fairbanks
University of Georgia
University of Minnesota—
Twin Cities
University of North Carolina—
Chapel Hill
University of Oklahoma
University of Texas—Austin
University of Waterloo
University of Wisconsin Extension

Classics
Indiana University
Laurentian University
Louisiana State University
Memorial University of
Newfoundland
Pennsylvania State University
University of Alabama
University of Georgia
University of Iowa
University of Manitoba
University of Minnesota—
Twin Cities
University of Missouri
University of Nebraska—Lincoln
University of North Carolina—
Chapel Hill

University of Oklahoma
University of Pittsburgh
University of Waterloo
University of Wisconsin Extension

Climatology
See Atmospheric Sciences

Clinical Laboratory Science
Weber State University

Coaching
University of Alabama

College and Graduate School Preparation
University of Arizona
University of California—Los Angeles

Commerce
See International Business

Communication Disorders
Arizona State University
Central Michigan University
Fort Hays State University
Northeastern Arizona University
Northern State University
Texas Woman's University
University of Colorado—Boulder
University of Pittsburgh
University of Utah

Communications
Arizona State University
Athabasca University
Auburn University
Bellevue Community College
Black Hills State University
Brevard Community College
Brigham Young University

Bucks County Community College
Burlington County College
California State University—Sacramento
Central Texas College
Charter Oak State College
College of DuPage
Colorado Electronic Community College
Columbus State Community College
Dallas TeleCollege
Emporia State University
Fort Hays State University
George Brown College
The Hadley School for the Blind
Home Study International
Indiana State University
Indiana University
Kennesaw State University
New School University
Northampton Community College
Northeastern Arizona University
Ohio University
Parkland College
Pennsylvania State University
Rensselaer Polytechnic Institute
Rio Salado College
Rutgers University
San Jose State University
Simon Fraser University
Sinclair Community College
Southwest Missouri State University
State University of New York
State University of New York—Empire State College
State University of West Georgia
Taylor University
Teikyo Post University
Troy State University—Montgomery
Ulster County Community College
University of Alabama
University of Alaska—Southeast

University of California—Los
Angeles
University of Colorado—Boulder
University of Delaware
University of Idaho
University of Iowa
University of Missouri
University of North Carolina—
Chapel Hill
University of Northern Iowa
University of Pittsburgh
University of Southern Indiana
University of Tennessee—Knoxville
University of Utah
University of Wisconsin Extension
Upper Iowa University
Utah Electronic Community
College
Weber State University
Western Illinois University

Comparative Literature

Indiana University
Montana State University—Billings
Pennsylvania State University
University of Delaware

Computer Art

New School University
University of California—Los
Angeles

Computer Information Systems

Atlantic Cape Community College
Black Hills State University
Cochise College
College of DuPage
Foothill College
Fort Hays State University
Kansas State University
National-Louis University
New Jersey Institute of Technology
North Carolina Central University

Northampton Community College
Northern State University
Parkland College
Portland Community College
Sinclair Community College
Southwest Missouri State University
State University of New York
State University of New York—
Empire State College
State University of West Georgia
Strayer University
Troy State University—
Montgomery
Tulsa Community
College/Emporia State University
University of Alaska—Fairbanks
University of Alaska—Southeast
Western Piedmont Community
College

Computer Programming

Columbus State Community
College
University of California Extension
University of California—
Los Angeles

Computer Science

Athabasca University
Bellevue Community College
Black Hills State University
Boise State University
Brevard Community College
Bucks County Community College
Burlington County College
California State University—
Bakersfield
California State University—
Sacramento
Central Texas College
Charles County Community
College
Chemeketa Community College
Christopher Newport University

City University
Coastal Carolina University
Colorado State University
Community College of Denver
Dakota State University
Dallas TeleCollege
Emporia State University
Florida Gulf Coast University
Floyd College
Front Range Community College
George Brown College
The Hadley School for the Blind
Houston Community College
Illinois Institute of Technology
Indiana State University
Indiana University
Indiana Wesleyan University
Iowa State University
Iowa Western Community College
J. Sargeant Reynolds Community
College
Kennesaw State University
Lane Community College
Memorial University of
Newfoundland
Michigan State University
Mississippi State University
Mohawk Valley Community College
Mott Community College
National American University
New School University
Niagara College
North Carolina Central University
North Carolina State University
Northwest Missouri State University
Oklahoma State University
Palm Beach Community College
Parkland College
Pennsylvania State University
Portland Community College
Rensselaer Polytechnic Institute
Rio Salado College
Rogers State University
Simon Fraser University

State University of New York
Tarrant County College District
Tompkins Cortland Community
College
Tulsa Community
College/Emporia State University
University of Alabama
University of Alaska—Fairbanks
University of California Extension
University of California—
Los Angeles
University of Central Florida
University of Colorado—Boulder
University of Florida
University of Manitoba
University of Maryland—
University College
University of Massachusetts—
Lowell
University of Minnesota—
Twin Cities
University of Missouri
University of North Carolina—
Chapel Hill
University of Southern California
University of Southern Colorado
University of Waterloo
Utah Electronic Community
College
Virginia Tech
West Virginia Wesleyan College
Western Illinois University
Western Michigan University

Conflict Resolution
University of Waterloo

Conservation and Wildlife
University of Alaska—Southeast

Construction
Colorado State University
Indiana State University
New York University

North Dakota State College of
Science
Portland Community College
University of Florida
Weber State University

Consumer Studies

Portland Community College
University of Arizona
University of Delaware
University of Idaho

Counseling

Hope International University
Kansas State University
Mississippi State University
North Carolina Central University
Pennsylvania State University
Prairie Bible Institute
Reformed Theological Seminary
Rio Salado College
Texas Tech University
University of Alabama
University of Georgia
University of Idaho
Western Michigan University

Creative Writing

Palm Beach Community College
University of California—
Los Angeles
University of Minnesota—
Twin Cities
University of Tennessee—Knoxville

Criminal Justice

Arizona State University
Athabasca University
Atlantic Cape Community College
Auburn University
Ball State University
Bemidji State University
Black Hills State University
Brevard Community College

California State University—
Bakersfield
California State University—
Sacramento
Central Texas College
Coastal Carolina University
Cochise College
College of DuPage
Daytona Beach Community College
Florida Gulf Coast University
Fort Hays State University
Fox Valley Technical College
Herkimer County Community
College
Houston Community College
Indiana State University
Indiana University
Memorial University of
Newfoundland
Michigan State University
New River Community College
North Carolina Central University
Northeastern Arizona University
Northern State University
Northern Virginia Community
College
Ohio University
Pennsylvania State University
Piedmont Technical College
Portland Community College
Portland State University
Simon Fraser University
State University of New York
State University of New York—
Empire State College
Tarrant County College District
Taylor University
Teikyo Post University
University of Alabama
University of Central Florida
University of Florida
University of Idaho
University of Massachusetts—
Lowell
University of Nevada—Reno

University of Pittsburgh
University of Tennessee—Knoxville
University of Wisconsin Extension
Utah Electronic Community
College
Weber State University
Western Illinois University
Western Oregon University

Criminology
See Criminal Justice

Critical Thinking
Charter Oak State College
City University
State University of New York—
Empire State College

Culinary Arts
New School University

Cultural Studies
See Ethnic Studies

Dairy Science
Louisiana State University
Pennsylvania State University

Dance
Brigham Young University
University of Iowa
University of Waterloo
University of Wisconsin Extension

Data Processing
Northwestern College (Ohio)

Dental Assisting
State University of New York

Dental Hygiene
Northeastern Arizona University
Portland Community College

Dentistry
J. Sargeant Reynolds Community
College

Diesel Mechanics
North Dakota State College of
Science

Dietetics
Kansas State University
Pennsylvania State University
Sinclair Community College
University of Delaware
University of Nebraska—Lincoln
University of North Dakota

Drama
See Theatre

Drafting and Design
Brevard Community College
Central Texas College
Chemeketa Community College
Dallas TeleCollege
Houston Community College
Sinclair Community College
University of Alaska—Fairbanks

Early Childhood Education
Central Texas College
Northampton Community College
Texas Tech University

Earth and Space Sciences
Indiana Wesleyan University
Pennsylvania State University
State University of New York
University of North Carolina—
Chapel Hill
University of Waterloo

Ecology
See Environmental Studies

Economics

Adams State College
Athabasca University
Atlantic Cape Community College
Auburn University
Ball State University
Bellevue Community College
Bemidji State University
Black Hills State University
Boise State University
Brevard Community College
Brigham Young University
Bucks County Community College
Burlington County College
California State University—Bakersfield
California State University—Sacramento
Central Carolina Community College
Central Michigan University
Charles County Community College
Charter Oak State College
Chemeketa Community College
Christopher Newport University
Cochise College
College of DuPage
Colorado Electronic Community College
Colorado State University
Columbus State Community College
Community College of Denver
Dallas TeleCollege
Daytona Beach Community College
East Carolina University
Eastern Oregon University
Foothill College
Fox Valley Technical College
Front Range Community College

Houston Community College
Indiana State University
Indiana University
Iowa State University
J. Sargeant Reynolds Community College
Lane Community College
Laurentian University
Louisiana State University
Marywood University
Memorial University of Newfoundland
Mercy College
Michigan State University
Mississippi State University
National American University
New Jersey Institute of Technology
New River Community College
Niagara College
North Carolina Central University
North Carolina State University
Northampton Community College
Northern State University
Northern Virginia Community College
Ohio University
Oklahoma State University
Oregon State University
Palm Beach Community College
Parkland College
Pennsylvania State University
Piedmont Technical College
Portland Community College
Portland State University
Rio Salado College
Rogers State University
San Jose State University
Simon Fraser University
Sinclair Community College
State University of New York
State University of New York—Empire State College
State University of West Georgia
Strayer University

Tarrant County College District
Teikyo Post University
Texas Tech University
Troy State University—
Montgomery
Tulsa Community
College/Emporia State University
University College of Cape Breton
University of Alabama
University of Alaska—Fairbanks
University of Arizona
University of California Extension
University of Colorado—Boulder
University of Delaware
University of Florida
University of Georgia
University of Idaho
University of Iowa
University of Manitoba
University of Maryland—University
College
University of Massachusetts—
Lowell
University of Minnesota—
Twin Cities
University of Missouri
University of Nebraska—Lincoln
University of Nevada—Reno
University of North Carolina—
Chapel Hill
University of North Dakota
University of Northern Iowa
University of Oklahoma
University of Pittsburgh
University of Southern Colorado
University of Tennessee—Knoxville
University of Texas—Austin
University of Utah
University of Waterloo
University of Wisconsin Extension
Utah Electronic Community
College
Utah State University
Weber State University

West Virginia Wesleyan College
Western Illinois University
Western Michigan University
Western Piedmont Community
College

Education

Adams State College
Arizona State University
Athabasca University
Bemidji State University
Black Hills State University
Boise State University
Brigham Young University
Bucks County Community College
Burlington County College
California State University—Chico
California State University—
Dominguez Hills
California State University—
Los Angeles
California State University—
Sacramento
California State University—
San Marcos
Capella University
Charles County Community
College
Chemeketa Community College
Christopher Newport University
Coastal Carolina University
Cochise College
College of DuPage
Colorado Electronic Community
College
Colorado State University
Columbus State Community
College
Dallas TeleCollege
Daytona Beach Community
College
East Carolina University
Emporia State University
Florida Gulf Coast University

Fort Hays State University
Fox Valley Technical College
Home Study International
Houston Community College
Indiana State University
Indiana University
Iowa State University
Kansas State University
Lakehead University
Louisiana State University
McGill University
Memorial University of
Newfoundland
Mercy College
Michigan State University
Montana State University—Billings
Montana State University—
Bozeman
Mott Community College
Niagara College
North Carolina Central University
North Carolina State University
Northeastern Arizona University
Northern State University
Oklahoma State University
Oregon State University
Palm Beach Community College
Pennsylvania State University
Portland Community College
Rio Salado College
San Diego State University
San Jose State University
Simon Fraser University
State University of New York
State University of New York—
Empire State College
Taylor University
Texas A&M University
Texas Tech University
University College of Cape Breton
University of Alabama
University of Alaska—Fairbanks
University of Alaska—Southeast
University of Arizona
University of California Extension

University of California—
Los Angeles
University of Central Florida
University of Colorado—Boulder
University of Delaware
University of Florida
University of Georgia
University of Idaho
University of Manitoba
University of Missouri
University of Nevada—Reno
University of North Carolina—
Chapel Hill
University of Northern Iowa
University of Oklahoma
University of Southern Colorado
University of Southern Indiana
University of Tennessee—Knoxville
University of Utah
University of Wisconsin Extension
Utah Electronic Community
College
Western Michigan University
Western Oregon University

Educational Administration

National-Louis University
State University of West Georgia
Texas Woman's University
University of Nevada—Reno

Educational Psychology

Kansas State University
Mississippi State University
Pennsylvania State University
Texas Tech University
University of Georgia
University of Minnesota—
Twin Cities
University of Pittsburgh
University of Texas—Austin
University of Utah
University of Wisconsin Extension

Educational Technology

California State University—
Los Angeles
Emporia State University
San Jose State University
Texas A&M University
Texas Tech University

Electrician

North Dakota State College of
Science

Electronic Commerce

Christopher Newport University
Kennesaw State University

Electronics

Central Texas College
East Carolina University
Indiana State University
Niagara College
North Dakota State College of
Science
Oklahoma State University
Portland Community College
Sinclair Community College
University of California Extension
Western Piedmont Community
College

Elementary and Secondary Education

Mississippi State University
Utah State University
Western Illinois University

Emergency Medicine

University of Texas—Austin

Emergency Services

Chemeketa Community College
State University of New York
State University of New York—

Empire State College
University of Wisconsin Extension

Engineering

Arizona State University
Auburn University
Black Hills State University
Boise State University
Brigham Young University
California State University—
Los Angeles
California State University—
Northridge
California State University—
Sacramento
Illinois Institute of Technology
Indiana University
Iowa State University
Kansas State University
Lehigh University
Memorial University of
Newfoundland
Michigan State University
Montana State University—
Bozeman
North Carolina State University
Northeastern Arizona University
Northern State University
Northern Virginia Community
College
Oklahoma State University
Pennsylvania State University
Rensselaer Polytechnic Institute
Rochester Institute of Technology
State University of New York
Syracuse University
Texas Tech University
Tulsa Community College/
Emporia State University
University of Alabama
University of Arizona
University of California Extension
University of Central Florida
University of Florida

University of Missouri
University of Oklahoma
University of Southern California
University of Wisconsin Extension
Weber State University

Engineering—Aerospace

University of Arizona
University of Southern California
University of Tennessee—
Knoxville

Engineering—Architectural

Pennsylvania State University

Engineering—Bioengineering

University of Utah

Engineering—Biological and Agricultural

University of Missouri

Engineering—Chemical

New Jersey Institute of Technology
University of Alabama
University of Delaware
University of Tennessee—Knoxville

Engineering—Civil

Pennsylvania State University
University of Arizona

Engineering—Civil and Environmental

University of Delaware

Engineering—Electrical

Pennsylvania State University
State University of New York
University of Southern California

Engineering—Electrical and Computer

University of Arizona
University of Delaware

Engineering—Environmental

University College of Cape Breton
University of Tennessee—Knoxville

Engineering—Industrial

New Jersey Institute of Technology
State University of New York
University of Tennessee—Knoxville
Western Michigan University

Engineering—Industrial and Systems

University of Arizona
University of Nebraska—Lincoln
University of Southern California

Engineering—Management

New Jersey Institute of Technology
University of Tennessee—Knoxville

Engineering—Manufacturing

Western Michigan University

Engineering—Mechanical

Indiana University
Louisiana State University
Pennsylvania State University
San Jose State University
University of Arizona
University of Delaware
University of Minnesota—
Twin Cities
University of Southern California
University of Tennessee—Knoxville

Engineering—Nuclear

Pennsylvania State University

Engineering—Petroleum

Texas A&M University

Engineering—Quality

University of Arizona

Engineering Sciences

University of Tennessee—Knoxville

Engineering—Software

Carnegie Mellon University
University of Southern California

Engineering—Systems

Rensselaer Polytechnic Institute

Engineering—Systems Science

State University of New York

Engineering Technology

University of Delaware
Western Illinois University

English

Adams State College
Arizona State University
Athabasca University
Atlantic Cape Community College
Ball State University
Bellevue Community College
Bemidji State University
Black Hills State University
Boise State University
Brigham Young University
Bucks County Community College
Burlington County College
California State University—
Bakersfield
Cambrian College

Central Carolina Community
College
Central Michigan University
Central Wyoming College
Charles County Community
College
Charter Oak State College
Chemeketa Community College
Christopher Newport University
City University
Coastal Carolina University
Cochise College
College of DuPage
Colorado Electronic Community
College
Columbus State Community
College
Community College of Denver
Dakota State University
Dallas TeleCollege
Daytona Beach Community
College
Eastern Oregon University
Emporia State University
Foothill College
Fort Hays State University
Front Range Community College
Herkimer County Community
College
Home Study International
Houston Community College
Indiana State University
Indiana University
Indiana Wesleyan University
Iowa State University
J. Sargeant Reynolds Community
College
Laurentian University
Louisiana State University
Memorial University of
Newfoundland
Mercy College
Mohawk Valley Community College
New Jersey Institute of Technology

New River Community College
Niagara College
North Carolina Central University
North Carolina State University
Northampton Community College
Northern State University
Northern Virginia Community
College
Oklahoma State University
Palm Beach Community College
Parkland College
Pennsylvania State University
Piedmont Technical College
Portland Community College
Portland State University
Rio Salado College
Rogers State University
San Jose State University
Simon Fraser University
Sinclair Community College
State University of New York—
Empire State College
State University of West Georgia
Syracuse University
Tarrant County College District
Taylor University
Teikyo Post University
Tennessee Temple University
Texas Tech University
Texas Woman's University
Tompkins Cortland Community
College
Troy State University—
Montgomery
Tulsa Community College/
Emporia State University
University College of Cape Breton
University of Alabama
University of Alaska—Fairbanks
University of Alaska—Southeast
University of Arizona
University of California Extension
University of California—
Los Angeles
University of Central Florida

University of Colorado—Boulder
University of Delaware
University of Florida
University of Georgia
University of Idaho
University of Iowa
University of Manitoba
University of Minnesota—
Twin Cities
University of Missouri
University of Nebraska—Lincoln
University of Nevada—Reno
University of North Carolina—
Chapel Hill
University of North Dakota
University of Northern Iowa
University of Oklahoma
University of Pittsburgh
University of Southern Colorado
University of Southern Indiana
University of Tennessee—Knoxville
University of Texas—Austin
University of Utah
University of Waterloo
University of Wisconsin Extension
Upper Iowa University
Utah Electronic Community
College
Utah State University
Virginia Tech
Weber State University
West Virginia Wesleyan College
Western Illinois University
Western Michigan University
Western Oregon University
Western Piedmont Community
College

English as a Second Language

Athabasca University
Atlantic Cape Community College
California State University—
Los Angeles
Chemeketa Community College

Portland Community College
State University of New York
University of Arizona
Utah Electronic Community
College

English Language
New School University
Ohio University

English Literature
Ohio University
State University of New York
University of Minnesota—
Twin Cities
University of Pittsburgh

Entomology
Auburn University
North Carolina State University
Pennsylvania State University
University of Arizona
University of Missouri
Virginia Tech

Entrepreneurship
See Small Business Management

Environmental Resources Management
California State University—
Bakersfield
Colorado State University
University of Arizona
University of Florida

Environmental Studies
Adams State College
Athabasca University
Bellevue Community College
Bemidji State University
Charles County Community
College
Colorado State University

Indiana University
Iowa State University
Lakehead University
Louisiana State University
Montana State University—
Bozeman
New Jersey Institute of Technology
State University of New York
University of Alaska—Southeast
University of California Extension
University of Florida
University of Georgia
University of Idaho
University of Minnesota—
Twin Cities
University of Nevada—Reno
University of North Carolina—
Chapel Hill
University of Waterloo
Utah Electronic Community
College

Epidemiology
State University of New York

Ethnic Studies
Hope International University
Indiana University
Memorial University of
Newfoundland
Mercy College
New School University
Taylor University

Exercise Studies
See Sports Sciences

Facilities Management
See Building Management

Family and Consumer Sciences
Colorado State University
Iowa State University

Mississippi State University
Ohio University
University of Alabama
University of Colorado—Boulder
University of Idaho
University of Missouri
University of Nebraska—Lincoln
University of Northern Iowa
West Virginia Wesleyan College
Western Illinois University
Western Michigan University

Family Studies
See Human Development

Farm Management
See Agribusiness

Fashion Design and Merchandising
Burlington County College
Colorado State University
New School University
North Carolina Central University
North Carolina State University
State University of New York
Syracuse University
University of Florida

Film Studies
Auburn University
Burlington County College
Charter Oak State College
University of Alabama
University of California Extension
University of Utah

Finance
Athabasca University
Ball State University
California State University—
Bakersfield
Central Michigan University
Coastal Carolina University

Columbus State Community
College
East Carolina University
Floyd College
Indiana State University
Iowa State University
Iowa Western Community College
ISIM University
J. Sargeant Reynolds Community
College
Kansas State University
Louisiana State University
Mississippi State University
Mortgage Bankers Association of
America
National American University
New River Community College
North Carolina Central University
Northern Virginia Community
College
Northwestern College (Ohio)
Ohio University
Oklahoma State University
Pennsylvania State University
State University of New York—
Empire State College
State University of West Georgia
Teikyo Post University
Troy State University—
Montgomery
University of Alabama
University of California Extension
University of California—
Los Angeles
University of Minnesota—
Twin Cities
University of Nebraska—Lincoln
University of Oklahoma
University of Utah
Weber State University
Western Illinois University

Fine Arts
See Art and Design

Fire Protection and Security Services

California State University—
Los Angeles
Chemeketa Community College
Floyd College
Fox Valley Technical College
Iowa Western Community College
Ohio University
Oklahoma State University
Portland Community College
State University of New York
State University of New York—
Empire State College
Western Oregon University

Flight Attendant

Hospitality Training Center

Food Science

See Nutrition and Food Science

Food Service Management

New School University
North Dakota State College of
Science
State University of New York

Folklore

See Ethnic Studies

Forensic Science

See Criminal Justice

Forestry

Oregon State University
Pennsylvania State University
University of Georgia
University of Tennessee—Knoxville
University of Wisconsin Extension

French

Arizona State University
Athabasca University

Burlington County College
California State University—
Sacramento
College of DuPage
Columbus State Community
College
Daytona Beach Community
College
Indiana University
J. Sargeant Reynolds Community
College
Louisiana State University
North Carolina Central University
Northern Virginia Community
College
Oklahoma State University
Pennsylvania State University
Simon Fraser University
Tarrant County College District
Tulsa Community
College/Emporia State University
Ulster County Community College
University of Arizona
University of Georgia
University of Iowa
University of Manitoba
University of Minnesota—
Twin Cities
University of Nevada—Reno
University of North Carolina—
Chapel Hill
University of North Dakota
University of Oklahoma
University of Tennessee—Knoxville
University of Texas—Austin
University of Waterloo
University of Wisconsin Extension
Weber State University

Gaming Management

University of Nevada—Reno

GED

College of DuPage
Portland Community College

Genealogy
Brigham Young University
Coastal Carolina University
National Genealogical Society

Genetics
North Carolina State University
University of California Extension
University of Minnesota—
Twin Cities

Geography
Athabasca University
Auburn University
Ball State University
Bellevue Community College
Bemidji State University
Black Hills State University
Boise State University
Brigham Young University
California State University—Chico
California State University—
Sacramento
Central Michigan University
Central Wyoming College
Charter Oak State College
Colorado Electronic Community
College
Community College of Denver
Daytona Beach Community College
Foothill College
Front Range Community College
Home Study International
Houston Community College
Indiana State University
Indiana University
Lane Community College
Laurentian University
Louisiana State University
Memorial University of
Newfoundland
Michigan State University
North Carolina Central University
Northampton Community College

Northeastern Arizona University
Northern State University
Northern Virginia Community
College
Ohio University
Oklahoma State University
Pennsylvania State University
Portland Community College
Portland State University
Rio Salado College
Rogers State University
San Jose State University
Simon Fraser University
State University of New York
Syracuse University
Texas Tech University
Troy State University—
Montgomery
Tulsa Community College/
Emporia State University
University of Alabama
University of Alaska—Fairbanks
University of Alaska—Southeast
University of Arizona
University of Colorado—Boulder
University of Florida
University of Georgia
University of Iowa
University of Manitoba
University of Minnesota—
Twin Cities
University of Missouri
University of Nebraska—Lincoln
University of Nevada—Reno
University of North Carolina—
Chapel Hill
University of North Dakota
University of Northern Iowa
University of Oklahoma
University of Southern Colorado
University of Tennessee—Knoxville
University of Texas—Austin
University of Utah
University of Waterloo

University of Wisconsin Extension
Utah State University
Weber State University
Western Illinois University
Western Michigan University
Western Piedmont Community
College

Geology

Athabasca University
Ball State University
Bellevue Community College
Bemidji State University
Black Hills State University
Boise State University
Brigham Young University
Burlington County College
California State University—
Sacramento
Charles County Community
College
Colorado Electronic Community
College
Community College of Denver
Front Range Community College
Houston Community College
Indiana State University
Indiana University
Laurentian University
Louisiana State University
New River Community College
Northern State University
Palm Beach Community College
Portland State University
Rio Salado College
State University of West Georgia
Tarrant County College District
Tulsa Community
College/Emporia State University
University of Alaska—Southeast
University of California Extension
University of Colorado—Boulder
University of Florida
University of Georgia

University of Manitoba
University of Minnesota—
Twin Cities
University of Missouri
University of North Dakota
University of Northern Iowa
University of Oklahoma
University of Pittsburgh
University of Southern Colorado
University of Tennessee—Knoxville
University of Wisconsin Extension
Utah State University
Weber State University
Western Illinois University

Geosciences

Fort Hays State University
Oregon State University
Pennsylvania State University
Texas A&M University
University of Arizona
University of Minnesota—
Twin Cities
Western Michigan University

German

Arizona State University
Athabasca University
Brigham Young University
Burlington County College
Indiana University
Louisiana State University
Oklahoma State University
Pennsylvania State University
University of Alabama
University of Arizona
University of Florida
University of Georgia
University of Iowa
University of Minnesota—
Twin Cities
University of Missouri
University of Nevada—Reno
University of Oklahoma

University of Pittsburgh
University of Tennessee—Knoxville
University of Texas—Austin
University of Waterloo
University of Wisconsin Extension
Western Oregon University

Germanic Languages

University of Waterloo

Gerontology

Community College of Denver
Florida Gulf Coast University
Laurentian University
Simon Fraser University
University of Iowa
University of Utah
University of Waterloo
Weber State University

Golf Management

State University of New York

Government

See Political Science

Grant Writing

Floyd College
Iowa Western Community College
Syracuse University
University of Southern Colorado

Graphic Design

Mohawk Valley Community College
New School University
Rochester Institute of Technology
State University of New York
University of California—Los
Angeles
Weber State University

Greek

North Carolina State University
Northwestern College (Minnesota)

University of Alaska—Fairbanks
University of Oklahoma
University of Texas—Austin
University of Waterloo
University of Wisconsin Extension

Gunsmithing

Modern Gun School

Hazardous Materials

Brevard Community College
University of California Extension

Health

Athabasca University
Atlantic Cape Community College
Auburn University
Ball State University
Bemidji State University
Black Hills State University
Boise State University
Brevard Community College
Brigham Young University
Bucks County Community College
California State University—
Sacramento
Central Michigan University
Charles County Community
College
Chemeketa Community College
Christopher Newport University
Coastal Carolina University
College of DuPage
Columbus State Community
College
Daytona Beach Community College
Eastern Oregon University
Emporia State University
Florida Gulf Coast University
George Brown College
Herkimer County Community
College
Home Study International
Indiana University

J. Sargeant Reynolds Community
College
Lane Community College
Mercy College
Montana State University—
Bozeman
Mott Community College
New River Community College
New York University
Niagara College
Northampton Community College
Ohio University
Oklahoma State University
Palm Beach Community College
Pennsylvania State University
Portland Community College
Rio Salado College
Sinclair Community College
State University of New York
Tarrant County College District
Texas Woman's University
Tompkins Cortland Community
College
University of Alaska—Fairbanks
University of California Extension
University of Central Florida
University of Colorado—Boulder
University of Delaware
University of Florida
University of Nebraska—Lincoln
University of Nevada—Reno
University of Northern Iowa
University of Oklahoma
University of Pittsburgh
University of Tennessee—Knoxville
University of Waterloo
University of Wisconsin Extension
Utah Electronic Community
College
Utah State University
Weber State University
West Virginia Wesleyan College

Health and Fitness

See Physical Education

Health Education

North Carolina Central University
Portland Community College
University of Alabama
University of Arizona
University of Georgia
University of Texas—Austin
University of Utah
University of Wisconsin Extension

Health Information Administration

Columbus State Community
College
Dakota State University
University of Alaska—Southeast
Weber State University

Health Information Technician

Northern Virginia Community
College
Portland Community College

Health Services

Chemeketa Community College
Mohawk Valley Community College
New School University
Northern State University
Northwestern College (Ohio)
Pennsylvania State University
Piedmont Technical College
State University of New York
State University of New York—
Empire State College
University of California Extension
University of Central Florida
University of Idaho
University of Maryland—University
College
University of Missouri
University of Nevada—Reno
University of North Carolina—
Chapel Hill

University of Wisconsin Extension
Weber State University
Western Michigan University

Hebrew

Brigham Young University
University of Wisconsin Extension

High School Subjects

Brigham Young University
California State University—
Dominguez Hills
Citizens' High School
The Hadley School for the Blind
Home Study International
Indiana University
Keystone National High School
Louisiana State University
Mississippi State University
North Dakota Division of
Independent Study
Oklahoma State University
Phoenix Special Programs and
Academies
Portland State University
Richard Milburn High School
Texas Tech University
University of Alabama
University of California Extension
University of Colorado—Boulder
University of Florida
University of Idaho
University of Missouri
University of Nebraska—Lincoln
University of Nevada—Reno
University of Oklahoma
University of Tennessee—Knoxville
University of Texas—Austin
University of Wisconsin Extension

History

Arizona State University
Athabasca University
Atlantic Cape Community College

Ball State University
Bellevue Community College
Bemidji State University
Black Hills State University
Boise State University
Brevard Community College
Brigham Young University
Bucks County Community College
Burlington County College
California State University—Chico
California State University—
Sacramento
California State University—
San Marcos
Central Carolina Community
College
Central Wyoming College
Charles County Community
College
Charter Oak State College
Chemeketa Community College
Christopher Newport University
College of DuPage
Colorado Electronic Community
College
Colorado State University
Community College of Denver
Dallas TeleCollege
Daytona Beach Community College
East Carolina University
Eastern Oregon University
Florida Gulf Coast University
Foothill College
Fort Hays State University
Front Range Community College
Home Study International
Hope International University
Houston Community College
Indiana State University
Indiana University
Iowa State University
J. Sargeant Reynolds Community
College
Kansas State University
Lakehead University

Lane Community College
Laurentian University
Louisiana State University
Memorial University of
Newfoundland
Mississippi State University
New River Community College
North Carolina State University
Northampton Community College
Northeastern Arizona University
Northern State University
Northern Virginia Community
College
Northwestern College (Minnesota)
Ohio University
Oklahoma State University
Oregon State University
Parkland College
Pennsylvania State University
Portland Community College
Portland State University
Prairie Bible Institute
Rio Salado College
Rogers State University
San Diego State University
Simon Fraser University
Sinclair Community College
State University of New York
State University of New York—
Empire State College
Tarrant County College District
Taylor University
Teikyo Post University
Tennessee Temple University
Texas Tech University
Troy State University—
Montgomery
Tulsa Community
College/Emporia State University
Ulster County Community College
University of Alabama
University of Alaska—Fairbanks
University of Alaska—Southeast
University of Arizona
University of California Extension

University of California—
Los Angeles
University of Colorado—Boulder
University of Delaware
University of Florida
University of Georgia
University of Idaho
University of Iowa
University of Manitoba
University of Maryland—University
College
University of Minnesota—
Twin Cities
University of Missouri
University of Nebraska—Lincoln
University of Nevada—Reno
University of North Carolina—
Chapel Hill
University of North Dakota
University of Northern Iowa
University of Oklahoma
University of Pittsburgh
University of Southern Colorado
University of Tennessee—Knoxville
University of Texas—Austin
University of Utah
University of Waterloo
University of Wisconsin Extension
Upper Iowa University
Utah State University
Weber State University
West Virginia Wesleyan College
Western Illinois University
Western Michigan University

HIV/AIDS Education
University of California Extension
University of Idaho

Home Economics
See Family and Consumer Sciences

Horticulture
Auburn University
Brigham Young University

Colorado State University
Iowa State University
Kansas State University
Oklahoma State University
Pennsylvania State University
University of Georgia

Hospitality

Atlantic Cape Community College
Auburn University
Brevard Community College
Bucks County Community College
Central Texas College
Chemeketa Community College
Columbus State Community
College
Front Range Community College
Herkimer County Community
College
Hospitality Training Center
International Aviation and Travel
Academy
J. Sargeant Reynolds Community
College
Kansas State University
New York University
Niagara College
Northeastern Arizona University
Northwestern College (Ohio)
Pennsylvania State University
State University of New York
Texas Tech University
Tompkins Cortland Community
College
University of Alabama
University of Delaware
University of Nevada—Reno
University of North Carolina—
Chapel Hill
Utah Electronic Community
College

Hotel, Restaurant, and Institutional Management

See Hospitality

Human Development

Bellevue Community College
Chemeketa Community College
Colorado State University
The Hadley School for the Blind
Iowa State University
Kansas State University
Oklahoma State University
Pennsylvania State University
Rio Salado College
State University of New York—
Empire State College
Texas Tech University
University of Alabama
University of Alaska—Southeast
University of Delaware
University of Florida
University of Georgia
University of Missouri
Utah Electronic Community
College
Utah State University
Virginia Tech
Weber State University

Human Environments

University of Alabama

Human Resource Management

Columbus State Community
College
Dallas TeleCollege
Houston Community College
New Jersey Institute of Technology
New School University
Niagara College
Ohio University
Oklahoma State University
University of California Extension
University of Delaware
University of Tennessee—Knoxville
Utah State University

Human Sciences
See Social Sciences

Human Services
See Social Services/Social Work

Humanities
Arizona State University
Athabasca University
Atlantic Cape Community College
Bemidji State University
Black Hills State University
Brevard Community College
Brigham Young University
Bucks County Community College
Central Texas College
Chemeketa Community College
College of DuPage
Columbus State Community
College
Community College of Denver
Dallas TeleCollege
Eastern Oregon University
Florida Gulf Coast University
Foothill College
Front Range Community College
George Brown College
Herkimer County Community
College
Lane Community College
Mott Community College
New Jersey Institute of Technology
New School University
Northeastern Arizona University
Northern State University
Northern Virginia Community
College
Northwest Missouri State University
Ohio University
Portland Community College
Rio Salado College
Simon Fraser University
Tennessee Temple University

Tulsa Community
College/Emporia State University
University of Minnesota—
Twin Cities
University of North Dakota
University of Northern Iowa
University of Southern Indiana
Utah Electronic Community
College
Virginia Tech

Independent Living
The Hadley School for the Blind

Industrial Operations
Niagara College
Northwest Missouri State University
Ohio University
Weber State University

Industrial Relations
See Labor Studies

Industrial Technology
Bemidji State University
Central Texas College
Coastal Carolina University
Colorado State University
East Carolina University
Indiana State University

Information Management/Systems
See Management Information Systems

Information Technology
Bellevue Community College
Black Hills State University
Floyd College
Fort Hays State University
Indiana Wesleyan University
Iowa Western Community College
New River Community College

New York University
Northern State University
Northern Virginia Community
College
Syracuse University
University of California Extension
University of Southern Colorado
Weber State University

Instructional Design

Emporia State University
Pennsylvania State University
University of Nebraska—Lincoln
University of Nevada—Reno
University of Pittsburgh
University of Tennessee—Knoxville
University of Texas—Austin

Insurance

Ball State University
Indiana State University
University of Florida

Interdisciplinary Studies

Florida Gulf Coast University
Fort Hays State University
Reformed Theological Seminary
State University of New York—
Empire State College
University of California Extension
University of Florida
University of Manitoba
University of North Carolina—
Chapel Hill

Interior Design

New School University
University of Wisconsin Extension
Weber State University

International Business

Caldwell College
Laurentian University
University of California Extension

University of California—
Los Angeles

International Relations/International Affairs

New York University
University of Central Florida
University of Delaware

Internet Technology

See Information Technology

Italian

Arizona State University
Indiana University
Tulsa Community
College/Emporia State University
University of Iowa
University of Nevada—Reno
University of North Carolina—
Chapel Hill
University of Tennessee—Knoxville
University of Wisconsin Extension

Japanese

Simon Fraser University
Sinclair Community College
University of Alabama
University of Oklahoma

Journalism

Ball State University
Central Michigan University
Colorado Electronic Community
College
Indiana University
Ohio University
Oklahoma State University
University of Alabama
University of Alaska—Fairbanks
University of California—
Los Angeles
University of Colorado—Boulder

University of Florida
University of Georgia
University of Iowa
University of Maryland—University College
University of Minnesota—Twin Cities
University of Nebraska—Lincoln
University of Nevada—Reno
University of North Carolina—Chapel Hill
University of Oklahoma
University of Wisconsin Extension
Western Illinois University
Western Michigan University

Judaic Studies

University of Wisconsin Extension

K–12 Subjects

Home Study International
North Dakota Division of Independent Study
Phoenix Special Programs and Academies
Texas Tech University
University of Missouri

Kinesiology

Lakehead University
Louisiana State University
Pennsylvania State University
Simon Fraser University
University of Colorado—Boulder
University of Texas—Austin
University of Waterloo

Knowledge Management

See Management Information Systems

Labor Studies

Athabasca University
Indiana University

Northwest Missouri State University
Pennsylvania State University
State University of New York
State University of New York—Empire State College

Landscaping

University of Idaho
Utah State University

Languages

Central Wyoming College
Fort Hays State University
The Hadley School for the Blind
Home Study International
Mississippi State University
Montana State University—Bozeman
New River Community College
New School University
New York University
Niagara College
North Carolina State University
Ohio University
State University of New York
Tennessee Temple University
Texas Tech University
University of Alaska—Fairbanks
University of California Extension
University of Delaware
University of Missouri
University of Oklahoma
Utah Electronic Community College
Western Illinois University

Latin American Studies

University of Florida

Law

Athabasca University
Bucks County Community College
City University

College of DuPage
Daytona Beach Community College
Laurentian University
National American University
Niagara College
Ohio University
Pennsylvania State University
Sinclair Community College
State University of New York
Texas Tech University
Troy State University—
Montgomery
University of Alabama
University of Alaska—Southeast
University of California Extension
University of Idaho
Utah Electronic Community
College

Law Enforcement

See Criminal Justice

Legal Secretarial

National Distance Education
Center
Northwestern College (Ohio)

Legal Studies

Brevard Community College
Columbus State Community
College
Front Range Community College
Hospitality Training Center
Iowa Western Community College
National Distance Education
Center
Northwestern College (Ohio)
State University of New York
Teikyo Post University
Texas Tech University
Tompkins Cortland Community
College
University of Central Florida
University of Pittsburgh

Utah Electronic Community
College
Western Piedmont Community
College

Leisure Studies

*See Recreation, Park Resources, and
Leisure Studies*

Liberal Arts

Northeastern Arizona University
Rochester Institute of Technology
Simon Fraser University
Texas A&M University
University of Florida

Library Science

California State University—
Los Angeles
East Carolina University
Eastern Oregon University
Indiana University
Louisiana State University
Memorial University of
Newfoundland
North Carolina Central University
Northampton Community College
Northern Virginia Community
College
Rutgers University
State University of New York
State University of West Georgia
Texas A&M University
Texas Woman's University
University of Alabama
University of Alaska—Fairbanks
University of Arizona
University of California Extension
University of Florida
University of Idaho
University of North Carolina—
Chapel Hill
University of Oklahoma

University of Tennessee—Knoxville
Weber State University

Life Sciences
Indiana State University
San Diego State University
Texas A&M University
University of Florida

Linguistics
Indiana University
Iowa State University
Simon Fraser University
University of Alaska—Fairbanks
University of Florida
University of Iowa
University of Oklahoma

Logistics
See Transportation and Logistics

Management
Athabasca University
Ball State University
Boise State University
Bucks County Community College
Caldwell College
California State University—
Bakersfield
California State University—Chico
California State University—
Dominguez Hills
Central Michigan University
City University
Coastal Carolina University
College of DuPage
Columbus State Community
College
Dallas TeleCollege
Daytona Beach Community
College
Emporia State University
Florida Gulf Coast University
Fort Hays State University

Front Range Community College
Houston Community College
Iowa State University
Iowa Western Community College
ISIM University
Kansas State University
Louisiana State University
Montana State University—Billings
National American University
New Jersey Institute of Technology
Northern Virginia Community
College
Northwestern College (Ohio)
Ohio University
Oklahoma State University
Pennsylvania State University
Piedmont Technical College
Portland Community College
Rensselaer Polytechnic Institute
Rio Salado College
Sinclair Community College
Southwest Missouri State University
State University of New York
State University of New York—
Empire State College
State University of West Georgia
Syracuse University
Tarrant County College District
Teikyo Post University
Texas Tech University
Troy State University—
Montgomery
Tulsa Community
College/Emporia State University
University of Alabama
University of California Extension
University of California—
Los Angeles
University of Central Florida
University of Florida
University of Georgia
University of Massachusetts—
Lowell
University of Minnesota—
Twin Cities

University of Missouri
University of Nebraska—Lincoln
University of Nevada—Reno
University of North Dakota
University of Northern Iowa
University of Oklahoma
University of Southern Colorado
University of Tennessee—Knoxville
Utah State University
Weber State University
Western Illinois University

Management Information Systems

Athabasca University
Brigham Young University
Bucks County Community College
California State University—Sacramento
Central Michigan University
Dakota State University
Emporia State University
Florida Gulf Coast University
Foothill College
Herkimer County Community College
ISIM University
J. Sargeant Reynolds Community College
Louisiana State University
Memorial University of Newfoundland
Mohawk Valley Community College
Montana State University—Billings
New Jersey Institute of Technology
Northwest Missouri State University
Ohio University
Oklahoma State University
Pennsylvania State University
State University of New York
Teikyo Post University
University of California Extension
University of California—Los Angeles

University of Massachusetts—Lowell
University of Pittsburgh
University of Tennessee—Knoxville
Upper Iowa University
Utah State University
Western Michigan University

Manufacturing
See Industrial Technology

Marine Sciences
University of North Carolina—Chapel Hill

Marketing

Athabasca University
Black Hills State University
Boise State University
Bucks County Community College
Caldwell College
California State University—Bakersfield
California State University—Chico
California State University—Dominguez Hills
Central Carolina Community College
Central Michigan University
College of DuPage
Colorado State University
Columbus State Community College
Dallas TeleCollege
Daytona Beach Community College
Fort Hays State University
Fox Valley Technical College
Front Range Community College
Houston Community College
Iowa State University
Louisiana State University
Mississippi State University
Montana State University—Billings
New Jersey Institute of Technology

New River Community College
Niagara College
Northern State University
Northern Virginia Community
College
Northwestern College (Ohio)
Ohio University
Oklahoma State University
Pennsylvania State University
Sinclair Community College
State University of New York
State University of New York—
Empire State College
Teikyo Post University
Texas Tech University
Troy State University—
Montgomery
Tulsa Community College/
Emporia State University
University of Arizona
University of California Extension
University of California—
Los Angeles
University of Florida
University of Georgia
University of Minnesota—
Twin Cities
University of Missouri
University of Nebraska—Lincoln
University of Northern Iowa
University of Oklahoma
University of Southern Colorado
Weber State University
Western Illinois University
Western Piedmont Community
College

Marriage and Family Services

University of Tennessee—Knoxville

Masonry

North Dakota State College of
Science

Mass Communications

Bellevue Community College
Black Hills State University
Daytona Beach Community
College
Louisiana State University
New School University
Northern State University
State University of New York
State University of West Georgia
Texas Tech University
University of Alabama
University of Florida
University of Georgia
University of Iowa
University of Minnesota—
Twin Cities
University of North Carolina—
Chapel Hill
University of Oklahoma
University of Wisconsin Extension

Materials Management

*See Production and Inventory
Management*

Materials Science

University of Alabama

Mathematics

Arizona State University
Athabasca University
Atlantic Cape Community College
Auburn University
Ball State University
Bellevue Community College
Black Hills State University
Boise State University
Brevard Community College
Brigham Young University
Bucks County Community College
Burlington County College
California State University—
Bakersfield

California State University—Chico
Central Carolina Community
College
Central Texas College
Charles County Community
College
Charter Oak State College
Chemeketa Community College
Christopher Newport University
Coastal Carolina University
Cochise College
College of DuPage
Colorado Electronic Community
College
Colorado State University
Columbus State Community
College
Community College of Denver
Dakota State University
Dallas TeleCollege
Daytona Beach Community College
East Carolina University
Eastern Oregon University
Foothill College
Fort Hays State University
Fox Valley Technical College
Front Range Community College
Herkimer County Community
College
Home Study International
Houston Community College
Indiana State University
Indiana University
Iowa State University
Laurentian University
Louisiana State University
Memorial University of
Newfoundland
Mercy College
Michigan State University
Mississippi State University
Mohawk Valley Community College
Montana State University—
Bozeman
Mott Community College

National American University
National-Louis University
New Jersey Institute of Technology
New River Community College
New School University
North Carolina Central University
North Carolina State University
Northampton Community College
Northeastern Arizona University
Northern State University
Northern Virginia Community
College
Northwestern College (Minnesota)
Northwestern College (Ohio)
Ohio University
Oklahoma State University
Oregon State University
Palm Beach Community College
Parkland College
Pennsylvania State University
Piedmont Technical College
Portland Community College
Portland State University
Rio Salado College
Rogers State University
Simon Fraser University
Sinclair Community College
State University of New York
State University of New York—
Empire State College
Tarrant County College District
Taylor University
Teikyo Post University
Tennessee Temple University
Texas Tech University
Troy State University—
Montgomery
Tulsa Community College/
Emporia State University
Ulster County Community College
University of Alabama
University of Alaska—Fairbanks
University of Alaska—Southeast
University of Arizona
University of California Extension

University of California—
Los Angeles
University of Colorado—Boulder
University of Delaware
University of Florida
University of Georgia
University of Idaho
University of Iowa
University of Manitoba
University of Maryland—University
College
University of Massachusetts—
Lowell
University of Minnesota—
Twin Cities
University of Missouri
University of Nebraska—Lincoln
University of Nevada—Reno
University of North Carolina—
Chapel Hill
University of North Dakota
University of Northern Iowa
University of Oklahoma
University of Pittsburgh
University of Tennessee—Knoxville
University of Texas—Austin
University of Utah
University of Waterloo
University of Wisconsin Extension
Utah Electronic Community
College
Utah State University
Virginia Tech
Weber State University
West Virginia Wesleyan College
Western Illinois University
Western Michigan University
Western Piedmont Community
College

Media Studies
See Mass Communications

Medical Assisting
Portland Community College

Medical Office Management
Hospitality Training Center
Northwestern College (Ohio)

Medical Record Administration
See Health Information Administration

Medical Record Technician
See Health Information Technician

Medical Secretarial
Northwestern College (Ohio)

Medical Spanish for Health Care Professionals
University of Texas—Austin

Medical Technology
See Clinical Laboratory Science

Medical Terminology
Rio Salado College
State University of New York

Medical Transcription
National Distance Education
Center

Medicine
Memorial University of
Newfoundland
University of Florida
Western Michigan University

Mental Health Services
Central Texas College
Houston Community College
University of Florida

Meteorology
See Atmospheric Sciences

Microbiology
Mississippi State University
North Carolina State University
University of Idaho
University of Manitoba

Microcomputer Technology
Columbus State Community
College

Microsoft Certification
American Institute of Commerce
Baker College
Bucks County Community College
Dallas TeleCollege
University of Texas—Austin
Vatterott College

Middle- and Near-Eastern Studies
Brigham Young University

Military Science
State University of West Georgia
University of Missouri

Ministry
Berean University
Life Bible College
Moody Bible Institute
Prairie Bible Institute

Missionary Studies
Prairie Bible Institute
Reformed Theological Seminary
Taylor University
Tennessee Temple University

Mortuary Science
Piedmont Technical College

Multimedia Authoring
Columbus State Community
College
Dallas TeleCollege
Eastern Oregon University
Niagara College

Museum Studies
University of Arizona

Music
Athabasca University
Atlantic Cape Community College
Bemidji State University
Black Hills State University
Boise State University
Brigham Young University
Bucks County Community College
Burlington County College
Central Michigan University
Chemeketa Community College
Coastal Carolina University
College of DuPage
Colorado Electronic Community
College
Dakota State University
Dallas TeleCollege
Eastern Oregon University
Emporia State University
Foothill College
Fort Hays State University
Front Range Community College
The Hadley School for the Blind
Indiana University
Indiana Wesleyan University
Laurentian University
Louisiana State University
New River Community College
New School University
North Carolina Central University
Northeastern Arizona University
Northwest Missouri State University
Ohio University
Parkland College

Pennsylvania State University
Portland Community College
San Diego State University
Sinclair Community College
State University of New York
Tarrant County College District
Texas Tech University
Troy State University—
Montgomery
Tulsa Community College/
Emporia State University
University of Alabama
University of Alaska—Fairbanks
University of Alaska—Southeast
University of Arizona
University of California Extension
University of Colorado—Boulder
University of Delaware
University of Idaho
University of Minnesota—
Twin Cities
University of Nevada—Reno
University of North Carolina—
Chapel Hill
University of North Dakota
University of Northern Iowa
University of Oklahoma
University of Pittsburgh
University of Utah
University of Wisconsin Extension
Weber State University
West Virginia Wesleyan College
Western Michigan University

Native American Studies
Athabasca University
Laurentian University
Simon Fraser University
University of Alaska—Fairbanks
University of Arizona
University of Iowa
University of Manitoba
University of Minnesota—
Twin Cities
University of Waterloo

Natural Sciences
See Biological Sciences

Nonprofit Management
New School University
University of California—Los
Angeles

Novell Certification
University of Texas—Austin

Nurse-Midwife
Laurentian University

Nursing
Arizona State University
Athabasca University
Atlantic Cape Community College
Bemidji State University
Black Hills State University
Boise State University
Brigham Young University
California State University—
Bakersfield
California State University—Chico
California State University—
Sacramento
Cambrian College
Central Wyoming College
Columbus State Community
College
Florida Gulf Coast University
Floyd College
Fort Hays State University
Indiana State University
Indiana University
Lakehead University
Laurentian University
Memorial University of
Newfoundland
Michigan State University
Montana State University—
Bozeman

North Carolina Central University
Northeastern Arizona University
Northern State University
Parkland College
Pennsylvania State University
Piedmont Technical College
Portland Community College
San Jose State University
State University of New York
Texas Woman's University
University of Alabama
University of Central Florida
University of Delaware
University of Florida
University of Manitoba
University of Minnesota—
Twin Cities
University of Nebraska—Lincoln
University of North Carolina—
Chapel Hill
University of Pittsburgh
University of Southern Colorado
University of Southern Indiana
University of Tennessee—Knoxville
University of Texas—Austin
Weber State University
West Virginia Wesleyan College

Nutrition and Food Science

American Academy of Nutrition
Athabasca University
Auburn University
Brevard Community College
Brigham Young University
Burlington County College
Chemeketa Community College
Colorado State University
Community College of Denver
Dallas TeleCollege
Daytona Beach Community College
East Carolina University
Front Range Community College
Home Study International

Iowa State University
Kansas State University
Michigan State University
Mississippi State University
North Carolina State University
Oklahoma State University
Oregon State University
Pennsylvania State University
Portland Community College
Portland State University
Rio Salado College
San Diego State University
State University of New York
Texas Tech University
Texas Woman's University
University of California Extension
University of Delaware
University of Florida
University of Georgia
University of Minnesota—
Twin Cities
University of Nebraska—Lincoln
University of Nevada—Reno
University of North Carolina—
Chapel Hill
University of North Dakota
University of Tennessee—Knoxville
University of Texas—Austin
University of Utah
Weber State University

Occupational Health Studies

McGill University

Occupational Therapy

Colorado State University
San Jose State University
Texas Woman's University
Tulsa Community
College/Emporia State University
University of North Dakota
Western Michigan University

Oceanography
Bellevue Community College

Office Management and Technology
Atlantic Cape Community College
Bellevue Community College
Brevard Community College
Bucks County Community College
Central Texas College
Charles County Community College
Columbus State Community College
Dallas TeleCollege
Daytona Beach Community College
Eastern Oregon University
Louisiana State University
Parkland College
Portland Community College
Rio Salado College
Sinclair Community College
Tarrant County College District
Western Piedmont Community College

Operations Research
University of Delaware

Opticianry
J. Sargeant Reynolds Community College
University of Arizona

Organization
Athabasca University
New York University

Paralegal Studies
See Legal Studies

Paramedic
See Emergency Medicine

Parks and Recreation
See Recreation, Park Resources, and Leisure Studies

Pastoral Ministries and Counseling
Seminary Extension Independent Study Institute
Taylor University
Tennessee Temple University

Peace Studies
See Conflict Resolution

Performing Arts
Texas Woman's University
University of Utah

Pest Management
University of Missouri

Pharmacology
Indiana University
University of Arizona
University of California Extension

Pharmacy
Auburn University
University of Florida

Pharmacy Technology
Hospitality Training Center
National Distance Education Center
Northwestern College (Ohio)

Philosophy
Athabasca University
Ball State University
Bellevue Community College
Bemidji State University
Brigham Young University
Bucks County Community College

California State University—Chico
California State University—
Sacramento
Central Carolina Community
College
Charles County Community
College
Charter Oak State College
Chemeketa Community College
Christopher Newport University
Cochise College
College of DuPage
Colorado Electronic Community
College
Colorado State University
Community College of Denver
Dallas TeleCollege
Daytona Beach Community College
Foothill College
Fort Hays State University
Franciscan University of
Steubenville
Front Range Community College
Houston Community College
Indiana University
Indiana Wesleyan University
Iowa State University
Lakehead University
Laurentian University
Louisiana State University
Memorial University of
Newfoundland
National-Louis University
North Carolina State University
Northampton Community College
Northern Virginia Community
College
Northwest Missouri State University
Northwestern College (Minnesota)
Ohio University
Oklahoma State University
Oregon State University
Pennsylvania State University
Piedmont Technical College

Rio Salado College
Simon Fraser University
State University of New York
State University of New York—
Empire State College
Syracuse University
Tarrant County College District
Taylor University
Tennessee Temple University
Tulsa Community
College/Emporia State University
University of Alabama
University of Alaska—Fairbanks
University of Alaska—Southeast
University of California Extension
University of California—
Los Angeles
University of Colorado—Boulder
University of Delaware
University of Florida
University of Georgia
University of Idaho
University of Manitoba
University of Minnesota—
Twin Cities
University of Missouri
University of Nebraska—Lincoln
University of North Carolina—
Chapel Hill
University of North Dakota
University of Oklahoma
University of Pittsburgh
University of Tennessee—Knoxville
University of Texas—Austin
University of Utah
University of Waterloo
University of Wisconsin Extension
Utah Electronic Community
College
Virginia Tech
Weber State University
West Virginia Wesleyan College
Western Illinois University
Western Michigan University

Photography

Houston Community College
New School University

Physical Education

Adams State College
Atlantic Cape Community College
Ball State University
Bemidji State University
Brevard Community College
Brigham Young University
California State University—Chico
Central Carolina Community
College
Central Wyoming College
Chemeketa Community College
Dallas TeleCollege
Eastern Oregon University
Indiana University
Laurentian University
Mississippi State University
North Carolina State University
Northampton Community College
Northern Virginia Community
College
Ohio University
Parkland College
State University of New York
Tarrant County College District
University of Idaho
University of Iowa
University of Pittsburgh
Utah Electronic Community
College
Utah State University
Weber State University
West Virginia Wesleyan College
Western Illinois University
Western Michigan University

Physical Science

Adams State College
Arizona State University
Bemidji State University

Black Hills State University
Brevard Community College
Brigham Young University
Bucks County Community College
College of DuPage
East Carolina University
Emporia State University
Louisiana State University
Ohio University
State University of New York
Upper Iowa University
Utah Electronic Community
College
West Virginia Wesleyan College

Physical Therapy

Texas Woman's University
University of Minnesota—
Twin Cities

Physician Assisting

University of Florida

Physics

Athabasca University
Ball State University
Boise State University
Brigham Young University
Bucks County Community College
California State University—Chico
Central Michigan University
Chemeketa Community College
Christopher Newport University
College of DuPage
Columbus State Community
College
Front Range Community College
Illinois Institute of Technology
Indiana University
Laurentian University
Louisiana State University
Michigan State University
Mississippi State University

Montana State University—
Bozeman
New Jersey Institute of Technology
North Carolina Central University
North Carolina State University
Northern Virginia Community
College
Ohio University
Pennsylvania State University
Rogers State University
Sinclair Community College
State University of New York
University of Alabama
University of Arizona
University of California Extension
University of Idaho
University of Minnesota—
Twin Cities
University of Missouri
University of Nebraska—Lincoln
University of North Carolina—
Chapel Hill
University of Texas—Austin
University of Utah
University of Waterloo
University of Wisconsin Extension

Plant Pathology
Pennsylvania State University
University of Arizona
University of Missouri

Plant Sciences
Texas Tech University
University of Missouri

Plant Utilities Technology
State University of New York

Plastics
Northampton Community College
Sinclair Community College

Plumbing
North Dakota State College of
Science

Political Science
Arizona State University
Athabasca University
Atlantic Cape Community College
Auburn University
Ball State University
Bellevue Community College
Bemidji State University
Black Hills State University
Boise State University
Brigham Young University
Bucks County Community College
Burlington County College
California State University—
Bakersfield
California State University—Chico
California State University—
Los Angeles
California State University—
Sacramento
Central Michigan University
Central Wyoming College
Charles County Community
College
Christopher Newport University
Coastal Carolina University
Cochise College
College of DuPage
Community College of Denver
Dallas TeleCollege
Daytona Beach Community College
Eastern Oregon University
Foothill College
Fort Hays State University
Front Range Community College
Home Study International
Houston Community College
Indiana State University
Indiana University
Iowa State University

J. Sargeant Reynolds Community
College
Kansas State University
Lakehead University
Laurentian University
Louisiana State University
Memorial University of
Newfoundland
Mississippi State University
New River Community College
North Carolina State University
Northampton Community College
Northeastern Arizona University
Northern State University
Northern Virginia Community
College
Ohio University
Oklahoma State University
Oregon State University
Palm Beach Community College
Parkland College
Pennsylvania State University
Piedmont Technical College
Portland Community College
Rio Salado College
San Jose State University
Simon Fraser University
Southwest Missouri State University
State University of New York
State University of New York—
Empire State College
State University of West Georgia
Syracuse University
Tarrant County College District
Teikyo Post University
Tennessee Temple University
Texas Tech University
Troy State University—
Montgomery
Tulsa Community
College/Emporia State University
University College of Cape Breton
University of Alabama

University of Alaska—Fairbanks
University of Alaska—Southeast
University of Arizona
University of California Extension
University of California—
Los Angeles
University of Colorado—Boulder
University of Delaware
University of Florida
University of Georgia
University of Idaho
University of Iowa
University of Manitoba
University of Minnesota—
Twin Cities
University of Missouri
University of Nebraska—Lincoln
University of Nevada—Reno
University of North Carolina—
Chapel Hill
University of Northern Iowa
University of Oklahoma
University of Pittsburgh
University of Southern Colorado
University of Southern Indiana
University of Tennessee—Knoxville
University of Texas—Austin
University of Utah
University of Wisconsin Extension
Upper Iowa University
Virginia Tech
Weber State University
West Virginia Wesleyan College
Western Illinois University
Western Michigan University
Western Oregon University

Portuguese
University of Iowa
University of Wisconsin Extension

Poultry Science
Pennsylvania State University

Preschool Subjects

John Tracy Clinic

Problem-Centered Studies

University College of Cape Breton

Production and Inventory Management

Northwest Missouri State University
University of Wisconsin Extension
Weber State University

Property Management

See Building Management

Psychology

Adams State College
Arizona State University
Athabasca University
Atlantic Cape Community College
Auburn University
Ball State University
Bellevue Community College
Bemidji State University
Black Hills State University
Boise State University
Brevard Community College
Brigham Young University
Bucks County Community College
Burlington County College
California State University—Chico
California State University—
Dominguez Hills
California State University—
Sacramento
Cambrian College
Capella University
Central Carolina Community
College
Central Michigan University
Central Wyoming College
Charles County Community
College
Chemeketa Community College

Coastal Carolina University
Cochise College
College of DuPage
Colorado Electronic Community
College
Colorado State University
Columbus State Community
College
Community College of Denver
Dakota State University
Dallas TeleCollege
Daytona Beach Community College
East Carolina University
Eastern Oregon University
Emporia State University
Florida Gulf Coast University
Foothill College
Fort Hays State University
Fox Valley Technical College
Front Range Community College
Home Study International
Houston Community College
Illinois Institute of Technology
Indiana State University
Indiana University
J. Sargeant Reynolds Community
College
Kansas State University
Lakehead University
Lane Community College
Laurentian University
Louisiana State University
Memorial University of
Newfoundland
Mercy College
Mississippi State University
Mohawk Valley Community College
Montana State University—Billings
National-Louis University
New River Community College
New York University
Niagara College
North Carolina State University
Northampton Community College

Northern State University
Northern Virginia Community
College
Northwestern College (Minnesota)
Ohio University
Oklahoma State University
Oregon State University
Palm Beach Community College
Parkland College
Pennsylvania State University
Piedmont Technical College
Portland Community College
Portland State University
Rio Salado College
San Jose State University
Simon Fraser University
Sinclair Community College
Southwest Missouri State University
State University of New York
State University of New York—
Empire State College
Syracuse University
Tarrant County College District
Taylor University
Teikyo Post University
Tennessee Temple University
Texas Tech University
Texas Woman's University
Tompkins Cortland Community
College
Troy State University—
Montgomery
Tulsa Community
College/Emporia State University
Ulster County Community College
University College of Cape Breton
University of Alabama
University of Alaska—Fairbanks
University of Arizona
University of California Extension
University of Central Florida
University of Colorado—Boulder
University of Florida
University of Georgia

University of Idaho
University of Iowa
University of Manitoba
University of Massachusetts—
Lowell
University of Minnesota—
Twin Cities
University of Missouri
University of Nebraska—Lincoln
University of Nevada—Reno
University of North Carolina—
Chapel Hill
University of North Dakota
University of Northern Iowa
University of Oklahoma
University of Pittsburgh
University of Southern Colorado
University of Southern Indiana
University of Tennessee—Knoxville
University of Texas—Austin
University of Utah
University of Waterloo
University of Wisconsin Extension
Upper Iowa University
Utah Electronic Community
College
Weber State University
West Virginia Wesleyan College
Western Illinois University
Western Michigan University
Western Oregon University
Western Piedmont Community
College

Public Administration/ Public Affairs

Athabasca University
Indiana University
Memorial University of
Newfoundland
Northeastern Arizona University
State University of New York—
Empire State College
University College of Cape Breton

University of Alaska—Southeast
University of Florida
University of Pittsburgh
University of Waterloo
Upper Iowa University

Public Health

Oregon State University
State University of New York
University of California—
Los Angeles
University of Minnesota—
Twin Cities

Public Relations

University of Alabama
University of California—
Los Angeles
University of Florida
University of Tennessee—Knoxville

Publishing

Simon Fraser University

Purchasing

Sinclair Community College
University of California Extension
University of Texas—Austin

Quality Management

California State University—
Dominguez Hills
Rio Salado College
Troy State University—
Montgomery

Radio/Television/ Motion Pictures

See Broadcasting

Radiologic Science

Portland Community College
University of California Extension
Weber State University

Railroad Operations

Utah Electronic Community
College

Ranch Management

See Agribusiness

Range Science

Brigham Young University
Colorado State University
Oregon State University

Real Estate

Houston Community College
Louisiana State University
Mississippi State University
New York University
Portland Community College
Texas Tech University
University of Arizona
University of California Extension
University of California—
Los Angeles
University of Colorado—Boulder
University of Idaho
University of Nebraska—Lincoln
University of North Dakota

Recreation, Park Resources, and Leisure Studies

Adams State College
California State University—
Dominguez Hills
The Hadley School for the Blind
Indiana University
North Carolina Central University
Northeastern Arizona University
University of Georgia
University of Idaho
University of Iowa
University of Manitoba
University of Missouri

University of North Carolina—
Chapel Hill
University of Utah
Utah State University
Western Illinois University

Rehabilitation Services

University of Alabama
University of Minnesota—
Twin Cities
University of Tennessee—Knoxville

Religion

Athabasca University
Ball State University
Brigham Young University
California State University—Chico
The Catholic Distance University
Central Michigan University
Christopher Newport University
Coastal Carolina University
Home Study International
Indiana University
Laurentian University
Memorial University of
Newfoundland
Pennsylvania State University
Portland State University
Southwest Missouri State University
State University of New York—
Empire State College
Troy State University—
Montgomery
University of Alabama
University of California Extension
University of Florida
University of Georgia
University of Iowa
University of Manitoba
University of North Carolina—
Chapel Hill
University of North Dakota
University of Northern Iowa
University of Pittsburgh
University of Tennessee—Knoxville

University of Waterloo
Western Illinois University
Western Michigan University

Religious Education

Northwestern College (Minnesota)
Taylor University
Tennessee Temple University

Respiratory Therapy

J. Sargeant Reynolds Community
College
Weber State University

Retailing

State University of New York

Rural Development

Michigan State University

Russian

California State University—
Sacramento
University of Arizona
University of Minnesota—
Twin Cities
University of Missouri
University of Oklahoma
University of Waterloo
University of Wisconsin Extension

Safety Education

University of Tennessee—Knoxville
Western Illinois University

Sales and Service Technology

Weber State University

Scandinavian Languages

University of Minnesota—
Twin Cities
University of North Dakota

University of Waterloo
University of Wisconsin Extension

Science

Chemeketa Community College
Coastal Carolina University
Eastern Oregon University
George Brown College
Herkimer County Community
College
Iowa State University
Mott Community College
National-Louis University
Northwestern College (Minnesota)
Northwestern College (Ohio)
Portland Community College
Rochester Institute of Technology
State University of New York—
Empire State College
Texas A&M University
Troy State University—
Montgomery
University of Colorado—Boulder
University of Maryland—University
College
University of Waterloo

Secondary Education

*See Elementary and Secondary
Education*

Security Services

See Fire Protection and Security Services

Secretarial

See Administrative Assistance

Sign Language

New River Community College

Slavic Languages

University of Arizona
University of Texas—Austin
University of Waterloo

Small Business Management

Athabasca University
California State University—Los
Angeles
Coastal Carolina University
Floyd College
Iowa Western Community College
Portland Community College
University of Southern Colorado

Social Sciences

Athabasca University
California State University—Chico
Central Texas College
Charter Oak State College
Columbus State Community
College
Emporia State University
Herkimer County Community
College
Mott Community College
National-Louis University
New Jersey Institute of Technology
New School University
Ohio University
San Diego State University
State University of New York
Taylor University
Tennessee Temple University
University of Colorado—Boulder
University of Florida
University of Minnesota—
Twin Cities
University of Northern Iowa
University of Southern Colorado
University of Waterloo
University of Wisconsin Extension
Utah Electronic Community
College

Social Services/ Social Work

Arizona State University
Bemidji State University

Brigham Young University
California State University—Chico
Capella University
College of DuPage
Florida Gulf Coast University
Fort Hays State University
Kansas State University
Lakehead University
Laurentian University
Memorial University of
Newfoundland
Michigan State University
National-Louis University
Ohio University
State University of New York
State University of New York—
Empire State College
Texas Tech University
Texas Woman's University
University of Alaska—Southeast
University of Iowa
University of Manitoba
University of Minnesota—
Twin Cities
University of Missouri
University of Northern Iowa
University of Tennessee—Knoxville
University of Waterloo
University of Wisconsin Extension
Weber State University
Western Michigan University

Sociology

Adams State College
Athabasca University
Atlantic Cape Community College
Ball State University
Bellevue Community College
Bemidji State University
Black Hills State University
Boise State University
Brigham Young University
Bucks County Community College
Burlington County College

California State University—
Bakersfield
California State University—Chico
California State University—
Sacramento
California State University—San
Marcos
Central Carolina Community
College
Central Michigan University
Charles County Community
College
Charter Oak State College
Christopher Newport University
Coastal Carolinà University
Cochise College
College of DuPage
Colorado Electronic Community
College
Colorado State University
Community College of Denver
Dakota State University
Dallas TeleCollege
Daytona Beach Community
College
Eastern Oregon University
Emporia State University
Foothill College
Fort Hays State University
Fox Valley Technical College
Front Range Community College
Home Study International
Houston Community College
Indiana State University
Indiana University
Iowa State University
J. Sargeant Reynolds Community
College
Kansas State University
Lakehead University
Lane Community College
Laurentian University
Louisiana State University
Memorial University of
Newfoundland

Mercy College
Mississippi State University
Mohawk Valley Community College
New River Community College
New York University
Niagara College
North Carolina Central University
Northampton Community College
Northeastern Arizona University
Northern State University
Northern Virginia Community
College
Ohio University
Oklahoma State University
Oregon State University
Parkland College
Pennsylvania State University
Piedmont Technical College
Portland Community College
Portland State University
Rio Salado College
Rogers State University
Simon Fraser University
Sinclair Community College
State University of New York—
Empire State College
State University of West Georgia
Syracuse University
Tarrant County College District
Teikyo Post University
Texas Tech University
Texas Woman's University
Tompkins Cortland Community
College
Troy State University—
Montgomery
Tulsa Community
College/Emporia State University
Ulster County Community College
University of Alabama
University of Alaska—Fairbanks
University of Alaska—Southeast
University of Arizona
University of California Extension

University of Colorado—Boulder
University of Delaware
University of Florida
University of Georgia
University of Idaho
University of Iowa
University of Manitoba
University of Massachusetts—
Lowell
University of Missouri
University of Nebraska—Lincoln
University of Nevada—Reno
University of North Carolina—
Chapel Hill
University of North Dakota
University of Northern Iowa
University of Oklahoma
University of Southern Colorado
University of Tennessee—Knoxville
University of Texas—Austin
University of Waterloo
University of Wisconsin Extension
Upper Iowa University
West Virginia Wesleyan College
Western Illinois University
Western Michigan University

Soil Science

Colorado State University
North Carolina State University
Oregon State University
Texas Tech University
University of Georgia
Weber State University

Spanish

Arizona State University
Athabasca University
Bellevue Community College
Bemidji State University
Black Hills State University
Boise State University
Brigham Young University
Burlington County College

Central Carolina Community
College
Central Michigan University
Charles County Community
College
Christopher Newport University
College of DuPage
Columbus State Community
College
Dallas TeleCollege
Daytona Beach Community
College
Front Range Community College
Houston Community College
Indiana University
Lane Community College
Louisiana State University
North Carolina Central University
Northern State University
Northern Virginia Community
College
Oklahoma State University
Palm Beach Community College
Pennsylvania State University
Piedmont Technical College
Portland Community College
Rio Salado College
Rogers State University
Tarrant County College District
Troy State University—
Montgomery
Tulsa Community College/
Emporia State University
Ulster County Community College
University of Alabama
University of Arizona
University of Central Florida
University of Florida
University of Georgia
University of Iowa
University of Maryland—University
College
University of Minnesota—
Twin Cities

University of North Carolina—
Chapel Hill
University of North Dakota
University of Oklahoma
University of Tennessee—Knoxville
University of Texas—Austin
University of Waterloo
University of Wisconsin Extension
Upper Iowa University
Weber State University

Special Education

California State University—Chico
Mississippi State University
State University of West Georgia
University of Florida
University of Idaho
University of Tennessee—Knoxville
Western Illinois University
Western Oregon University

Speech

Auburn University
Bellevue Community College
Black Hills State University
Brevard Community College
Coastal Carolina University
College of DuPage
Colorado Electronic Community
College
Dallas TeleCollege
Florida Gulf Coast University
Front Range Community College
Indiana University
Iowa State University
Louisiana State University
New River Community College
Northern Virginia Community
College
Parkland College
Pennsylvania State University
Piedmont Technical College
Portland Community College
State University of New York

Tarrant County College District
Troy State University—
Montgomery
Tulsa Community College/
Emporia State University
University of Georgia
University of Iowa
University of Maryland—University
College
University of Minnesota—
Twin Cities

Speech and Language Pathology
See Communication Disorders

Sports Medicine
See Athletic Training and Sports Medicine

Sports Sciences
Ohio University
University of Iowa
University of Oklahoma

Statistics
Black Hills State University
Brigham Young University
California State University—
Sacramento
Central Michigan University
Daytona Beach Community College
Iowa State University
Kansas State University
Louisiana State University
Memorial University of
Newfoundland
Mississippi State University
North Carolina State University
Northern State University
Oklahoma State University
Oregon State University
Palm Beach Community College
Pennsylvania State University

Portland State University
Simon Fraser University
University of Alabama
University of Alaska—Fairbanks
University of Alaska—Southeast
University of California Extension
University of Delaware
University of Florida
University of Iowa
University of Manitoba
University of Massachusetts—
Lowell
University of Minnesota—
Twin Cities
University of Missouri
University of Nebraska—Lincoln
University of North Carolina—
Chapel Hill
University of Pittsburgh
University of Waterloo
University of Wisconsin Extension
Utah State University

Studio Arts
See Art and Design

Study Skills
New River Community College
Ohio University
State University of New York
University of Colorado—Boulder
University of Maryland—University
College
University of Tennessee—Knoxville

Supermarket Management
Rio Salado College

Supervision
Indiana University

Surgical Technology
Central Wyoming College

Surveying and Mapping
Houston Community College
Utah Electronic Community
College

Taxation
National Tax Training School
New York University

Teacher Education
See Education

Teaching—English as a Second Language
University of Florida

Technical Communication
University of California Extension

Technical Writing
Coastal Carolina University
University of California—
Los Angeles
University of Minnesota—
Twin Cities

Technology
Brigham Young University
Indiana University
ISIM University
Memorial University of
Newfoundland
Michigan State University
Mott Community College
Oklahoma State University
Rochester Institute of Technology
State University of New York
University of Alaska—Southeast
University of Southern California
University of Texas—Austin

Telecommunications
Central Texas College

Fort Hays State University
Indiana University
ISIM University
Oklahoma State University
State University of New York
University of Alabama
University of California Extension
University of Southern California
Weber State University

Test Preparation
Coastal Carolina University
Floyd College
Iowa Western Community College

Textiles
See Fashion Design and Merchandising

Theatre
Ball State University
Black Hills State University
Boise State University
Brigham Young University
Burlington County College
Central Wyoming College
Foothill College
Louisiana State University
New School University
Northern State University
Northern Virginia Community
College
Ohio University
Pennsylvania State University
Rio Salado College
State University of New York
Tarrant County College District
University of Alabama
University of Alaska—Fairbanks
University of Georgia
University of Iowa
University of Minnesota—
Twin Cities
University of North Carolina—
Chapel Hill

University of Oklahoma
University of Pittsburgh

Theology
Franciscan University of
Steubenville
Home Study International
Hope International University
Life Bible College
Prairie Bible Institute
Reformed Theological Seminary
Seminary Extension Independent
Study Institute
Taylor University
Tennessee Temple University
Wheaton College

Trade
See International Business

Transportation and Logistics
Iowa Western Community College
Pennsylvania State University
Weber State University

Travel and Tourism
See Hospitality

Turf Management
Pennsylvania State University

Typing
The Hadley School for the Blind
Northwestern College (Ohio)

Urban Studies
University of Delaware

Veterinary Medicine
Auburn University
State University of New York

Texas A&M University
University of Georgia

Veterinary Technology
Portland Community College

Vocational Education
Louisiana State University
State University of New York
University of Idaho
University of North Dakota
Western Michigan University

Water Resources
Kansas State University
Rio Salado College

Waste Management
Rio Salado College
University of Florida

Web Site Development
Kennesaw State University
Pennsylvania State University
State University of New York

Welding
North Dakota State College of
Science

Western European Studies
University of Nevada—Reno

Wildlife and Fish Science
Colorado State University
Mississippi State University
Oregon State University
University of Tennessee—Knoxville
Utah State University

Women's Studies
Arizona State University
Athabasca University

Indiana University
Kansas State University
Laurentian University
Louisiana State University
Memorial University of
Newfoundland
Ohio University
Oregon State University
Simon Fraser University
Texas Woman's University
University of Alaska—Fairbanks
University of Georgia
University of Iowa
University of Minnesota—
Twin Cities
University of Missouri
University of Nevada—Reno
University of Southern Colorado
University of Texas—Austin
University of Waterloo
University of Wisconsin Extension

Word Processing
New River Community College
Northwestern College (Ohio)

World Studies
Athabasca University
Bellevue Community College
New York University
Northwest Missouri State University
University of Iowa

Writing
Chemeketa Community College
Coastal Carolina University
Eastern Oregon University
Floyd College
Fox Valley Technical College
Iowa Western Community College
Lane Community College
New School University
New York University
Oregon State University
Portland Community College
State University of New York—
Empire State College
University of Arizona
University of California Extension
University of Colorado—Boulder
University of Massachusetts—
Lowell
University of Tennessee—Knoxville
Western Oregon University

Yacht Design
Westlawn School of Yacht Design

Zoology
Brigham Young University
North Carolina State University
University of Texas—Austin
Weber State University

Nationally Recognized Accrediting Agencies

This appendix lists all of the regional accrediting agencies and professional accrediting agencies recognized by the U.S. Department of Education and/or by the Council for Higher Education Accreditation (CHEA). You should only take a distance-learning degree or certificate program from a school that is accredited by one or both of these agencies. Remember that just because a distance-learning program claims to be accredited by one of these agencies isn't proof that it is; take the extra step of contacting the agency directly and double-checking the school's accreditation.

Regional Accrediting Agencies

Middle States Association of Colleges and Schools (MSACS)
Commission on Higher Education
3624 Market St.
Philadelphia, PA 19104
215-662-5606
www.msache.org/default.htm
Accredits schools in Delaware, the District of Columbia, Maryland, New Jersey, New York, Pennsylvania, Puerto Rico, the Republic of Panama, and the Virgin Islands.

New England Association of Schools and Colleges (NEASC)
209 Burlington Rd.
Bedford, MA 01730-1433
781-271-0022
www.neasc.org/
Accredits schools in Connecticut, Maine, Massachusetts, New Hampshire, Rhode Island, and Vermont.

North Central Association of
Colleges and Schools (NCACS)
Commission on Institutions of
Higher Education
30 N. LaSalle St., Suite 2400
Chicago, IL 60602-2504
1-800-621-7440
www.ncacihe.org/
*Accredits schools in Arizona, Arkansas,
Colorado, Illinois, Indiana, Iowa,
Kansas, Michigan, Minnesota,
Missouri, Nebraska, New Mexico,
North Dakota, Ohio, Oklahoma, South
Dakota, West Virginia, Wisconsin,
Wyoming, and the Navajo Nation.*

Northwest Association of Schools
and Colleges (NASC)
Commission on Colleges
11130 NE. 33rd Place, Suite 120
Bellevue, WA 98004
425-827-2005
*Accredits schools in Alaska, Idaho,
Montana, Nevada, Oregon, Utah, and
Washington.*

Southern Association of Colleges
and Schools (SACS)
Commission on Colleges
1866 Southern Lane
Decatur, GA 30033
404-679-4500
www.sacscoc.org/
*Accredits schools in Alabama, Florida,
Georgia, Kentucky, Louisiana,
Mississippi, North Carolina, South
Carolina, Tennessee, Texas, Virginia,
and most of Latin America.*

Western Association of Schools and
Colleges (WASC)
The Senior College Commission
Box 9990, Mills College
Oakland, CA 94613
510-632-5000
www.wascweb.org/

*Accredits schools in California,
Hawaii, American Samoa, the
Federated States of Micronesia, Guam,
the Marshall Islands, Northern
Marianas, and the Republic of Palau.*

Professional Accrediting Agencies

Acupuncture and Oriental Medicine

National Accrediting Commission
for Schools and Colleges of
Acupuncture and Oriental
Medicine
1010 Wayne Ave., Suite 1270
Silver Spring, MD 20910
301-608-9680

Allied Health

Accrediting Bureau of Health
Education Schools (ABHES)
803 W. Broad St., Suite 730
Falls Church, VA 22046
703-533-2082
www.abhes.org/
*Note: Accredits programs for medical
laboratory technicians and medical
assistants.*

Art and Design

National Association of Schools of
Art and Design (NASAD)
11250 Roger Bacon Dr., Suite 21
Reston, VA 20190
703-437-0700
www.arts-accredit.org/nasad/
default.htm

Bible College Education

Accrediting Association of Bible
Colleges (AABC)
5890 S. Semoran Blvd.
Orlando, FL 32822
407-207-0808
www.aabc.org/

Business

Accrediting Council for
Independent Colleges and Schools
(ACICS)
750 First St. NE, Suite 980
Washington, DC 20002-4241
202-336-6780
www.acics.org/

Chiropractic Education

Council on Chiropractic Education
(CCE)
8049 N. 85th Way
Scottsdale, AZ 85258-4321
480-443-8877
www.cce-usa.org/

Christian Education

Transnational Association of
Christian Colleges
P.O. Box 328
Forest, VA 24551
804-525-9539
www.tracs.org/

Clinical Laboratory Science

National Accrediting Agency for
Clinical Laboratory Sciences
(NAACLS)
8410 W. Bryn Mawr Ave., Suite 670
Chicago, IL 60631-3415
773-714-8880
www.naacls.org/
*Note: Accredits programs for histologic
technician, medical laboratory technician, medical technologist, and patholo-
gist's assistant.*

Computer Science

Computing Sciences Accreditation
Board, Inc. (CSAB)
2 Landmark Square, Suite 209
Stamford, CT 06901
203-975-1117
www.csab.org/
*Note: Recognized by CHEA but not by
the U.S. Department of Education.*

Construction Education

American Council for Construction
Education (ACCE)
1300 Hudson Lane, Suite #3
Monroe, LA 71201
318-323-2816
www.calpoly.edu/~cm/acce/
*Note: Recognized by CHEA but not by
the U.S. Department of Education.*

Continuing Education

Accrediting Council for
Continuing Education and
Training (ACCET)
1722 N St. NW
Washington, DC 20036
202-955-1113
www.accet.org/

Cosmetology

National Accrediting Commission
of Cosmetology Arts and Sciences
(NACCAS)
901 N. Stuart St., Suite 900
Arlington, VA 22203
703-527-7600
www.naccas.org/

Counseling

Council for Accreditation of
Counseling and Related
Educational Programs (CACREP)
5999 Stevenson Ave., 4th Floor
Alexandria, VA 22304
1-800-347-6647, ext. 301
www.counseling.org/cacrep/
*Note: Recognized by CHEA but not by
the U.S. Department of Education.*

Culinary Arts

American Culinary Federation, Inc.
(ACF)
10 San Bartola Dr.
St. Augustine, FL 32086
1-800-624-9458
www.acfchefs.org/

Note: Recognized by CHEA but not by the U.S. Department of Education.

Dance

National Association of Schools of
Dance (NASD)
11250 Roger Bacon Dr., Suite 21
Reston, VA 20190
703-437-0700
www.arts-accredit.org/nasd/
default.htm

Dentistry

American Dental Association
(ADA)
Commission on Dental
Accreditation
211 E. Chicago Ave.
Chicago, IL 60611
312-440-2500
www.ada.org/index.html

Dietetics

American Dietetic Association
(ADiA)
Education and Accreditation Team
216 W. Jackson Blvd.
Chicago, IL 60606-6995
1-800-877-1600, ext. 5400
www.eatright.org/caade/

Distance Education

Distance Education and Training
Council (DETC)
1601 18th St. NW
Washington, DC 20009-2529
202-234-5100
www.detc.org/

Engineering

Accrediting Board for Engineering
and Technology (ABET)
111 Market Place, Suite 1050
Baltimore, MD 21202
410-347-7700
www.abet.org/

Environmental Science

National Environmental Health
Science and Protection
Accreditation Council (NEHSPAC)
6307 Huntover Lane
Rockville, MD 20852
301-231-5205

Family and Consumer Sciences

American Association of Family
and Consumer Sciences (AAFCS)
Council for Accreditation
1555 King St.
Alexandria, VA 22314
703-706-4600
www.aafcs.org/
Note: Recognized by CHEA but not by the U.S. Department of Education.

Forestry

Society of American Foresters
(SFA)
5400 Grosvenor Lane
Bethesda, MD 20814
301-897-8720
www.safnet.org/educate/index.
html
Note: Recognized by CHEA but not by the U.S. Department of Education.

Funeral Service Education

American Board of Funeral Service
Education (ABFSE)
38 Florida Ave.
Portland, ME 04103
207-878-6530
www.abfse.org/

Health Services Administration

Accrediting Commission on
Education for Health Services
Administration (ACEHSA)
730 11th St. NW, 4th Floor
Washington, DC 20001-4510
202-638-5131
monkey.hmi.missouri.edu/acehsa/

Interior Design

Foundation for Interior Design
Education Research (FIDER)
60 Monroe Center NW, Suite 300
Grand Rapids, MI 49503-2920
616-458-0400
www.fider.org/
*Note: Recognized by CHEA but not by
the U.S. Department of Education.*

Journalism and Mass Communications

Accrediting Council on Education
in Journalism and Mass
Communications (ACEJMC)
Stauffer-Flint Hall
University of Kansas
Lawrence, KS 66045
785-864-3986
www.ukans.edu/~acejmc/

Landscape Architecture

American Society of Landscape
Architects (ASLA)
636 Eye St. NW
Washington, DC 20001-3736
202-898-2444
www.asla.org/
*Note: Recognized by CHEA but not by
the U.S. Department of Education.*

Law

American Bar Association (ABA)
Section of Legal Education and
Admissions to the Bar
750 N. Lake Shore Dr.
Chicago, IL 60611
312-988-5674
www.abanet.org/legaled

Association of American Law
Schools (AALS)
1201 Connecticut Ave. NW
Suite 800
Washington, DC 20036-2605
202-296-8851
www.aals.org/

*Note: Recognized by CHEA but not by
the U.S. Department of Education.*

Liberal Education

American Academy for Liberal
Education (AALE)
1700 K St. NW, Suite 901
Washington, DC 20006
202-452-8611
www.aale.org/

Library and Information Science

American Library Association
(ALA)
Office for Accreditation
50 E. Huron St.
Chicago, IL 60611
1-800-545-2433
www.ala.org/accreditation.html
*Note: Recognized by CHEA but not by
the U.S. Department of Education.*

Marriage and Family Therapy

American Association for Marriage
and Family Therapy (AAMFT)
1133 15th St. NW, Suite 300
Washington, DC 20005-2710
202-452-0109
www.aamft.org/

Medical Education

Liaison Committee on Medical
Education (LCME)
Association of American Medical
Colleges
2450 N Street NW
Washington, DC 20037
202-828-0596
www.lcme.org/
*Note: Responsible for accreditation in
even-numbered years, beginning July 1.*

Liaison Committee on Medical
Education (LCME)
American Medical Association
515 N. State St.
Chicago, IL 60610

312-464-4657

www.lcme.org/

Note: Responsible for accreditation on odd-numbered years, beginning July 1.

Montessori Education

Montessori Accreditation Council for Teacher Education (MACTE)
University of Wisconsin—
Parkside Tallent Hall, Room 236
900 Wood Rd., Box 2000
Kenosha, WI 53141-2000
1-888-446-2283
email.uwp.edu/~warner/
mactecomm/

Music

National Association of Schools of Music (NASM)
11250 Roger Bacon Dr., Suite 21
Reston, VA 20190
703-437-0700
www.arts-accredit.org/nasm/
nasm.htm

Naturopathy

Council on Naturopathic Medical Education (CNME)
P.O. Box 11426
Eugene, OR 97440-3626
541-484-6028
www.cnme.org/

Nuclear Medicine Technology

Joint Review Committee on Educational Programs in Nuclear Medicine Technology
#1 2nd Ave. East, Suite C
Polson, MT 59860-2320
406-883-0003

Nurse Anesthesia

American Association of Nurse Anesthetists (AANA)
222 Prospect Ave.
Park Ridge, IL 60068-4001

847-692-7050
www.aana.com/

Nurse-Midwifery

American College of Nurse-Midwives (ACNM)
818 Connecticut Ave. NW
Suite 900
Washington, DC 20006
202-728-9877
www.acnm.org/

Nurse Practitioners

National Association of Nurse Practitioners in Reproductive Health (NANPRH)
1090 Vermont Ave., Suite 800
Washington, DC 20005
202-555-5555
www.nanprh.org/

Nursing

National League for Nursing Inc. (NLN)
61 Broadway
New York, NY 10006
1-800-669-9656
www.nln.org/

Occupational Therapy

American Occupational Therapy Association (AOTA)
4720 Montgomery Lane
Bethesda, MD 20824
301-652-AOTA
www.aota.org/

Occupational, Trade, and Technical Education

Accrediting Commission of Career Schools and Colleges of Technology (ACCSCT)
2101 Wilson Blvd., Suite 302
Arlington, VA 22201
703-247-4212
www.accsct.org/

Council on Occupational
Education
41 Perimeter Center East NE
Suite 640
Atlanta, GA 30346
1-800-917-2081
www.council.org/

Optometry and Opticianry

American Optometric Association
(AOA)
243 N. Lindbergh Blvd.
St. Louis, MO 63141
314-991-4100
www.aoanet.org/

Commission on Opticianry
Accreditation (COA)
10341 Democracy Lane
Fairfax, VA 22030
703-352-8028
www.coaccreditation.com/
Workshop/ppframe.htm

Osteopathy

American Osteopathic Association
(AOsA)
142 E. Ontario St.
Chicago, IL 60611
1-800-621-1773
www.aoa-net.org/

Parks and Recreation

National Recreation and Park
Association (NRPA)
Council on Accreditation
22377 Belmont Ridge Rd.
Ashburn, VA 20148
703-858-0784
www.nrpa.org/
*Note: Recognized by CHEA but not by
U.S. Department of Education.*

Pastoral Education

Association for Clinical Pastoral
Education Inc.
1549 Clairmont Rd., Suite 103

Decatur, GA 30033-4611
404-320-1472
www.acpe.edu/

Pharmacy

American Council on
Pharmaceutical Education (ACPE)
311 West Superior St., Suite 512
Chicago, IL 60610
312-664-3575
www.acpe-accredit.org/

Physical Therapy

American Physical Therapy
Association (APTA)
1111 N. Fairfax St.
Alexandria, VA 22314-1488
1-800-999-APTA
www.apta.org/home.shtml

Planning

Planning Accreditation Board
(PAB)
Merle Hay Tower
3800 Merle Hay Rd.
Des Moines, IA 50310
515-252-0729
www.netins.net/showcase/
pab_fi66/
*Note: Recognized by CHEA but not by
the U.S. Department of Education.*

Podiatry

American Podiatric Medical
Association (APMA)
9312 Old Georgetown Rd.
Bethesda, MD 20814-1698
301-571-9200
www.apma.org/

Psychology

American Psychological Association
(APA)
Program Consultation and
Accreditation
750 First St. NE
Washington, DC 20002

202-336-5979

www.apa.org/ed/accred.html

Public Affairs and Administration

National Association of Schools of Public Affairs and Administration (NASPA)

1875 Connecticut Ave. NW

Suite 418

Washington, DC 20009

202-265-7500

www.naspa.org/

Note: Recognized by CHEA but not by U.S. Department of Education.

Public Health

Council on Education for Public Health (CEPH)

1015 15th St. NW, Suite 403

Washington, DC 20005

202-789-1050

Rabbinical and Talmudic Education

Association of Advanced Rabbinical and Talmudic Schools (AARTS)

175 Fifth Ave., Room 711

New York, NY 10010

212-477-0950

Radiologic Technology

Joint Review Committee on Education in Radiologic Technology (JRCERT)

20 N. Wacker Dr., Suite 900

Chicago, IL 60606

312-704-5300

hudson.idt.net/~jrcert/

Rehabilitation Education

Council on Rehabilitation Education (CORE)

Commission on Standards and Accreditation

1835 Rohlwing Rd., Suite E

Rolling Meadows, IL 60008

847-394-1785

www.core-rehab.org/

Note: Recognized by CHEA but not by U.S. Department of Education.

Social Work

Council on Social Work Education (CSWE)

1600 Duke St., Suite 300

Alexandria, VA 22314

703-683-8080

www.cswe.org/

Note: Recognized by CHEA but not by the U.S. Department of Education.

Speech-Language Pathology and Audiology

American Speech-Language-Hearing Association (ASHA)

10801 Rockville Place

Rockville, MD 20852

301-897-5700

www.asha.org/

Teacher Education

National Council for Accreditation of Teacher Education (NCATE)

2010 Massachusetts Ave. NW

Suite 500

Washington, DC 20036-1023

202-466-7496

www.ncate.org/

Theater

National Association of Schools of Theater (NAST)

11250 Roger Bacon Dr., Suite 21

Reston, VA 20190

703-437-0700

www.arts-accredit.org/nast/default.htm

Theology

Association of Theological Schools in the United States and Canada (ATS)

10 Summit Park Dr.

Pittsburgh, PA 15275-1103

412-788-6505

www.ats.edu/

Veterinary Medicine

American Veterinary Medical
Association (AVMA)
1931 N. Meacham Rd., Suite 100
Schaumburg, IL 60173
847-925-8070
www.avma.org/

Recognized State-Run Accrediting Agency

New York State Board of Regents
State Education Department
Education Building
Albany, NY 12234
518-474-3852
www.nysed.gov/regents/

Glossary of Distance-Learning Terms

academic adviser College faculty member who assists degree students in selecting academic courses and programs.

academic year Period of study usually consisting of two semesters or three quarters or trimesters, each with a certain number of credit hours.

accreditation Seal of approval by a general regional accrediting agency or a specific academic-area accrediting agency, indicating that an institution of higher learning has been recognized as providing an adequate education.

accrediting agency Private organization that sets educational standards and accredits schools or academic programs that meet those standards. Colleges and universities, employers, certifying agencies, and licensing boards accept only accrediting agencies recognized by the U.S. Department of Education and/or CHEA.

ACT *See American College Testing Assessment.*

admission requirements Standards set by a college or university that applicants must meet to be considered for admission.

American College Testing (ACT) Assessment A national standardized college admission exam, widely given to high school students in the West and Midwest.

American Council on Education (ACE) Private association that recommends equivalent college credits for corporate educational programs and military training.

application Form that students fill out to request admission to colleges and universities, along with all supporting materials, including transcripts, test scores, essays, and letters of recommendation.

application fee The fee charged to cover the cost of processing a college application. Typical application fees range from $30 to $50.

associate's degree   Degree granted after completing a two-year undergraduate program, consisting of 60–64 semester hours of coursework. Associate's degrees are typically granted by community colleges for technical or vocational programs.

asynchronous   Not at the same time; refers to a distance-learning course in which there is no real-time interaction with the class, such as a correspondence course.

bachelor's degree   Degree awarded by a college upon successful completion of a four- or five-year program of study, consisting of 120–128 semester units. Depending on their majors, college graduates earn either a Bachelor of Arts (BA) or Bachelor of Science (BS) degree.

business school   Graduate-level professional school that awards students a Master of Business Administration (MBA) degree.

campus   The main facilities of a school, including class buildings, dorms, libraries, etc. The campus of a nontraditional school may consist entirely of offices.

certificate program   Nondegree program that trains and certifies students in a specific field.

college   Institute of higher learning that grants bachelor's degrees.

College Level Examination Program (CLEP)   Exam program that awards college credit for nontraditional college-level education, including independent study, correspondence, work, and on-the-job or military training.

community college   A two-year college; community colleges generally offer a transfer curriculum, in which credits can be transferred toward a bachelor's degree at a four-year college, and a vocational or technical curriculum that prepares students for a particular field of employment. Also called a *junior college*.

Continuing Education Unit (CEU)   Awarded for noncredit courses at the rate of one for every 10 hours of class time. CEUs are rarely considered as equivalent to college credit.

correspondence course   Class where students receive lessons and return completed assignments to instructors via the mail.

Council on Higher Education Accreditation (CHEA)   Private agency that, along with the U.S. Department of Education, recognizes accrediting agencies as qualified.

credit   Unit used to record successful completion of college courses. College courses are offered in one- to five-credit increments; each credit typically represents one hour spent in class each week. A certain number of credits is required to earn a degree.

Defense Activity for Nontraditional Education Support (DANTES)   Regulates financial aid programs and administers equivalency exams for members of the Armed Forces.

degree   Title conferred by a college or university to show that the student has completed a particular course of study.

Direct Loan   *See Federal Direct Student Loan Program.*

Distance Education and Training Council (DETC)   Nationally recognized accrediting agency that qualifies distance-learning programs.

distance learning   Education in which the students and instructor are physically separated from each other. Distance-learning classes can be taken through the Internet; via audiotapes, videotapes, and CD-ROMs; by correspondence; and over the television.

Doctorate   *See Ph.D.*

education loan   Type of financial aid that must be repaid with interest. Also called a student loan.

eligible program   Course of study that leads to a degree or certificate and meets the U.S. Department of Education's requirements. Students must be enrolled in an eligible program to receive federal financial aid.

expected family contribution (EFC)   Figure that indicates how much of the student's financial resources should be used to help pay for higher education. This number is subtracted from the cost of the educational program to determine financial need.

Federal Direct Student Loan Program   Part of the Stafford loan program, a type of federally guaranteed student loan that's administered directly by the government. Both subsidized and unsubsidized student Direct Loans are available. Not all schools participate in this program.

Federal Family Education Loan (FFEL) Program   Part of the Stafford loan program, a type of federally guaranteed student loan that's administered by a private institution, such as a bank or credit union. Both subsidized and unsubsidized FFEL loans are available.

fees   Money paid to a school for purposes other than academic tuition.

financial aid   The money provided to a student to help pay the costs of higher education. Major forms of financial aid include loans, grants, scholarships, and work-study. Financial aid comes from many sources, including federal and state government, the schools, and private organizations like companies, professional associations, and foundations.

financial aid officer   Person at the college who administers financial aid packages and determines how much aid to award to each student.

financial need   The difference between the cost of attending a particular degree program and a student's EFC (estimated family contribution). Financial aid awards are based on this amount.

Free Application for Federal Student Aid (FAFSA)   Form used to apply for Pell Grants and other federal financial aid programs.

full-time enrollment   Refers to students who enroll in 12 or more credit hours per semester.

General Educational Development (GED) Certificate   Certificate received by students who pass a preapproved high school equivalency test. Students without a high school diploma need to obtain a GED to be eligible for financial aid and to apply to college-level degree programs.

grade point average (GPA)   System of scoring student achievement. A student's GPA is computed by multiplying the numerical grade received in each course by the number of credits offered for each course, and then dividing by the total number of credit hours studied.

Graduate Management Aptitude Test (GMAT)   Standardized test required for admission to an MBA program.

graduate school   Collection of programs offered by a university to students pursuing master's and doctoral degrees.

graduate student   A student who has obtained a bachelor's degree and is continuing further study for a professional, master's, or doctoral degree.

Graduate Record Exam (GRE)   Standardized exam that tests verbal and math skills and is used as part of the admissions process for graduate school.

grant   Type of need-based financial aid that the recipient doesn't have to repay. Grant awards are typically based on financial need.

guaranty agency   Organization that administers FFEL Loans for state residents. Although the federal government sets loan limits and interest rates, each state is free to set its own additional limitations within federal guidelines.

half-time enrollment   Required for eligibility for federal financial aid programs. At schools measuring progress by credit hours and semesters, trimesters, or quarters, half-time enrollment is at least six semester or quarter hours per term. At schools measuring progress by credit hours but not using semesters, trimesters, or quarters, half-time enrollment is at least 12 semester hours or 18 quarter hours per year. At schools measuring progress by clock hours, half-time enrollment is at least 12 hours per week. Some schools set higher minimums than these.

HOPE Scholarship   Tax credit intended to enable all students to afford two years of postsecondary education. Eligible students can deduct up to $1,500 of tuition costs during the first two years of higher education.

independent study program   Degree or certificate program in which students complete course requirements at their own pace, rather than by academic term.

junior college   *See community college.*

Lifetime Learning Credit   Tax credit that enables qualified students to deduct a certain percentage of some of the cost of tuition. This credit is available for juniors and seniors in college, graduate students, and adults returning to school.

major   Academic area in which a student chooses to concentrate study when earning a bachelor's degree.

master's degree   Degree received after one or two years of study following a bachelor's degree.

Master of Business Administration (MBA)   Degree received after graduation from a business school.

merit-based aid   Financial aid—typically a scholarship—awarded based on academic, artistic, or athletic merit, rather than on financial need.

need-based aid   Financial aid based primarily on a student's financial need. All federal aid and most state aid is need-based.

noncredit course   A course which does not award college credit for successful completion. Noncredit courses include courses for skill development, fulfilling precollege requirements, or personal enrichment.

non-need-based aid   Broad category of financial aid that encompasses all aid awarded based on criteria other than financial need, including merit-based aid and aid based on a student's ethnicity, gender, religion, or affiliation with a group.

nontraditional   Education completed by methods other than attending classes on a school's campus, including distance learning.

nontraditional student   A college student who is pursuing a degree by means other than a traditional on-campus education, including distance learners. Nontraditional students are typically working adults who are continuing their college education.

open admission   Admissions program offered by some four-year colleges and most community colleges in which all students who apply and who have a high school diploma or GED are admitted.

origination fee   Fee charged by the federal government on Stafford loans and deducted from the loan before disbursement to partially offset administrative costs.

out-of-state student   Student who does not meet state residency requirements and must pay a higher tuition to attend one of the state's public colleges or universities.

part-time enrollment   Refers to students who enroll in fewer than 12 credit hours per semester.

Pell Grant   Federal program that awards grants to students with exceptional financial need. Most other financial aid awards are based on the application for the Pell Grant.

Ph.D.   The highest university degree. Also called a *doctorate.*

placement tests   Tests given to place students in the correct college-level courses for their levels of achievement. College credit is usually awarded for courses that students place out of.

prerequisite   Course or qualification required before a student may take an advanced course or declare a major in a specific area.

Prior Learning Assessment (PLA)   A portfolio presenting all of a student's prior learning experiences, with appropriate documentation. The portfolio is reviewed by the school faculty and used to award college credit for life experiences.

private loan   Education loan provided by a private lender, rather than by the federal government. Private loans are based on creditworthiness rather than financial need. Also called an alternative loan or supplemental loan.

professional accrediting agency   Nationally recognized accrediting agency that qualifies professional schools or academic programs in a specific field.

Accreditation of a particular program by a professional accrediting agency does not extend to the school that sponsors the program.

professional school   Graduate-level school that awards a professional degree, such as a business, law, or medical degree.

program   Group of courses leading to a degree or certificate.

public school   College or university that was founded by the state and is funded partly or fully by tax money. Public schools often give preference for admittance to in-state applicants.

quarter   Class term that generally lasts 12 weeks. Schools on the quarter system have four class terms during the academic year.

reach school   A college where an applicant may not necessarily meet admission standards, hence making it a "reach" for that applicant to gain admittance.

regional accrediting agency   One of six nationally recognized accrediting agencies that qualify entire schools and all the programs offered by those schools. Each agency is responsible for accrediting schools in a particular region of the country.

registrar   Office responsible for registration for classes and academic records.

registration   Enrolling in a course. Often, tuition and fees are due at the time of registration.

regular student   Student who is enrolled in an institution of higher learning to obtain a degree or certificate. Only regular students are eligible for federal financial aid.

safety school   A school for which an applicant is overqualified and is therefore well assured of admission.

SAT   National standardized college admissions test, widely given to high school students in the East and South.

scholarship   Form of financial aid that doesn't have to be repaid and is typically awarded based on merit or some other qualification instead of financial need.

score report   Report containing a student's standardized test scores.

semester   Class term that generally lasts 15–18 weeks. Schools on the semester system have two semesters during the academic year, plus one or more summer sessions.

Stafford loan   Federal education loan program that encompasses both Direct Loans and FFEL Loans.

standardized tests   Any of a number of formatted exams that all applicants to college, graduate school, and professional school must take. The SAT, ACT, CLEP exams, TOEFL, GRE, and GMAT are all examples of standardized tests. These tests are intended to enable colleges and graduate schools to equally compare applicants from all areas of the country.

subsidized loan   A federally guaranteed loan that is awarded to students based on financial need. The federal government pays the interest charges that accrue while the student is in school.

syllabus   A course outline that lists all the assignments, exams, and lecture topics for that course.

synchronous   At the same time; synchronous distance-learning programs include real-time class interaction.

Test of English as a Foreign Language (TOEFL)   Standardized test to demonstrate acceptable proficiency in English, given to college applicants for whom English is not the native language.

traditional education   Education at a residential college or university in which the student attends classes on campus.

transcript   The official record of a student's academic work.

trimester   Class term that generally lasts 17 weeks. Schools on the trimester system have three class terms during the academic year.

tuition   The cost of a college education and required institutional fees for services provided by the college.

undergraduate   A bachelor's or associate's degree candidate.

university   Institution of higher education that encompasses a liberal arts college, several professional programs, and various graduate programs, and graduate professional schools.

unsubsidized loan   A Stafford loan that is not awarded based on need and thus may be used to help pay the EFC. The student must pay all of the interest charges that accrue on the loan.

work-study   Type of financial aid that gives the student a part-time job, usually on campus. The student's paycheck is used to help pay college costs.

Internet Resources

You can find a lot more information about distance learning and returning to college on the Internet. I have culled the best of these Internet resources and listed them here for you.

Distance-Learning Resources

Distance Education Clearinghouse	www.uwex.edu/disted/home.html	Covers developments in distance learning and provides an introduction for newcomers.
Distance-Learning Home Page	distancelearn.about.com/	A good guide to online distance-learning resources, including timely program information.
Distance-Learning Newsgroup	alt.education.distance	Discuss distance-learning programs and get advice from distance learners.
Distance Learning on the Net	www.hoyle.com/distance.htm	Links to and describes distance-education resources on the Internet.
Disted.Com	www.disted.com/	A guide to distance and continuing education for students; includes a large bookstore where you can buy textbooks and course materials online.
United States Distance-Learning Association	www.usdla.org/	A leading source of information about the development of distance-learning programs.

General Resources for Nontraditional Students

ACT Assessment	www.act.org/	Provides information about the ACT test and how to obtain score reports.
American Council on Education	www.acenet.edu/	Recommends equivalent college credits for military and work training, and administers the GED Testing Service.
Back to College	www.back2college.com/	Provides resources for students who are returning to college.
CLEP Exams	www.collegeboard.org/clep/students/study/html/testl000.html	A thorough overview of the CLEP testing program, including information on what tests you can take, how to prepare for tests, and how to register.

Name	URL	Description
College and University Home Pages	www.mit.edu:8001/people/cdemello/univ.html	Comprehensive listing of the Web site addresses for all American colleges and universities.
Council for Adult and Experiential Learning	www.cael.org/	Provides information about the Prior Learning Assessment program for granting college credit for life experience.
Defense Activity for Nontraditional Educational Support (DANTES)	voled.doded.mil/	Provides information about nontraditional educational opportunities for members of the Armed Forces.
EduPoint.Com	www.edupoint.com/Features/pl970930.asp	Helps you locate adult, continuing education, and distance-learning programs in almost any subject.
Federal Student Financial Aid	www.ed.gov/offices/OSFAP/Students/	Find a guide to the federal financial aid program and apply for financial aid online.
FinAid	www.finaid.org/	A complete guide to obtaining federal and state financial aid, private scholarships, and educational loans.
GRE	www.gre.org/	Provides information about taking the GRE, how to prepare, and how to obtain score reports.
MBA Explorer	www.gmat.org/	Learn about MBA programs, financing your MBA, and taking the GMAT.
SAT	www.collegeboard.org/sat/html/students/indx001.html	Provides information about the SAT and how to obtain score reports.
TOEFL	www.toefl.org/	Provides a complete overview of the TOEFL and how to obtain information bulletins.

Study and Research Aids

Basic Guide to Essay Writing	members.tripod.com/~lklivingston/essay/
OneLook Dictionaries	www.onelook.com/
Online Writing Assistant	www.powa.org/
Research It!	www.iTools.com/research-it/research-it.html
ResearchPaper.Com	www.researchpaper.com/
Roget's Thesaurus	www.thesaurus.com/
Strunk and White's *Elements of Style*	www.bartleby.com/index.html
Study Skills Help Page	www.mtsu.edu/~studskl/